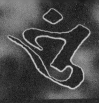

第5巻

RG VEDA

聖伝

蒼王飛翔篇

STORY BY
大川七瀬
AGEHA OHKAWA

COMIC BY
もこなあぱぱ
MOKONA

新書館

PLANNING
CLAMP

Publication

Serial Publication

WINGS

WINGS COMICS

SIX STARS WILL FALL TO THIS PLANE, THE DARK STARS THAT WILL DEFY THE HEAVENS.

AND YOU SHALL UNDERTAKE A JOURNEY, ONE THAT BEGINS WHEN YOU FIND THE CHILD OF A VANISHED RACE.

I CANNOT DISCERN THE CHILD'S ALIGNMENT... I ONLY KNOW THAT, IT IS HE ALONE WHO CAN TURN THE WHEEL OF TENKAI'S DESTINY.

FOR IT IS BY HEAVENLY MANDATE THAT THROUGH THIS CHILD, THE SIX STARS SHALL BEGIN TO GATHER.

AND THEN SOMEONE SHALL APPEAR FROM THE SHADOWS. EVEN MY POWERS CANNOT CLEARLY MAKE OUT HIS FIGURE, BUT HE KNOWS THE FUTURE AND CAN MANIPULATE BOTH EVIL AND HEAVENLY STARS.

A ROARING FLAME WILL RAZE THE WICKED.

SIX STARS WILL OVERPOWER ALL OTHERS...

AND INEVITABLY...THEY WILL BE THE SCHISM THAT SPLITS THE HEAVENS.

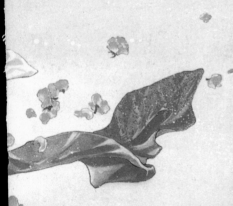

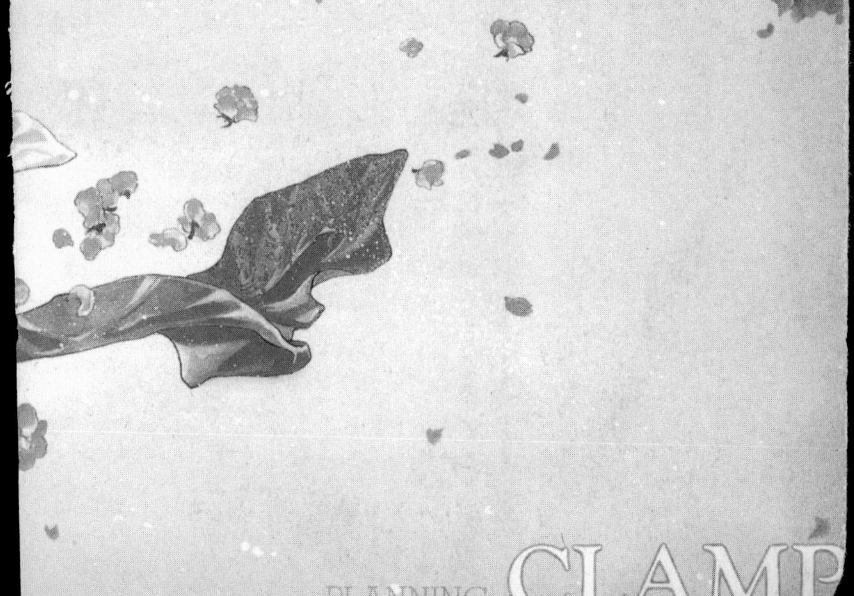

PLANNING CLAMP

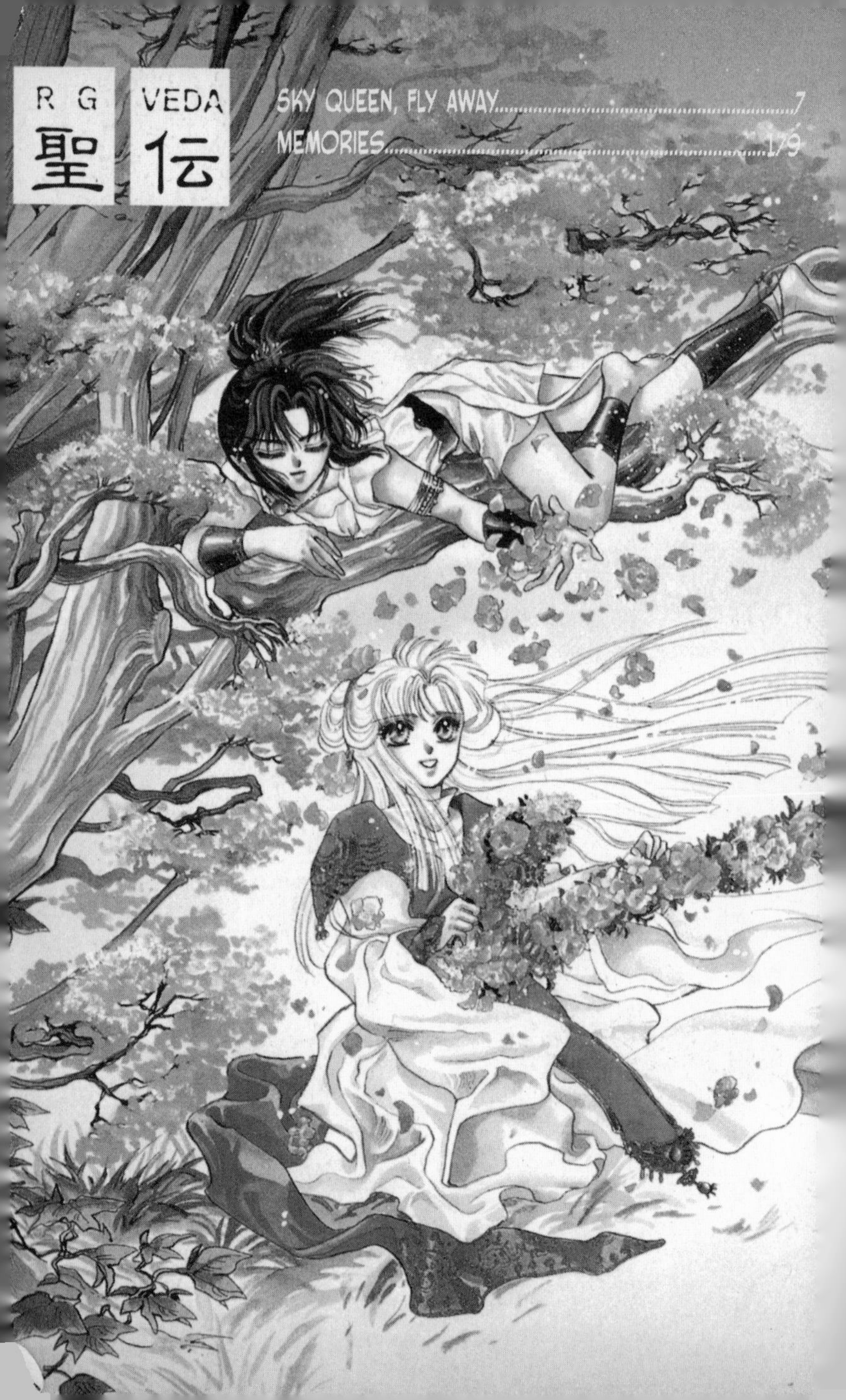

RG VEDA 聖伝

O S H I G A N A G A R E R U

CLAMP MEMBERS

Main

STORY
大川七瀬
AGEHA OHKAWA

COMIC
もこなあぱぱ
MOKONA

YOU WILL BE THE SCHISM THAT SPLITS HEAVEN.

Book Designer
大川七瀬
AGEHA OHKAWA

Director
こなあぱぱ
MOKONA

Short Comic
猫井みっく
TSUBAKI NEKOI

Art Assistants
猫井みっく
TSUBAKI NEKOI
五十嵐さつき
SATSUKI IGARASHI

PLANNING & PRESENTED by

CLAMP

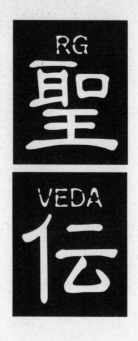

RG 聖 VEDA 伝

VOLUME 5

BY
CLAMP

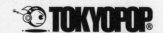

HAMBURG // LONDON // LOS ANGELES // TOKYO

RG Veda Vol. 5
created by CLAMP

Translation - Haruko Furukawa
English Adaptation - Christine Schilling
Copy Editor - Hope Donovan and Peter Ahlstrom
Retouch and Lettering - Jose Macasocol, Jr.
Production Artists - Jennifer Carbajal
Cover Design - Jorge Negrete

Editor - Troy Lewter
Digital Imaging Manager - Chris Buford
Production Manager - Jennifer Miller
Managing Editor - Lindsey Johnston
VP of Production - Ron Klamert
Publisher and E.I.C. - Mike Kiley
President and C.O.O. - John Parker
Chief Creative Officer and C.E.O. - Stuart Levy

A 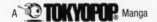 Manga

TOKYOPOP Inc.
5900 Wilshire Blvd. Suite 2000
Los Angeles, CA 90036

E-mail: info@TOKYOPOP.com
Come visit us online at www.TOKYOPOP.com

ISBN: 1-59532-488-7

First TOKYOPOP printing: April 2006
10 9 8 7 6 5 4 3 2 1
Printed in the USA

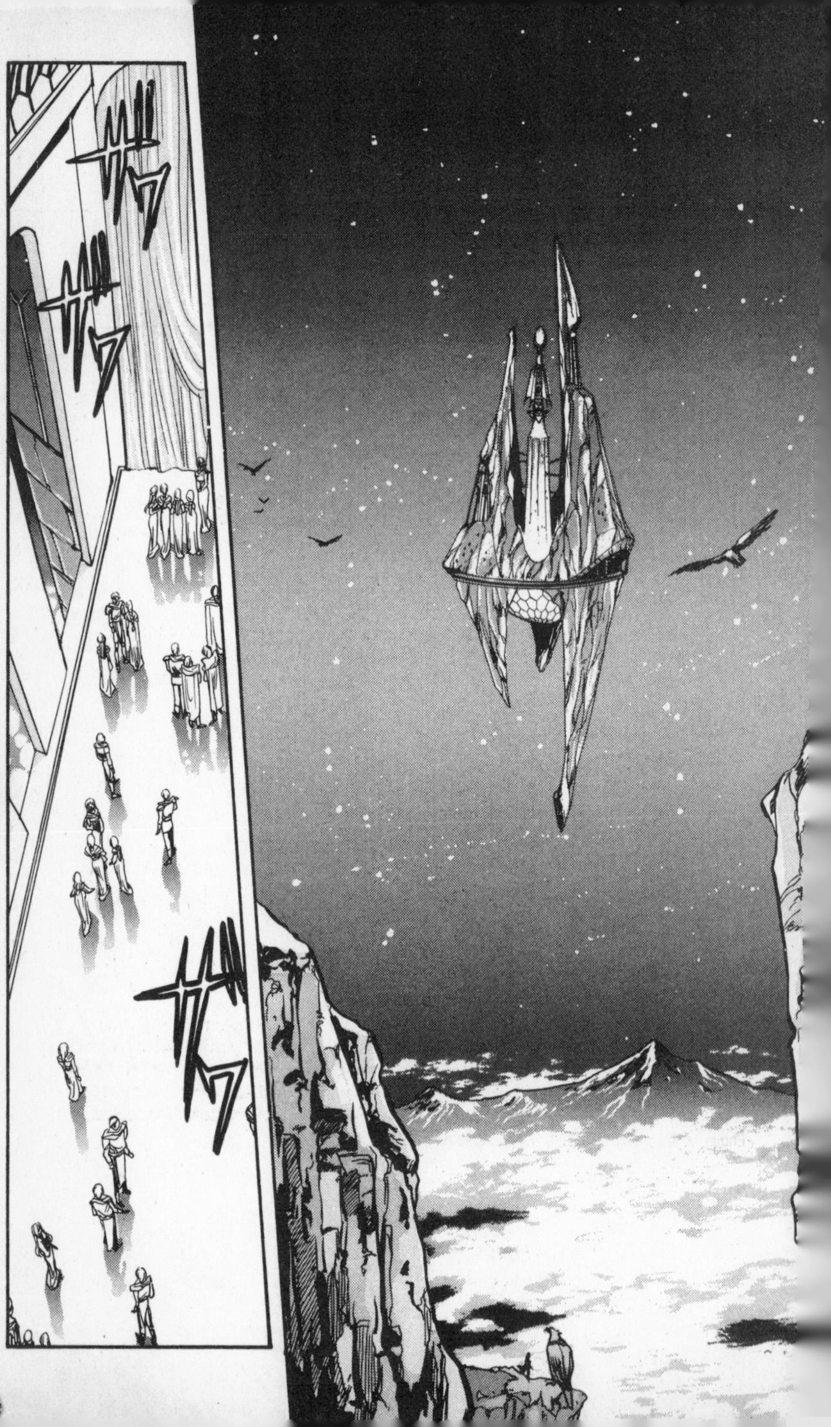
ザワ
ザワ
ザワ

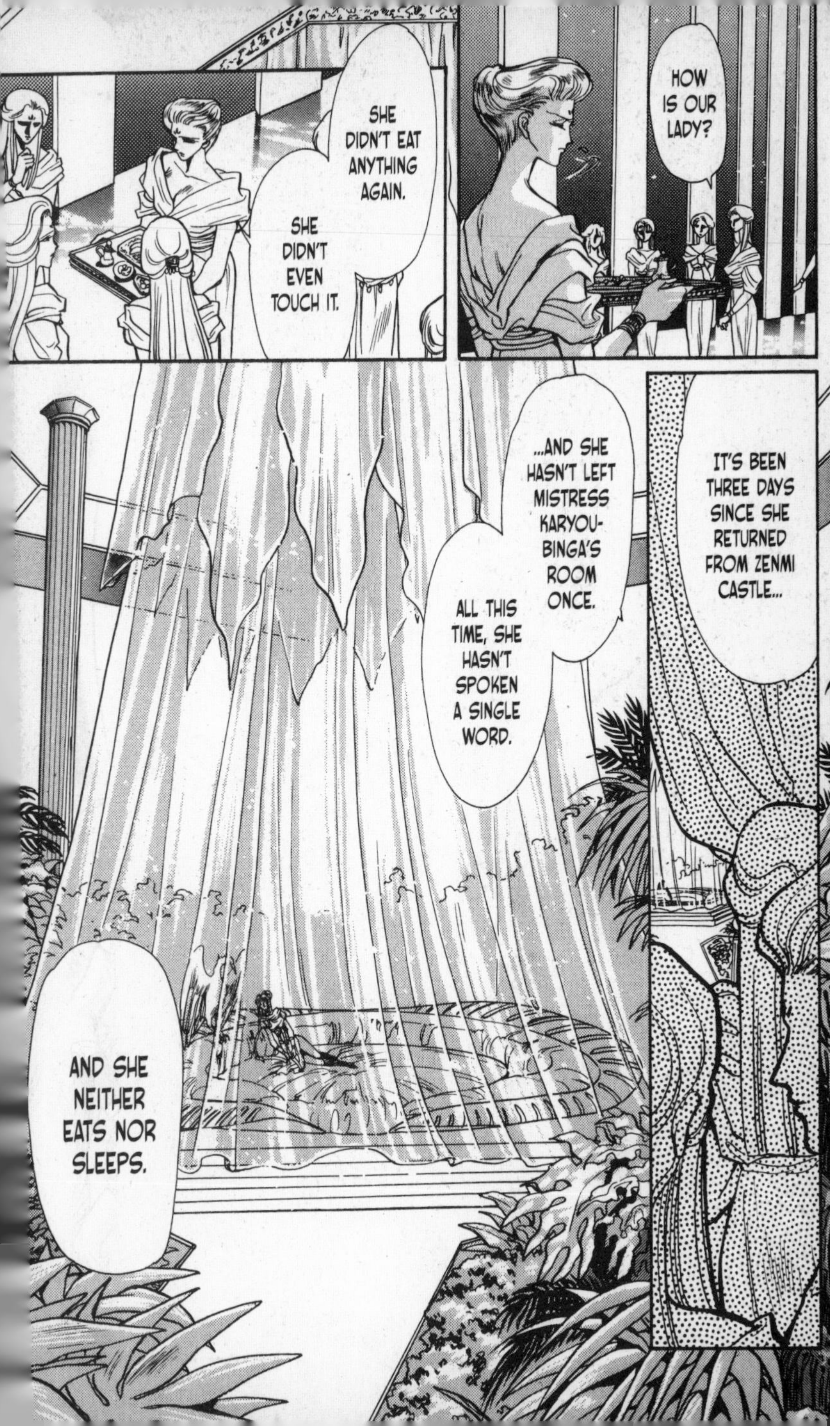
HOW IS OUR LADY?
SHE DIDN'T EAT ANYTHING AGAIN.
SHE DIDN'T EVEN TOUCH IT.
IT'S BEEN THREE DAYS SINCE SHE RETURNED FROM ZENMI CASTLE...
...AND SHE HASN'T LEFT MISTRESS KARYOU-BINGA'S ROOM ONCE.
ALL THIS TIME, SHE HASN'T SPOKEN A SINGLE WORD.
AND SHE NEITHER EATS NOR SLEEPS.

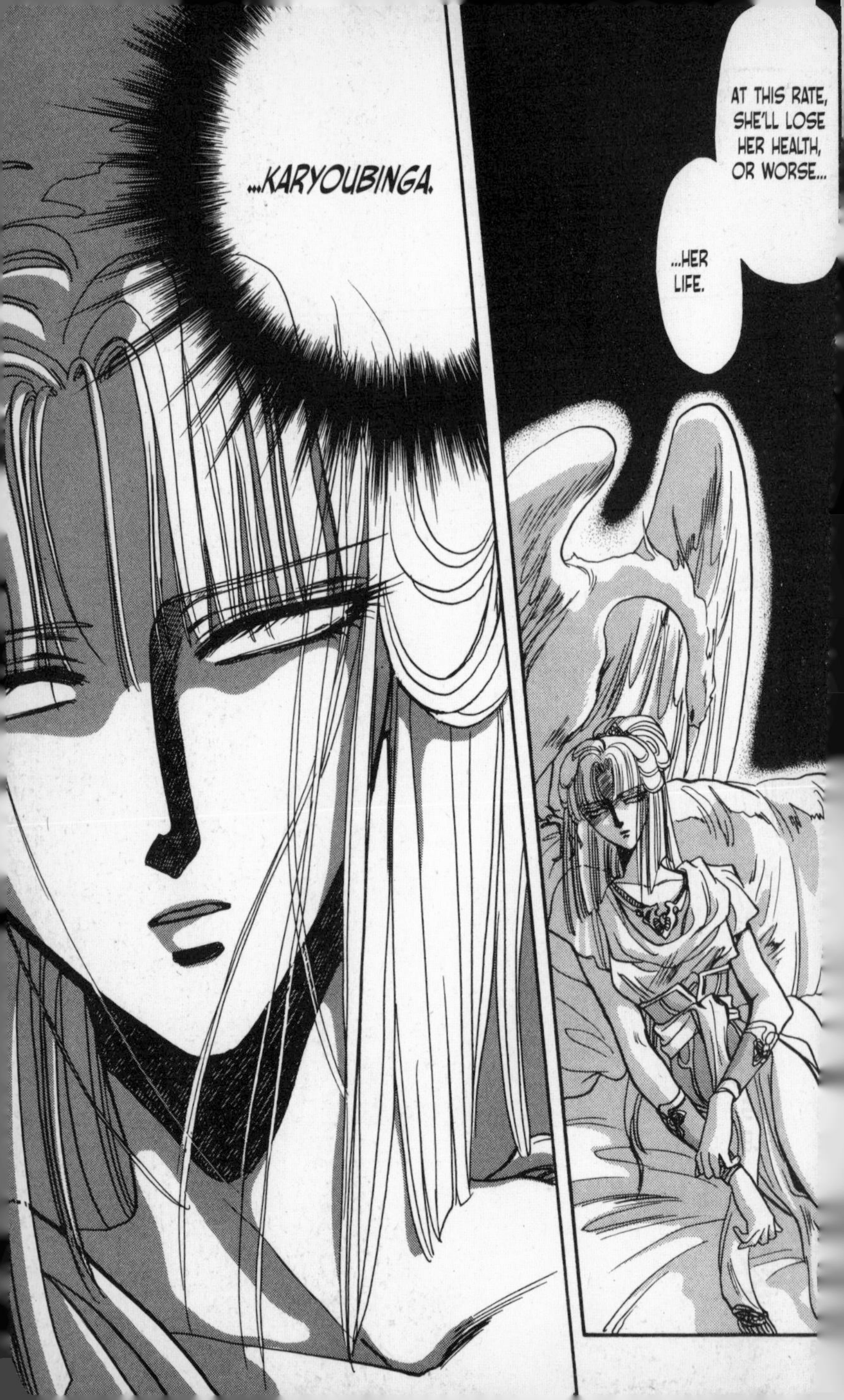
AT THIS RATE, SHE'LL LOSE HER HEALTH, OR WORSE...
...HER LIFE.
...KARYOUBINGA.

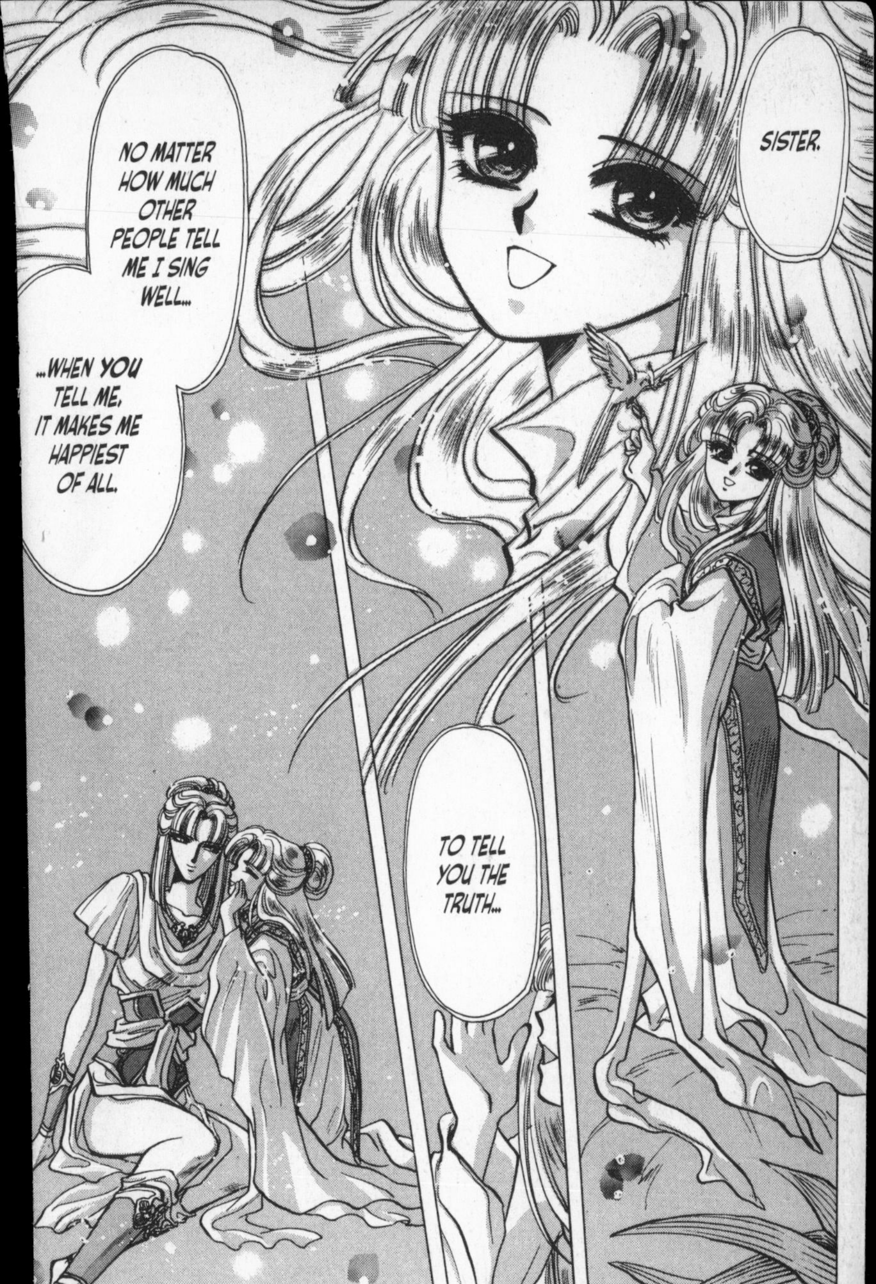
SISTER.
TO TELL YOU THE TRUTH...
NO MATTER HOW MUCH OTHER PEOPLE TELL ME I SING WELL...
...WHEN YOU TELL ME, IT MAKES ME HAPPIEST OF ALL.

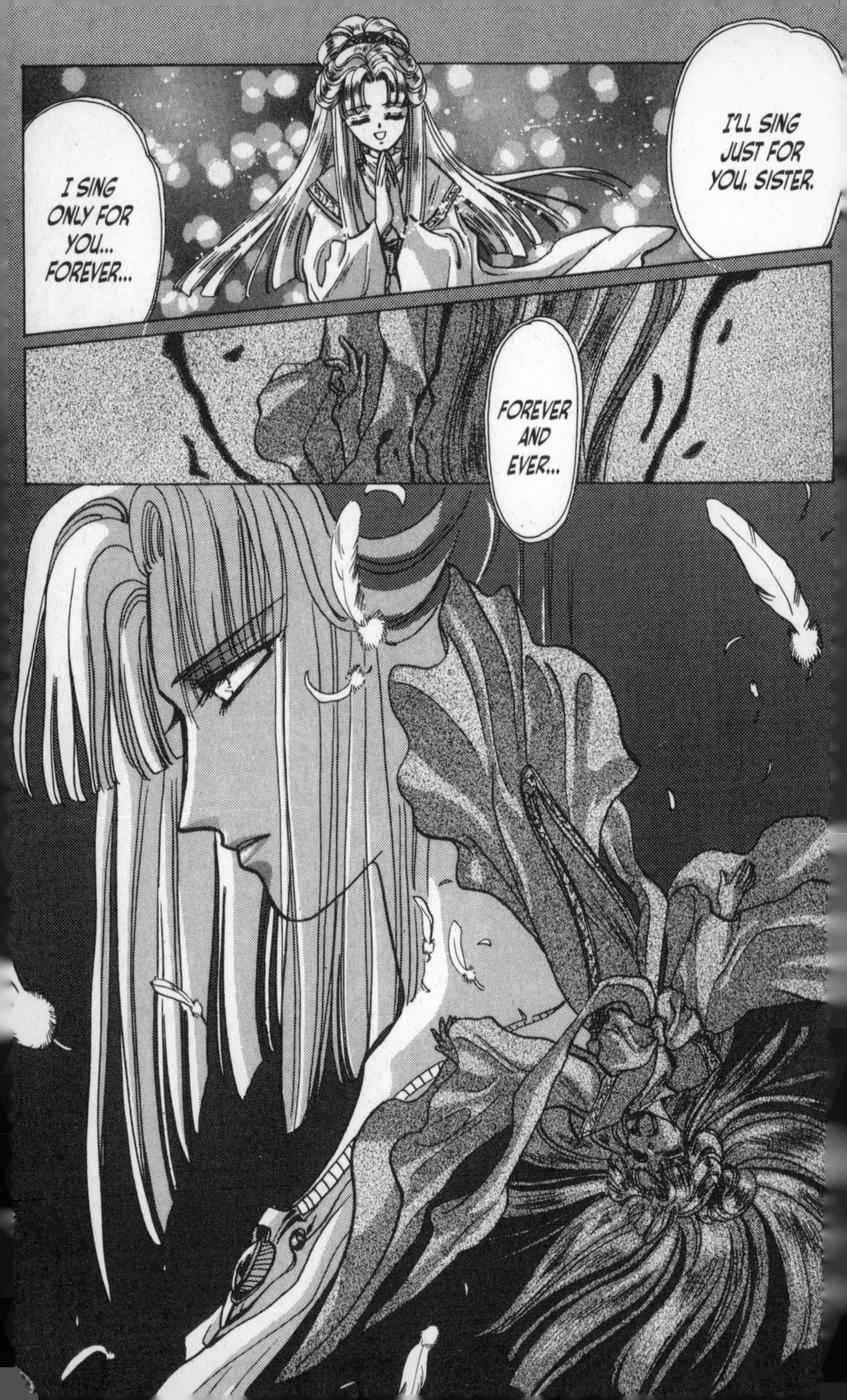
I'LL SING JUST FOR YOU, SISTER.
I SING ONLY FOR YOU... FOREVER...
FOREVER AND EVER...

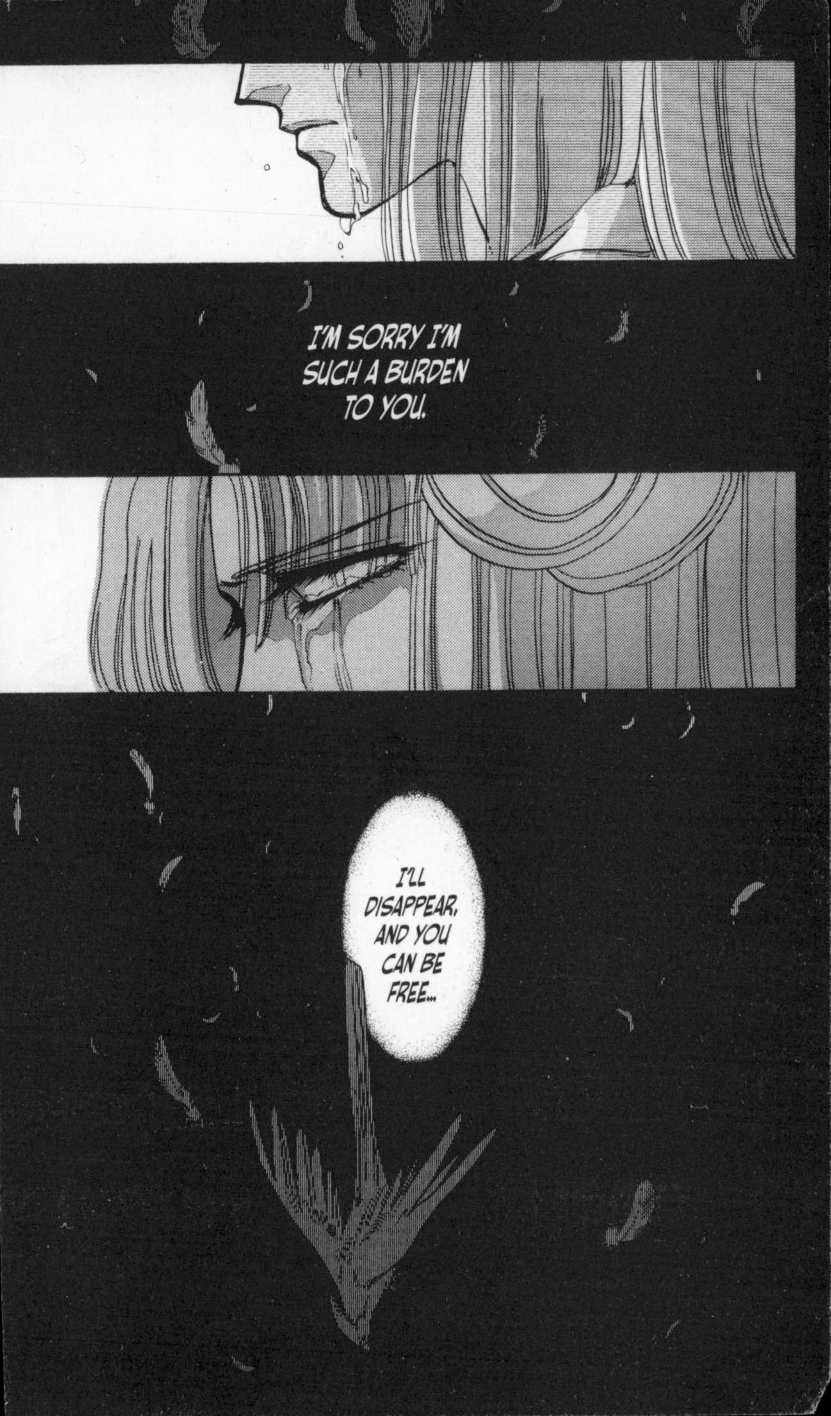
I'M SORRY I'M SUCH A BURDEN TO YOU.
I'LL DISAPPEAR, AND YOU CAN BE FREE...

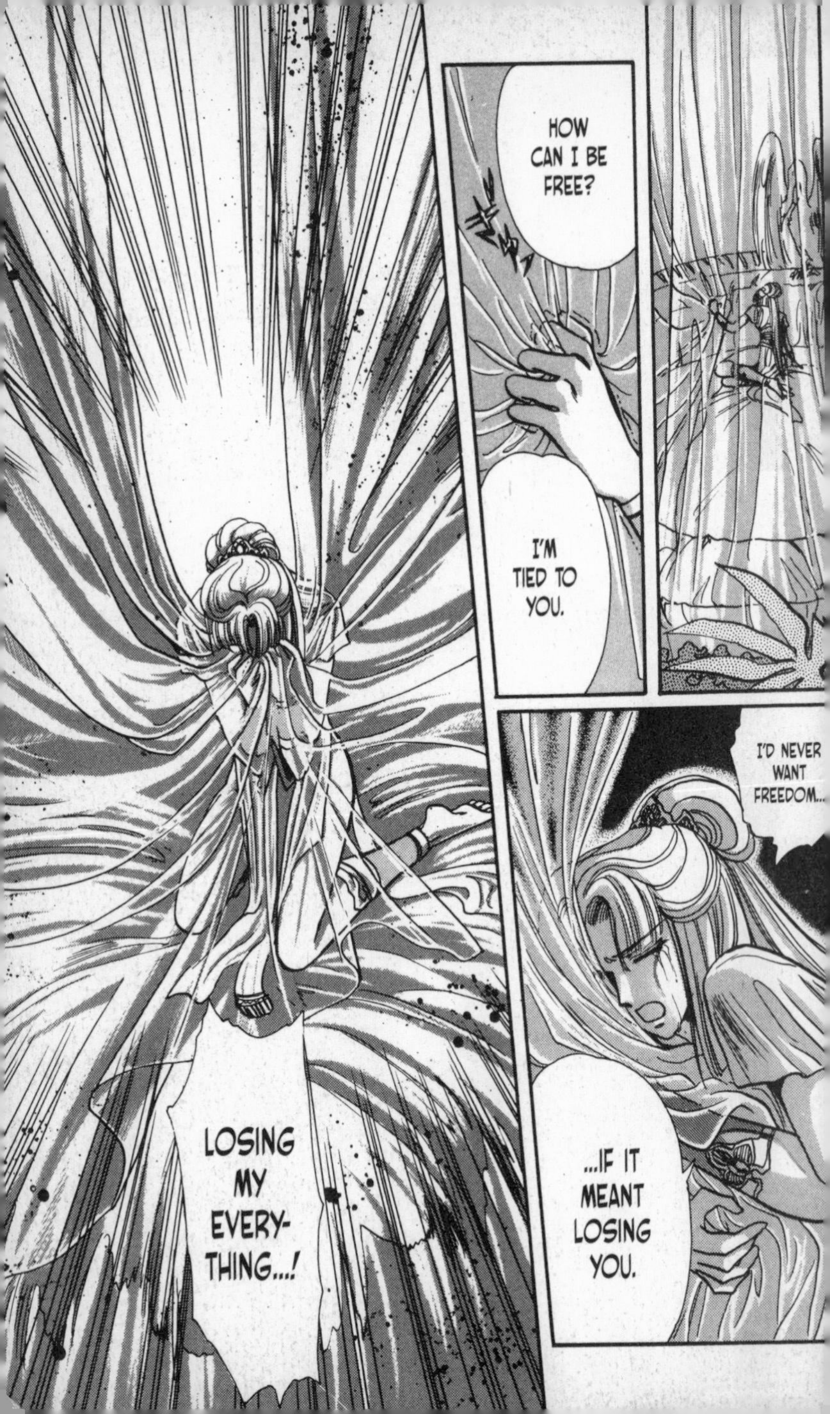
HOW CAN I BE FREE?
I'M TIED TO YOU.
I'D NEVER WANT FREEDOM...
...IF IT MEANT LOSING YOU.
LOSING MY EVERY-THING...!

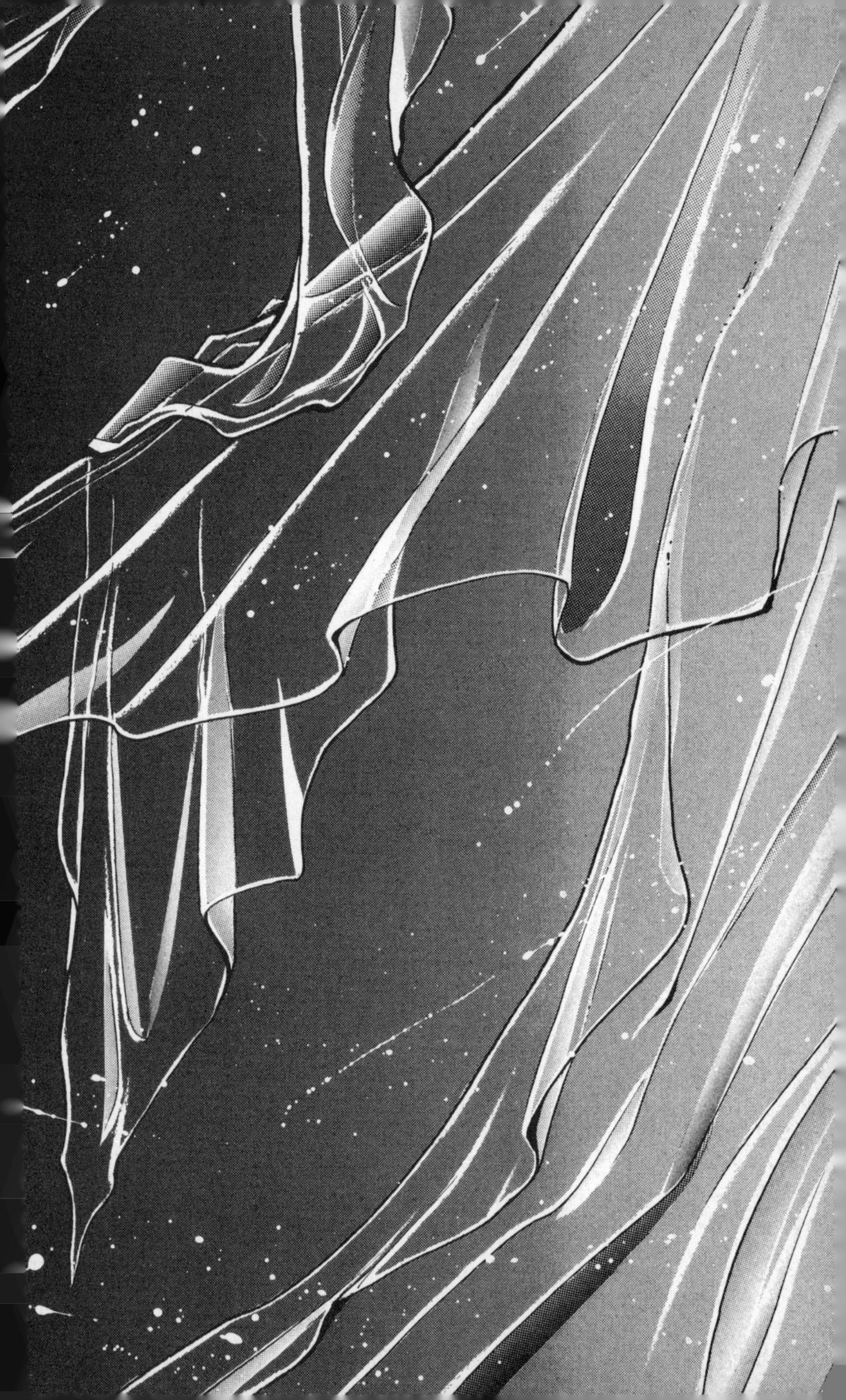

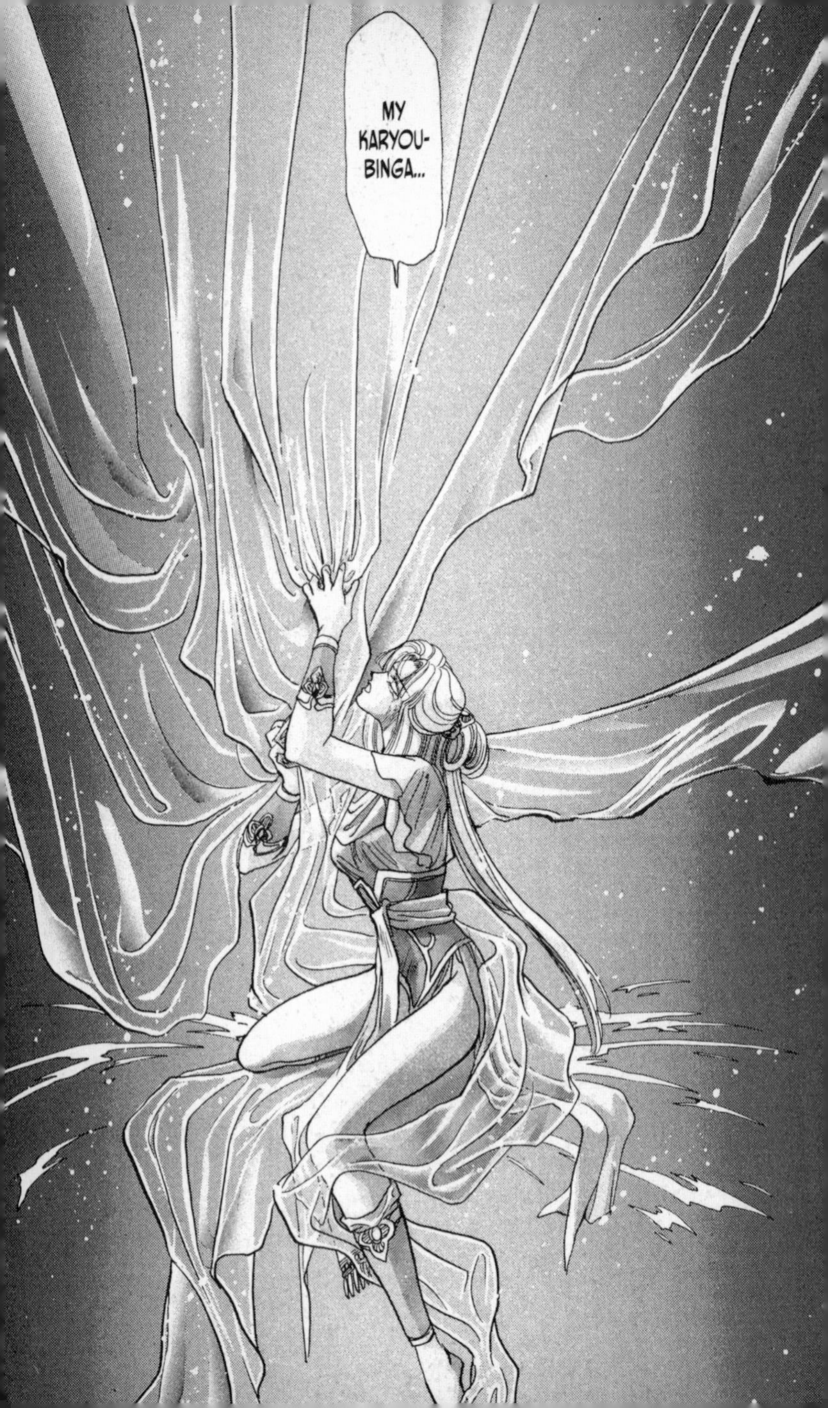
MY KARYOU-BINGA...

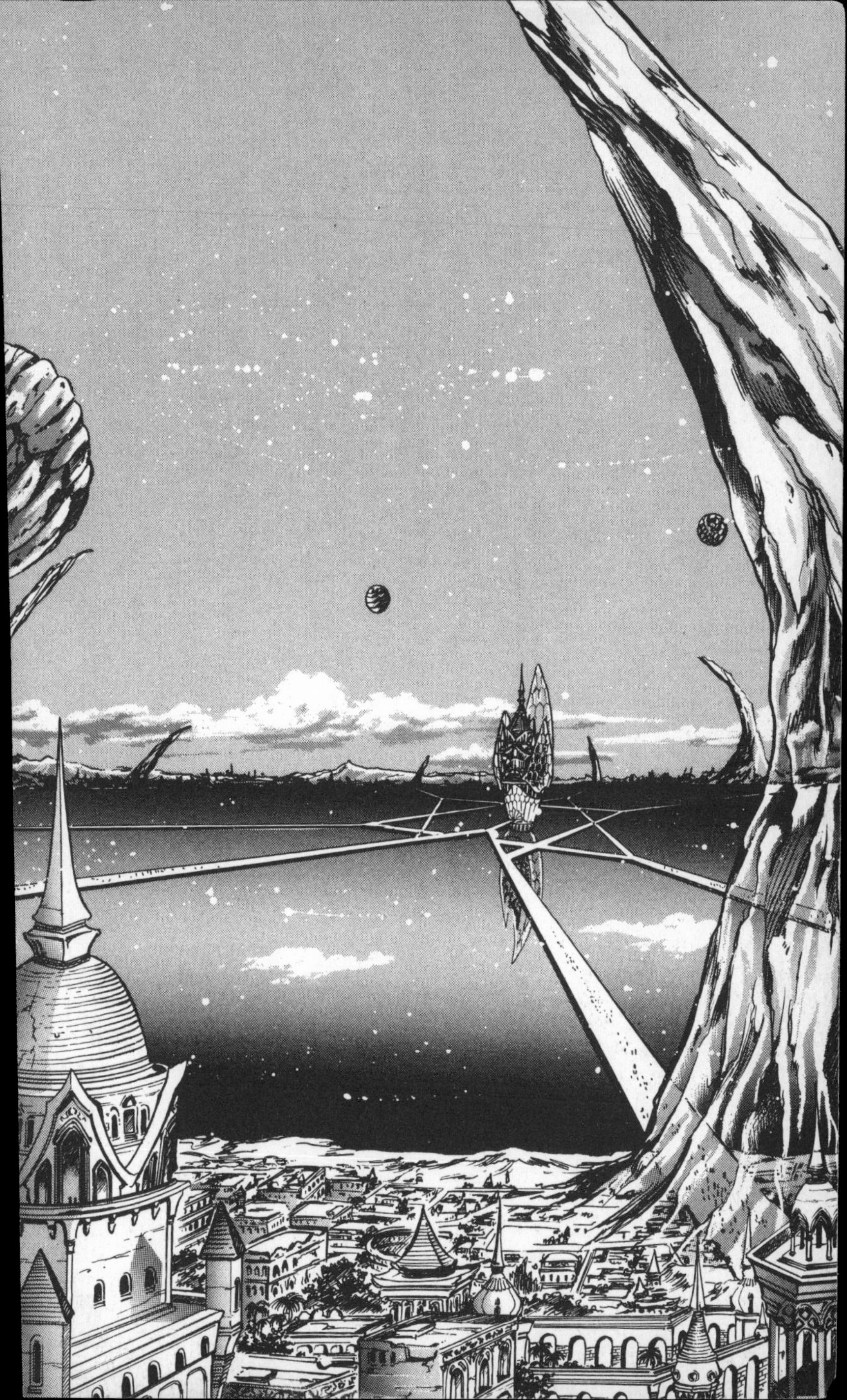

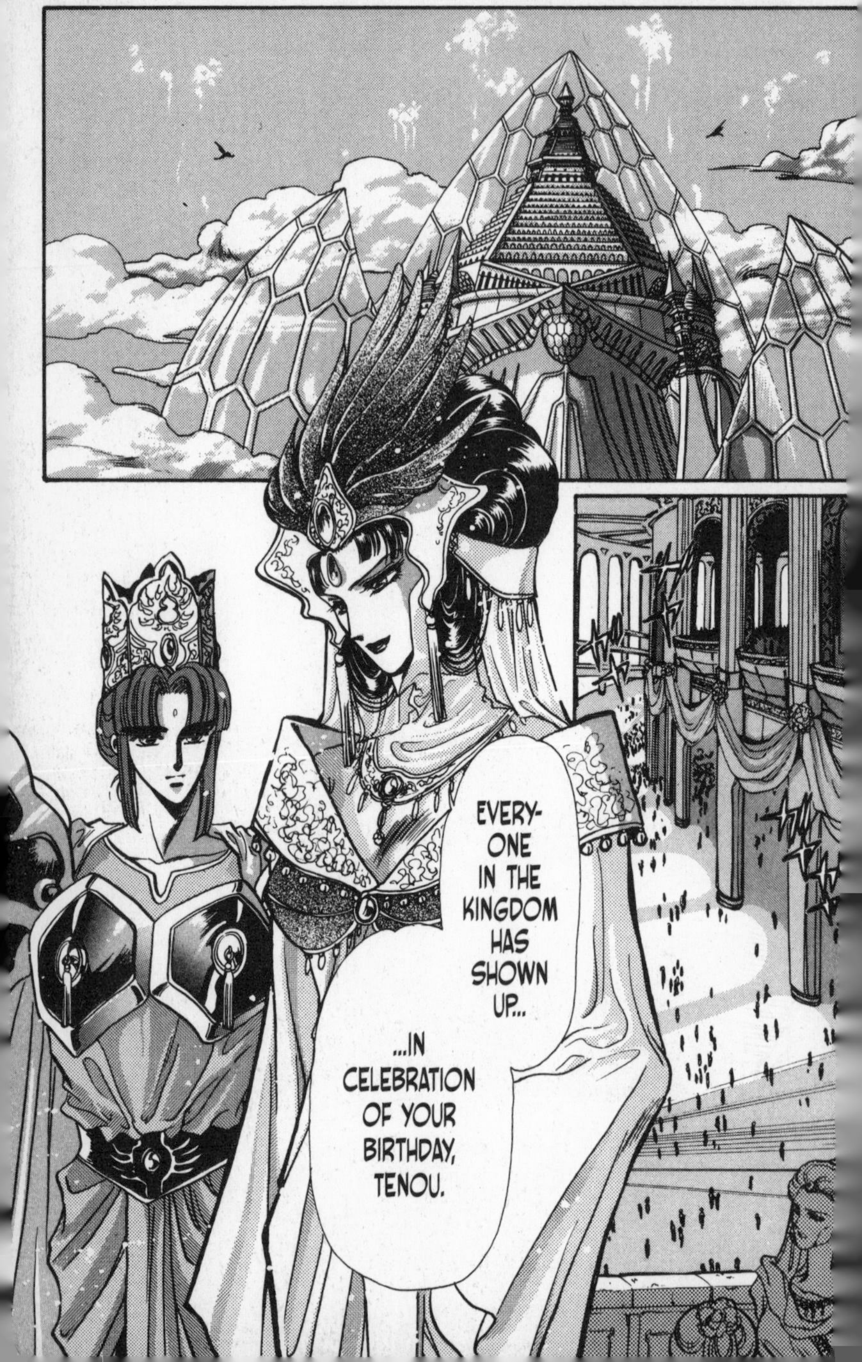
EVERY-ONE IN THE KINGDOM HAS SHOWN UP...
...IN CELEBRATION OF YOUR BIRTHDAY, TENOU.

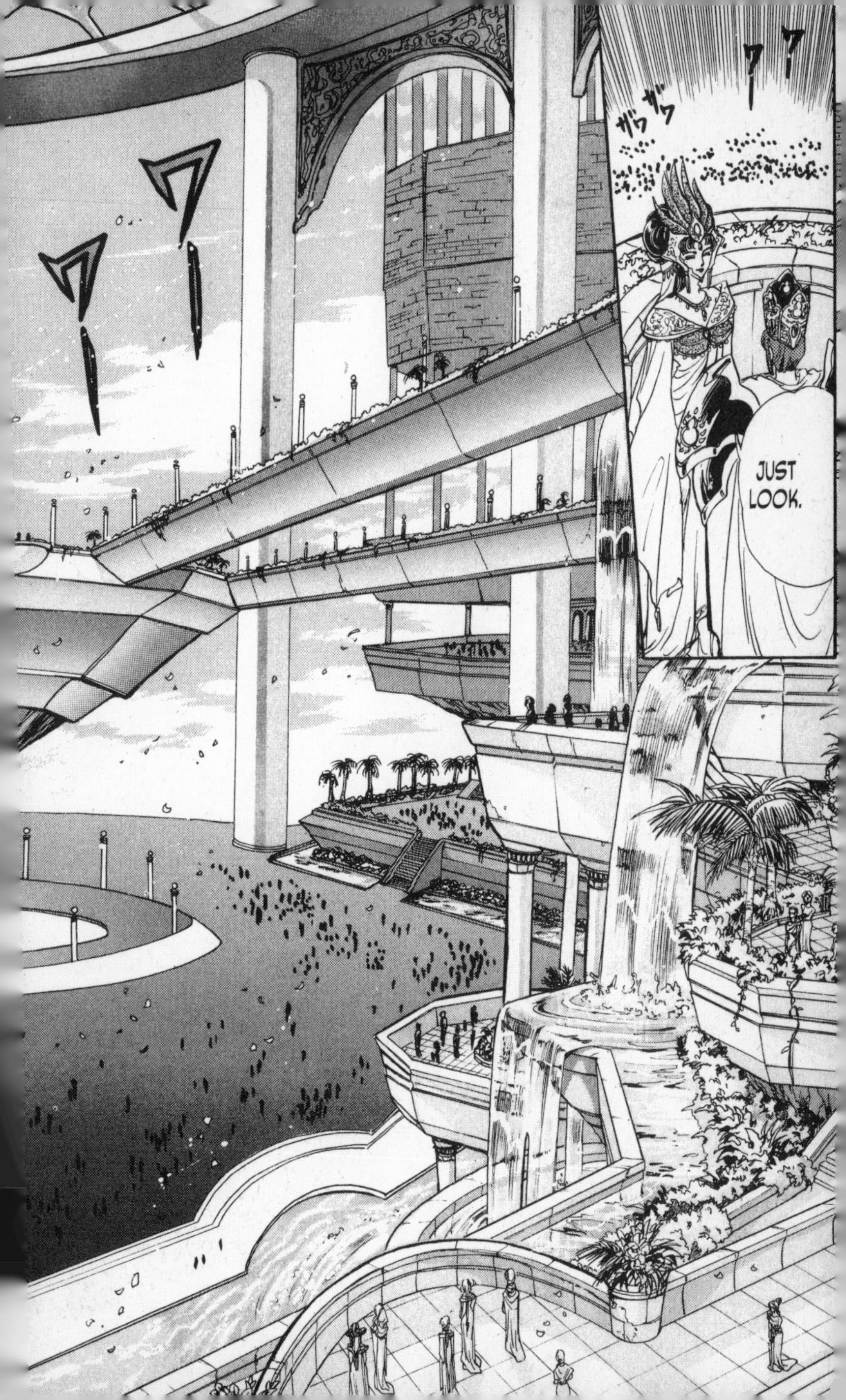
アア
ザワザワ
JUST LOOK.
ワーワー

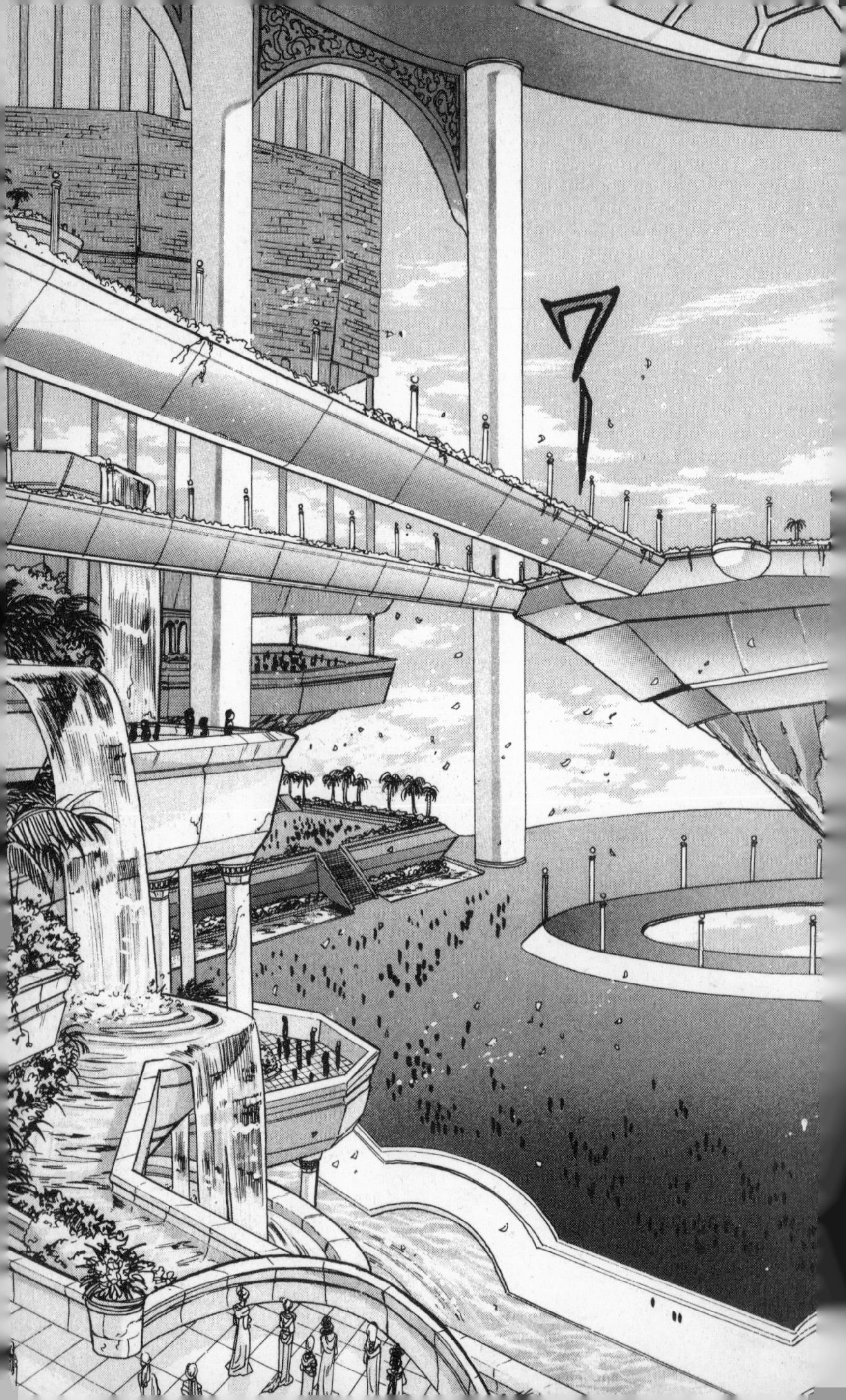
ワー

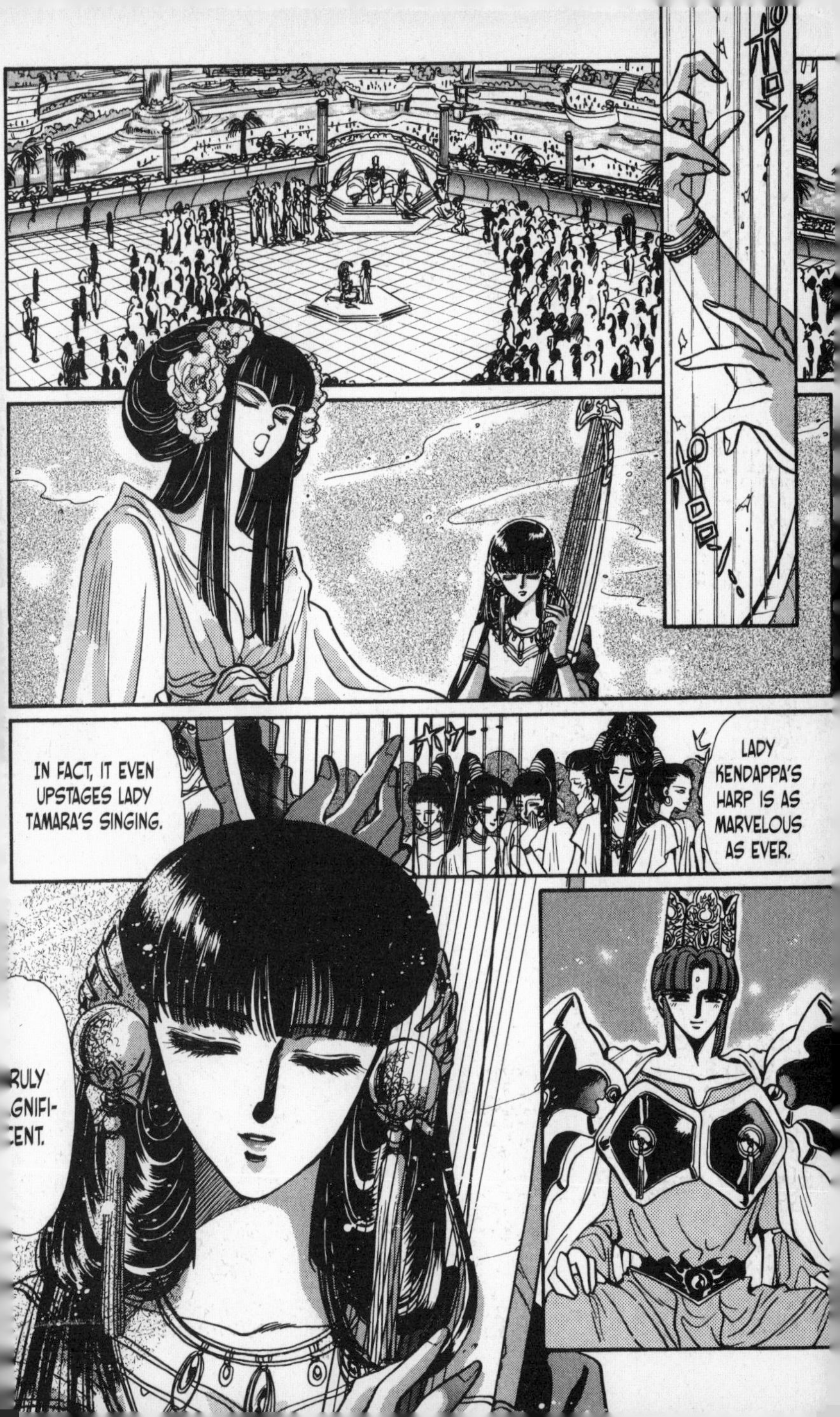
LADY KENDAPPA'S HARP IS AS MARVELOUS AS EVER.
IN FACT, IT EVEN UPSTAGES LADY TAMARA'S SINGING.
RULY GNIFI-CENT.

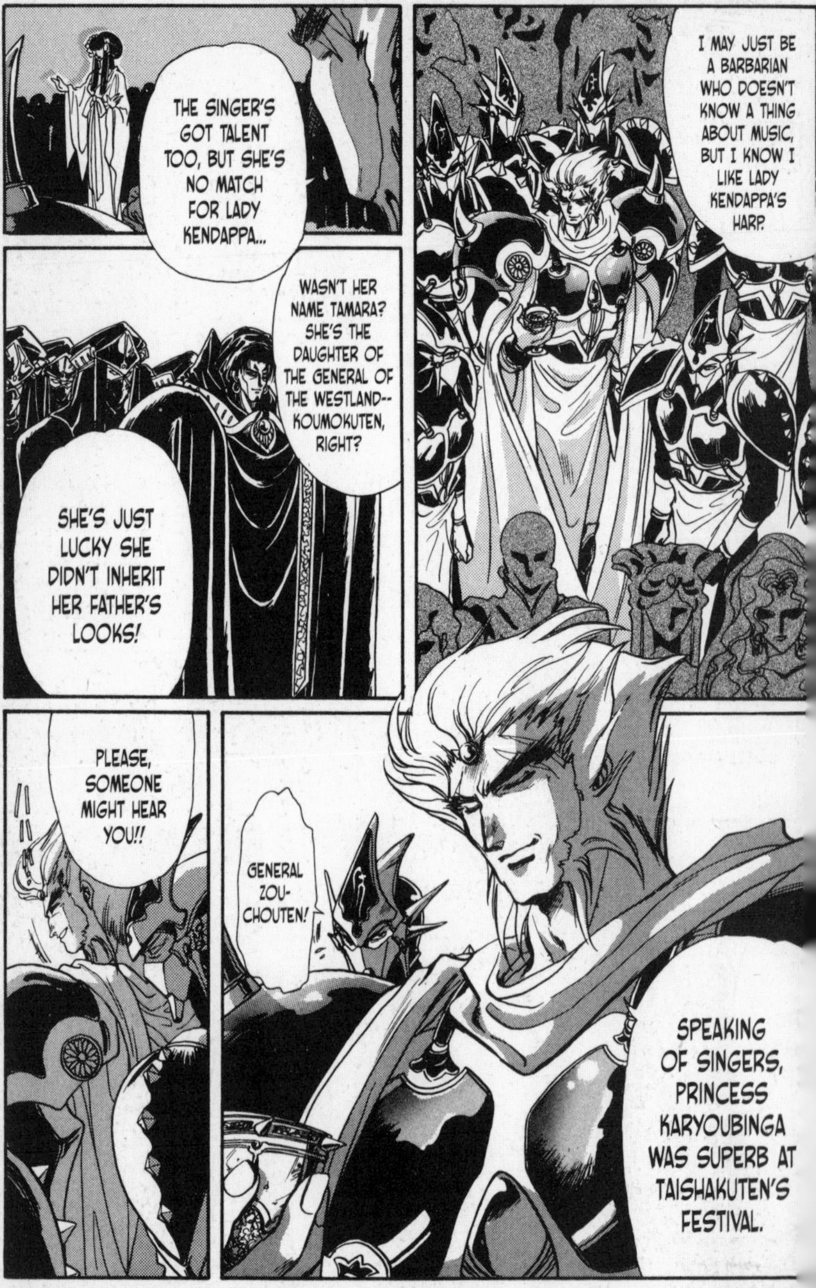
I MAY JUST BE A BARBARIAN WHO DOESN'T KNOW A THING ABOUT MUSIC, BUT I KNOW I LIKE LADY KENDAPPA'S HARP.
THE SINGER'S GOT TALENT TOO, BUT SHE'S NO MATCH FOR LADY KENDAPPA...
WASN'T HER NAME TAMARA? SHE'S THE DAUGHTER OF THE GENERAL OF THE WESTLAND--KOUMOKUTEN, RIGHT?
SHE'S JUST LUCKY SHE DIDN'T INHERIT HER FATHER'S LOOKS!
GENERAL ZOU-CHOUTEN!
SPEAKING OF SINGERS, PRINCESS KARYOUBINGA WAS SUPERB AT TAISHAKUTEN'S FESTIVAL.
PLEASE, SOMEONE MIGHT HEAR YOU!!

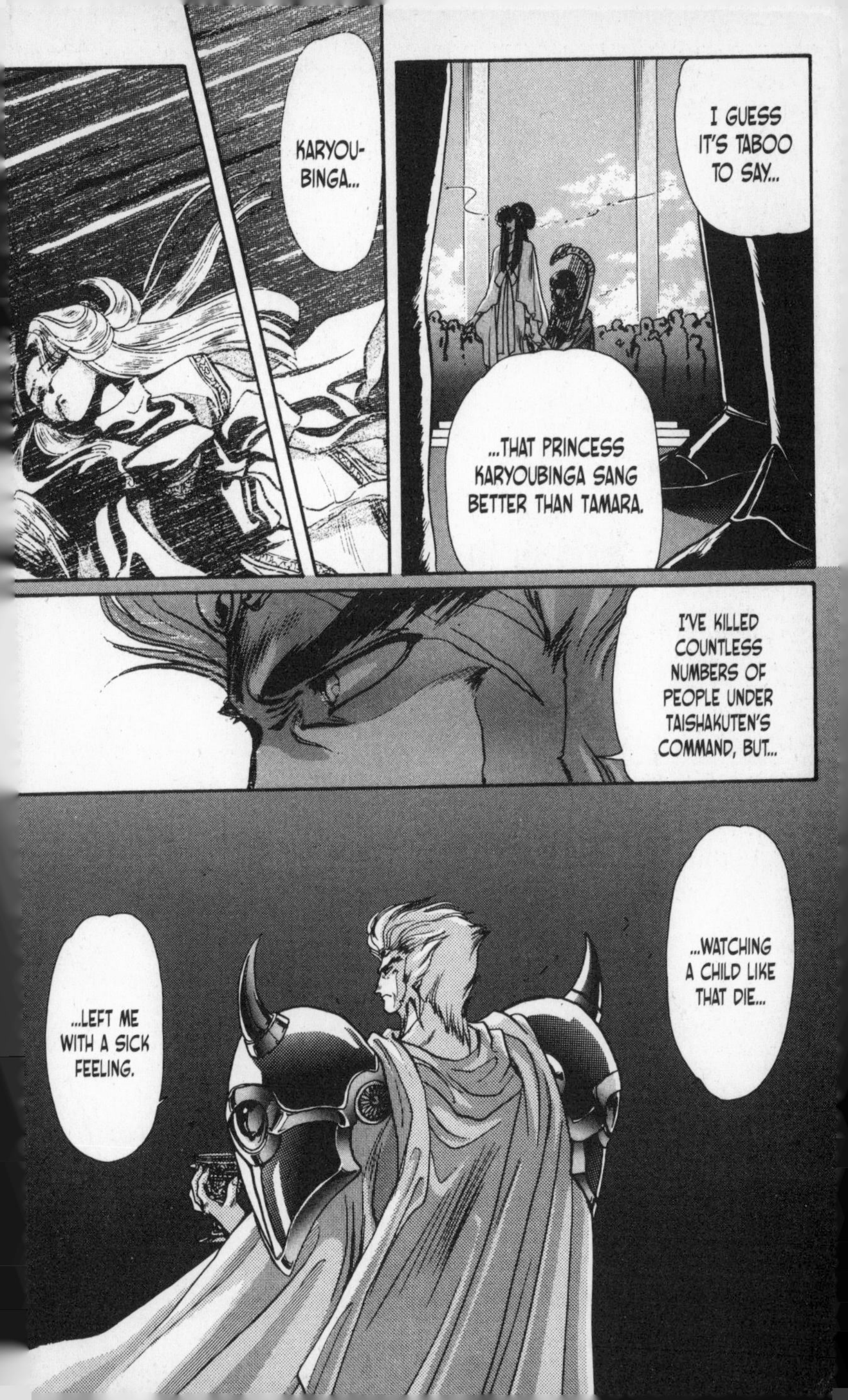
I GUESS IT'S TABOO TO SAY...
...THAT PRINCESS KARYOUBINGA SANG BETTER THAN TAMARA.
KARYOU-BINGA...
I'VE KILLED COUNTLESS NUMBERS OF PEOPLE UNDER TAISHAKUTEN'S COMMAND, BUT...
...WATCHING A CHILD LIKE THAT DIE...
...LEFT ME WITH A SICK FEELING.

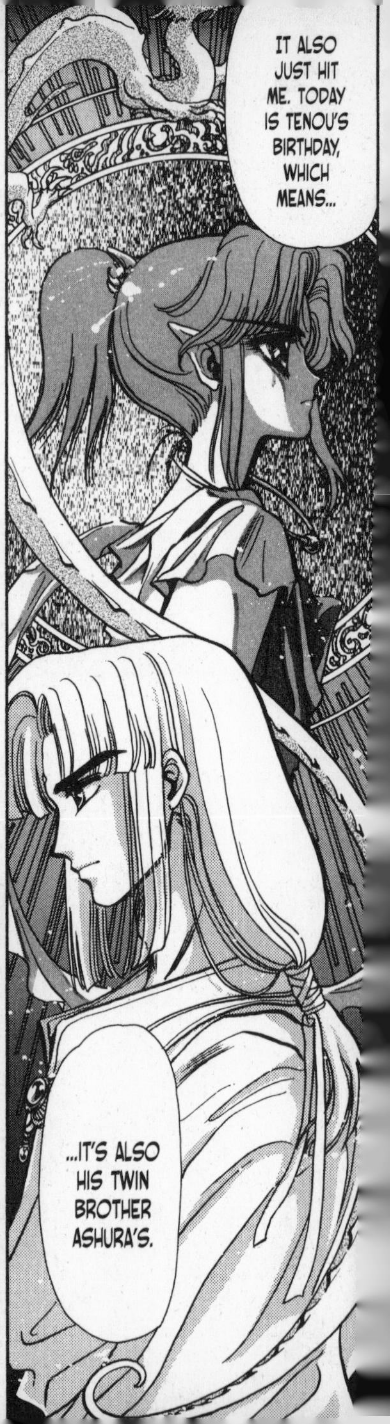
IT ALSO JUST HIT ME. TODAY IS TENOU'S BIRTHDAY, WHICH MEANS...
...IT'S ALSO HIS TWIN BROTHER ASHURA'S.

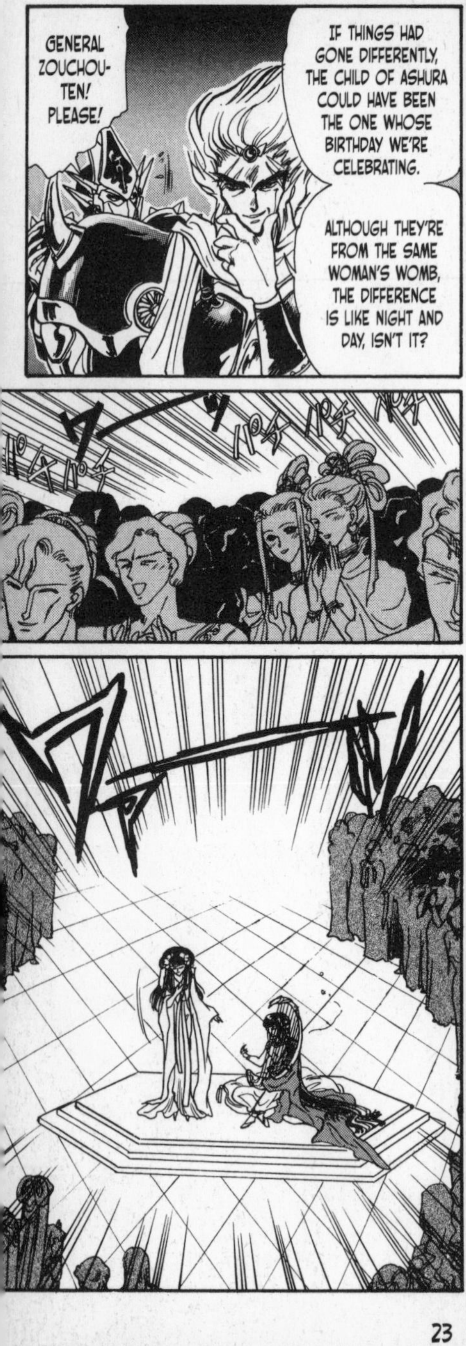
IF THINGS HAD GONE DIFFERENTLY, THE CHILD OF ASHURA COULD HAVE BEEN THE ONE WHOSE BIRTHDAY WE'RE CELEBRATING.
ALTHOUGH THEY'RE FROM THE SAME WOMAN'S WOMB, THE DIFFERENCE IS LIKE NIGHT AND DAY, ISN'T IT?
GENERAL ZOUCHOU-TEN! PLEASE!

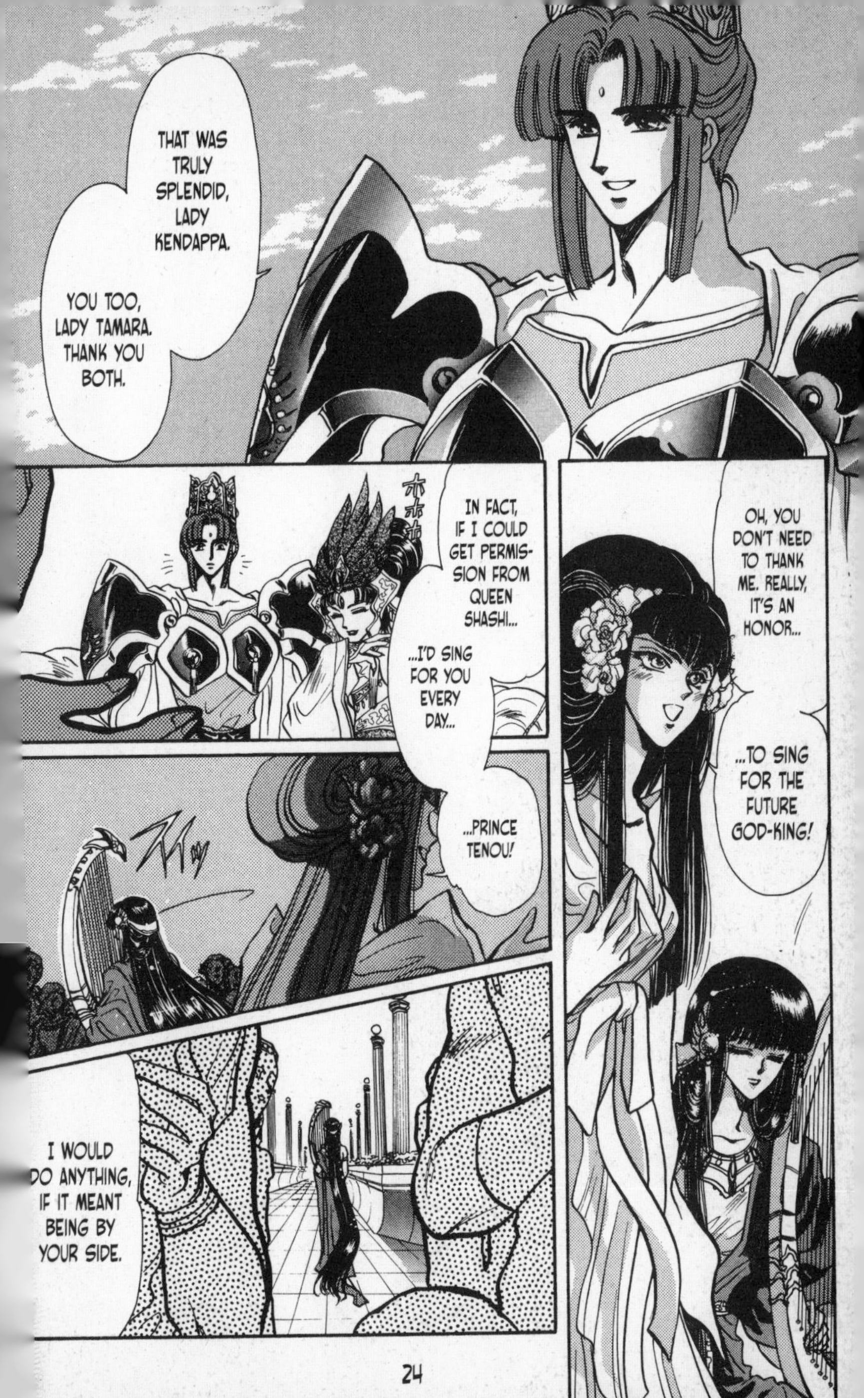
THAT WAS TRULY SPLENDID, LADY KENDAPPA.
YOU TOO, LADY TAMARA. THANK YOU BOTH.
OH, YOU DON'T NEED TO THANK ME. REALLY, IT'S AN HONOR...
...TO SING FOR THE FUTURE GOD-KING!
IN FACT, IF I COULD GET PERMIS-SION FROM QUEEN SHASHI...
...I'D SING FOR YOU EVERY DAY...
...PRINCE TENOU!
I WOULD DO ANYTHING, IF IT MEANT BEING BY YOUR SIDE.

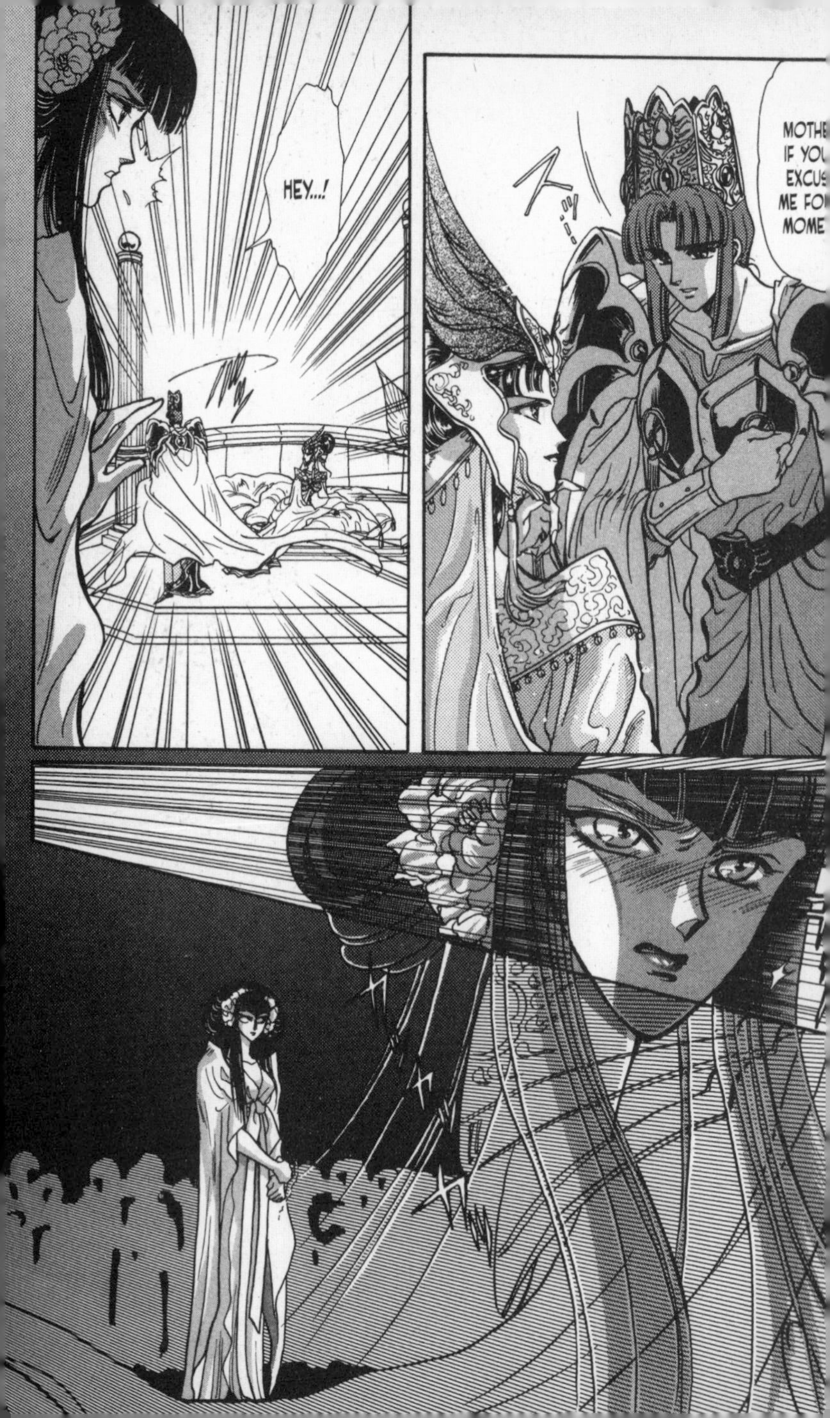
MOTHE IF YOU EXCUS ME FO MOME
HEY...!

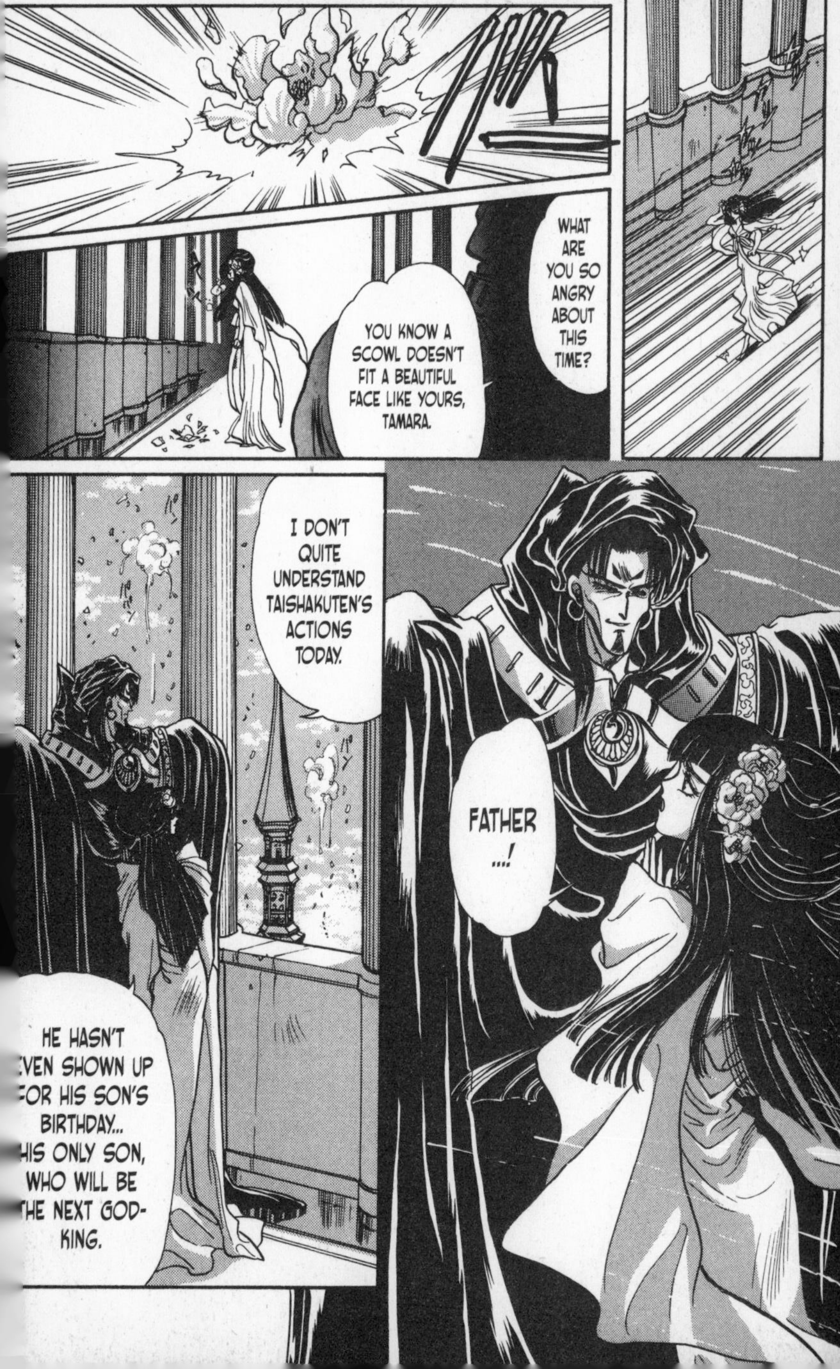

WHAT ARE YOU SO ANGRY ABOUT THIS TIME?
YOU KNOW A SCOWL DOESN'T FIT A BEAUTIFUL FACE LIKE YOURS, TAMARA.
FATHER ...!
I DON'T QUITE UNDERSTAND TAISHAKUTEN'S ACTIONS TODAY.
HE HASN'T EVEN SHOWN UP FOR HIS SON'S BIRTHDAY... HIS ONLY SON, WHO WILL BE THE NEXT GOD-KING.

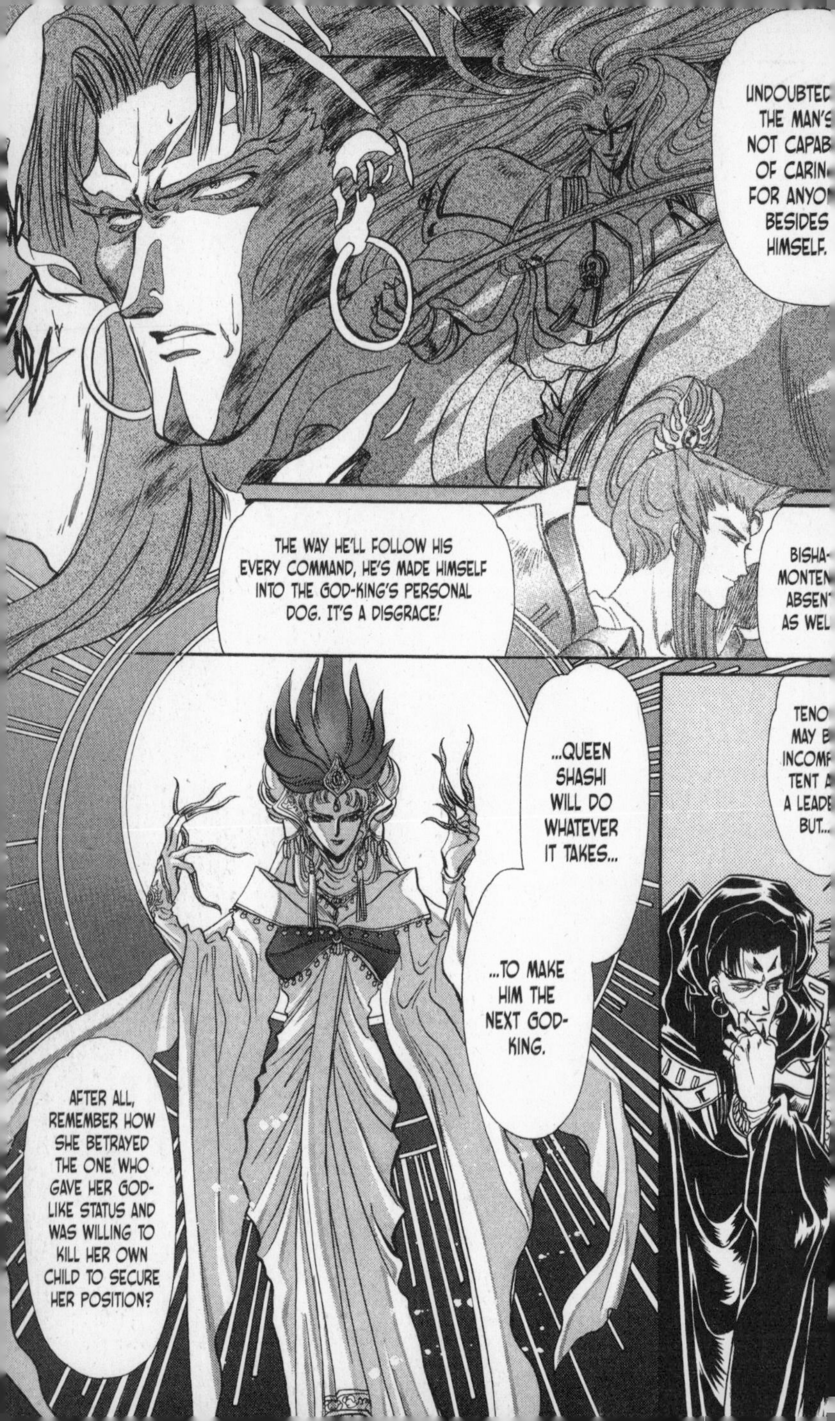
UNDOUBTED THE MAN'S NOT CAPAB OF CARIN FOR ANYO BESIDES HIMSELF.
THE WAY HE'LL FOLLOW HIS EVERY COMMAND, HE'S MADE HIMSELF INTO THE GOD-KING'S PERSONAL DOG. IT'S A DISGRACE!
BISHA-MONTEN ABSENT AS WEL
TENO MAY B INCOMP TENT A A LEADE BUT...
...QUEEN SHASHI WILL DO WHATEVER IT TAKES...
...TO MAKE HIM THE NEXT GOD-KING.
AFTER ALL, REMEMBER HOW SHE BETRAYED THE ONE WHO GAVE HER GOD-LIKE STATUS AND WAS WILLING TO KILL HER OWN CHILD TO SECURE HER POSITION?

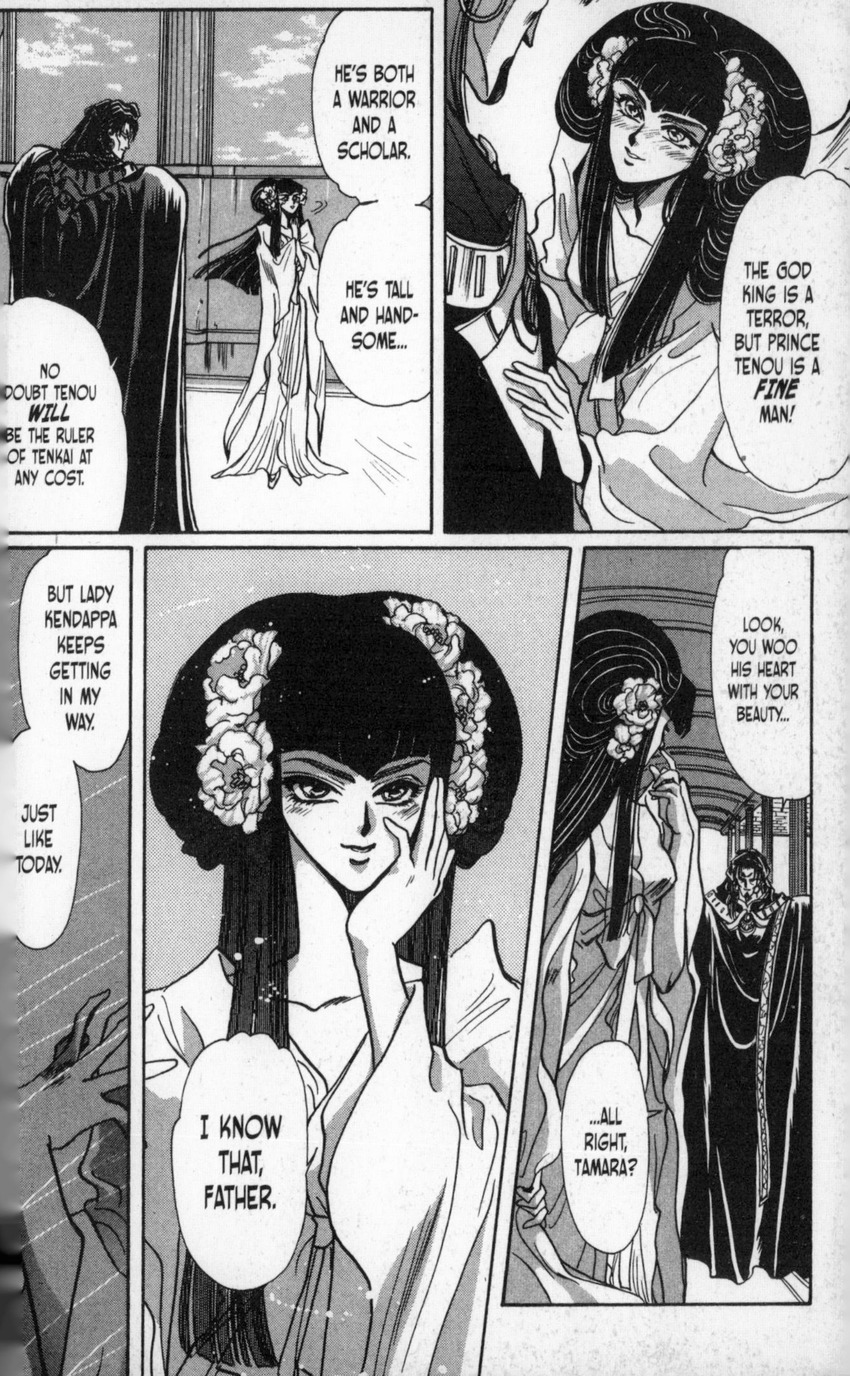
THE GOD KING IS A TERROR, BUT PRINCE TENOU IS A FINE MAN!
HE'S BOTH A WARRIOR AND A SCHOLAR.
HE'S TALL AND HAND-SOME...
NO DOUBT TENOU WILL BE THE RULER OF TENKAI AT ANY COST.
LOOK, YOU WOO HIS HEART WITH YOUR BEAUTY...
...ALL RIGHT, TAMARA?
I KNOW THAT, FATHER.
BUT LADY KENDAPPA KEEPS GETTING IN MY WAY.
JUST LIKE TODAY.

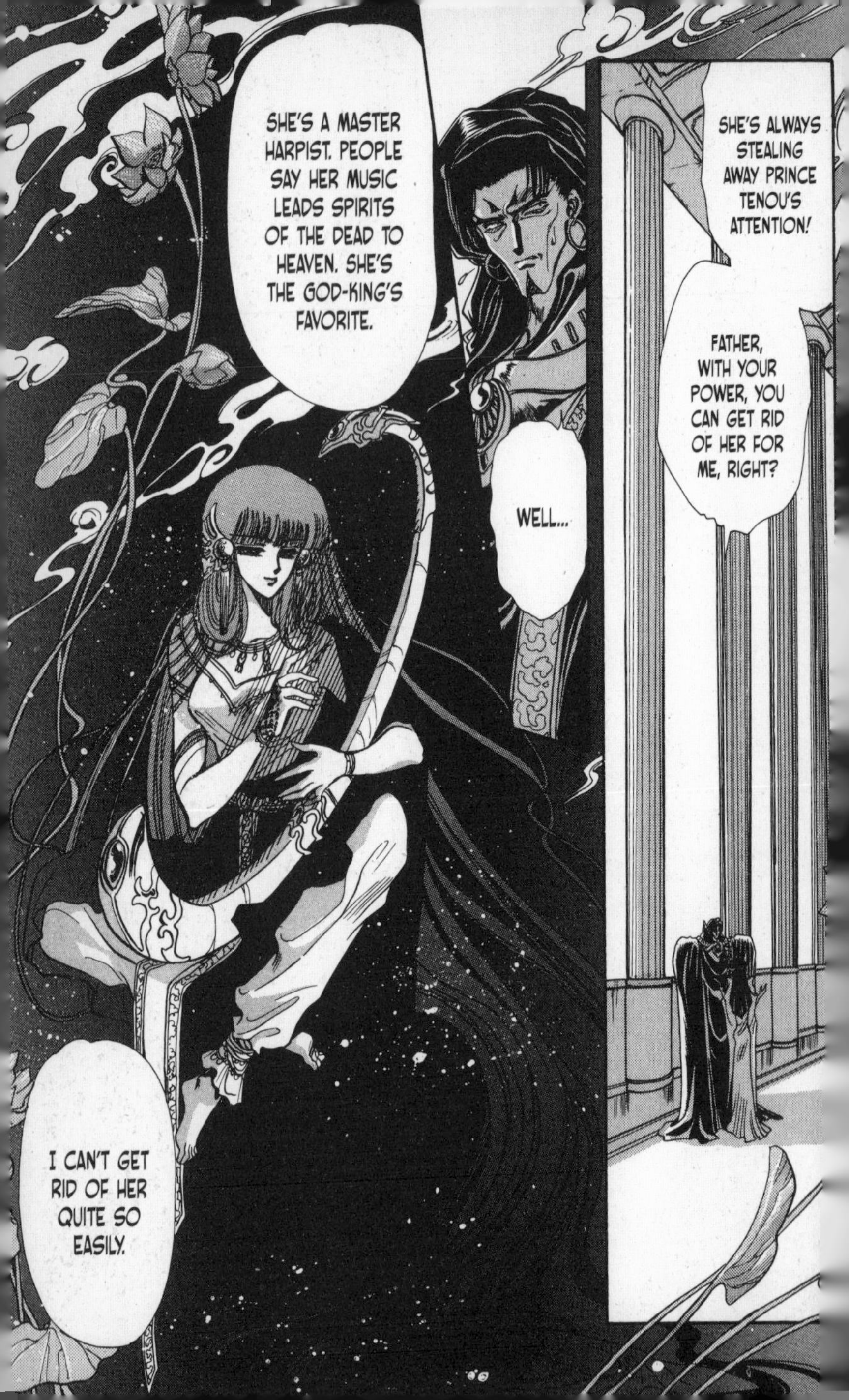
SHE'S ALWAYS STEALING AWAY PRINCE TENOU'S ATTENTION!
FATHER, WITH YOUR POWER, YOU CAN GET RID OF HER FOR ME, RIGHT?
WELL...
SHE'S A MASTER HARPIST. PEOPLE SAY HER MUSIC LEADS SPIRITS OF THE DEAD TO HEAVEN. SHE'S THE GOD-KING'S FAVORITE.
I CAN'T GET RID OF HER QUITE SO EASILY.

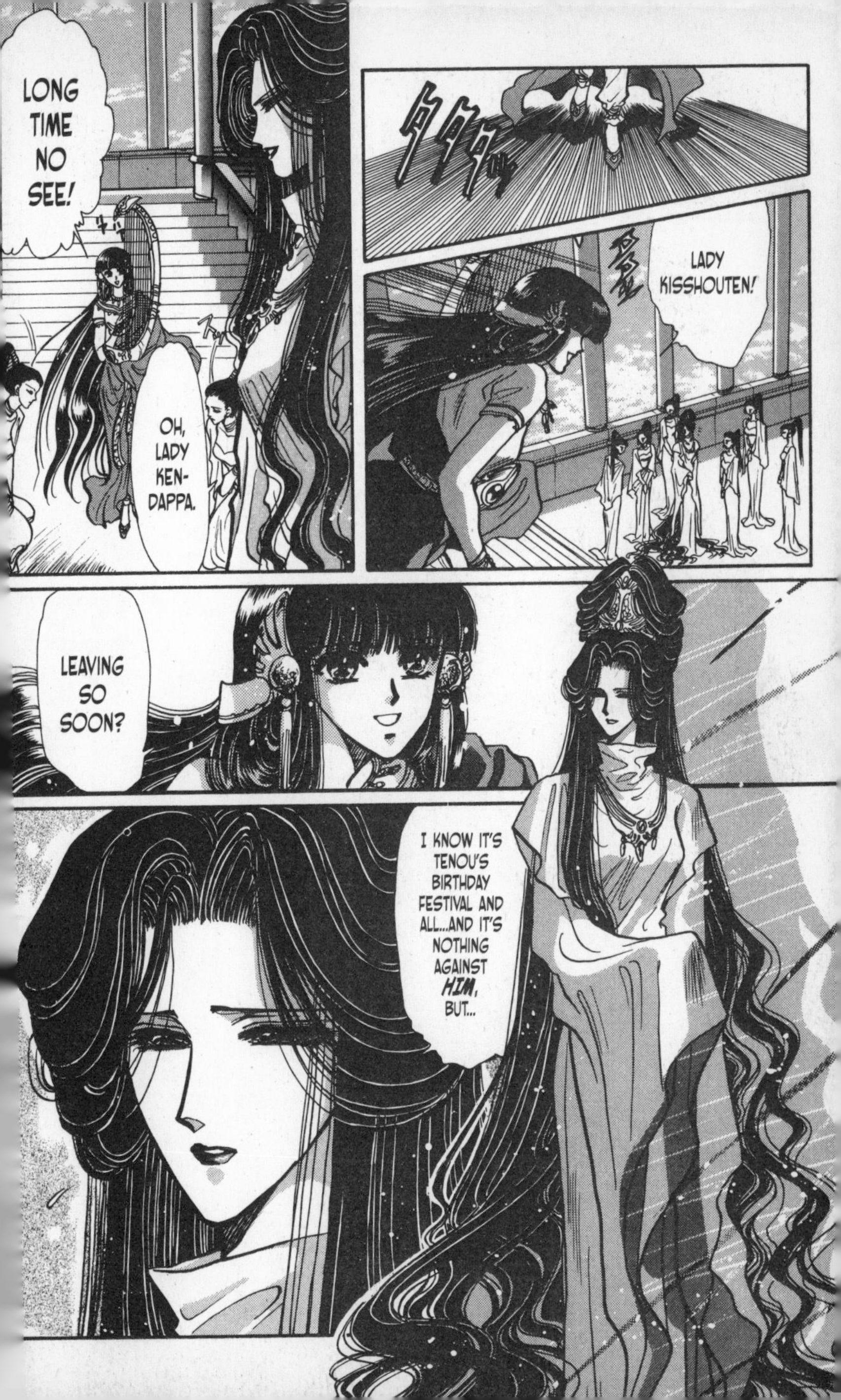
LADY KISSHOUTEN!
LONG TIME NO SEE!
OH, LADY KEN-DAPPA.
LEAVING SO SOON?
I KNOW IT'S TENOU'S BIRTHDAY FESTIVAL AND ALL...AND IT'S NOTHING AGAINST *HIM*, BUT...

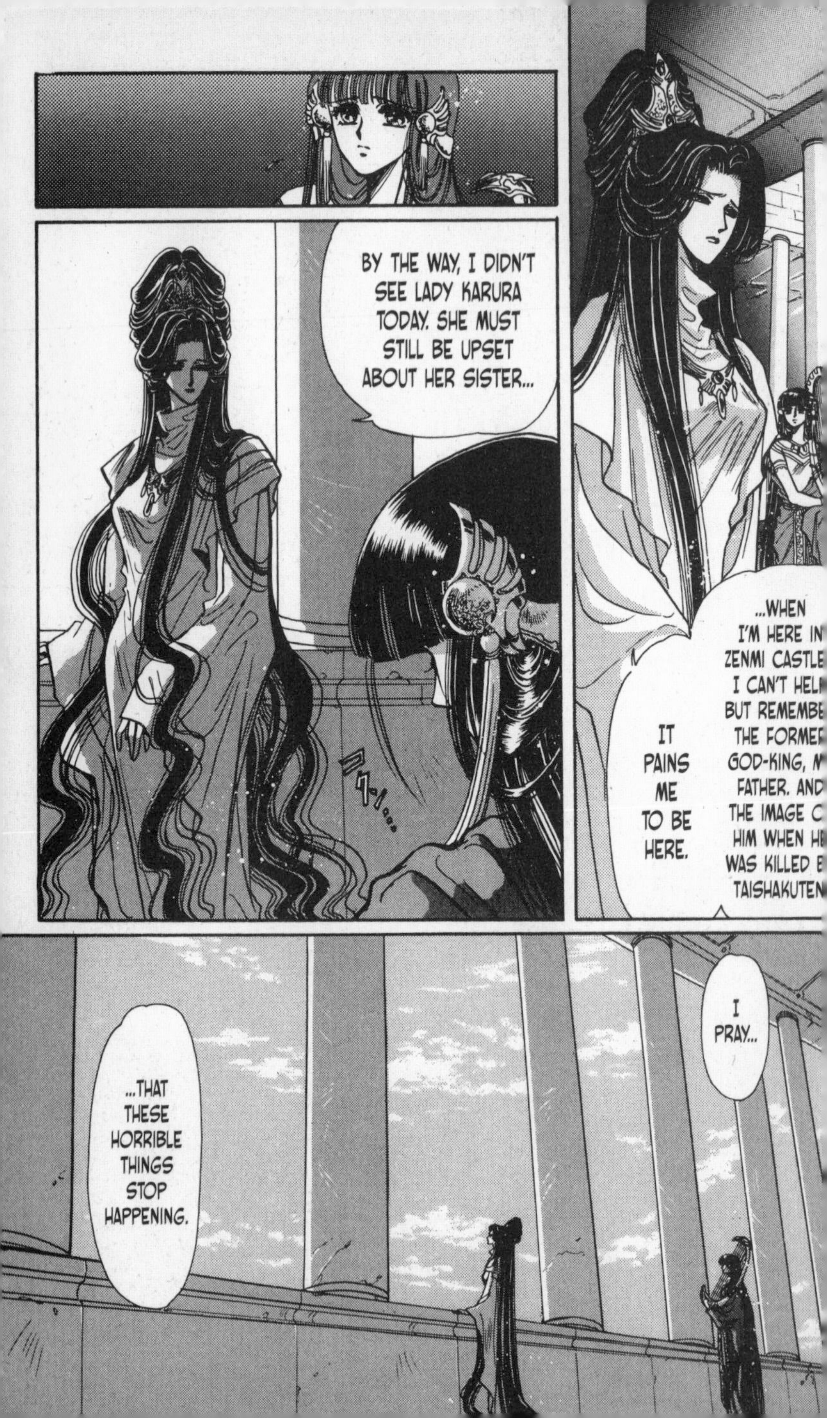
...WHEN I'M HERE IN ZENMI CASTLE I CAN'T HELP BUT REMEMBE THE FORMER GOD-KING, M FATHER. AND THE IMAGE C HIM WHEN HE WAS KILLED B TAISHAKUTEN
IT PAINS ME TO BE HERE.
BY THE WAY, I DIDN'T SEE LADY KARURA TODAY. SHE MUST STILL BE UPSET ABOUT HER SISTER...
I PRAY...
...THAT THESE HORRIBLE THINGS STOP HAPPENING.

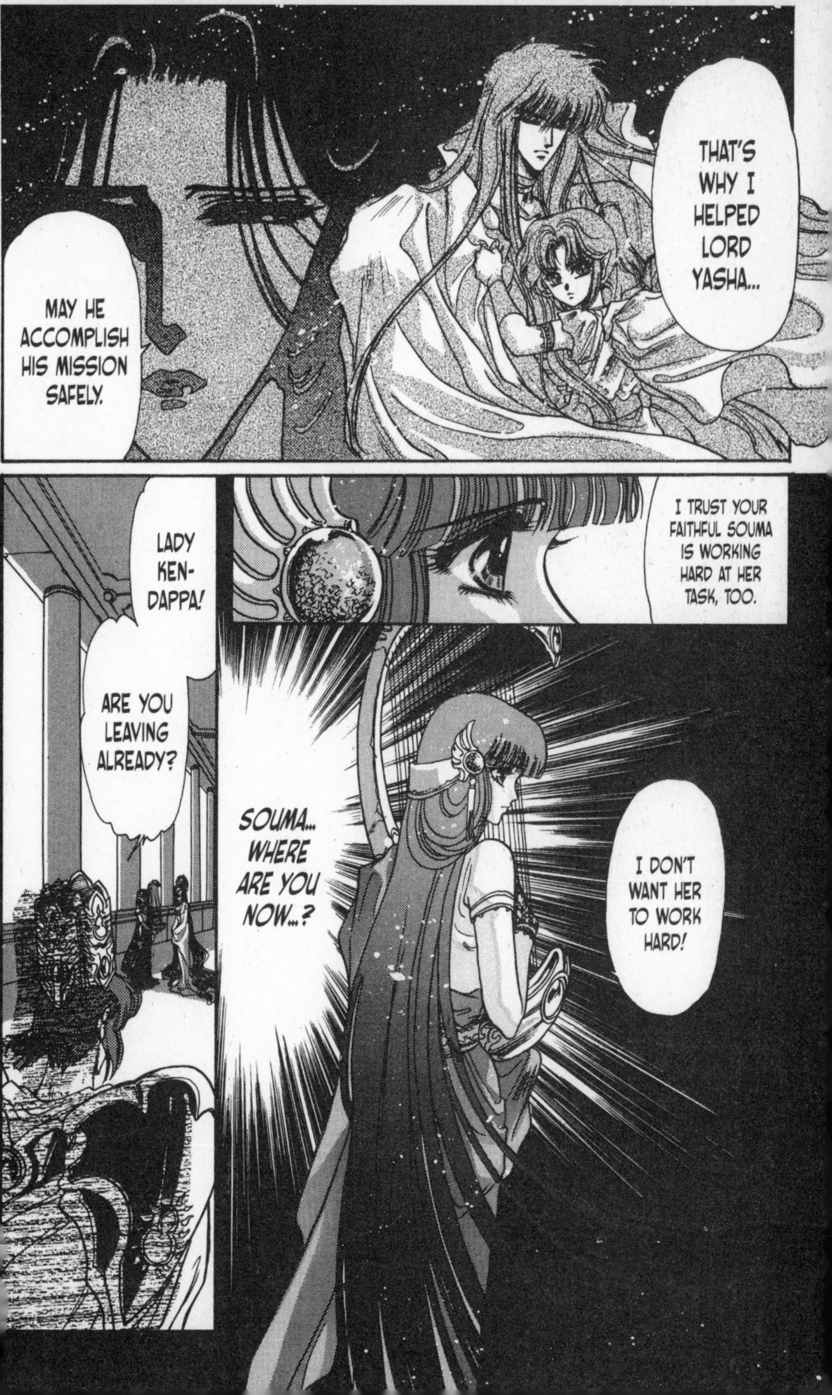
THAT'S WHY I HELPED LORD YASHA...
MAY HE ACCOMPLISH HIS MISSION SAFELY.
I TRUST YOUR FAITHFUL SOUMA IS WORKING HARD AT HER TASK, TOO.
I DON'T WANT HER TO WORK HARD!
SOUMA... WHERE ARE YOU NOW...?
LADY KEN-DAPPA!
ARE YOU LEAVING ALREADY?

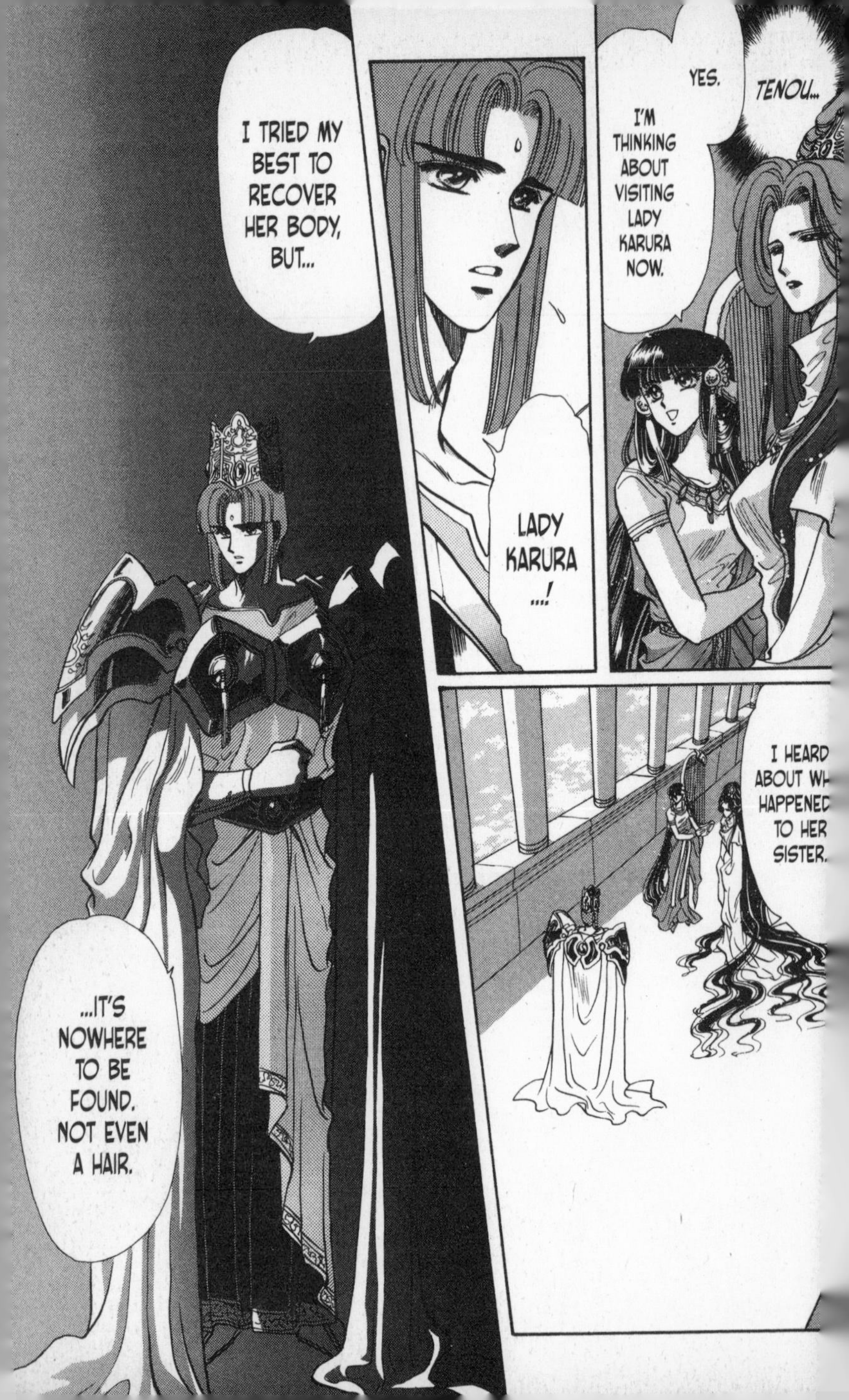
TENOU...
YES.
I'M THINKING ABOUT VISITING LADY KARURA NOW.
LADY KARURA ...!
I HEARD ABOUT WH HAPPENED TO HER SISTER.
I TRIED MY BEST TO RECOVER HER BODY, BUT...
...IT'S NOWHERE TO BE FOUND. NOT EVEN A HAIR.

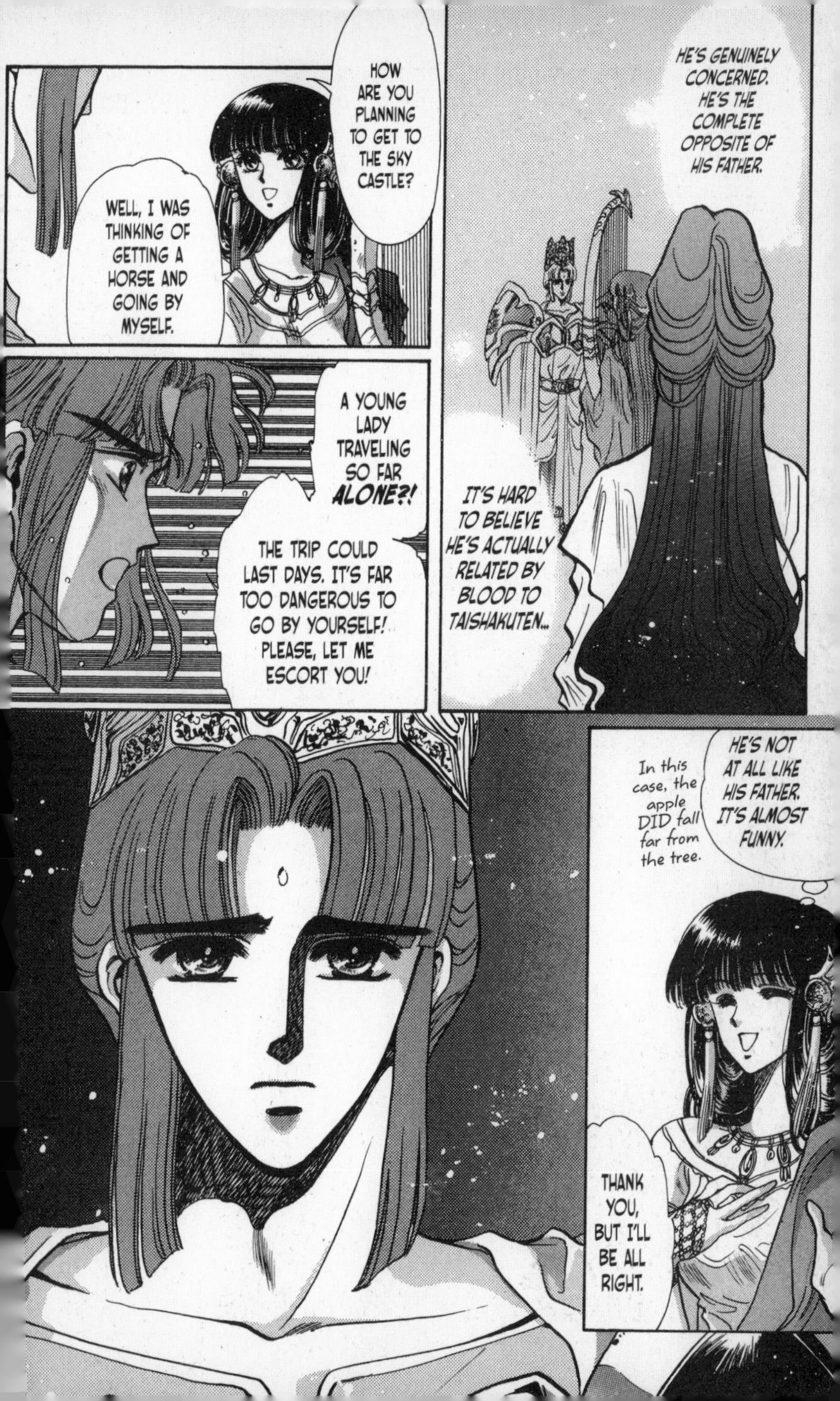
HE'S GENUINELY CONCERNED. HE'S THE COMPLETE OPPOSITE OF HIS FATHER.
IT'S HARD TO BELIEVE HE'S ACTUALLY RELATED BY BLOOD TO TAISHAKUTEN...
HOW ARE YOU PLANNING TO GET TO THE SKY CASTLE?
WELL, I WAS THINKING OF GETTING A HORSE AND GOING BY MYSELF.
A YOUNG LADY TRAVELING SO FAR ALONE?!
THE TRIP COULD LAST DAYS. IT'S FAR TOO DANGEROUS TO GO BY YOURSELF! PLEASE, LET ME ESCORT YOU!
HE'S NOT AT ALL LIKE HIS FATHER. IT'S ALMOST FUNNY.
In this case, the apple DID fall far from the tree.
THANK YOU, BUT I'LL BE ALL RIGHT.

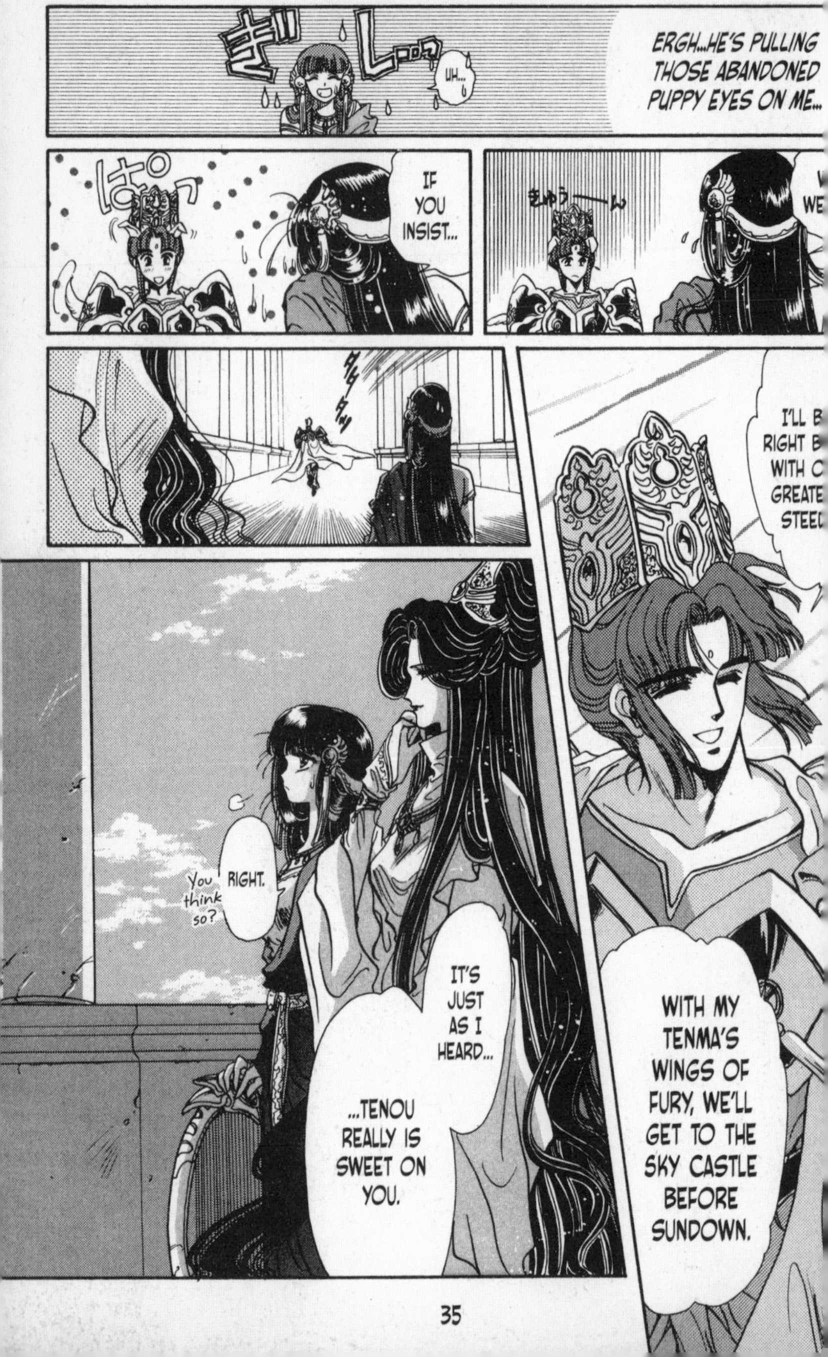
ERGH...HE'S PULLING THOSE ABANDONED PUPPY EYES ON ME...
UH...
ぱっ
IF YOU INSIST...
WITH MY TENMA'S WINGS OF FURY, WE'LL GET TO THE SKY CASTLE BEFORE SUNDOWN.
IT'S JUST AS I HEARD...
...TENOU REALLY IS SWEET ON YOU.
RIGHT.
You think so?

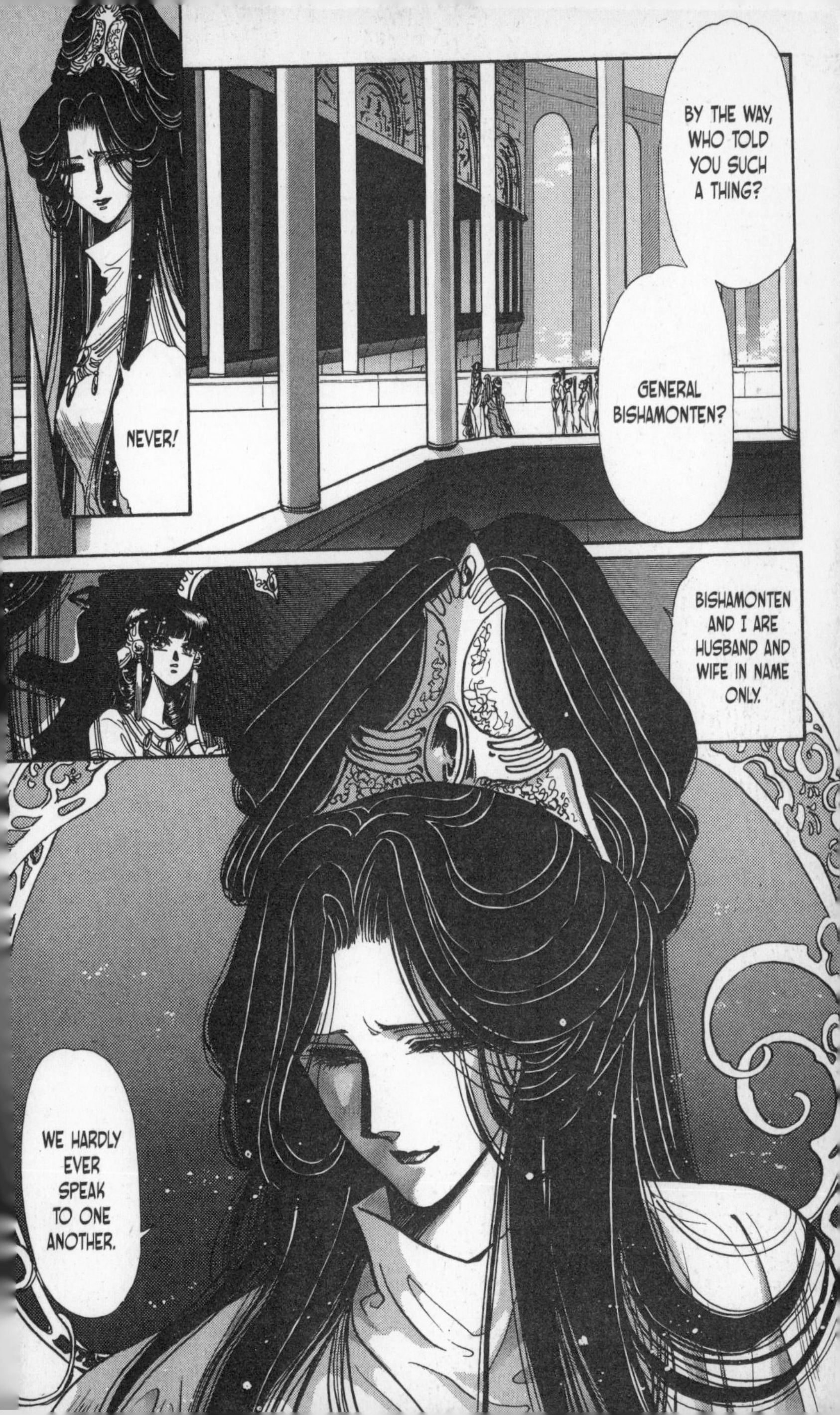
BY THE WAY, WHO TOLD YOU SUCH A THING?
GENERAL BISHAMONTEN?
NEVER!
BISHAMONTEN AND I ARE HUSBAND AND WIFE IN NAME ONLY.
WE HARDLY EVER SPEAK TO ONE ANOTHER.

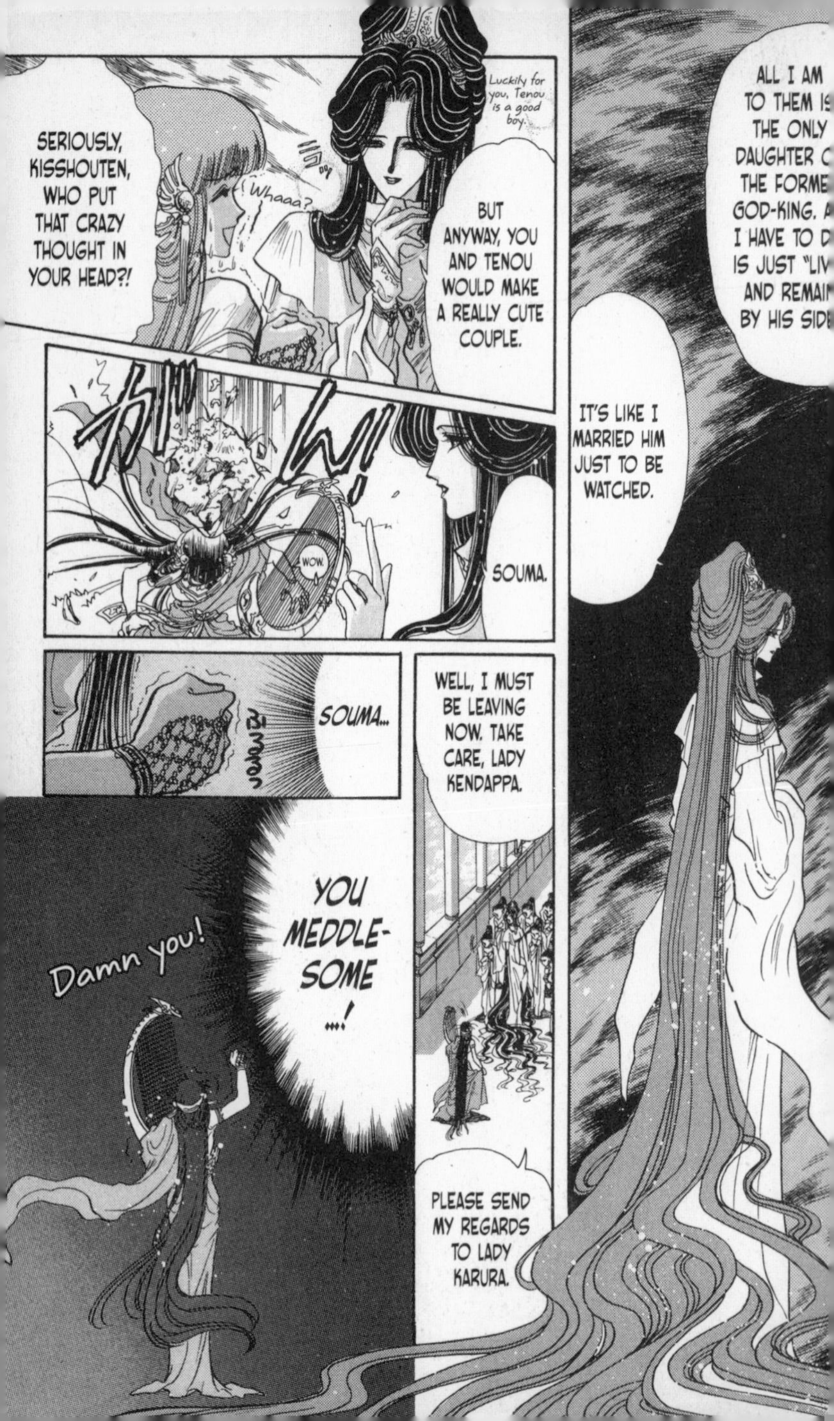
ALL I AM TO THEM IS THE ONLY DAUGHTER C THE FORME GOD-KING. A I HAVE TO D IS JUST "LIV AND REMAI BY HIS SIDE
IT'S LIKE I MARRIED HIM JUST TO BE WATCHED.
Luckily for you, Tenou is a good boy.
BUT ANYWAY, YOU AND TENOU WOULD MAKE A REALLY CUTE COUPLE.
Whaaa?
SERIOUSLY, KISSHOUTEN, WHO PUT THAT CRAZY THOUGHT IN YOUR HEAD?!
WOW.
SOUMA.
WELL, I MUST BE LEAVING NOW. TAKE CARE, LADY KENDAPPA.
PLEASE SEND MY REGARDS TO LADY KARURA.
SOUMA...
YOU MEDDLE-SOME ...!
Damn you!

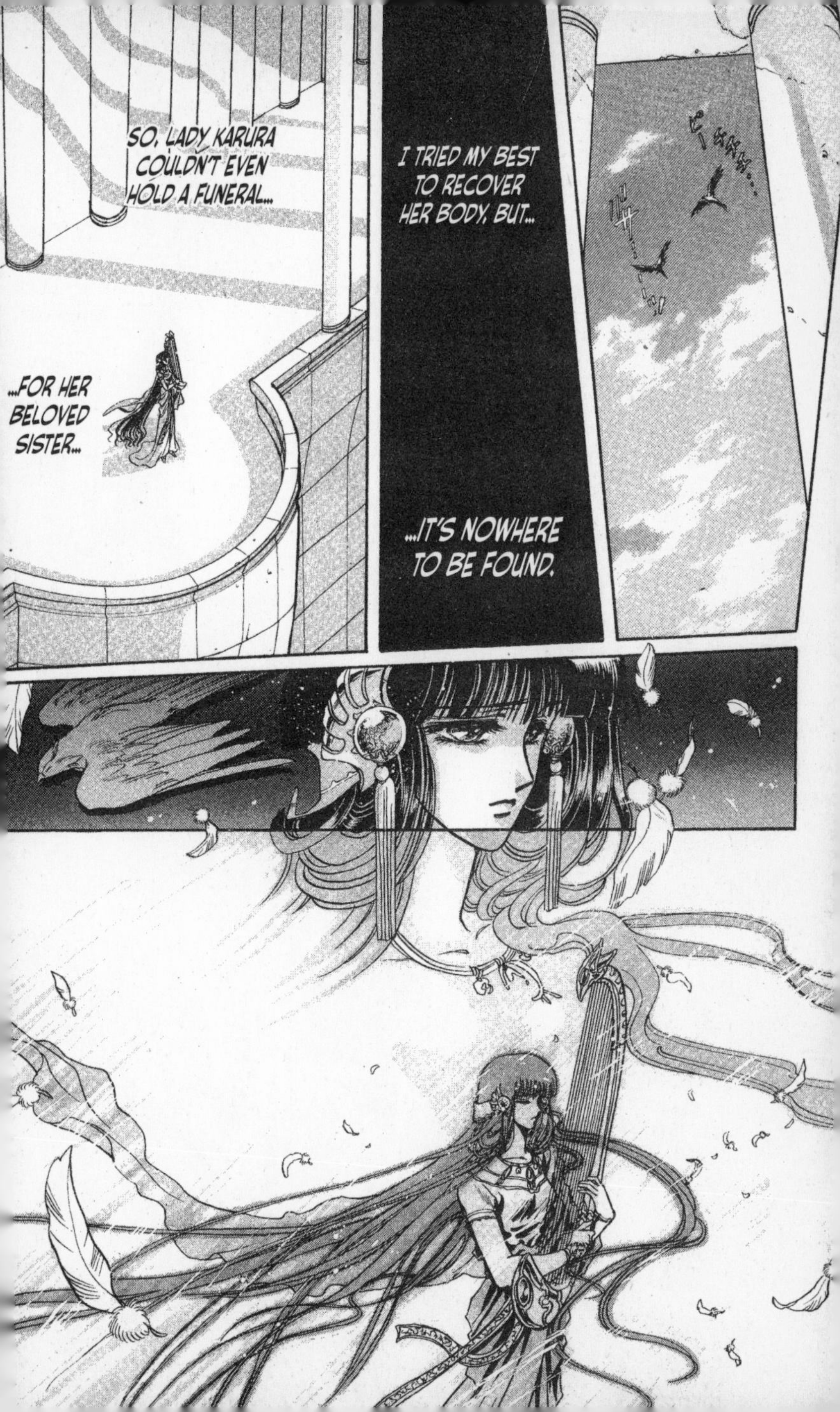
I TRIED MY BEST TO RECOVER HER BODY, BUT...
...IT'S NOWHERE TO BE FOUND.
SO, LADY KARURA COULDN'T EVEN HOLD A FUNERAL...
...FOR HER BELOVED SISTER...

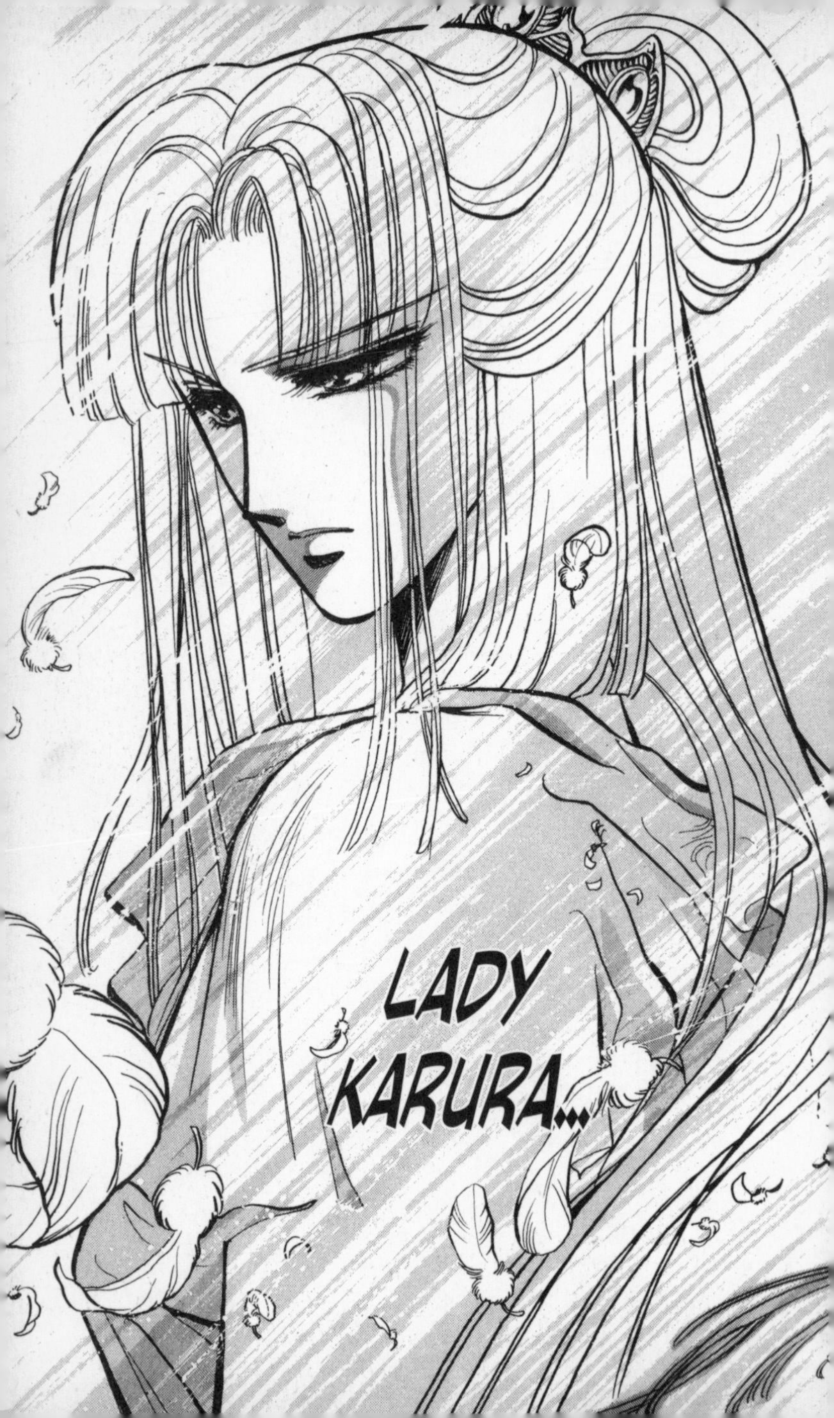
LADY KARURA...

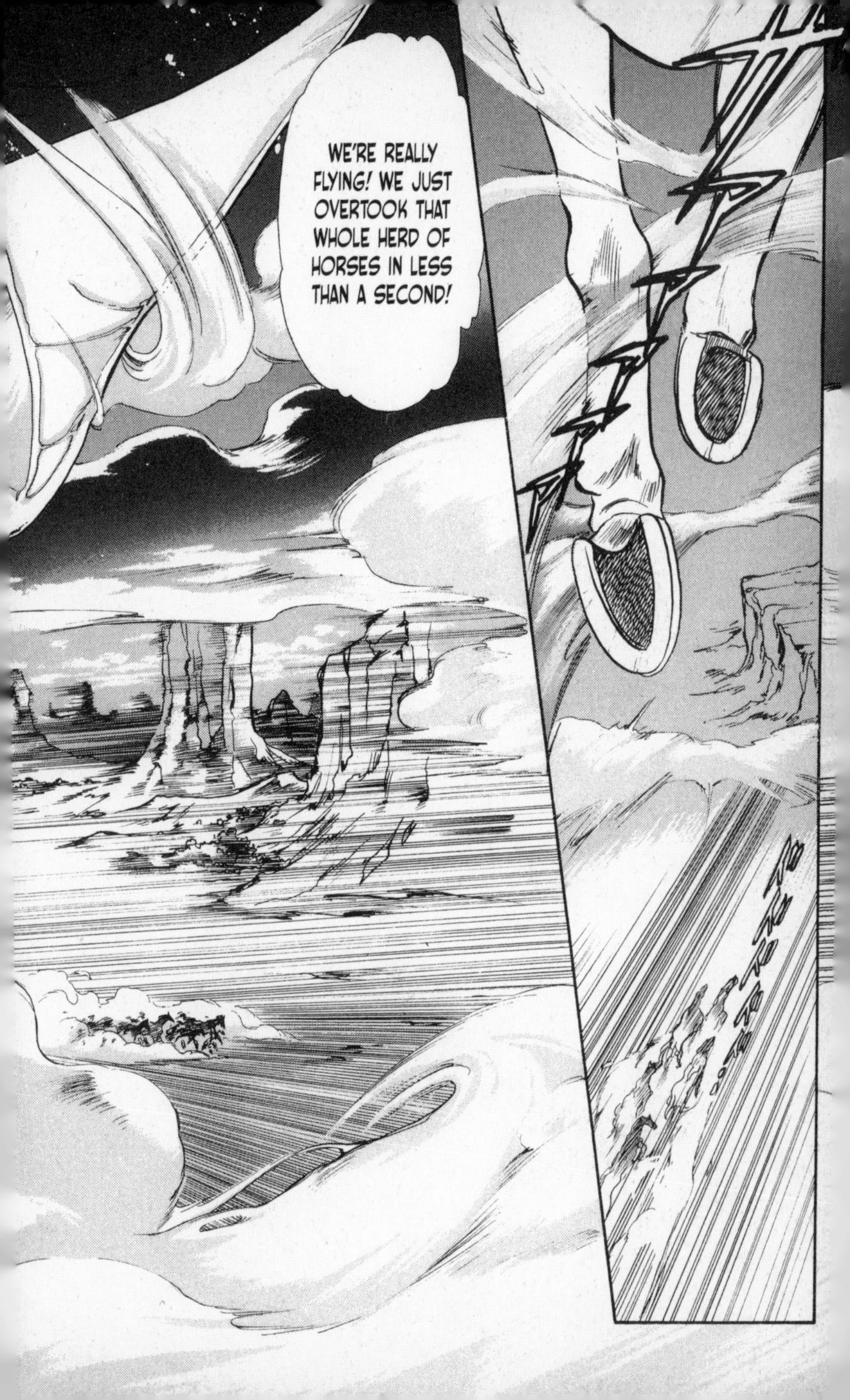
WE'RE REALLY FLYING! WE JUST OVERTOOK THAT WHOLE HERD OF HORSES IN LESS THAN A SECOND!

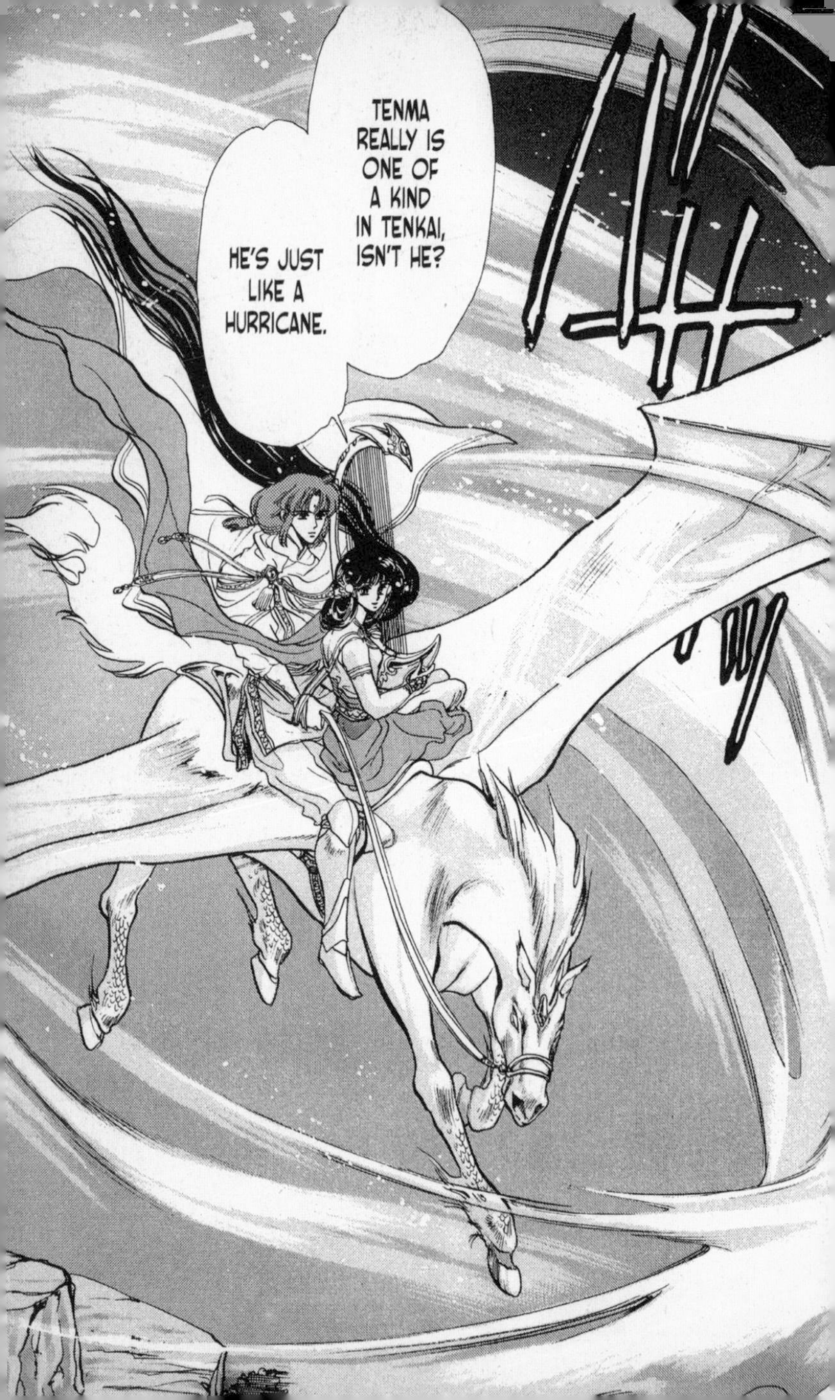
TENMA REALLY IS ONE OF A KIND IN TENKAI, ISN'T HE?
HE'S JUST LIKE A HURRICANE.

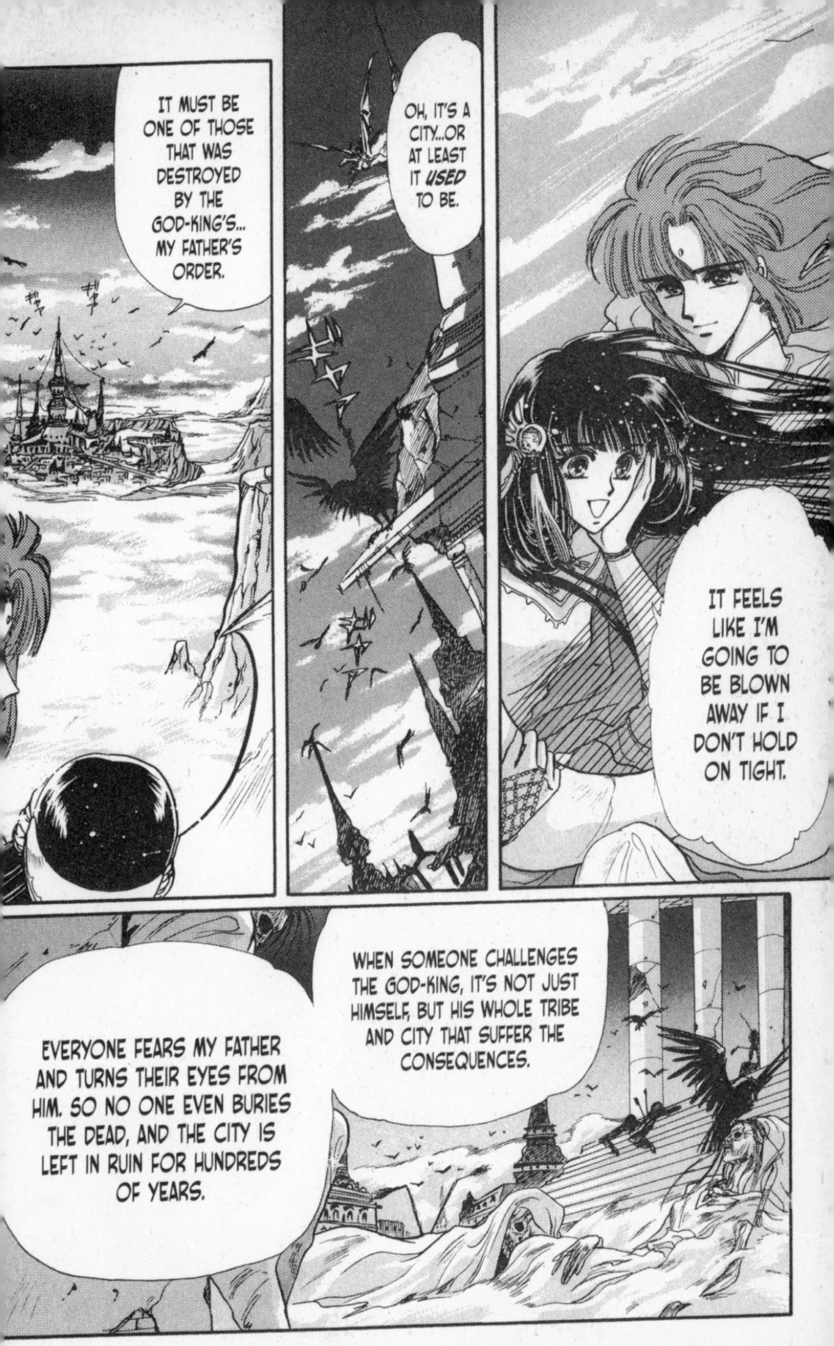
IT FEELS LIKE I'M GOING TO BE BLOWN AWAY IF I DON'T HOLD ON TIGHT.
OH, IT'S A CITY...OR AT LEAST IT *USED* TO BE.
IT MUST BE ONE OF THOSE THAT WAS DESTROYED BY THE GOD-KING'S... MY FATHER'S ORDER.
WHEN SOMEONE CHALLENGES THE GOD-KING, IT'S NOT JUST HIMSELF, BUT HIS WHOLE TRIBE AND CITY THAT SUFFER THE CONSEQUENCES.
EVERYONE FEARS MY FATHER AND TURNS THEIR EYES FROM HIM. SO NO ONE EVEN BURIES THE DEAD, AND THE CITY IS LEFT IN RUIN FOR HUNDREDS OF YEARS.

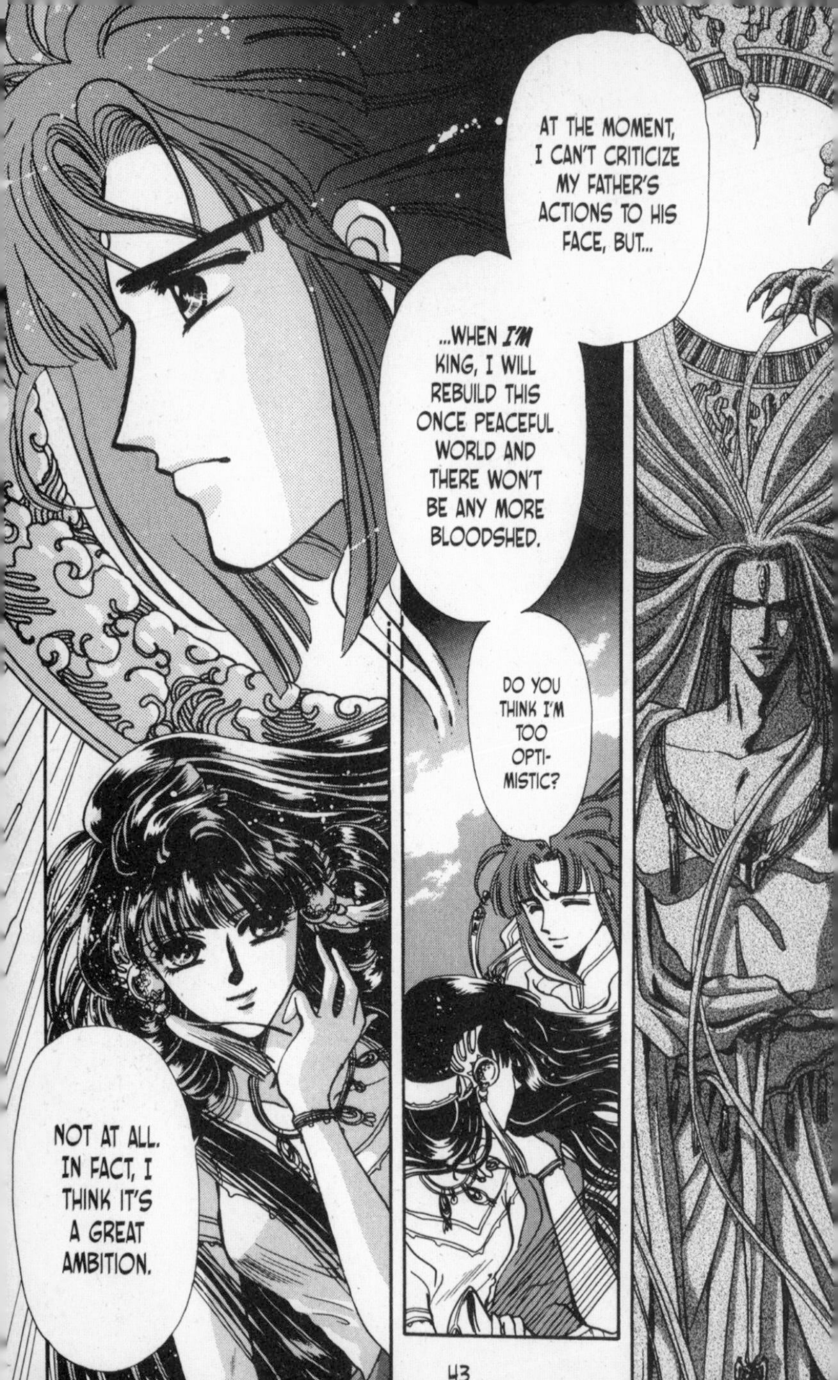
AT THE MOMENT, I CAN'T CRITICIZE MY FATHER'S ACTIONS TO HIS FACE, BUT...
...WHEN *I'M* KING, I WILL REBUILD THIS ONCE PEACEFUL WORLD AND THERE WON'T BE ANY MORE BLOODSHED.
DO YOU THINK I'M TOO OPTI-MISTIC?
NOT AT ALL. IN FACT, I THINK IT'S A GREAT AMBITION.

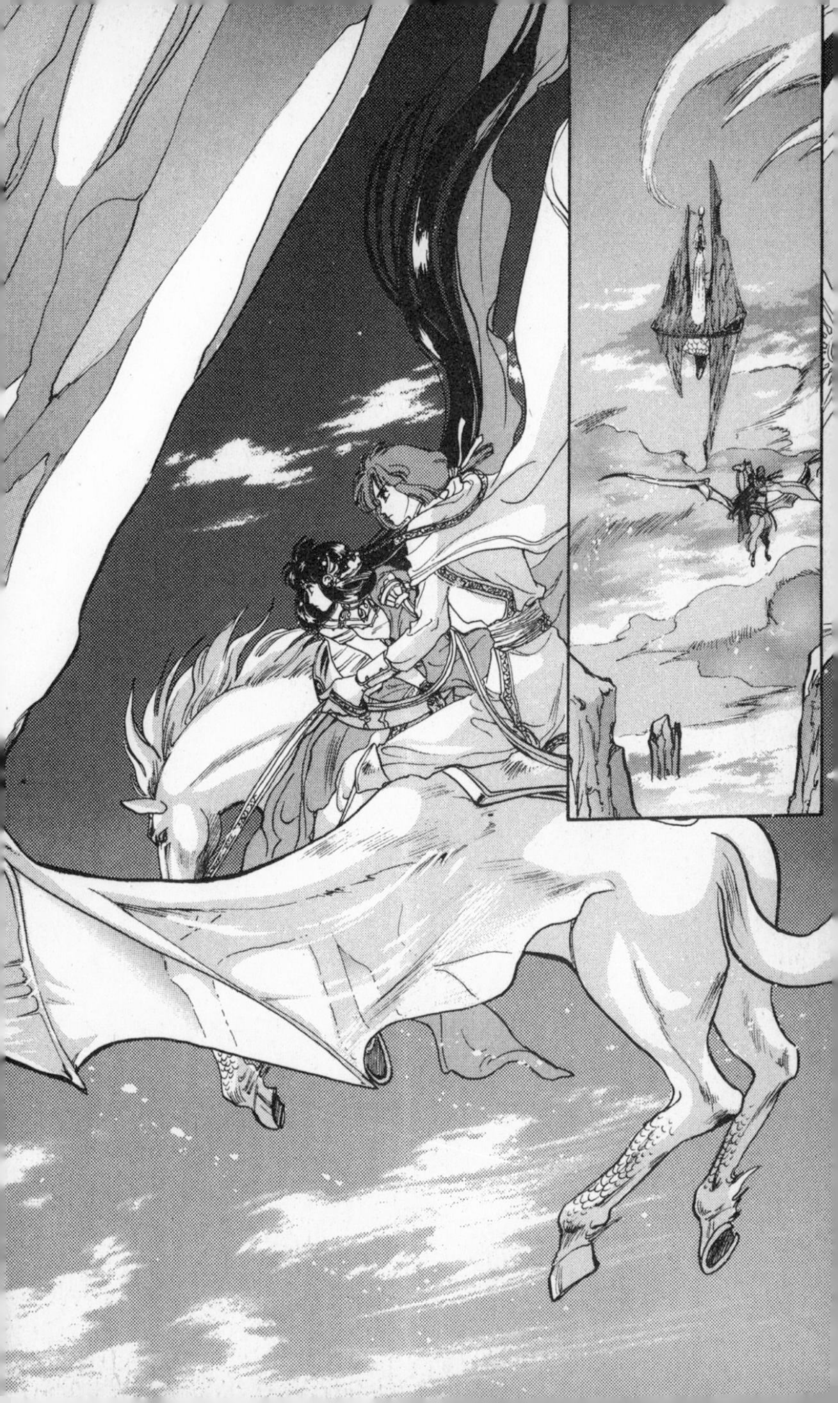

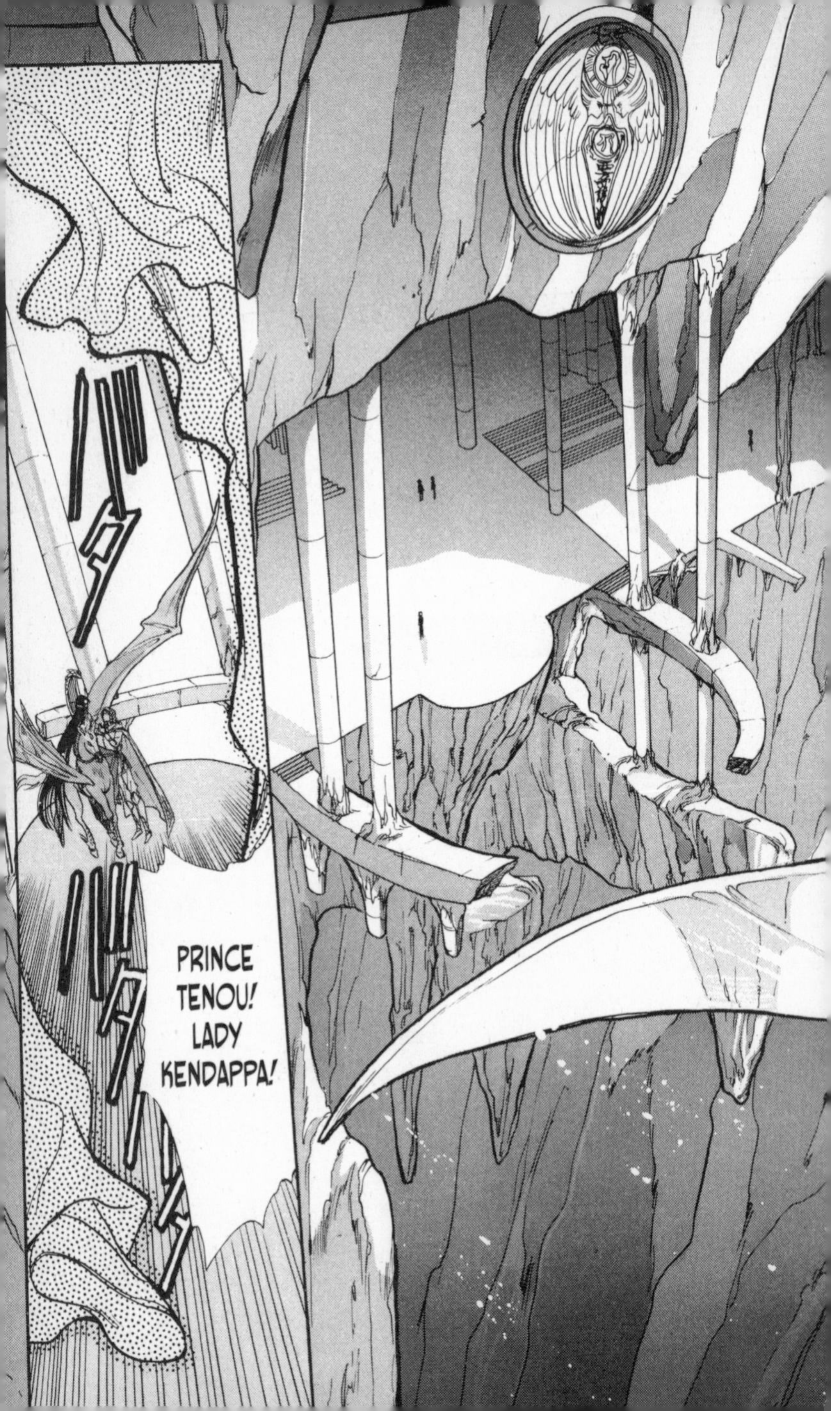
PRINCE TENOU! LADY KENDAPPA!

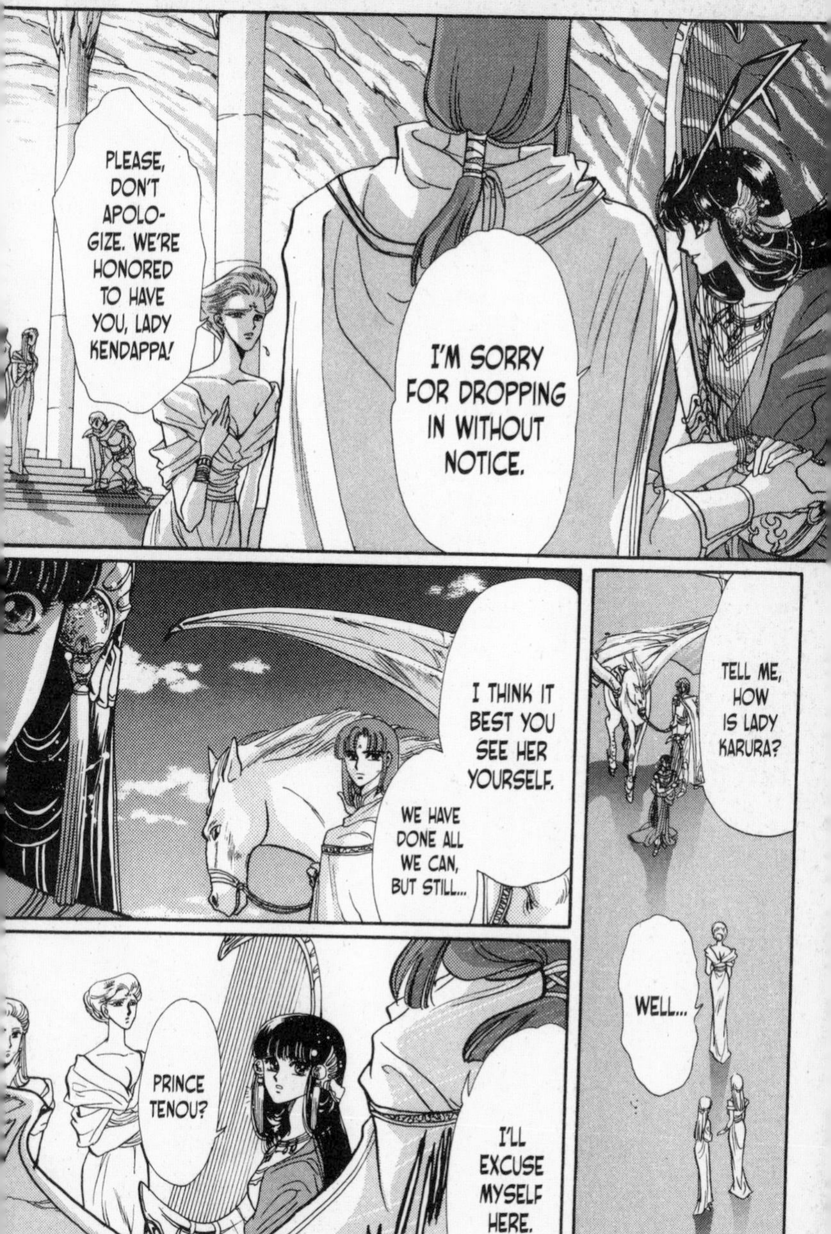
I'M SORRY FOR DROPPING IN WITHOUT NOTICE.
PLEASE, DON'T APOLO-GIZE. WE'RE HONORED TO HAVE YOU, LADY KENDAPPA!
TELL ME, HOW IS LADY KARURA?
WELL...
I THINK IT BEST YOU SEE HER YOURSELF.
WE HAVE DONE ALL WE CAN, BUT STILL...
I'LL EXCUSE MYSELF HERE.
PRINCE TENOU?

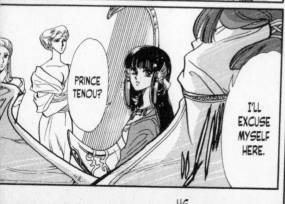

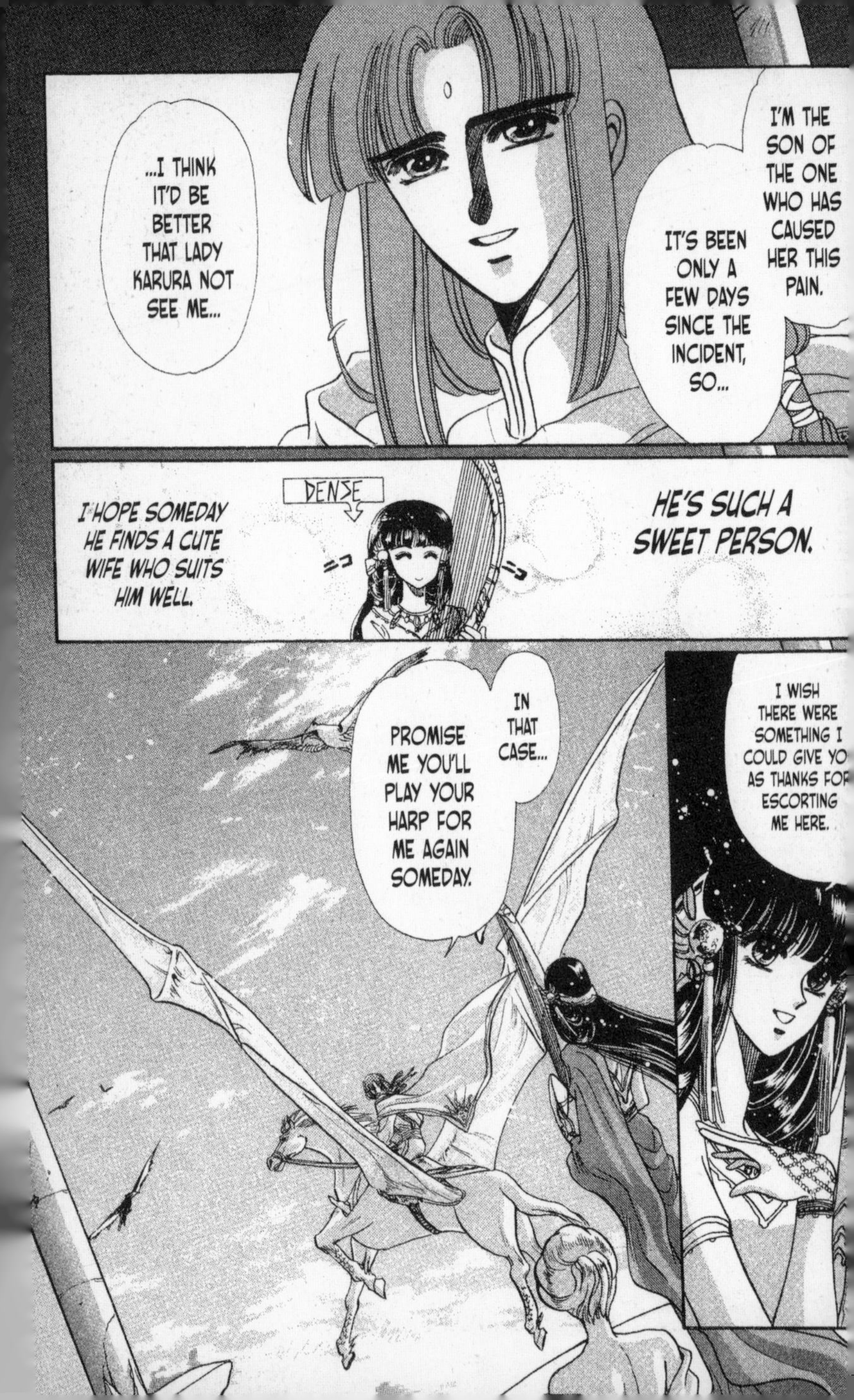
I'M THE SON OF THE ONE WHO HAS CAUSED HER THIS PAIN.
IT'S BEEN ONLY A FEW DAYS SINCE THE INCIDENT, SO...
...I THINK IT'D BE BETTER THAT LADY KARURA NOT SEE ME...
HE'S SUCH A SWEET PERSON.
DENSE
I HOPE SOMEDAY HE FINDS A CUTE WIFE WHO SUITS HIM WELL.
I WISH THERE WERE SOMETHING I COULD GIVE YO AS THANKS FOR ESCORTING ME HERE.
IN THAT CASE...
PROMISE ME YOU'LL PLAY YOUR HARP FOR ME AGAIN SOMEDAY.

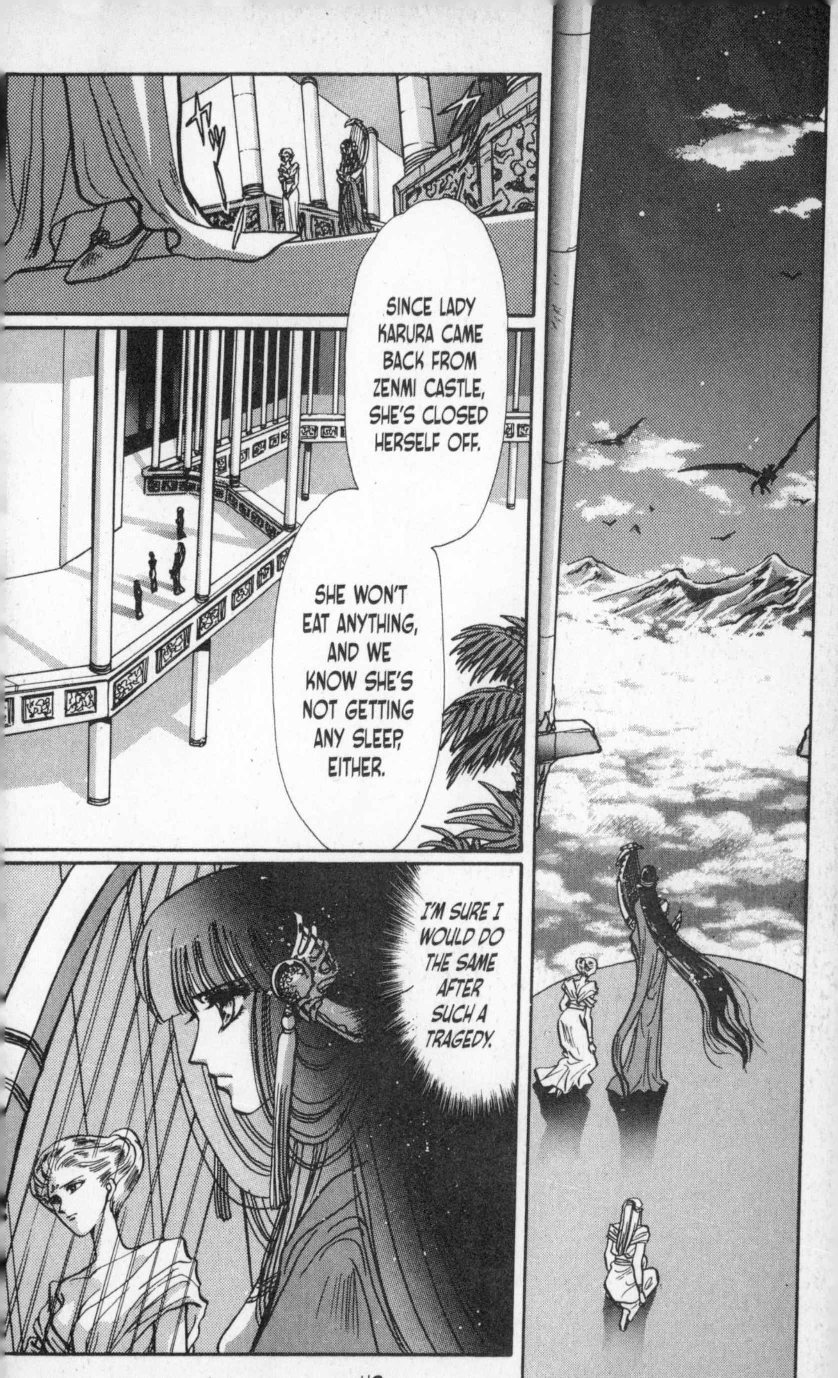
SINCE LADY KARURA CAME BACK FROM ZENMI CASTLE, SHE'S CLOSED HERSELF OFF.
SHE WON'T EAT ANYTHING, AND WE KNOW SHE'S NOT GETTING ANY SLEEP, EITHER.
I'M SURE I WOULD DO THE SAME AFTER SUCH A TRAGEDY.

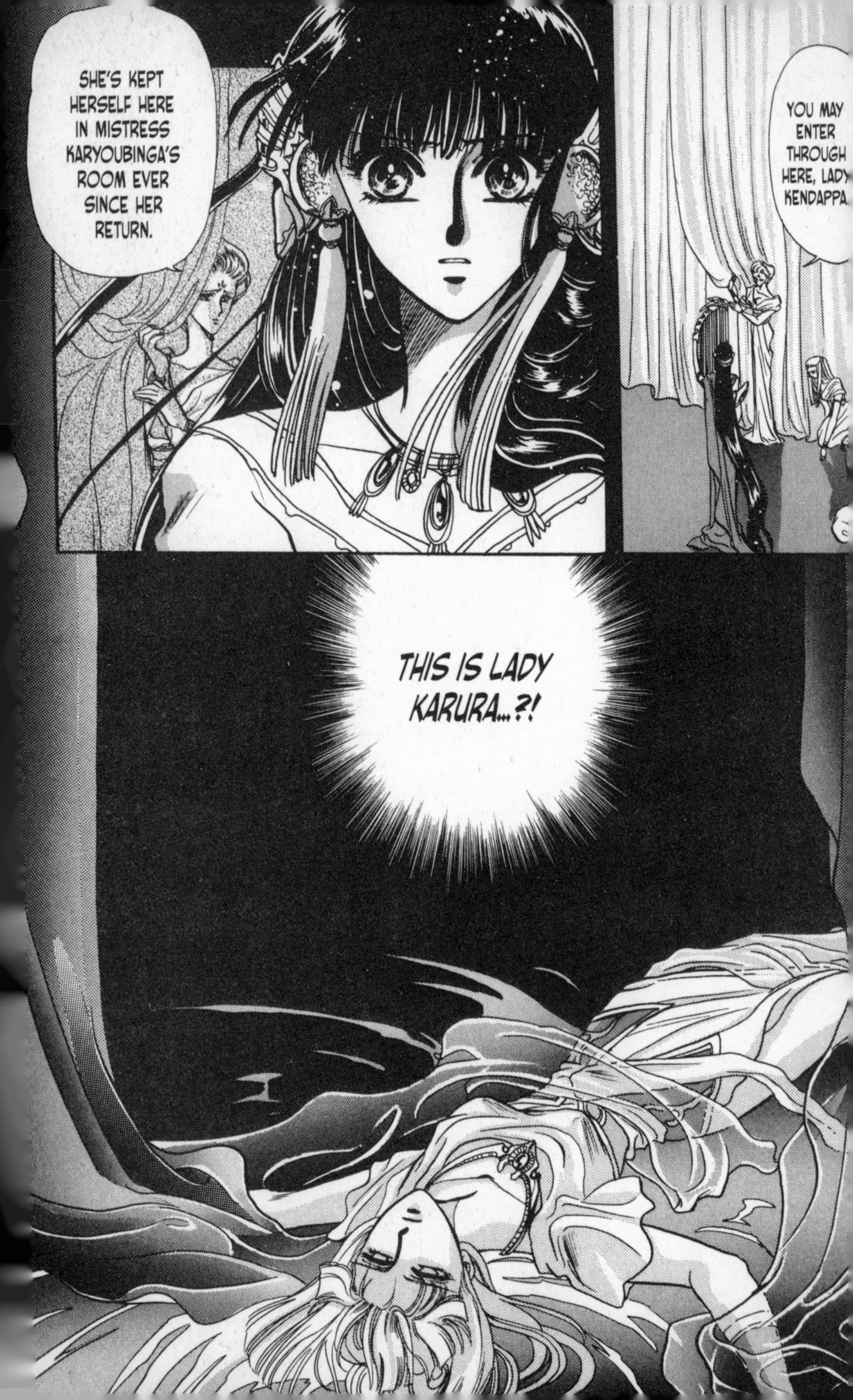
YOU MAY ENTER THROUGH HERE, LADY KENDAPPA.
SHE'S KEPT HERSELF HERE IN MISTRESS KARYOUBINGA'S ROOM EVER SINCE HER RETURN.
THIS IS LADY KARURA...?!

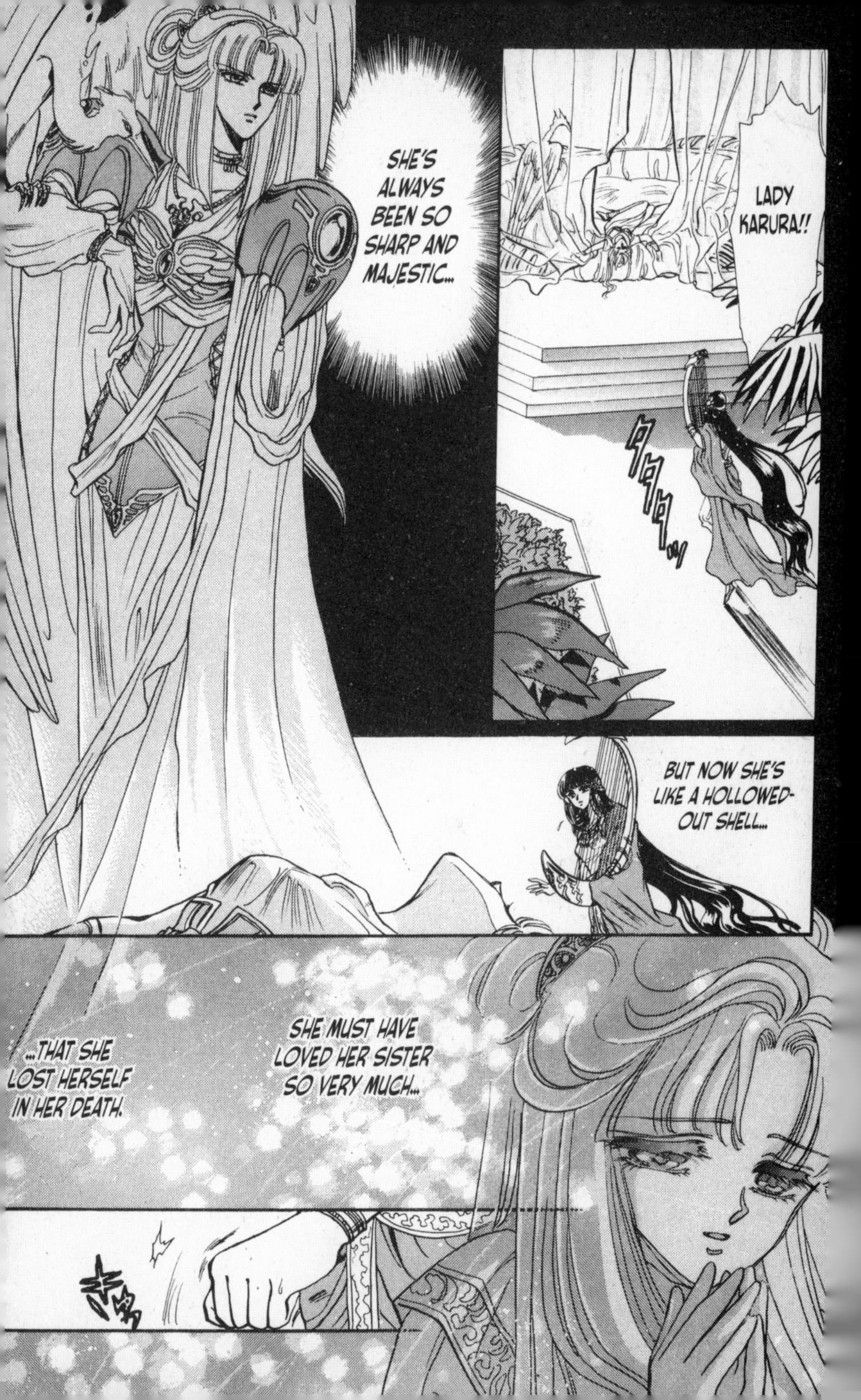
LADY KARURA!!
BUT NOW SHE'S LIKE A HOLLOWED-OUT SHELL...
SHE'S ALWAYS BEEN SO SHARP AND MAJESTIC...
SHE MUST HAVE LOVED HER SISTER SO VERY MUCH...
...THAT SHE LOST HERSELF IN HER DEATH.

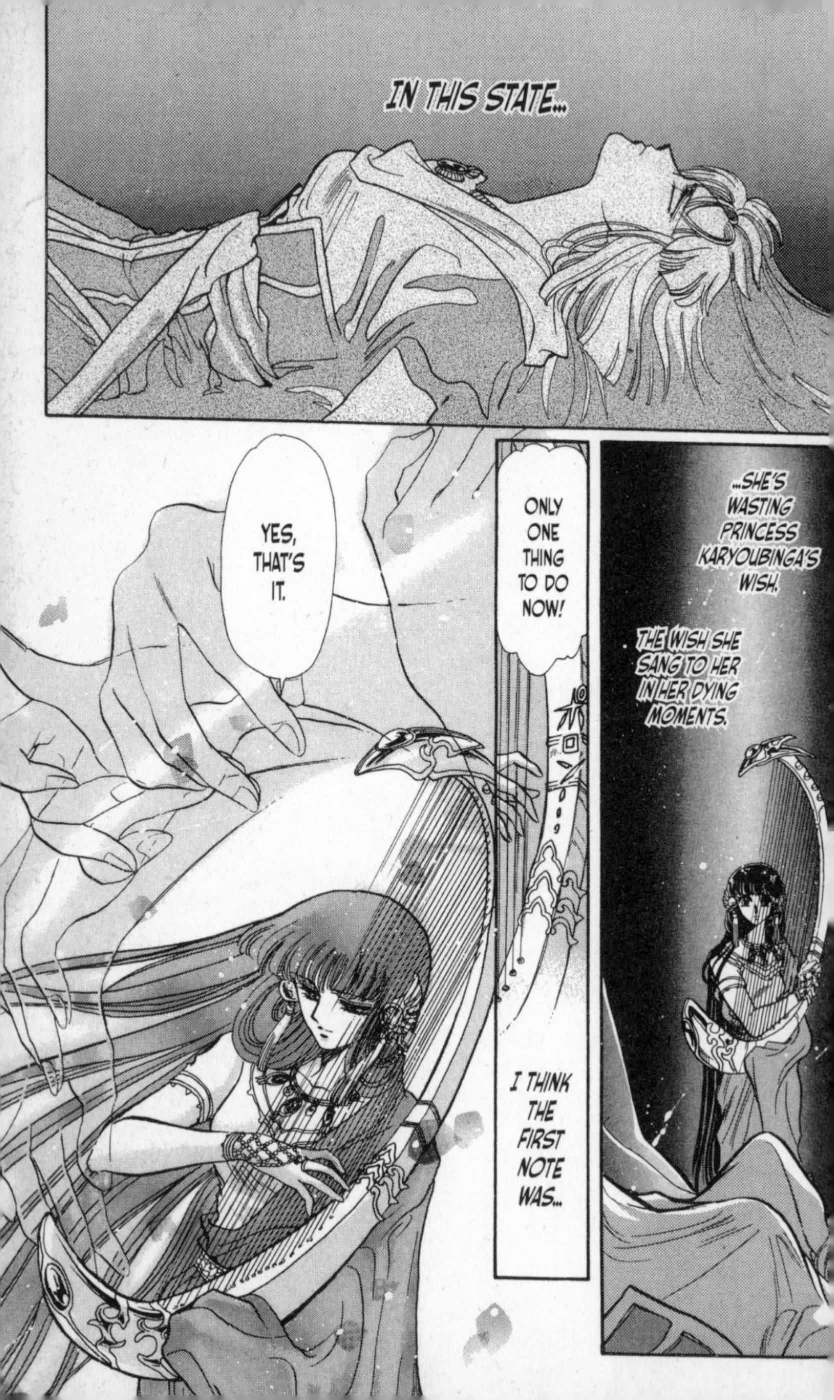
IN THIS STATE...
...SHE'S WASTING PRINCESS KARYOUBINGA'S WISH.
THE WISH SHE SANG TO HER IN HER DYING MOMENTS.
ONLY ONE THING TO DO NOW!
I THINK THE FIRST NOTE WAS...
YES, THAT'S IT.

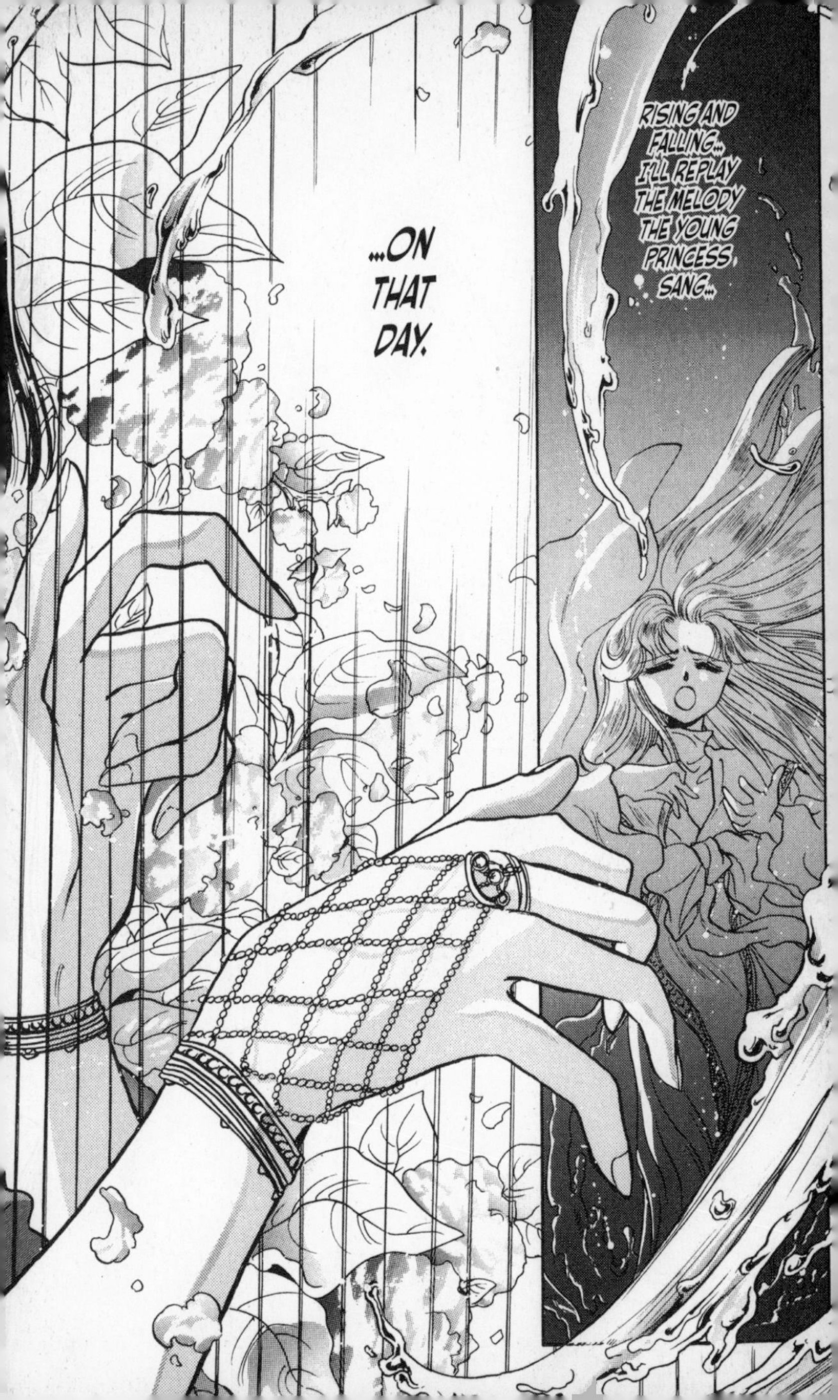
RISING AND FALLING... I'LL REPLAY THE MELODY THE YOUNG PRINCESS SANG...
...ON THAT DAY.

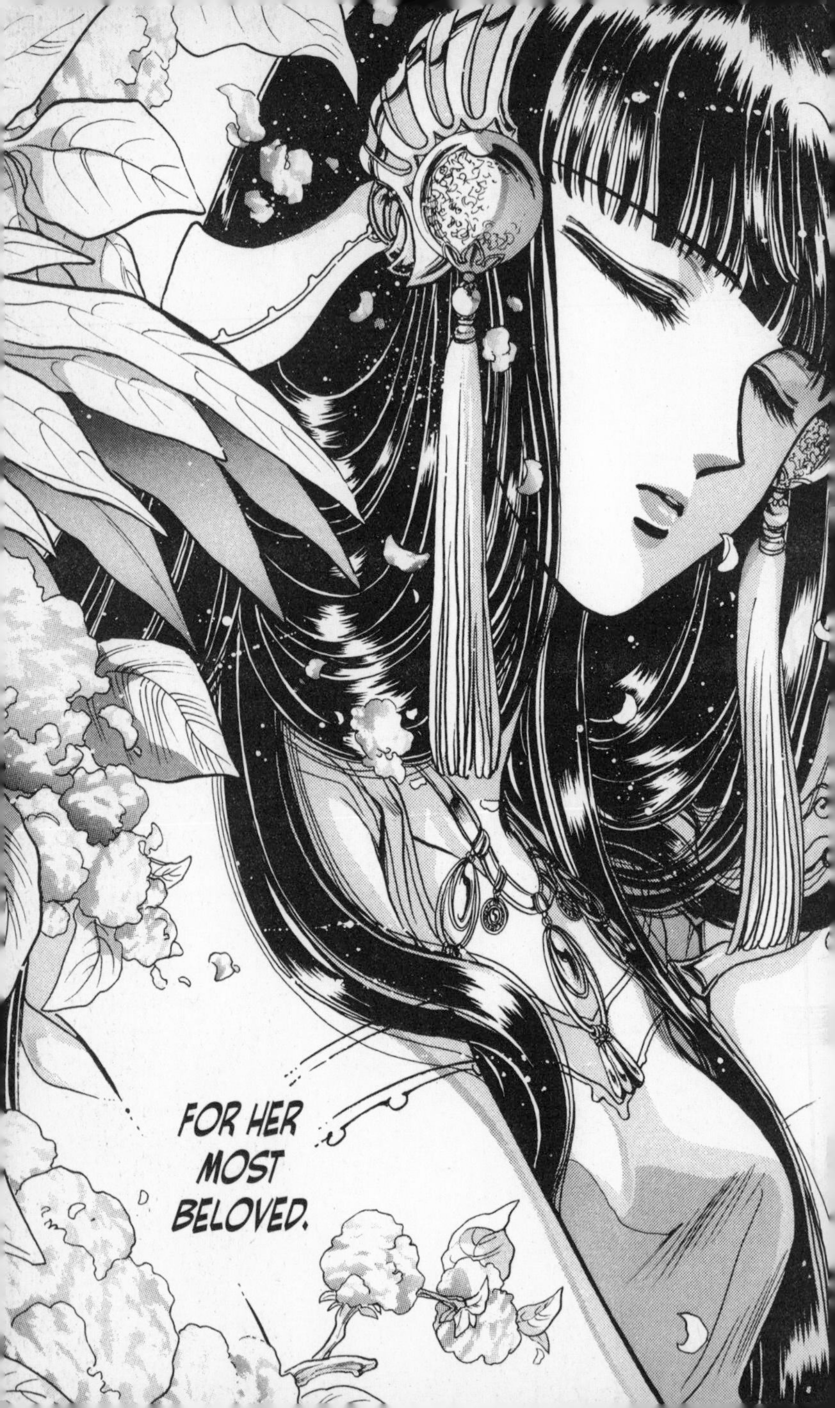
FOR HER MOST BELOVED.

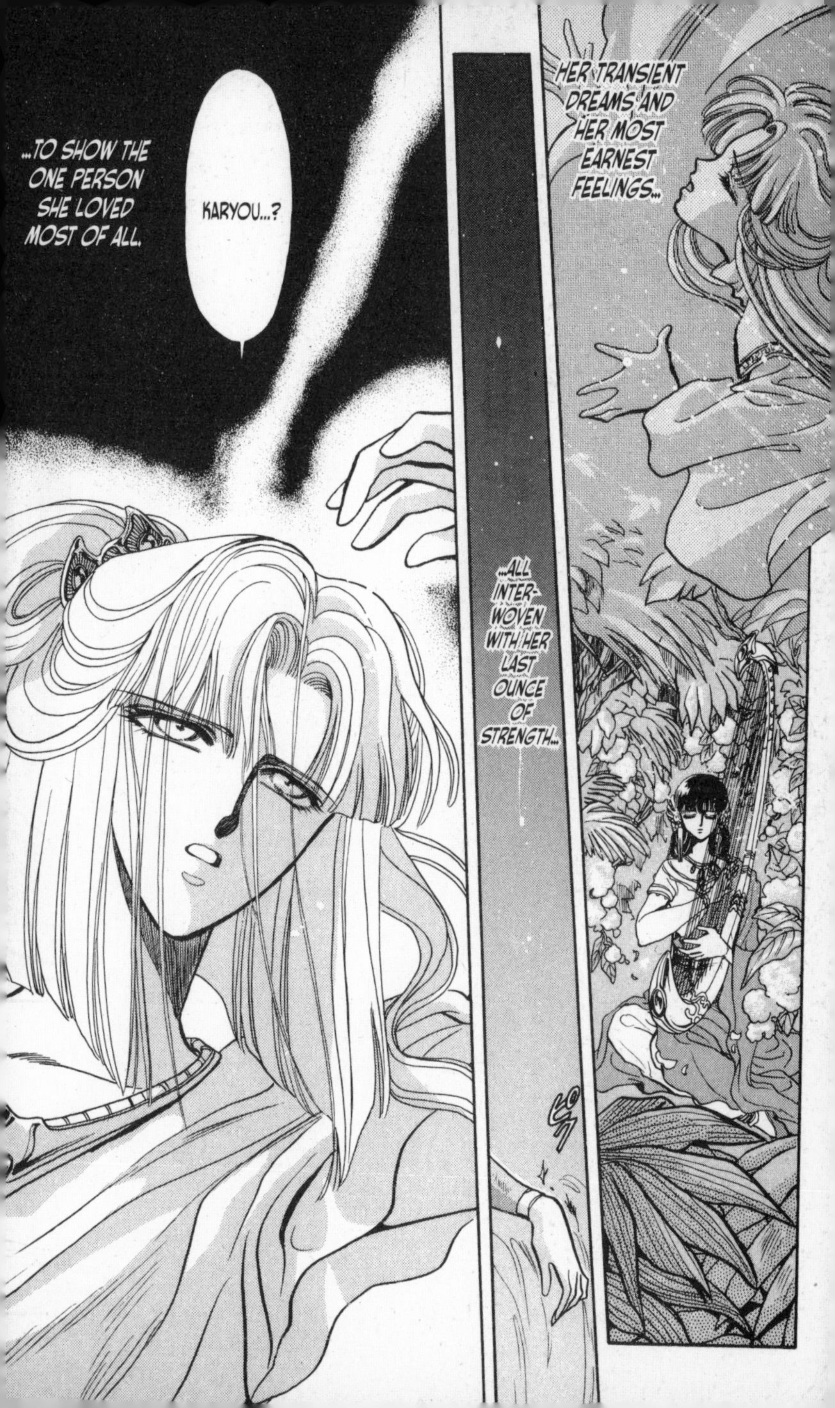
HER TRANSIENT DREAMS AND HER MOST EARNEST FEELINGS...
...ALL INTER-WOVEN WITH HER LAST OUNCE OF STRENGTH...
...TO SHOW THE ONE PERSON SHE LOVED MOST OF ALL.
KARYOU...?

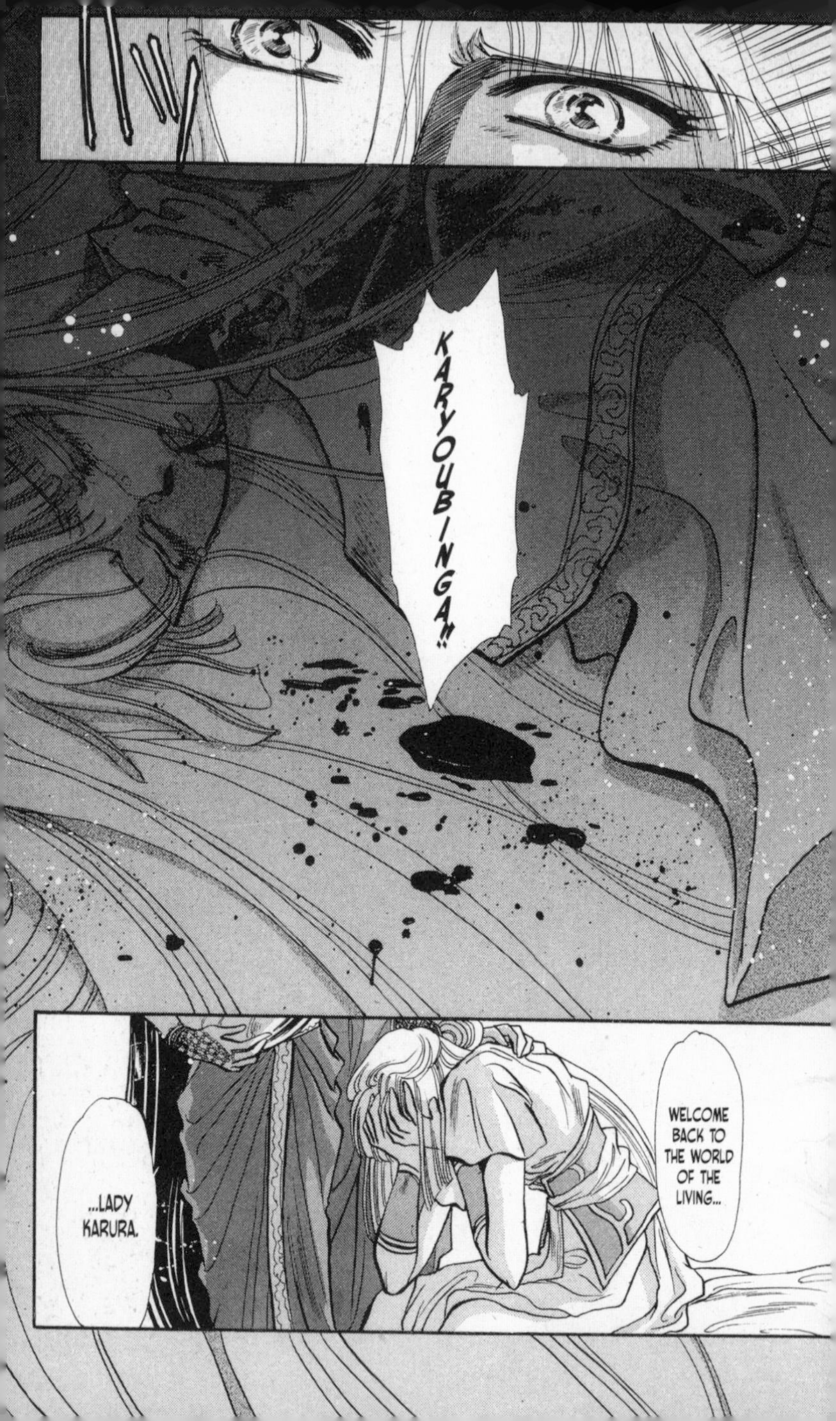
KARYOUBINGA!!
WELCOME BACK TO THE WORLD OF THE LIVING...
...LADY KARURA.

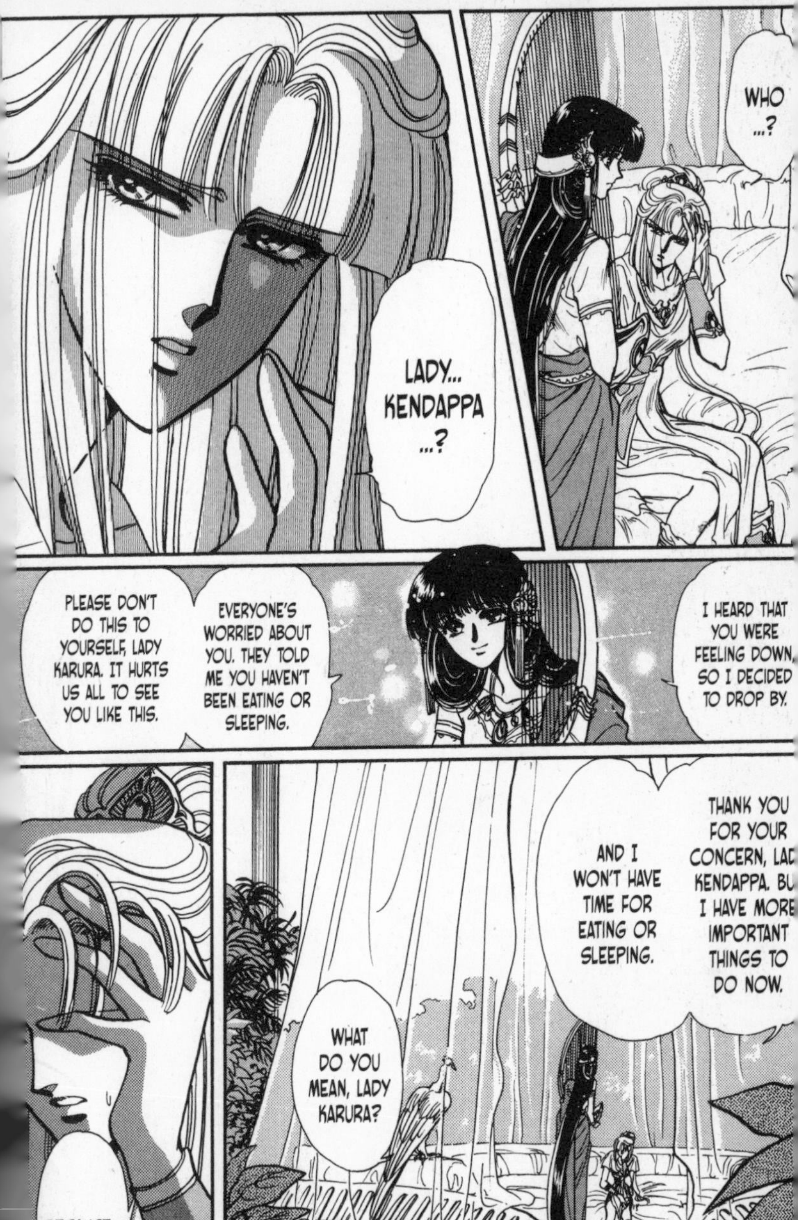
WHO ...?
LADY... KENDAPPA ...?
I HEARD THAT YOU WERE FEELING DOWN, SO I DECIDED TO DROP BY.
EVERYONE'S WORRIED ABOUT YOU. THEY TOLD ME YOU HAVEN'T BEEN EATING OR SLEEPING.
PLEASE DON'T DO THIS TO YOURSELF, LADY KARURA. IT HURTS US ALL TO SEE YOU LIKE THIS.
THANK YOU FOR YOUR CONCERN, LAD KENDAPPA. BU I HAVE MORE IMPORTANT THINGS TO DO NOW.
AND I WON'T HAVE TIME FOR EATING OR SLEEPING.
WHAT DO YOU MEAN, LADY KARURA?
BECAUSE...

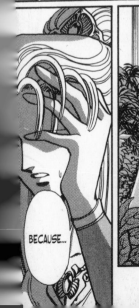

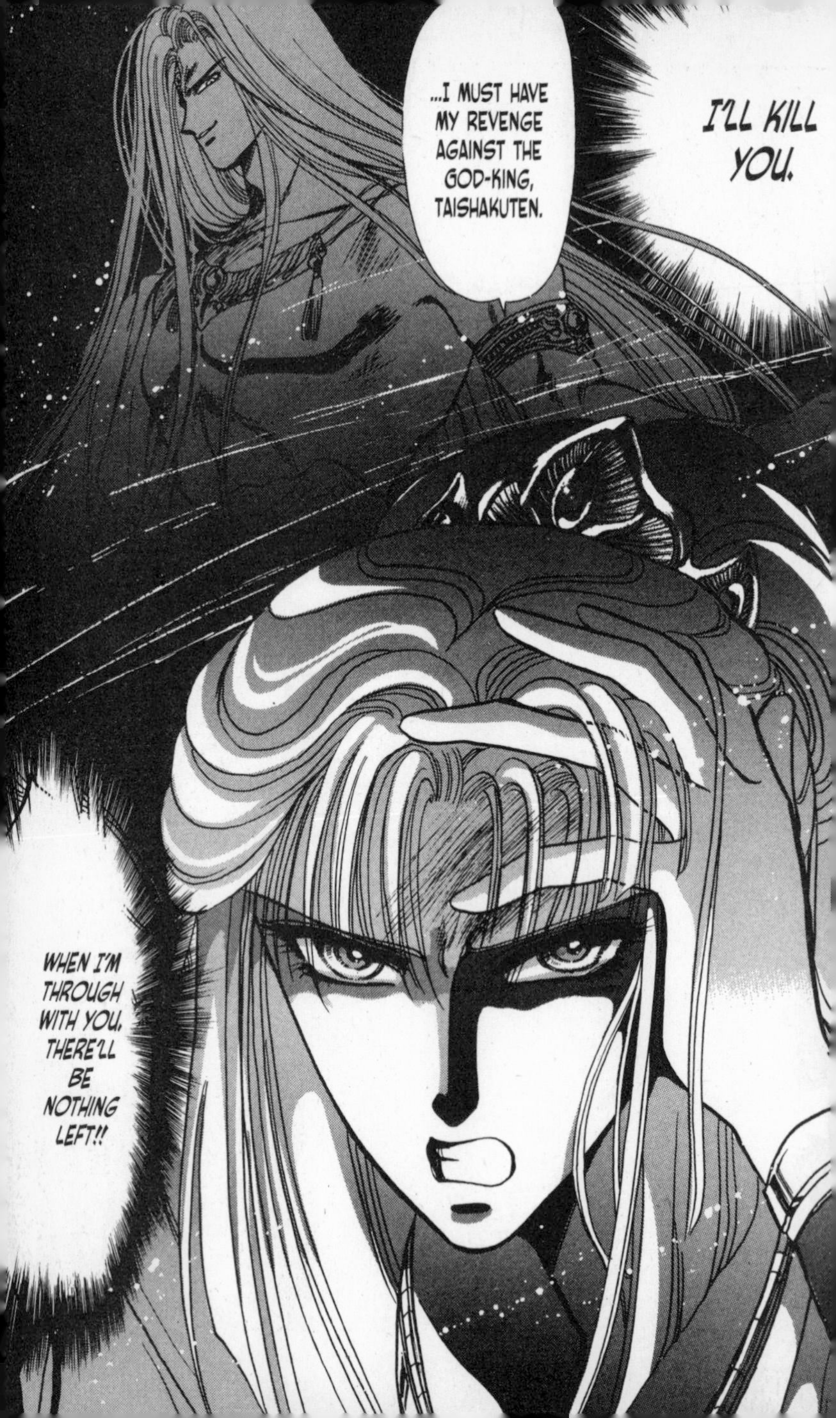
I'LL KILL YOU.
...I MUST HAVE MY REVENGE AGAINST THE GOD-KING, TAISHAKUTEN.
WHEN I'M THROUGH WITH YOU, THERE'LL BE NOTHING LEFT!!

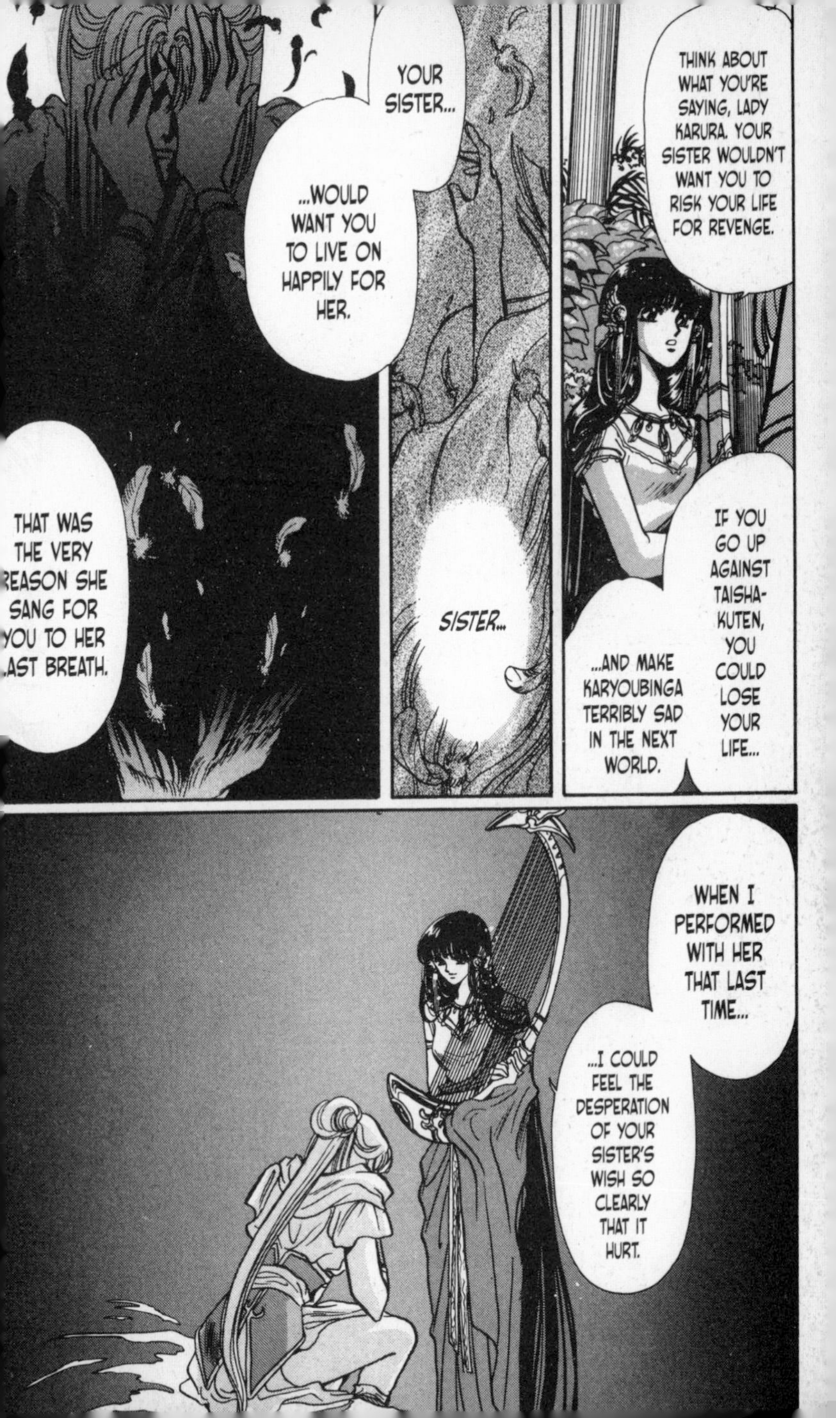
THINK ABOUT WHAT YOU'RE SAYING, LADY KARURA. YOUR SISTER WOULDN'T WANT YOU TO RISK YOUR LIFE FOR REVENGE.
IF YOU GO UP AGAINST TAISHA-KUTEN, YOU COULD LOSE YOUR LIFE...
...AND MAKE KARYOUBINGA TERRIBLY SAD IN THE NEXT WORLD.
YOUR SISTER...
...WOULD WANT YOU TO LIVE ON HAPPILY FOR HER.
SISTER...
THAT WAS THE VERY REASON SHE SANG FOR YOU TO HER LAST BREATH.
WHEN I PERFORMED WITH HER THAT LAST TIME...
...I COULD FEEL THE DESPERATION OF YOUR SISTER'S WISH SO CLEARLY THAT IT HURT.

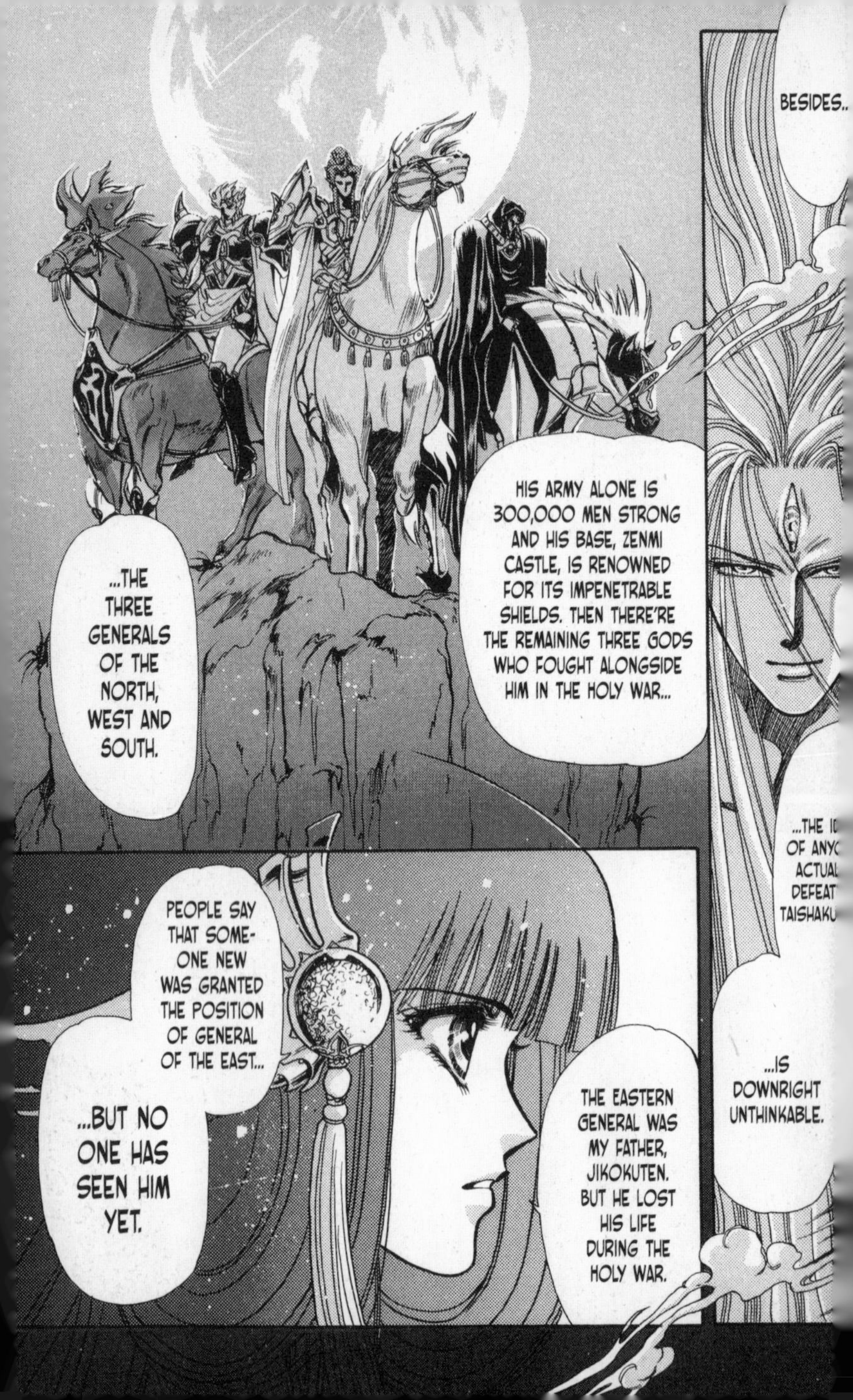
BESIDES..
...THE ID OF ANYO ACTUAL DEFEAT TAISHAKU
...IS DOWNRIGHT UNTHINKABLE.
HIS ARMY ALONE IS 300,000 MEN STRONG AND HIS BASE, ZENMI CASTLE, IS RENOWNED FOR ITS IMPENETRABLE SHIELDS. THEN THERE'RE THE REMAINING THREE GODS WHO FOUGHT ALONGSIDE HIM IN THE HOLY WAR...
...THE THREE GENERALS OF THE NORTH, WEST AND SOUTH.
THE EASTERN GENERAL WAS MY FATHER, JIKOKUTEN. BUT HE LOST HIS LIFE DURING THE HOLY WAR.
PEOPLE SAY THAT SOME-ONE NEW WAS GRANTED THE POSITION OF GENERAL OF THE EAST...
...BUT NO ONE HAS SEEN HIM YET.

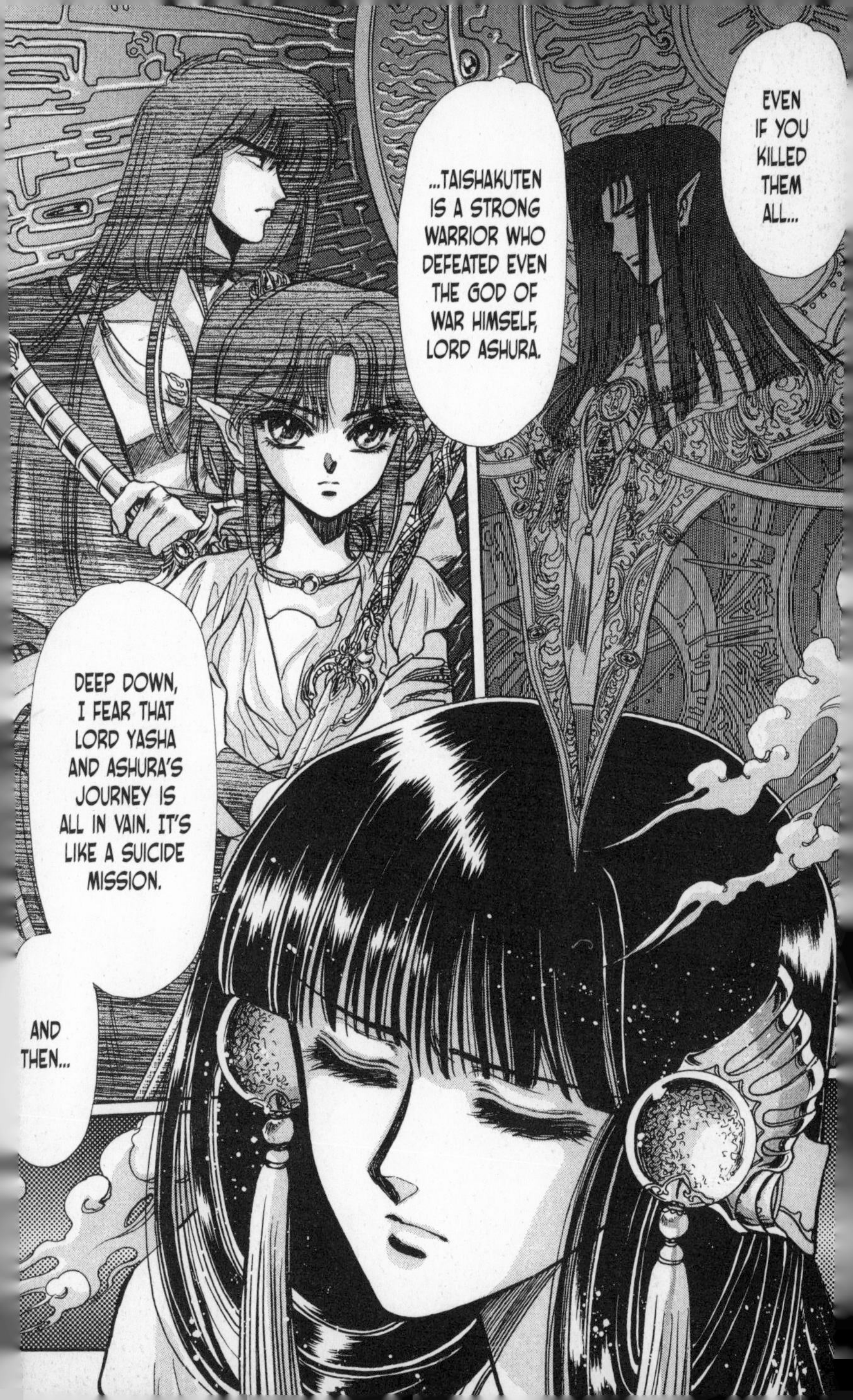
EVEN IF YOU KILLED THEM ALL...
...TAISHAKUTEN IS A STRONG WARRIOR WHO DEFEATED EVEN THE GOD OF WAR HIMSELF, LORD ASHURA.
DEEP DOWN, I FEAR THAT LORD YASHA AND ASHURA'S JOURNEY IS ALL IN VAIN. IT'S LIKE A SUICIDE MISSION.
AND THEN...

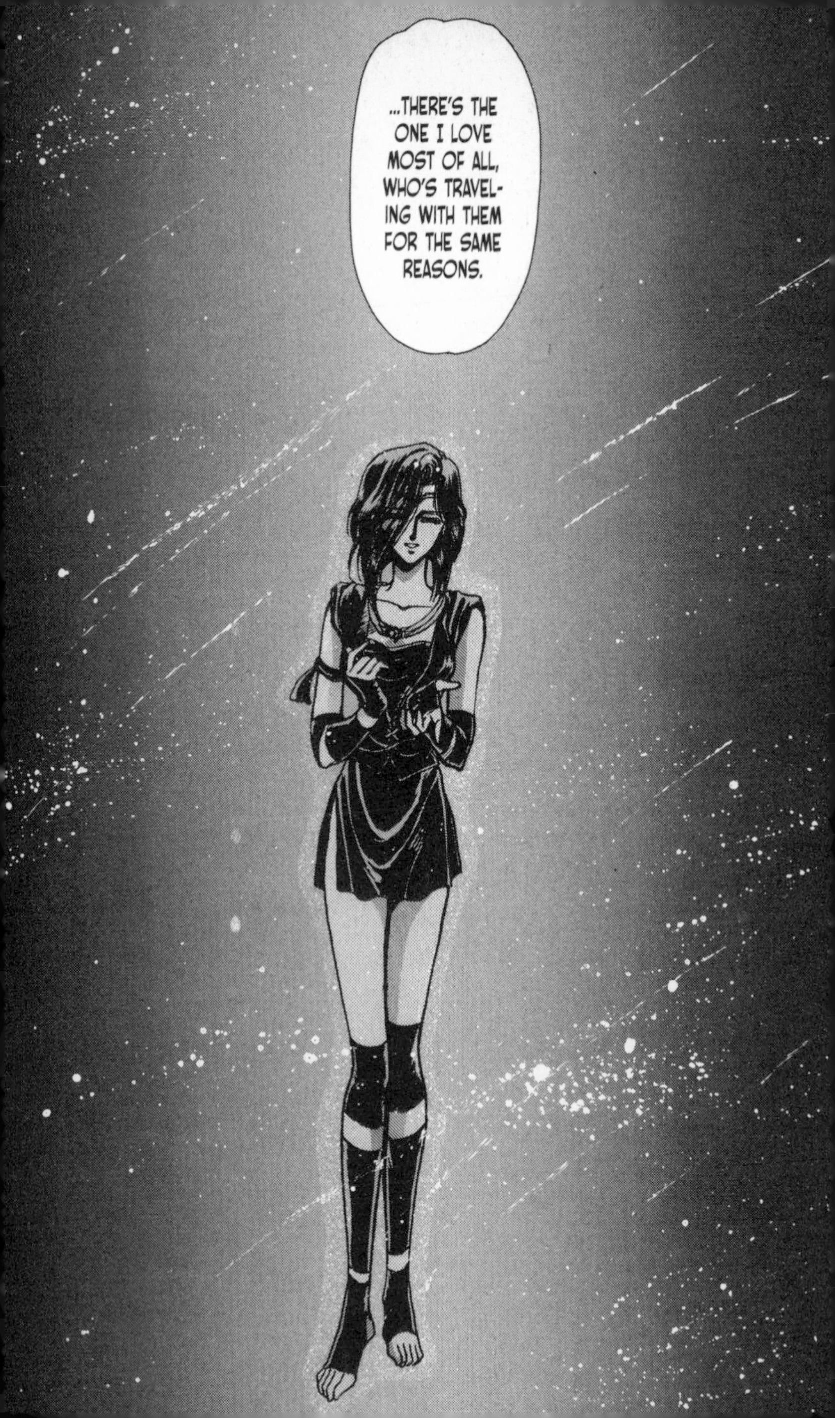
...THERE'S THE ONE I LOVE MOST OF ALL, WHO'S TRAVEL-ING WITH THEM FOR THE SAME REASONS.

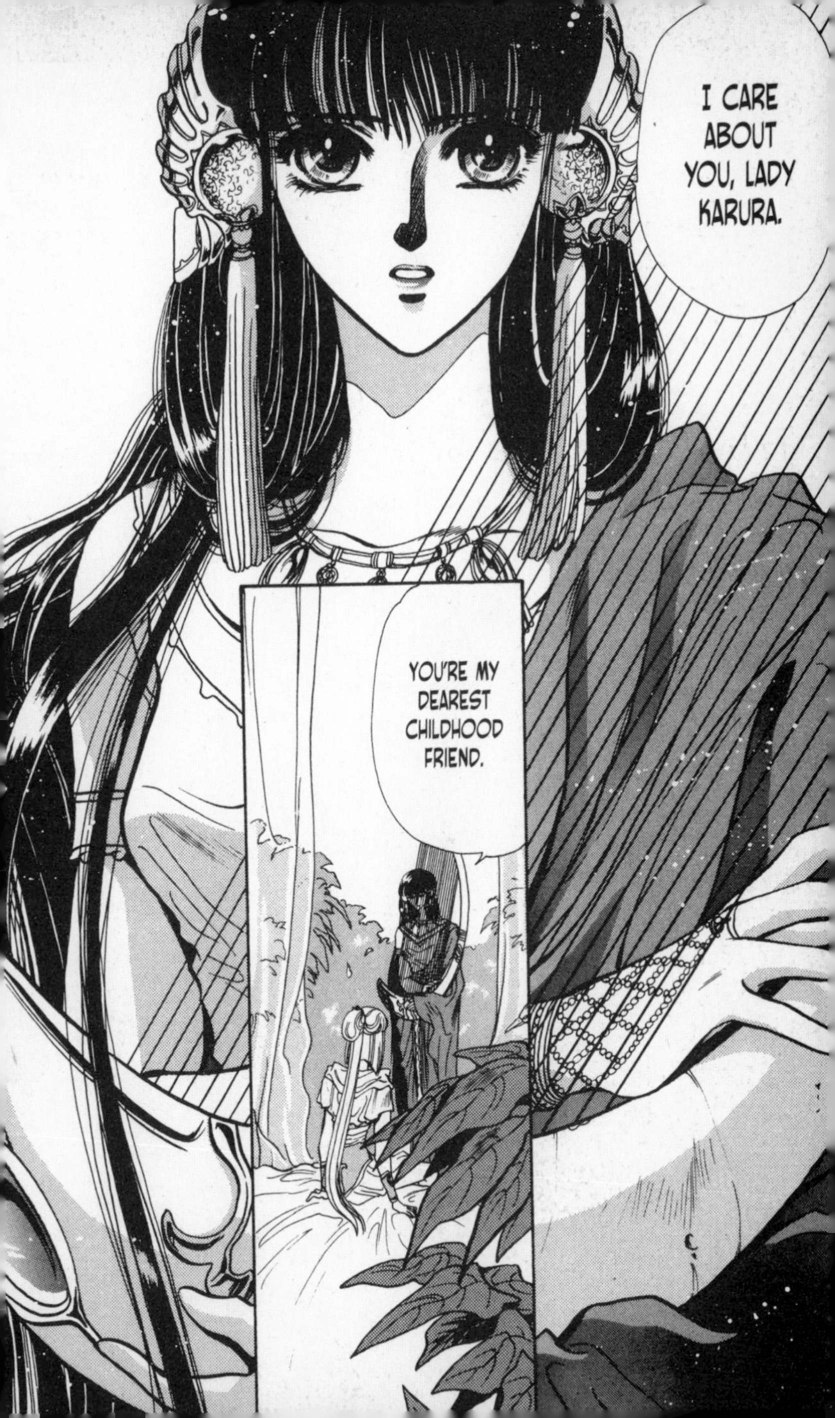
I CARE ABOUT YOU, LADY KARURA.
YOU'RE MY DEAREST CHILDHOOD FRIEND.

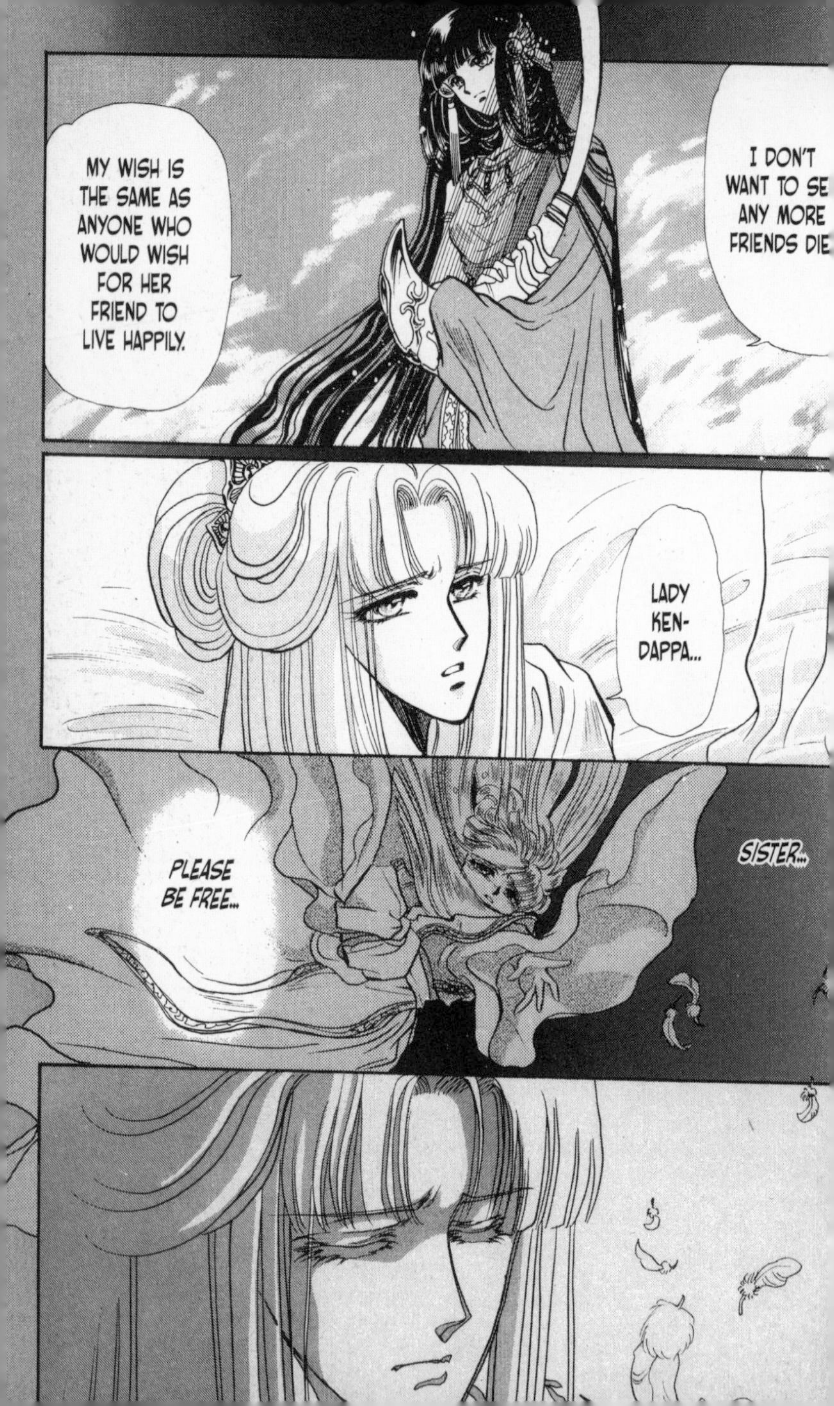
I DON'T WANT TO SE ANY MORE FRIENDS DIE
MY WISH IS THE SAME AS ANYONE WHO WOULD WISH FOR HER FRIEND TO LIVE HAPPILY.
LADY KEN-DAPPA...
SISTER...
PLEASE BE FREE...

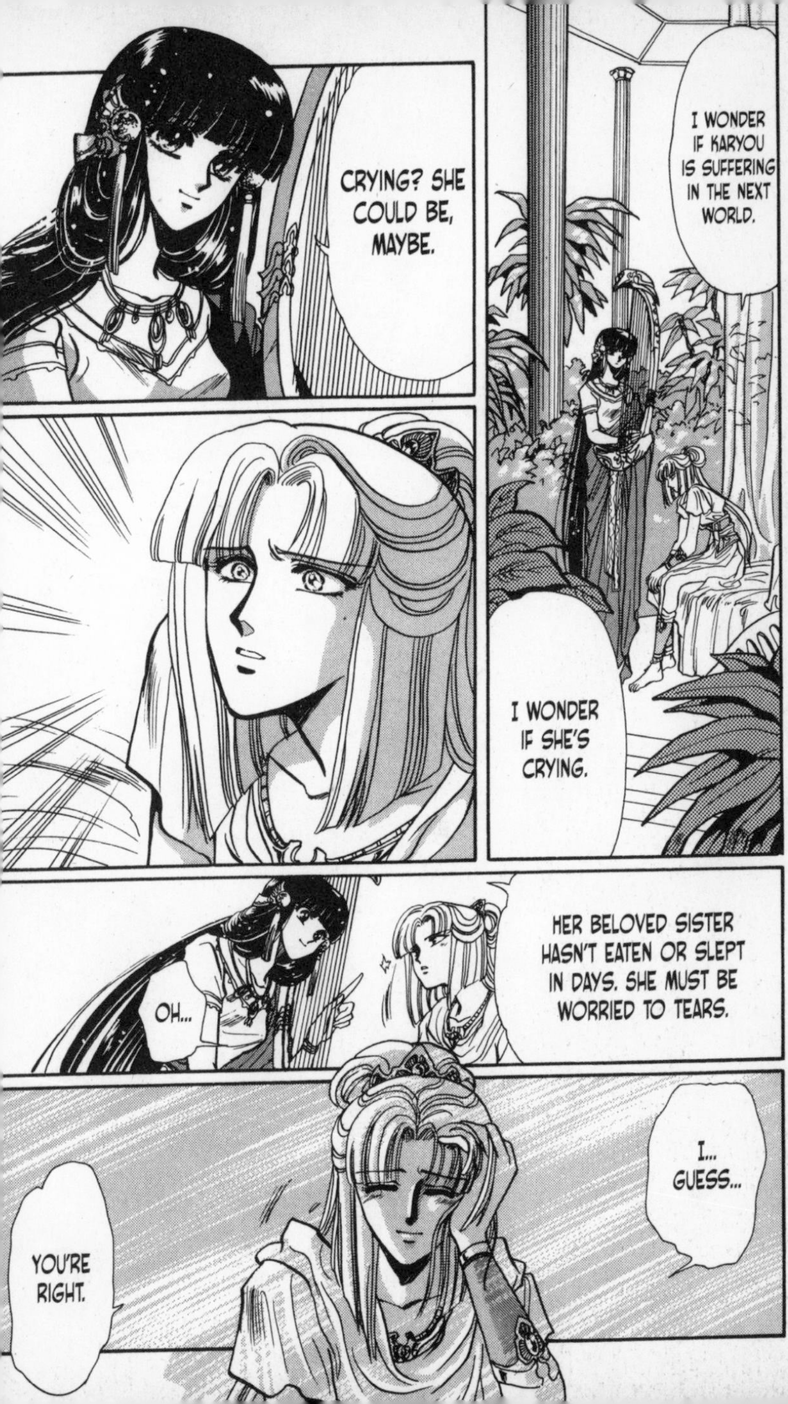
I WONDER IF KARYOU IS SUFFERING IN THE NEXT WORLD.
I WONDER IF SHE'S CRYING.
CRYING? SHE COULD BE, MAYBE.
HER BELOVED SISTER HASN'T EATEN OR SLEPT IN DAYS. SHE MUST BE WORRIED TO TEARS.
OH...
I... GUESS...
YOU'RE RIGHT.

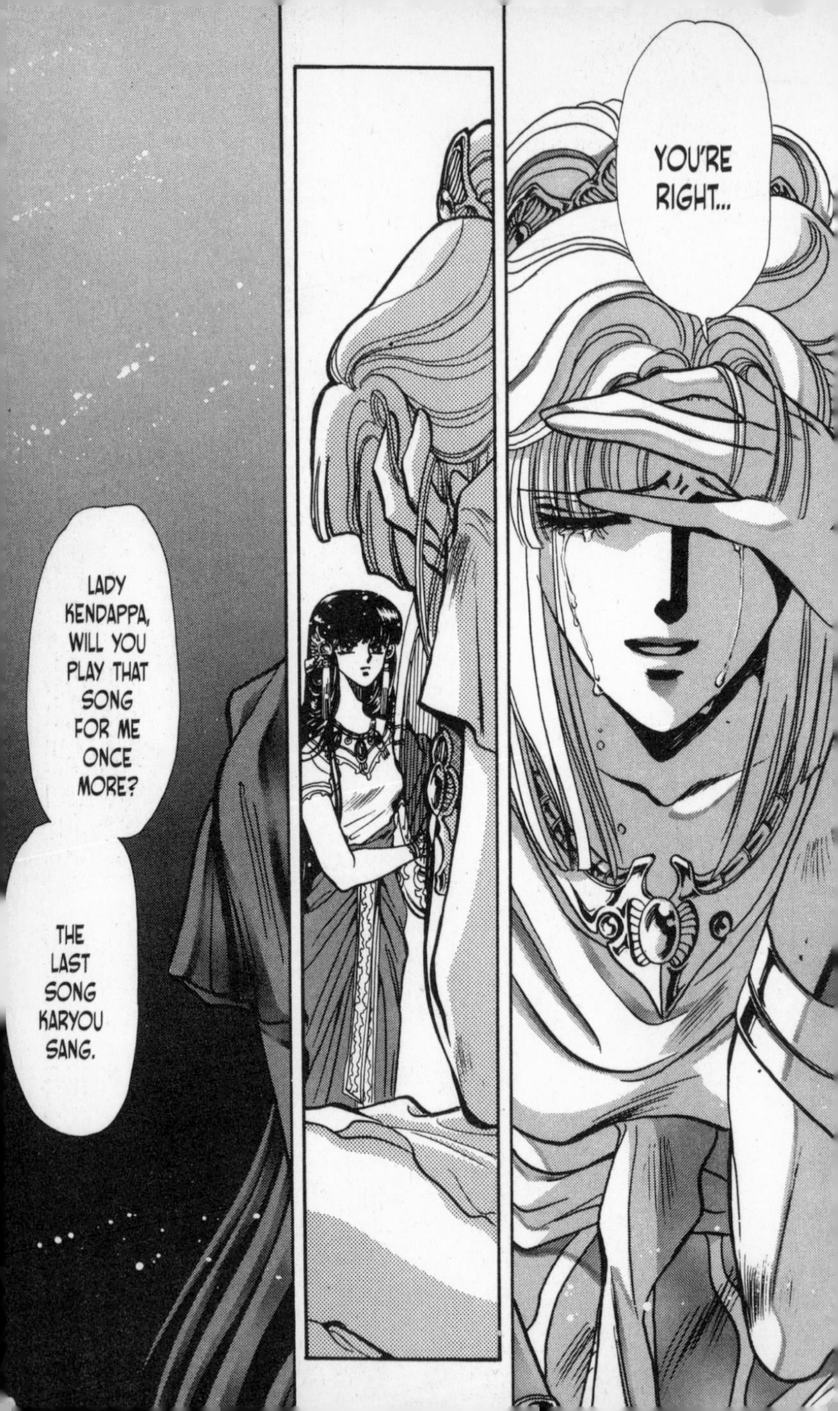
YOU'RE RIGHT...
LADY KENDAPPA, WILL YOU PLAY THAT SONG FOR ME ONCE MORE?
THE LAST SONG KARYOU SANG.

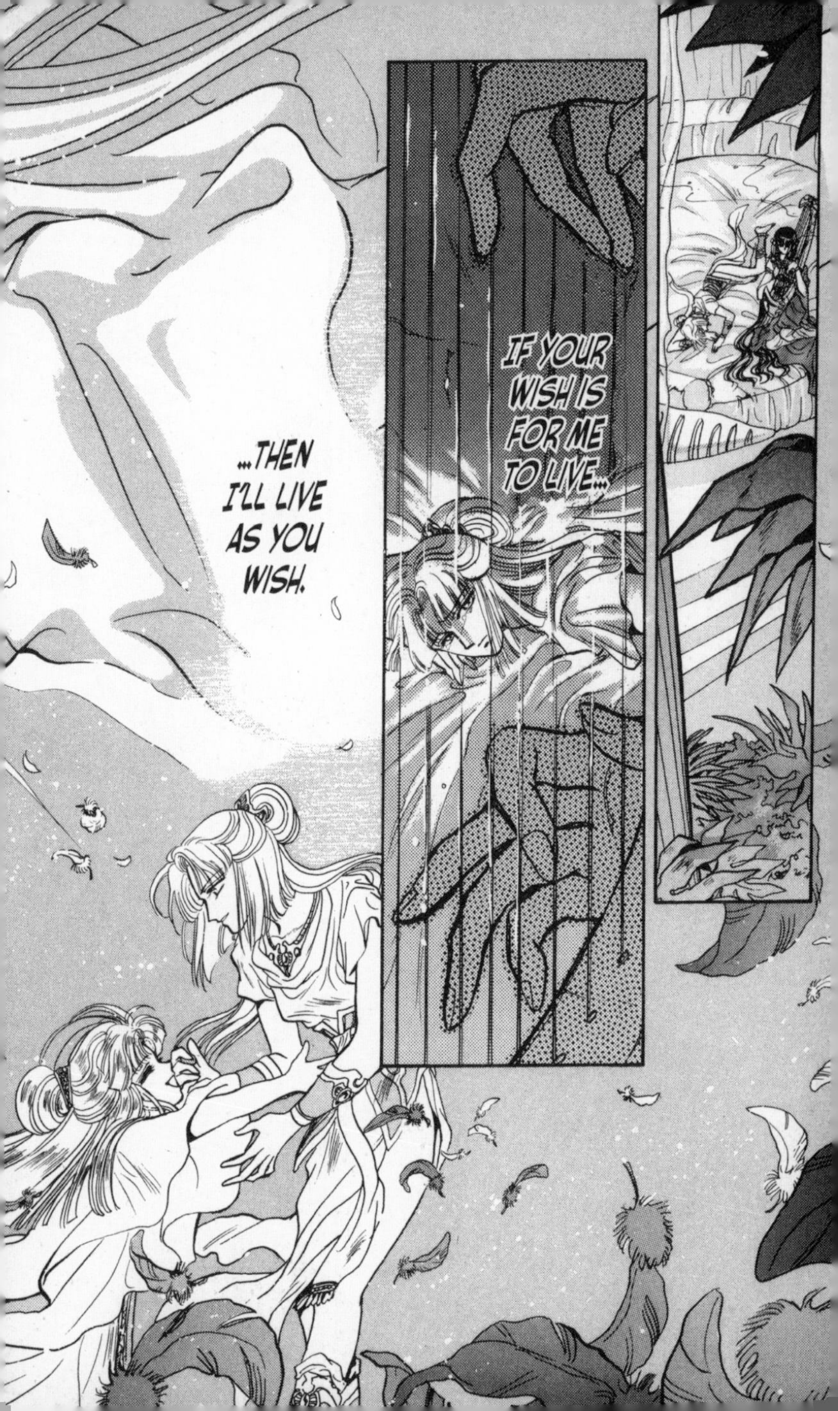
IF YOUR WISH IS FOR ME TO LIVE...
...THEN I'LL LIVE AS YOU WISH.

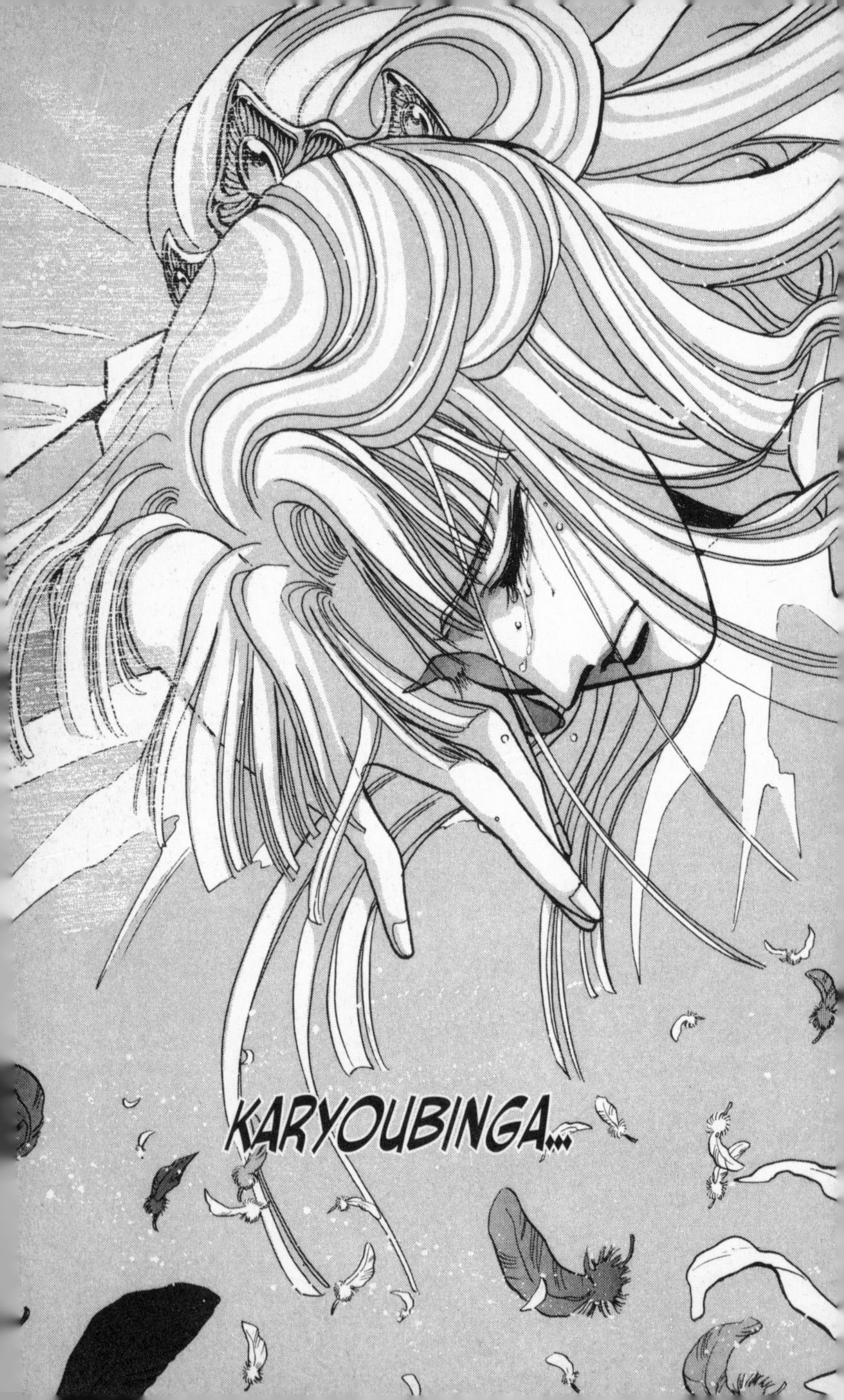
KARYOUBINGA...

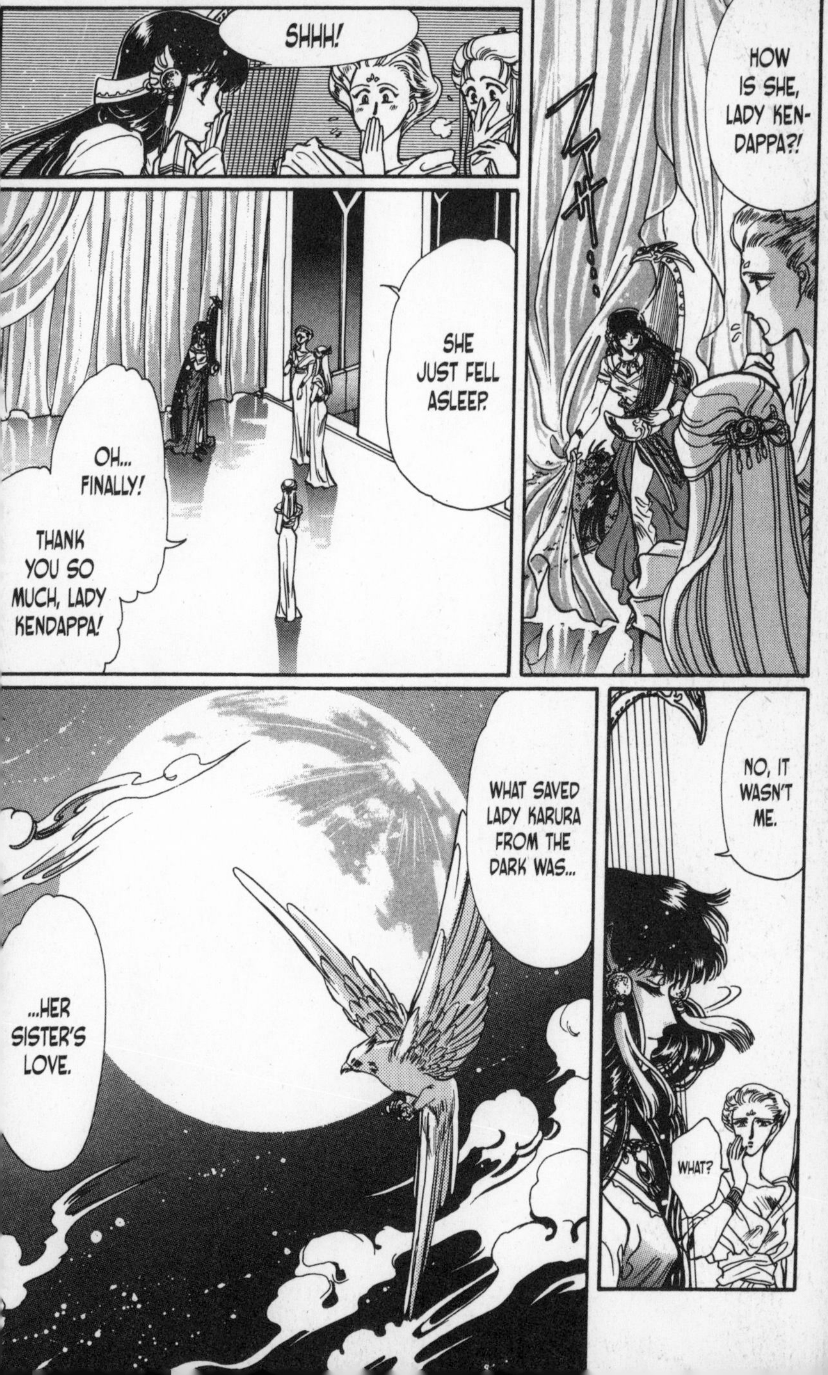
HOW IS SHE, LADY KEN-DAPPA?!
SHHH!
SHE JUST FELL ASLEEP.
OH... FINALLY!
THANK YOU SO MUCH, LADY KENDAPPA!
NO, IT WASN'T ME.
WHAT?
WHAT SAVED LADY KARURA FROM THE DARK WAS...
...HER SISTER'S LOVE.

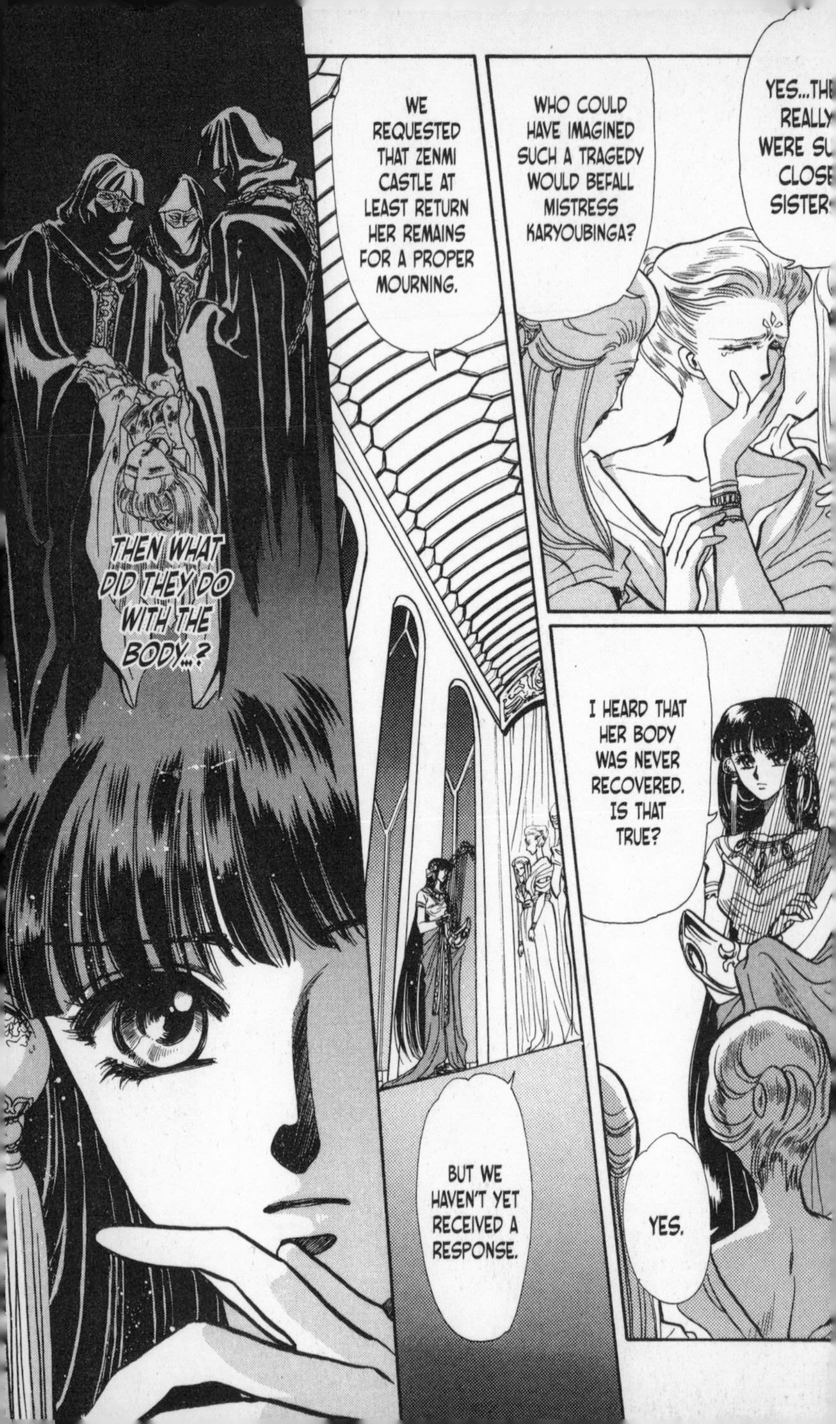
WHO COULD HAVE IMAGINED SUCH A TRAGEDY WOULD BEFALL MISTRESS KARYOUBINGA?
YES...THE REALLY WERE SU CLOSE SISTER
I HEARD THAT HER BODY WAS NEVER RECOVERED. IS THAT TRUE?
YES.
WE REQUESTED THAT ZENMI CASTLE AT LEAST RETURN HER REMAINS FOR A PROPER MOURNING.
BUT WE HAVEN'T YET RECEIVED A RESPONSE.
THEN WHAT DID THEY DO WITH THE BODY...?

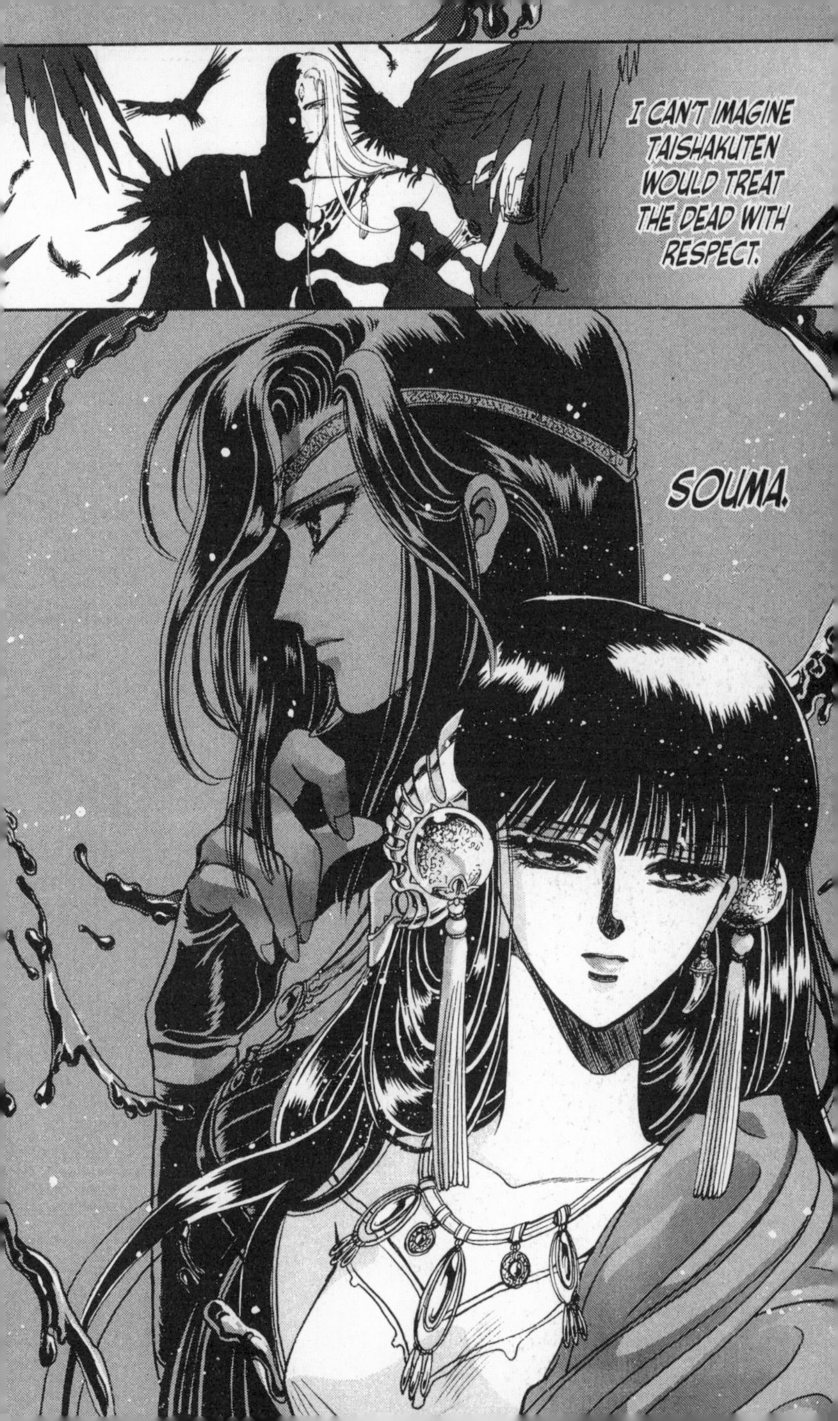
I CAN'T IMAGINE TAISHAKUTEN WOULD TREAT THE DEAD WITH RESPECT.
SOUMA.

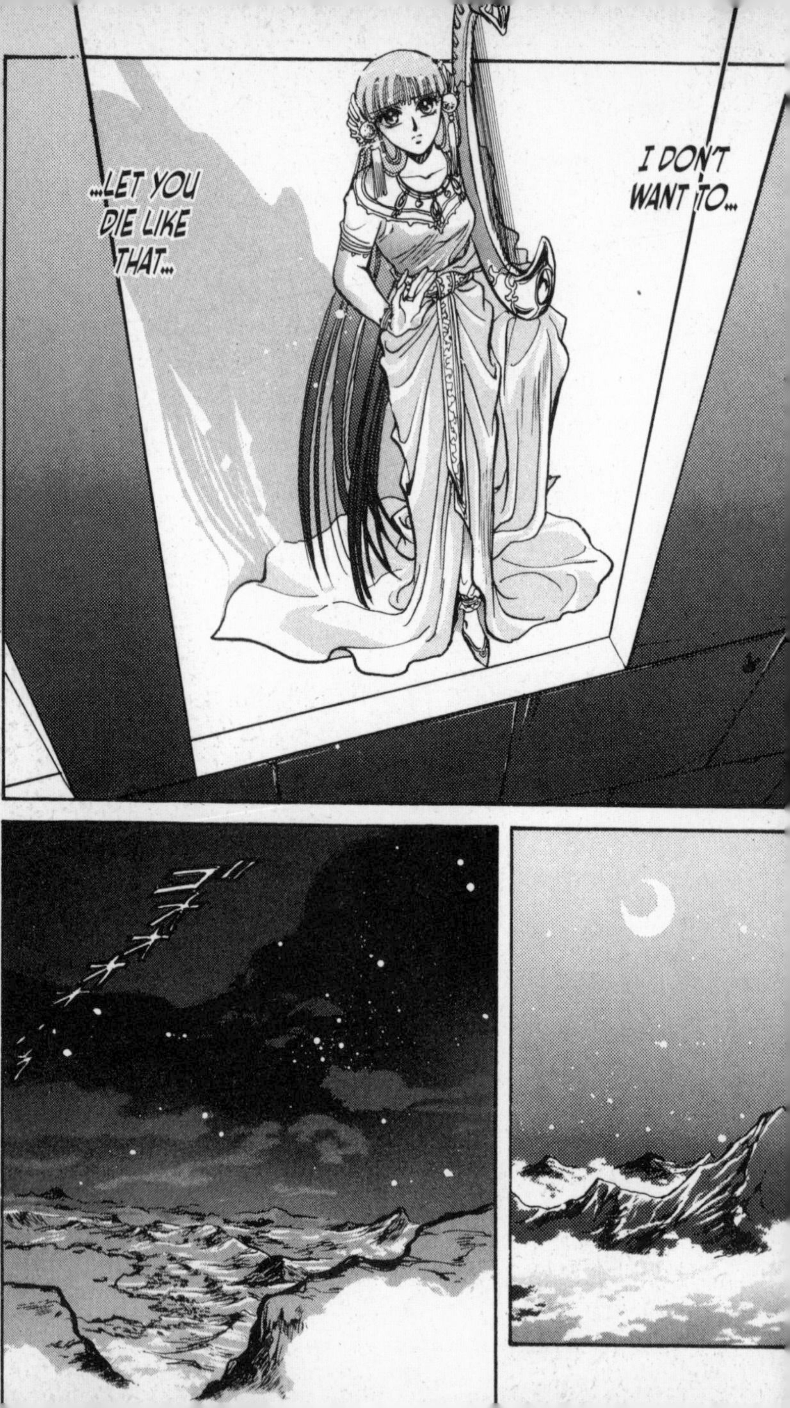
I DON'T WANT TO...
...LET YOU DIE LIKE THAT...

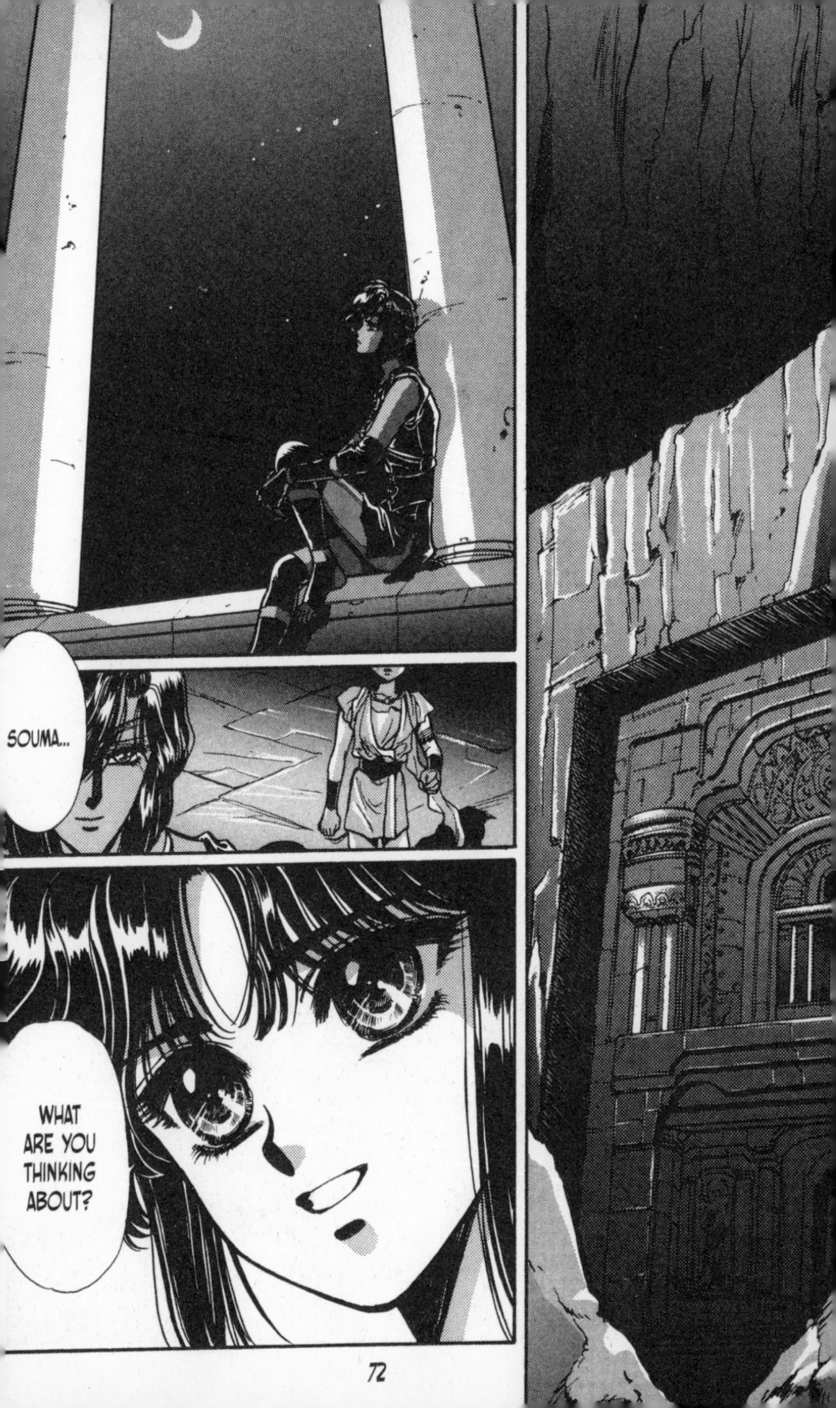
SOUMA...
WHAT ARE YOU THINKING ABOUT?

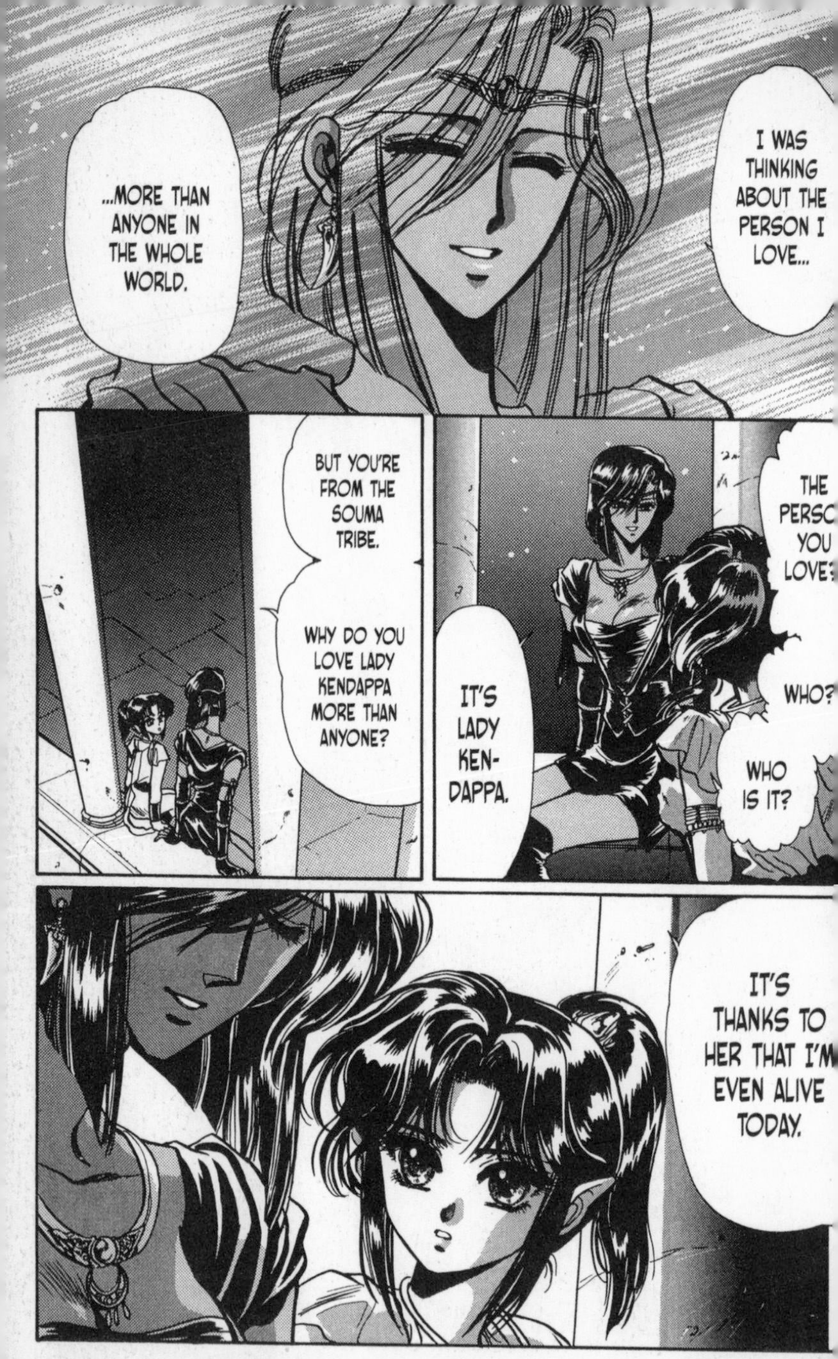
I WAS THINKING ABOUT THE PERSON I LOVE...
...MORE THAN ANYONE IN THE WHOLE WORLD.
THE PERSO YOU LOVE?
WHO?
WHO IS IT?
IT'S LADY KEN-DAPPA.
BUT YOU'RE FROM THE SOUMA TRIBE.
WHY DO YOU LOVE LADY KENDAPPA MORE THAN ANYONE?
IT'S THANKS TO HER THAT I'M EVEN ALIVE TODAY.

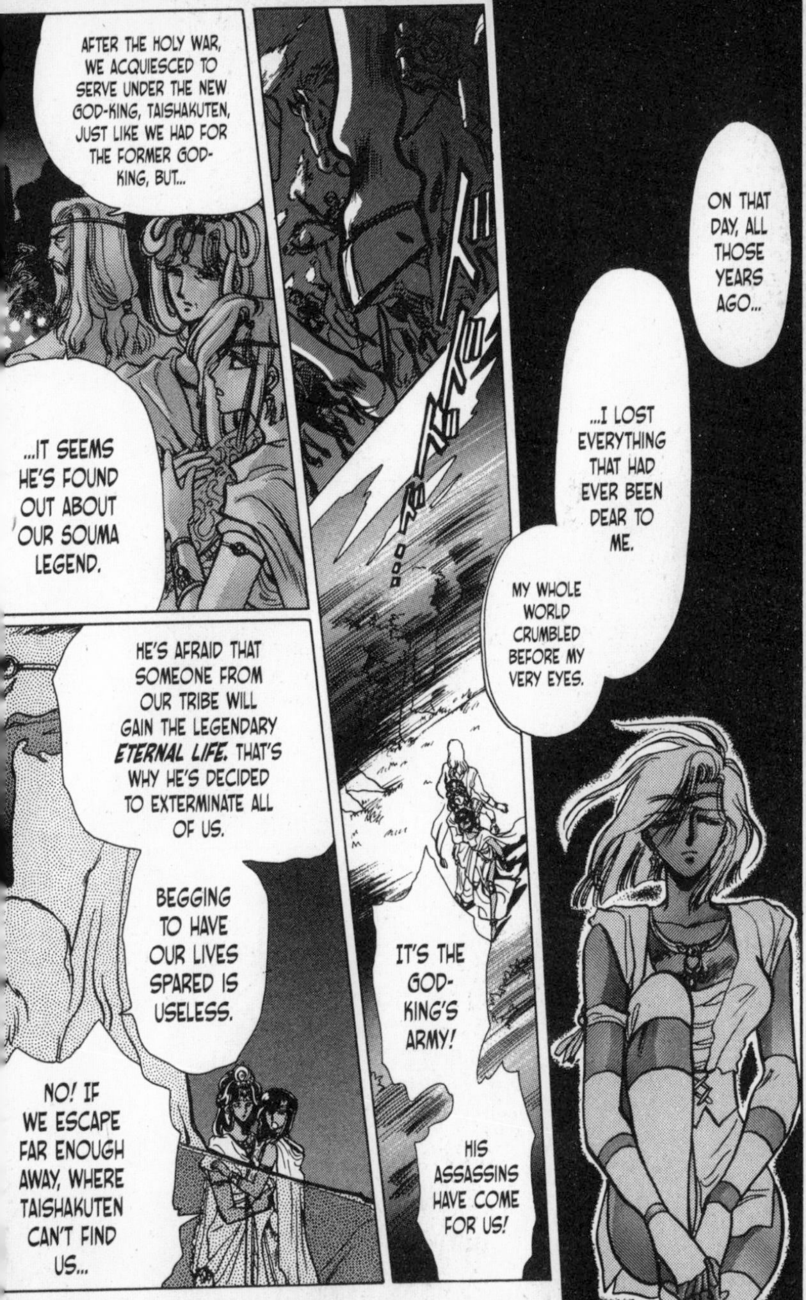
ON THAT DAY, ALL THOSE YEARS AGO...
...I LOST EVERYTHING THAT HAD EVER BEEN DEAR TO ME.
MY WHOLE WORLD CRUMBLED BEFORE MY VERY EYES.
IT'S THE GOD-KING'S ARMY!
HIS ASSASSINS HAVE COME FOR US!
AFTER THE HOLY WAR, WE ACQUIESCED TO SERVE UNDER THE NEW GOD-KING, TAISHAKUTEN, JUST LIKE WE HAD FOR THE FORMER GOD-KING, BUT...
...IT SEEMS HE'S FOUND OUT ABOUT OUR SOUMA LEGEND.
HE'S AFRAID THAT SOMEONE FROM OUR TRIBE WILL GAIN THE LEGENDARY ***ETERNAL LIFE.*** THAT'S WHY HE'S DECIDED TO EXTERMINATE ALL OF US.
BEGGING TO HAVE OUR LIVES SPARED IS USELESS.
NO! IF WE ESCAPE FAR ENOUGH AWAY, WHERE TAISHAKUTEN CAN'T FIND US...

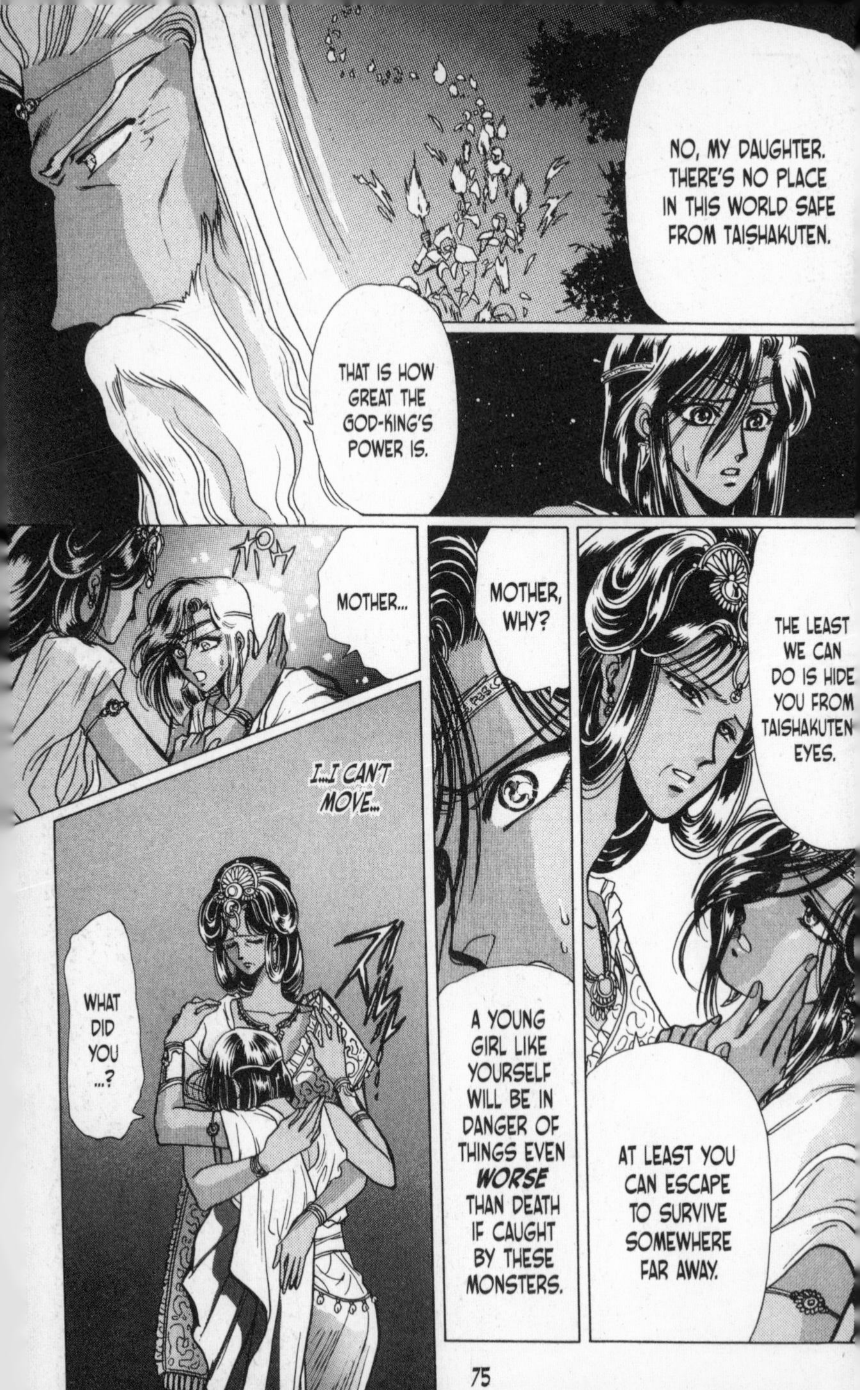
NO, MY DAUGHTER. THERE'S NO PLACE IN THIS WORLD SAFE FROM TAISHAKUTEN.
THAT IS HOW GREAT THE GOD-KING'S POWER IS.
THE LEAST WE CAN DO IS HIDE YOU FROM TAISHAKUTEN EYES.
AT LEAST YOU CAN ESCAPE TO SURVIVE SOMEWHERE FAR AWAY.
MOTHER, WHY?
A YOUNG GIRL LIKE YOURSELF WILL BE IN DANGER OF THINGS EVEN WORSE THAN DEATH IF CAUGHT BY THESE MONSTERS.
MOTHER...
I...I CAN'T MOVE...
WHAT DID YOU ...?

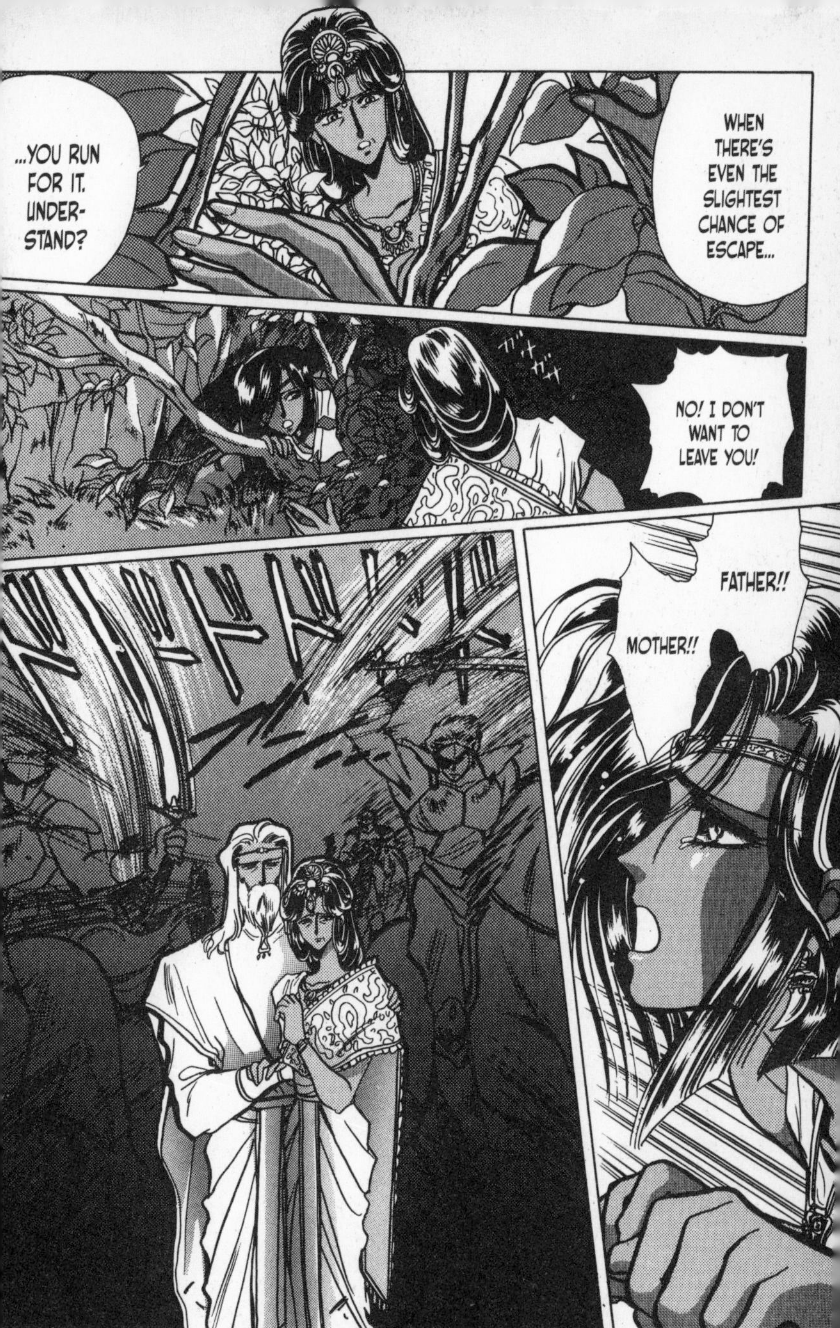
WHEN THERE'S EVEN THE SLIGHTEST CHANCE OF ESCAPE...
...YOU RUN FOR IT. UNDER-STAND?
NO! I DON'T WANT TO LEAVE YOU!
FATHER!!
MOTHER!!

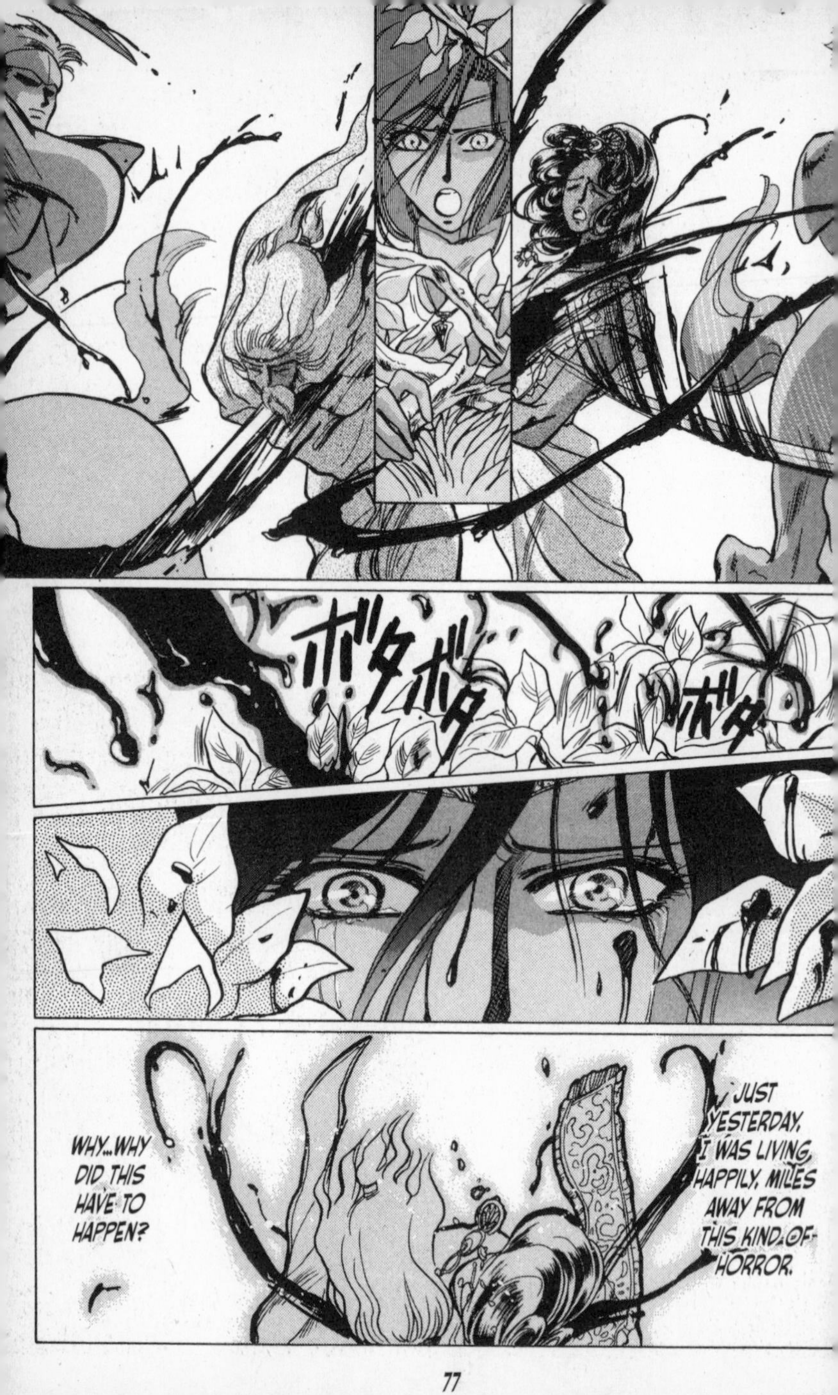
ボタ
ボタボタ
JUST YESTERDAY, I WAS LIVING HAPPILY, MILES AWAY FROM THIS KIND OF HORROR.
WHY...WHY DID THIS HAVE TO HAPPEN?

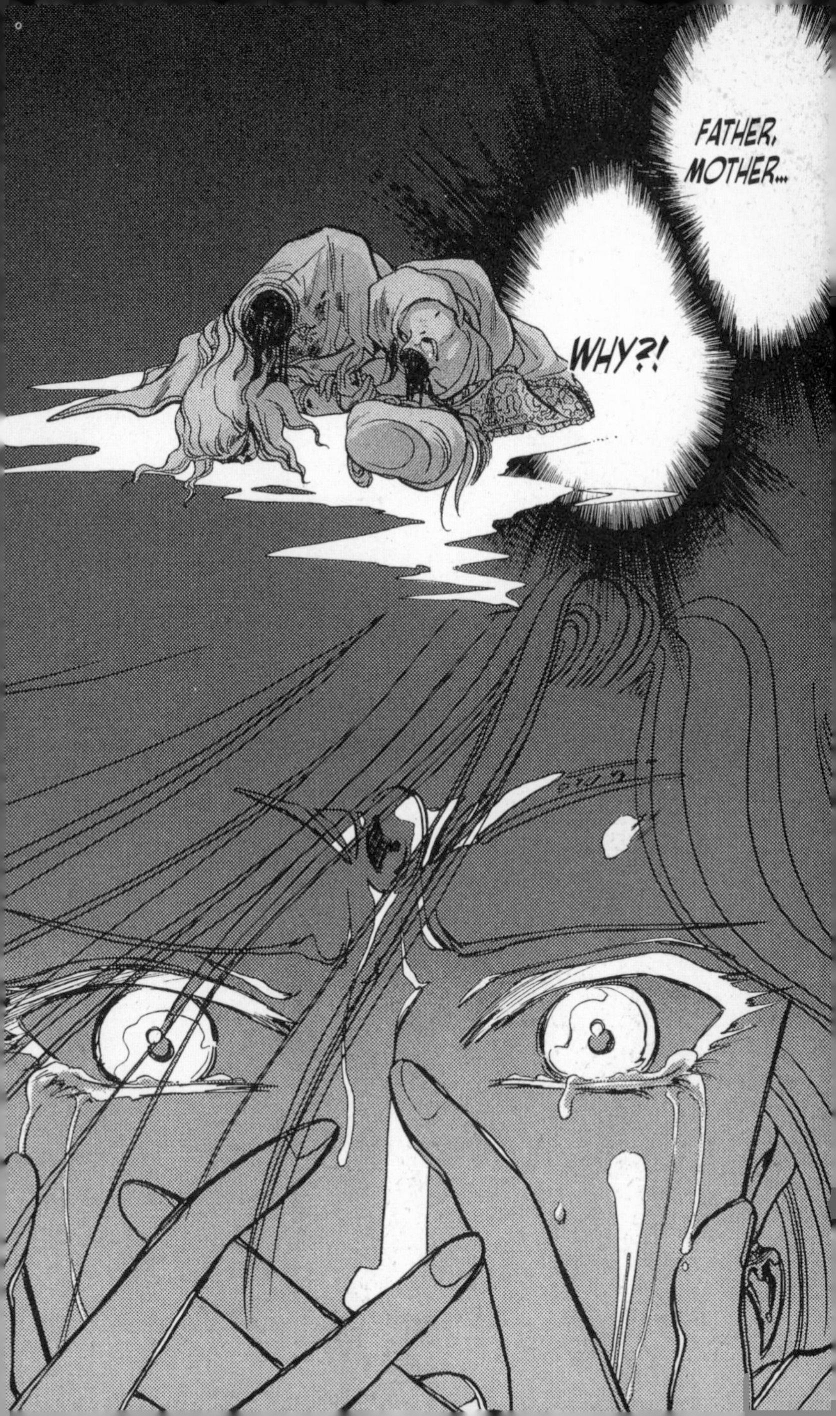
FATHER, MOTHER...
WHY?!

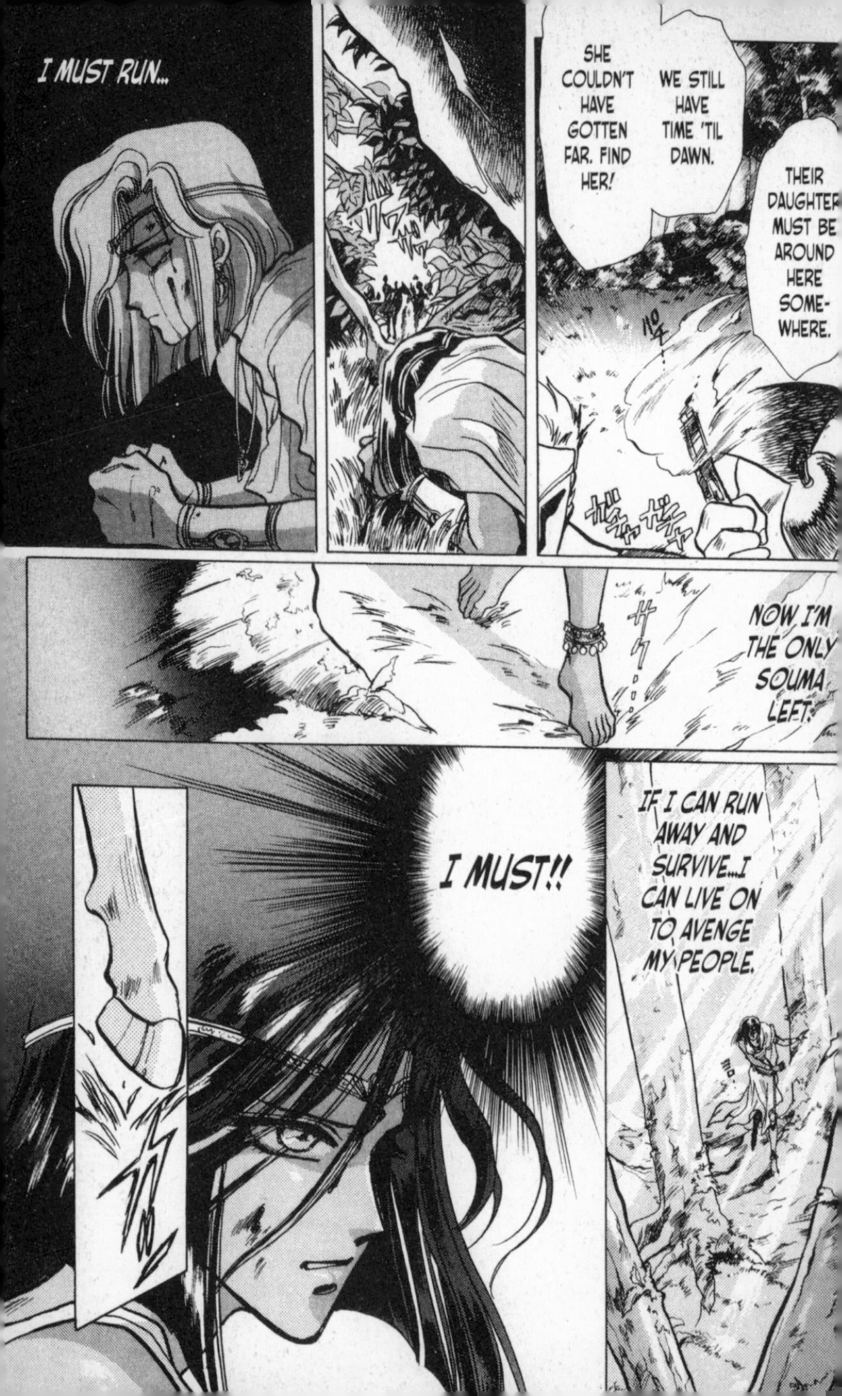
THEIR DAUGHTER MUST BE AROUND HERE SOMEWHERE.
WE STILL HAVE TIME 'TIL DAWN.
SHE COULDN'T HAVE GOTTEN FAR. FIND HER!
I MUST RUN...
NOW I'M THE ONLY SOUMA LEFT.
IF I CAN RUN AWAY AND SURVIVE...I CAN LIVE ON TO AVENGE MY PEOPLE.
I MUST!!

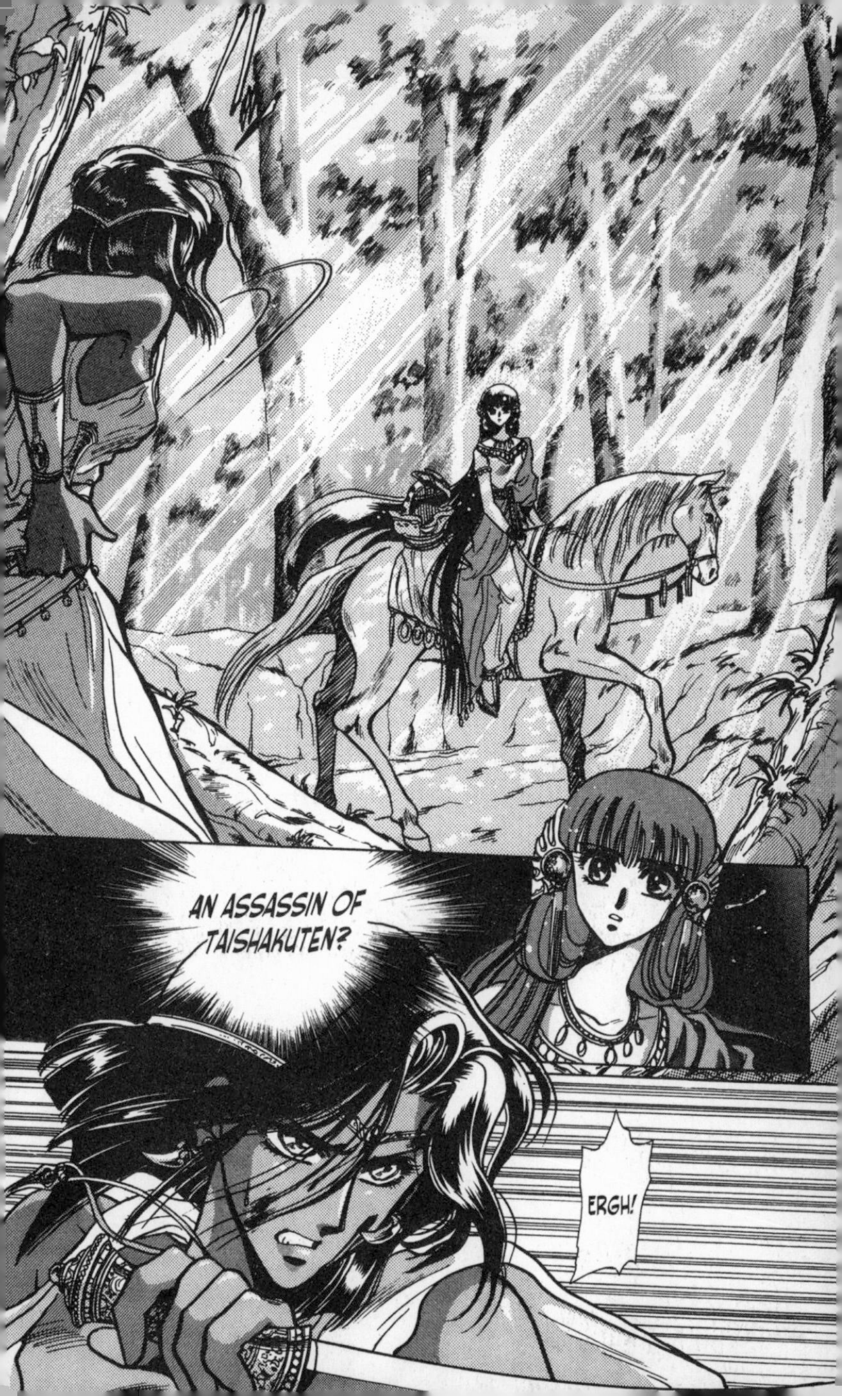
AN ASSASSIN OF TAISHAKUTEN?
ERGH!

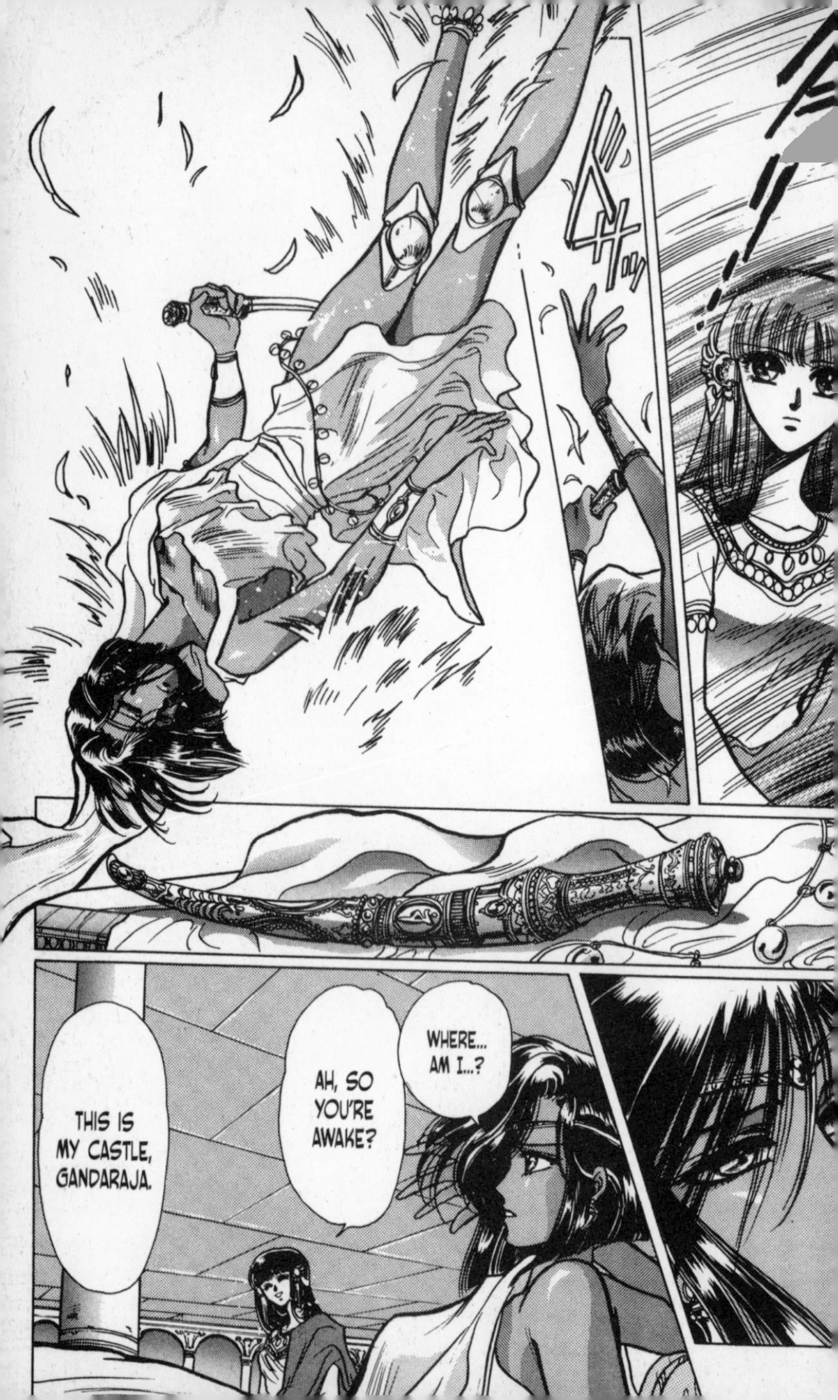
WHERE... AM I...?
AH, SO YOU'RE AWAKE?
THIS IS MY CASTLE, GANDARAJA.

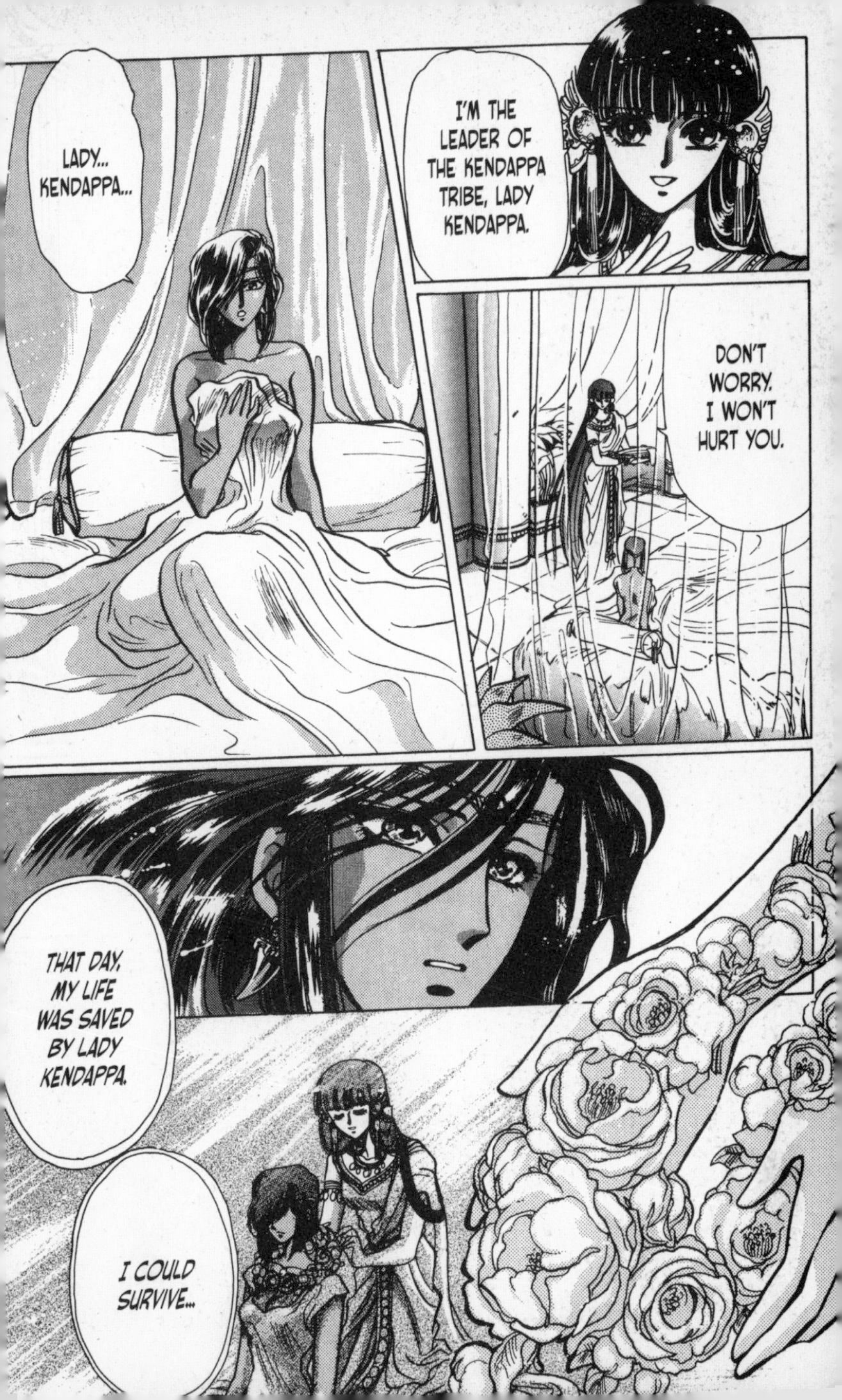

I'M THE LEADER OF THE KENDAPPA TRIBE, LADY KENDAPPA.
DON'T WORRY. I WON'T HURT YOU.
LADY... KENDAPPA...
THAT DAY, MY LIFE WAS SAVED BY LADY KENDAPPA.
I COULD SURVIVE...

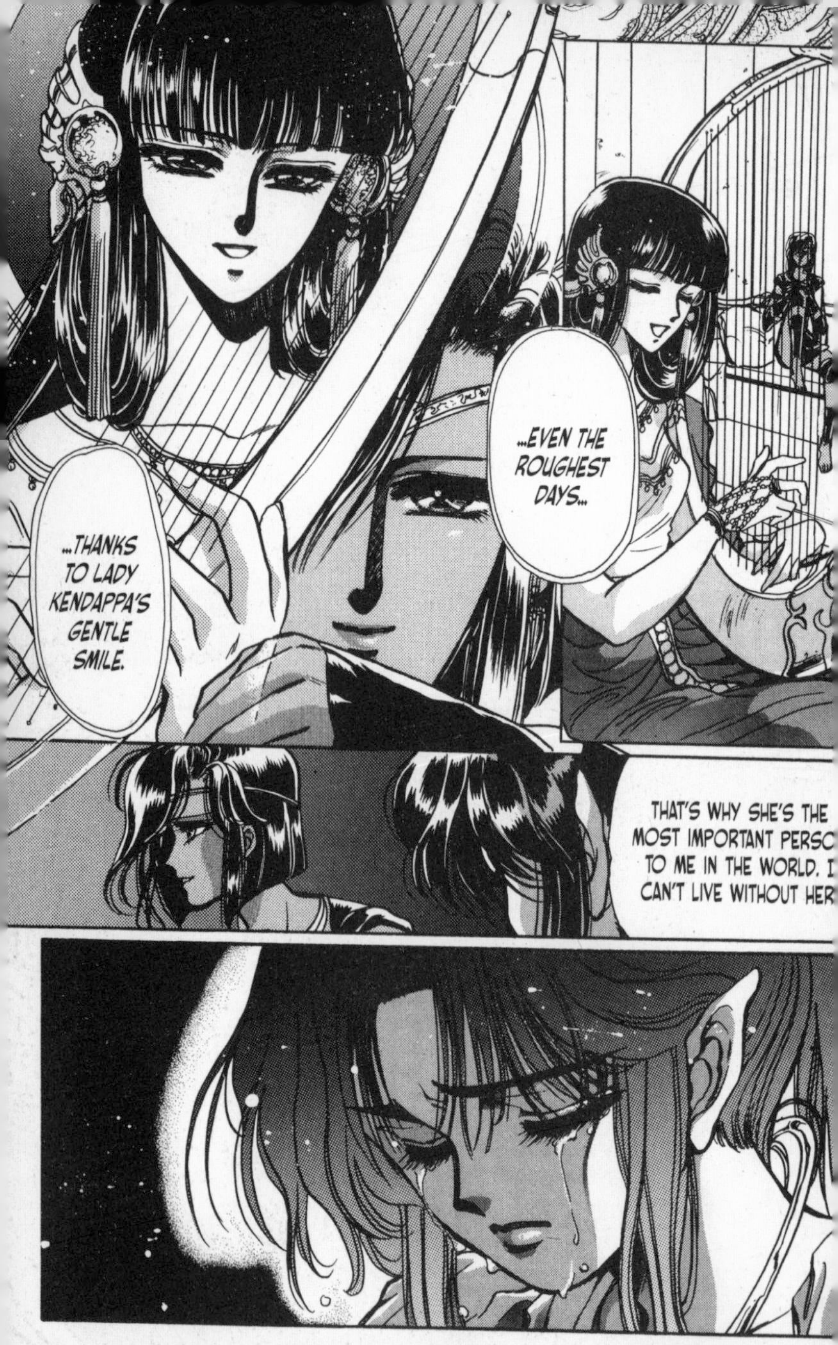
...EVEN THE ROUGHEST DAYS...
...THANKS TO LADY KENDAPPA'S GENTLE SMILE.
THAT'S WHY SHE'S THE MOST IMPORTANT PERSO TO ME IN THE WORLD. I CAN'T LIVE WITHOUT HER

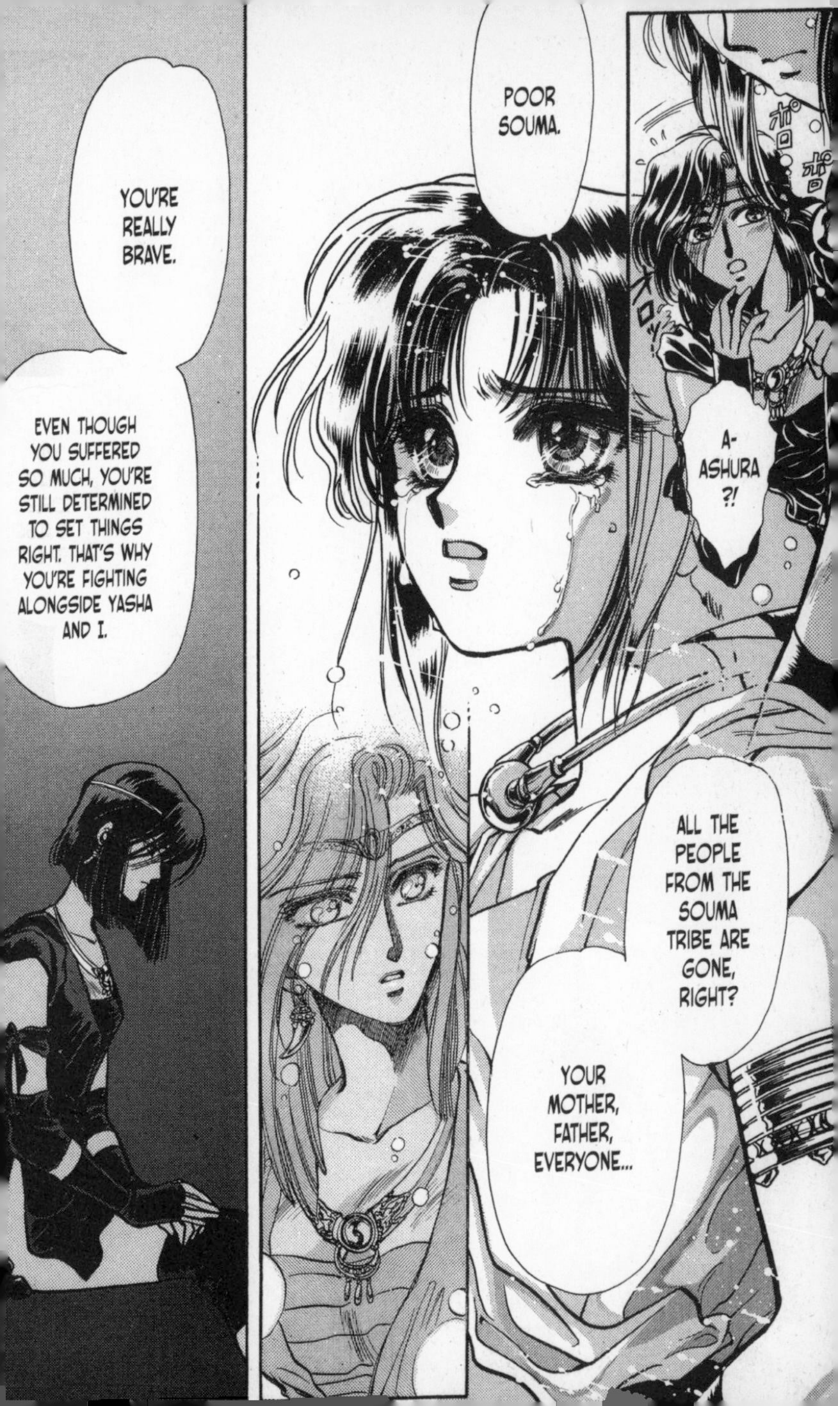

A-ASHURA ?!
POOR SOUMA.
ALL THE PEOPLE FROM THE SOUMA TRIBE ARE GONE, RIGHT?
YOUR MOTHER, FATHER, EVERYONE...
YOU'RE REALLY BRAVE.
EVEN THOUGH YOU SUFFERED SO MUCH, YOU'RE STILL DETERMINED TO SET THINGS RIGHT. THAT'S WHY YOU'RE FIGHTING ALONGSIDE YASHA AND I.

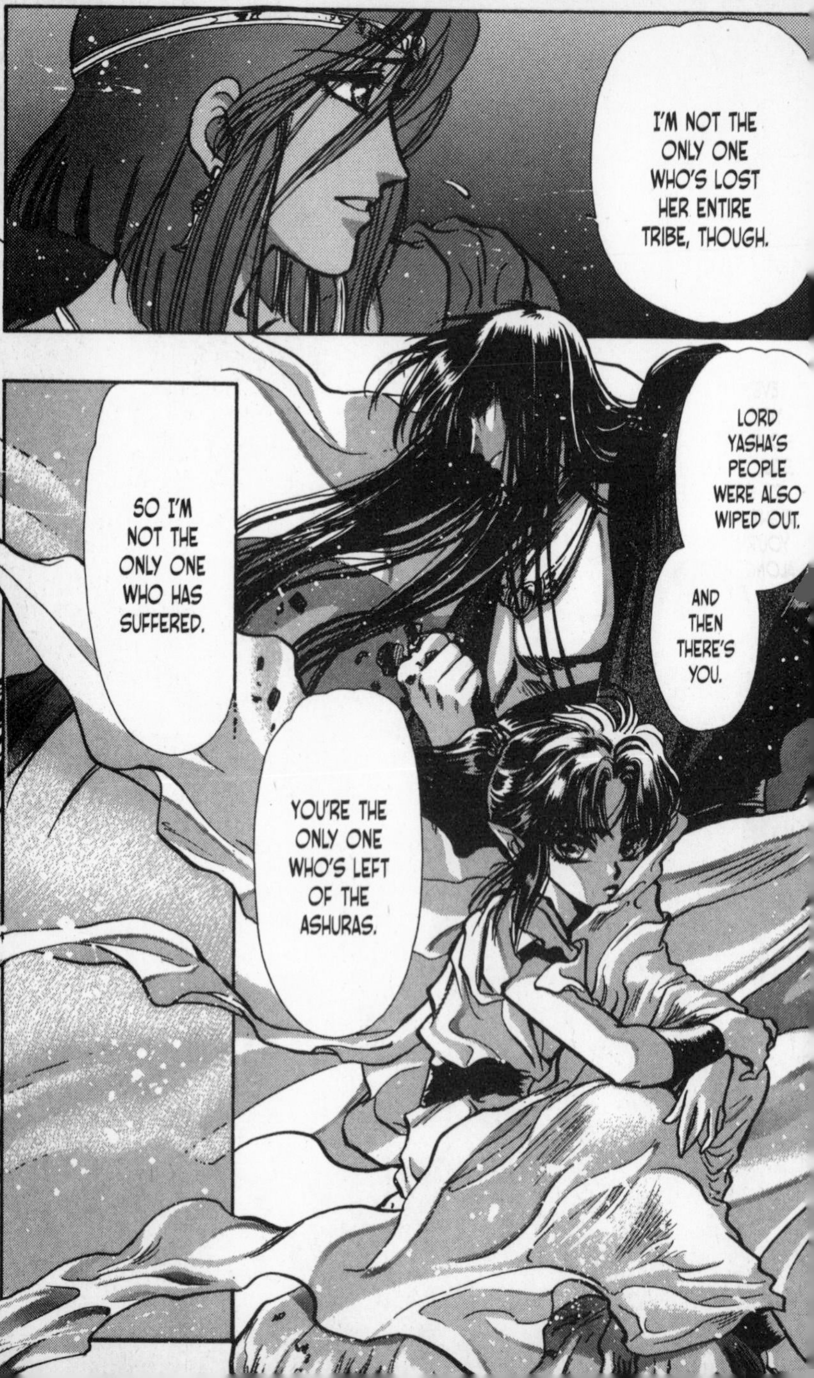
I'M NOT THE ONLY ONE WHO'S LOST HER ENTIRE TRIBE, THOUGH.
LORD YASHA'S PEOPLE WERE ALSO WIPED OUT.
AND THEN THERE'S YOU.
YOU'RE THE ONLY ONE WHO'S LEFT OF THE ASHURAS.
SO I'M NOT THE ONLY ONE WHO HAS SUFFERED.

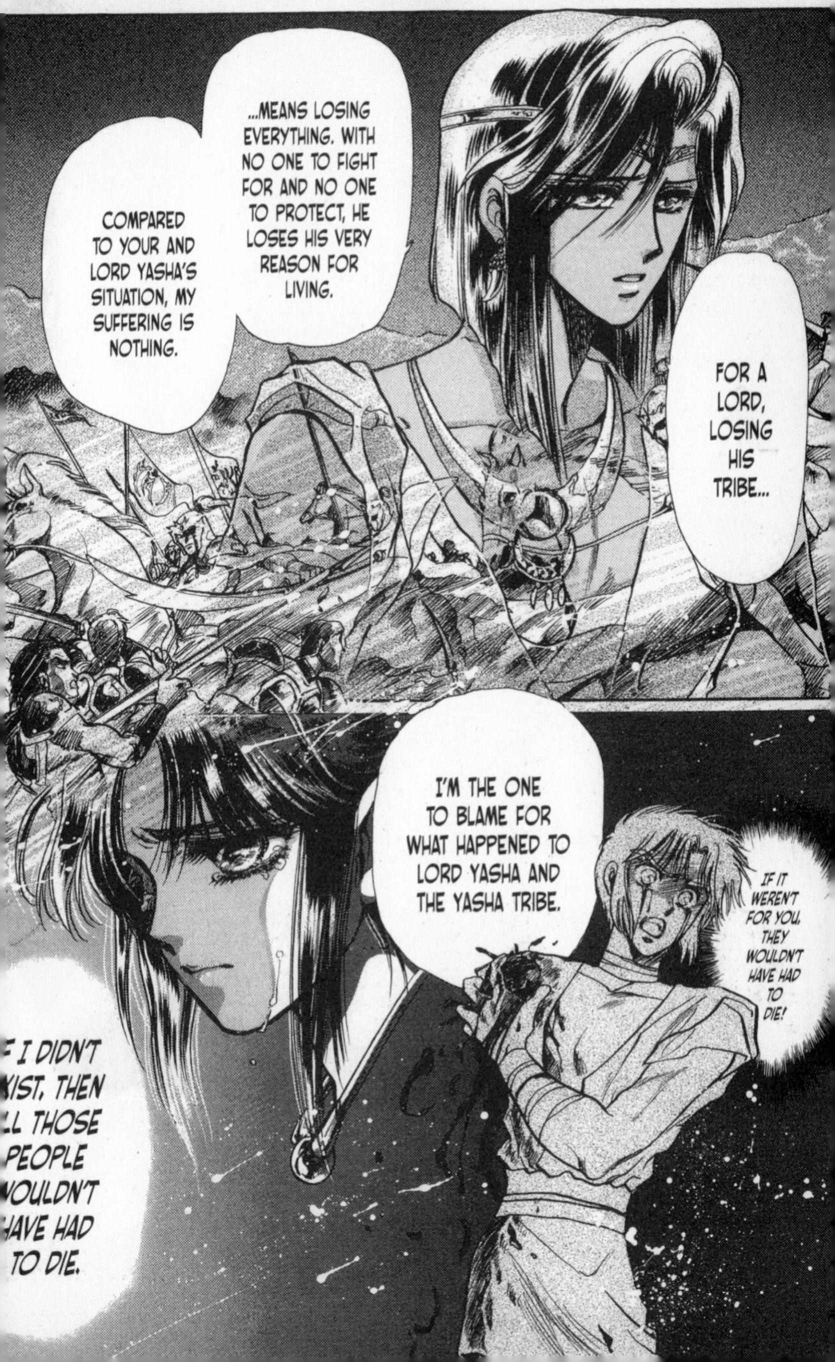
FOR A LORD, LOSING HIS TRIBE...
...MEANS LOSING EVERYTHING. WITH NO ONE TO FIGHT FOR AND NO ONE TO PROTECT, HE LOSES HIS VERY REASON FOR LIVING.
COMPARED TO YOUR AND LORD YASHA'S SITUATION, MY SUFFERING IS NOTHING.
I'M THE ONE TO BLAME FOR WHAT HAPPENED TO LORD YASHA AND THE YASHA TRIBE.
IF IT WEREN'T FOR YOU, THEY WOULDN'T HAVE HAD TO DIE!
F I DIDN'T XIST, THEN LL THOSE PEOPLE OULDN'T AVE HAD TO DIE.

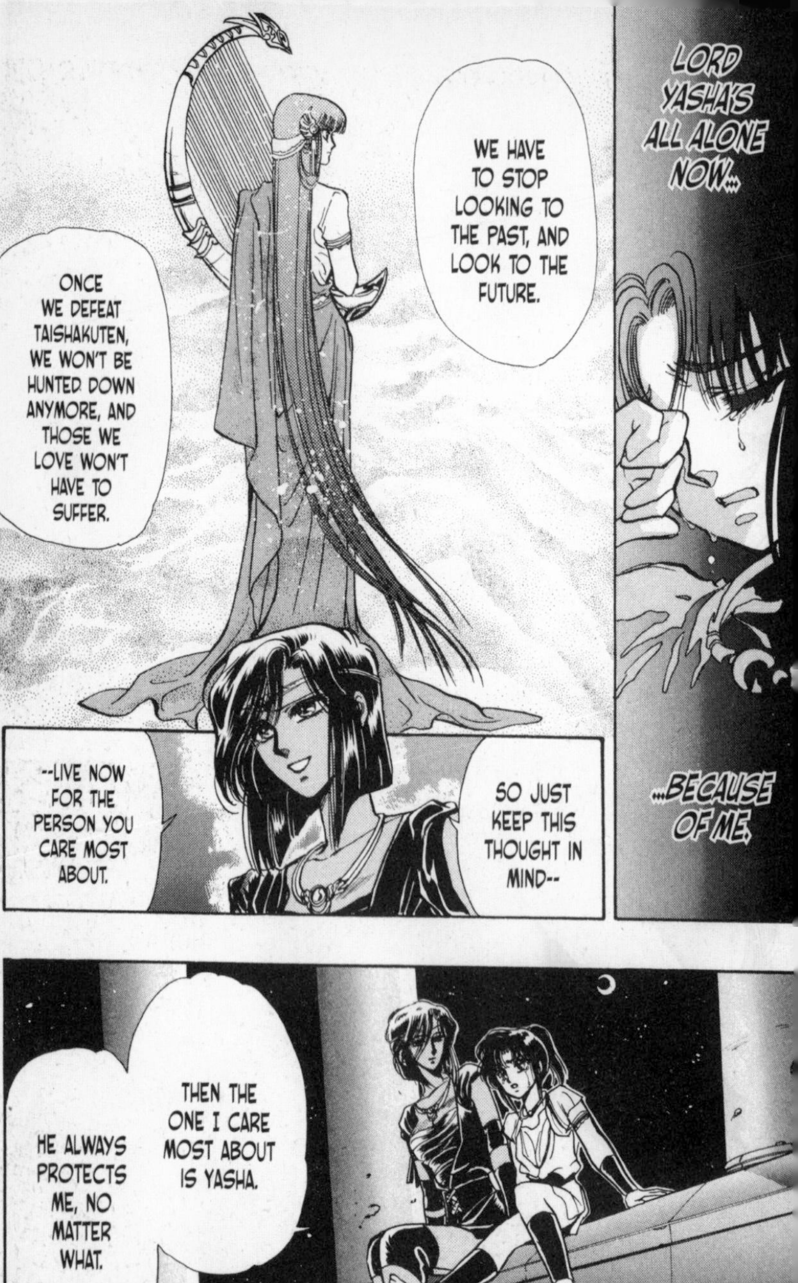
LORD YASHA'S ALL ALONE NOW...
...BECAUSE OF ME.
WE HAVE TO STOP LOOKING TO THE PAST, AND LOOK TO THE FUTURE.
ONCE WE DEFEAT TAISHAKUTEN, WE WON'T BE HUNTED DOWN ANYMORE, AND THOSE WE LOVE WON'T HAVE TO SUFFER.
SO JUST KEEP THIS THOUGHT IN MIND--
--LIVE NOW FOR THE PERSON YOU CARE MOST ABOUT.
THEN THE ONE I CARE MOST ABOUT IS YASHA.
HE ALWAYS PROTECTS ME, NO MATTER WHAT.

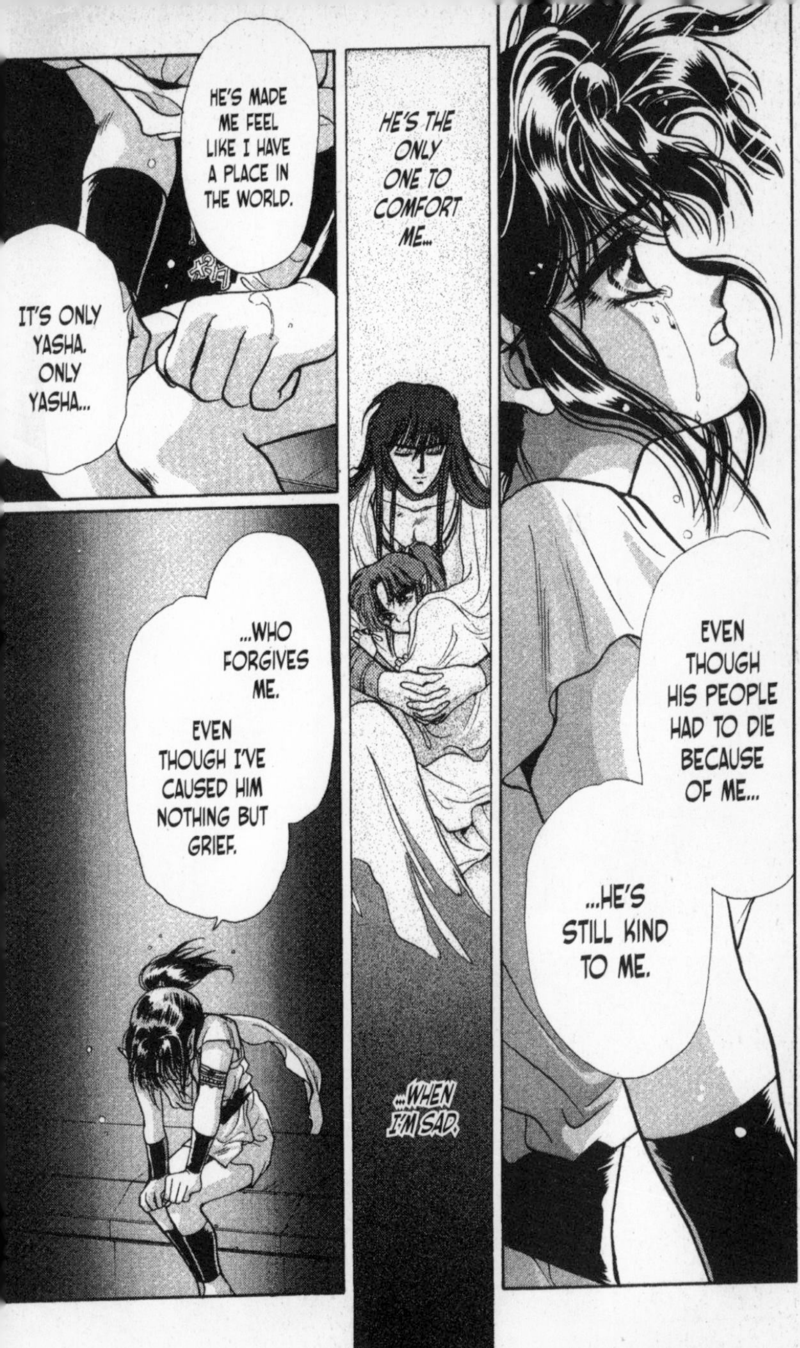
EVEN THOUGH HIS PEOPLE HAD TO DIE BECAUSE OF ME...
...HE'S STILL KIND TO ME.
HE'S THE ONLY ONE TO COMFORT ME...
...WHEN I'M SAD.
HE'S MADE ME FEEL LIKE I HAVE A PLACE IN THE WORLD.
IT'S ONLY YASHA. ONLY YASHA...
...WHO FORGIVES ME.
EVEN THOUGH I'VE CAUSED HIM NOTHING BUT GRIEF.

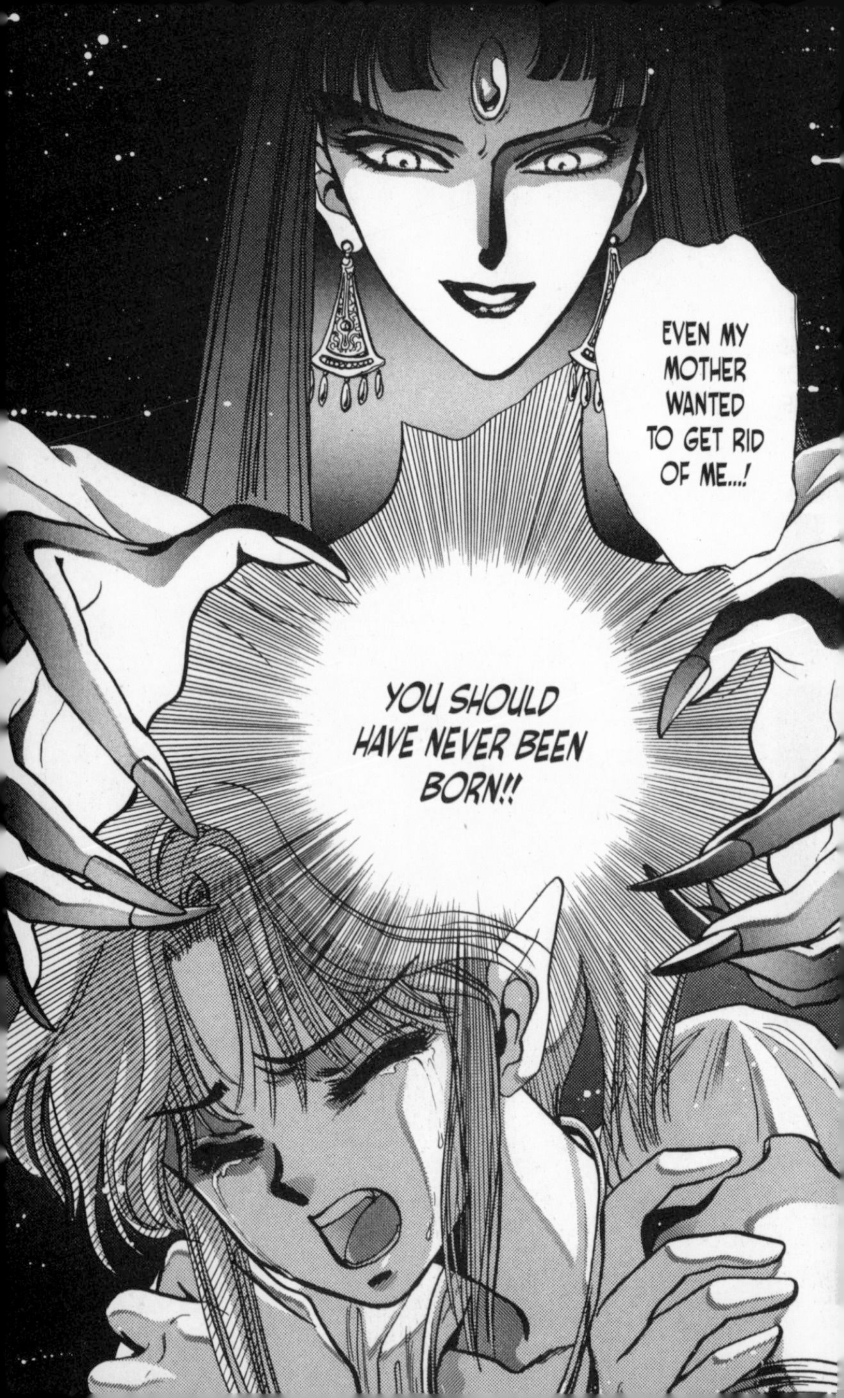
EVEN MY MOTHER WANTED TO GET RID OF ME...!
YOU SHOULD HAVE NEVER BEEN BORN!!

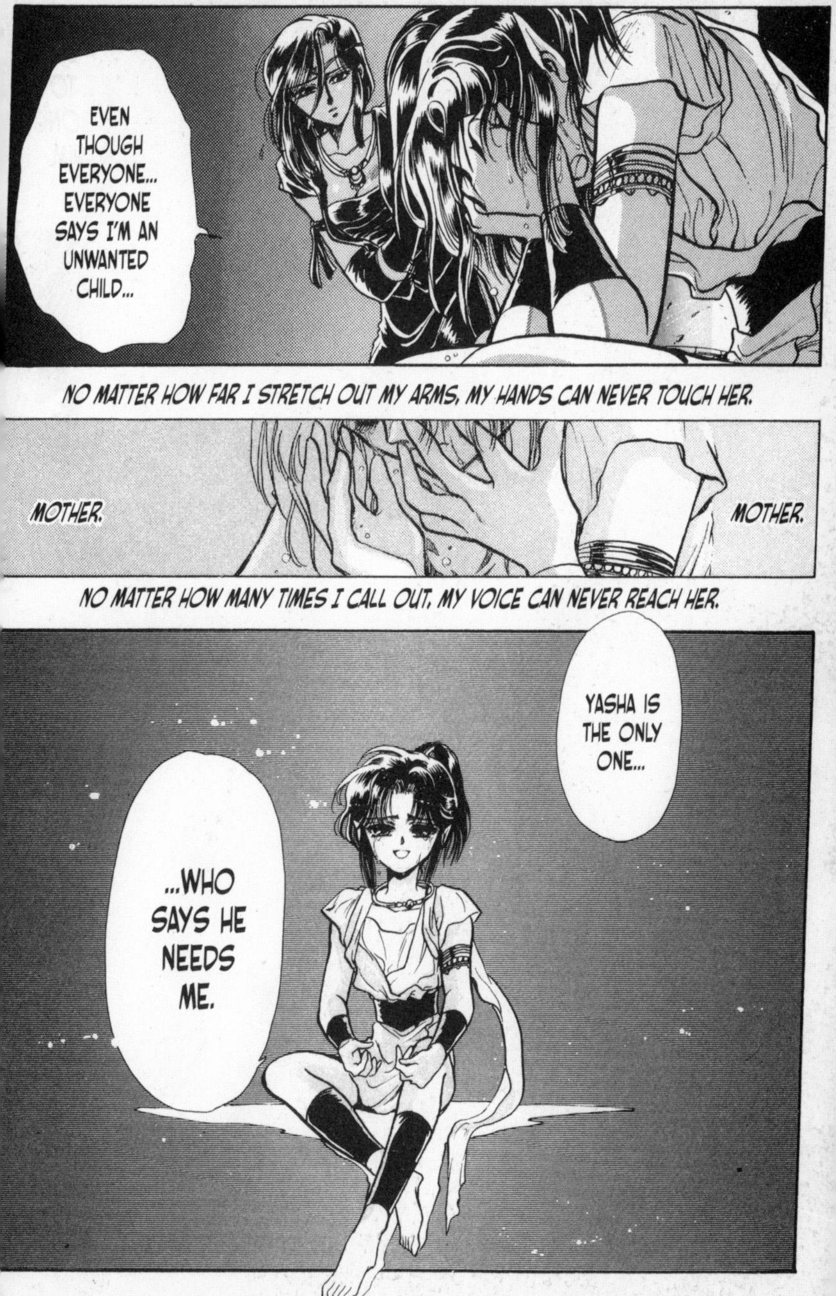
EVEN THOUGH EVERYONE... EVERYONE SAYS I'M AN UNWANTED CHILD...
NO MATTER HOW FAR I STRETCH OUT MY ARMS, MY HANDS CAN NEVER TOUCH HER.
MOTHER.
MOTHER.
NO MATTER HOW MANY TIMES I CALL OUT, MY VOICE CAN NEVER REACH HER.
YASHA IS THE ONLY ONE...
...WHO SAYS HE NEEDS ME.

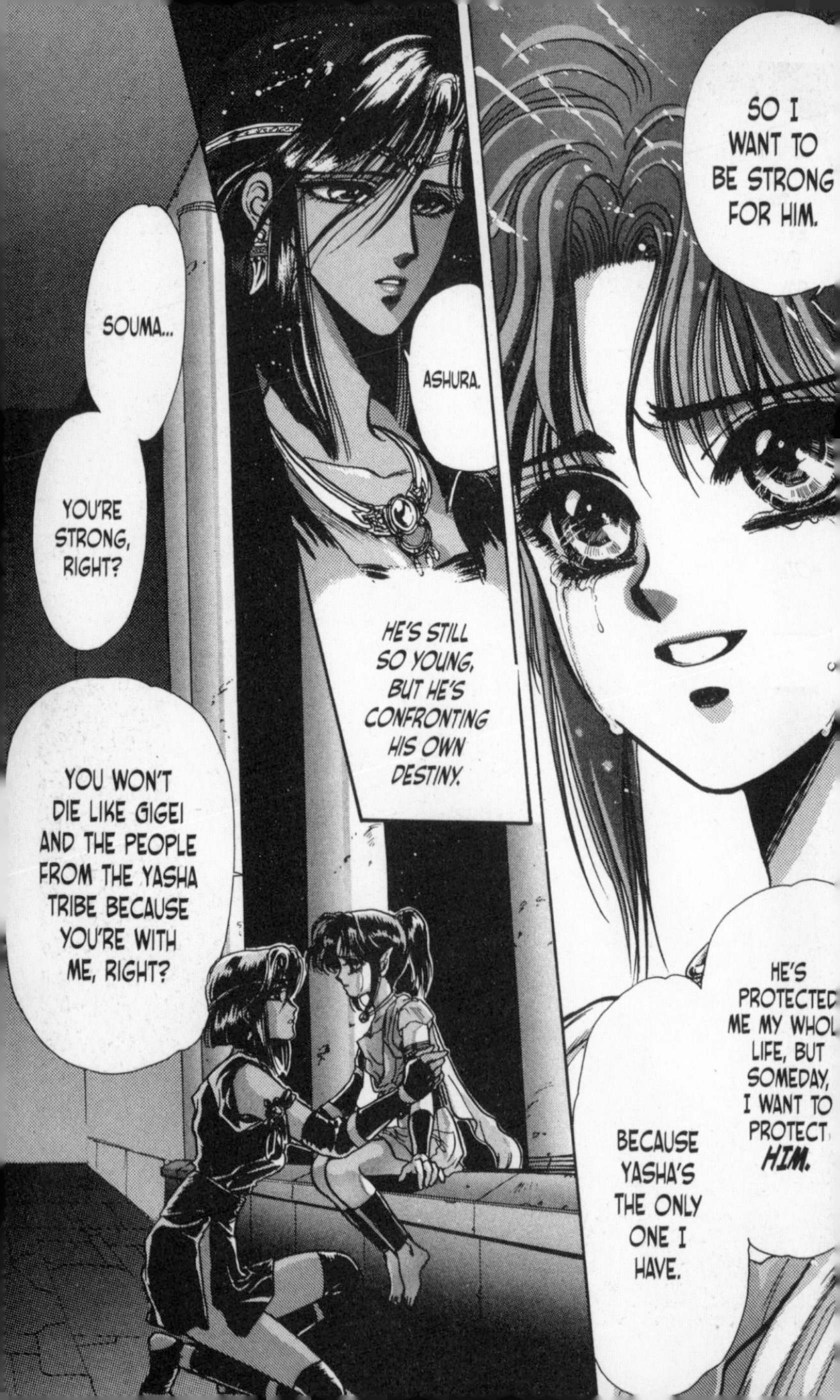
SO I WANT TO BE STRONG FOR HIM.
HE'S PROTECTED ME MY WHOL LIFE, BUT SOMEDAY, I WANT TO PROTECT *HIM.*
BECAUSE YASHA'S THE ONLY ONE I HAVE.
ASHURA.
HE'S STILL SO YOUNG, BUT HE'S CONFRONTING HIS OWN DESTINY.
SOUMA...
YOU'RE STRONG, RIGHT?
YOU WON'T DIE LIKE GIGEI AND THE PEOPLE FROM THE YASHA TRIBE BECAUSE YOU'RE WITH ME, RIGHT?

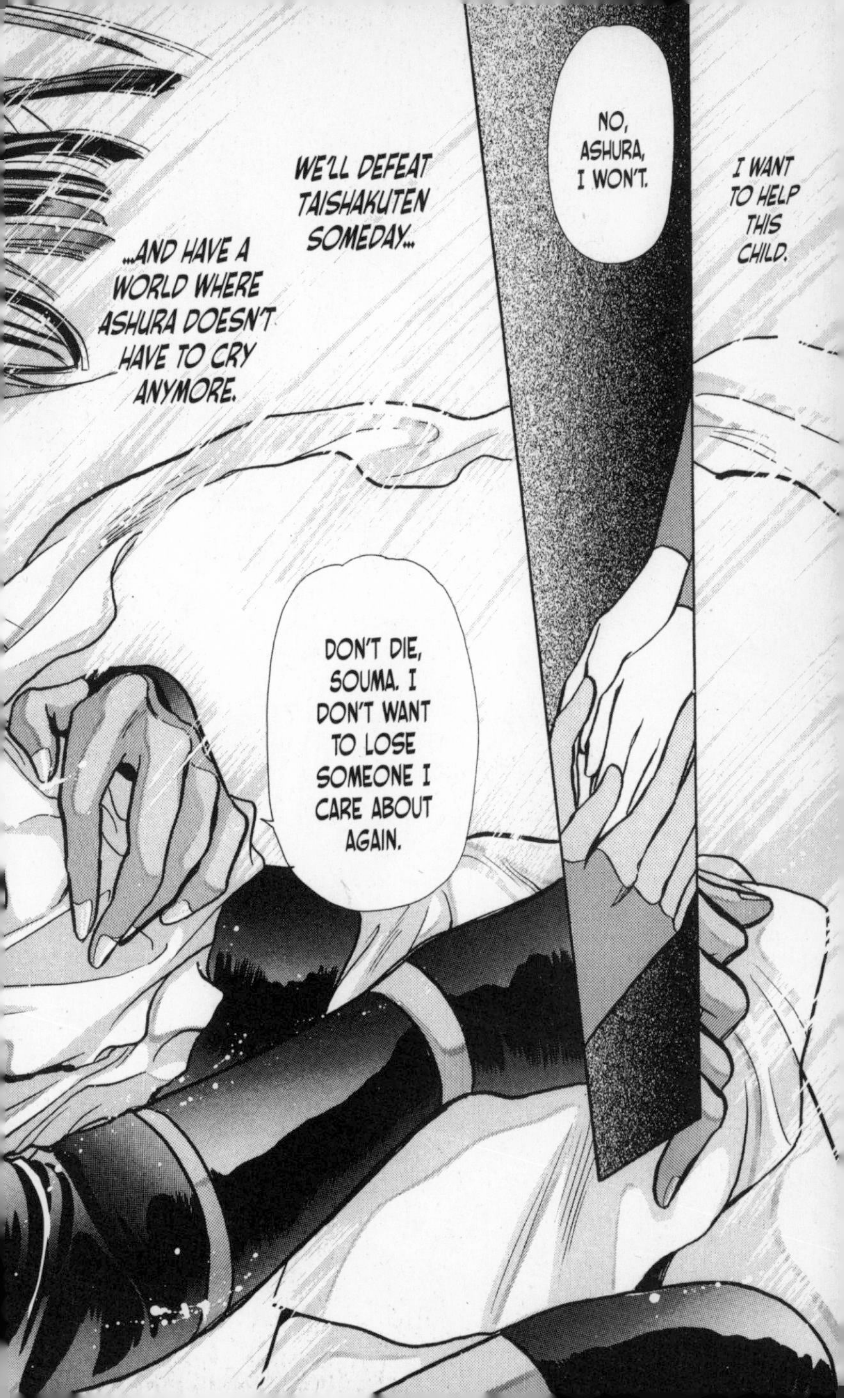
I WANT TO HELP THIS CHILD.
NO, ASHURA, I WON'T.
WE'LL DEFEAT TAISHAKUTEN SOMEDAY...
...AND HAVE A WORLD WHERE ASHURA DOESN'T HAVE TO CRY ANYMORE.
DON'T DIE, SOUMA. I DON'T WANT TO LOSE SOMEONE I CARE ABOUT AGAIN.

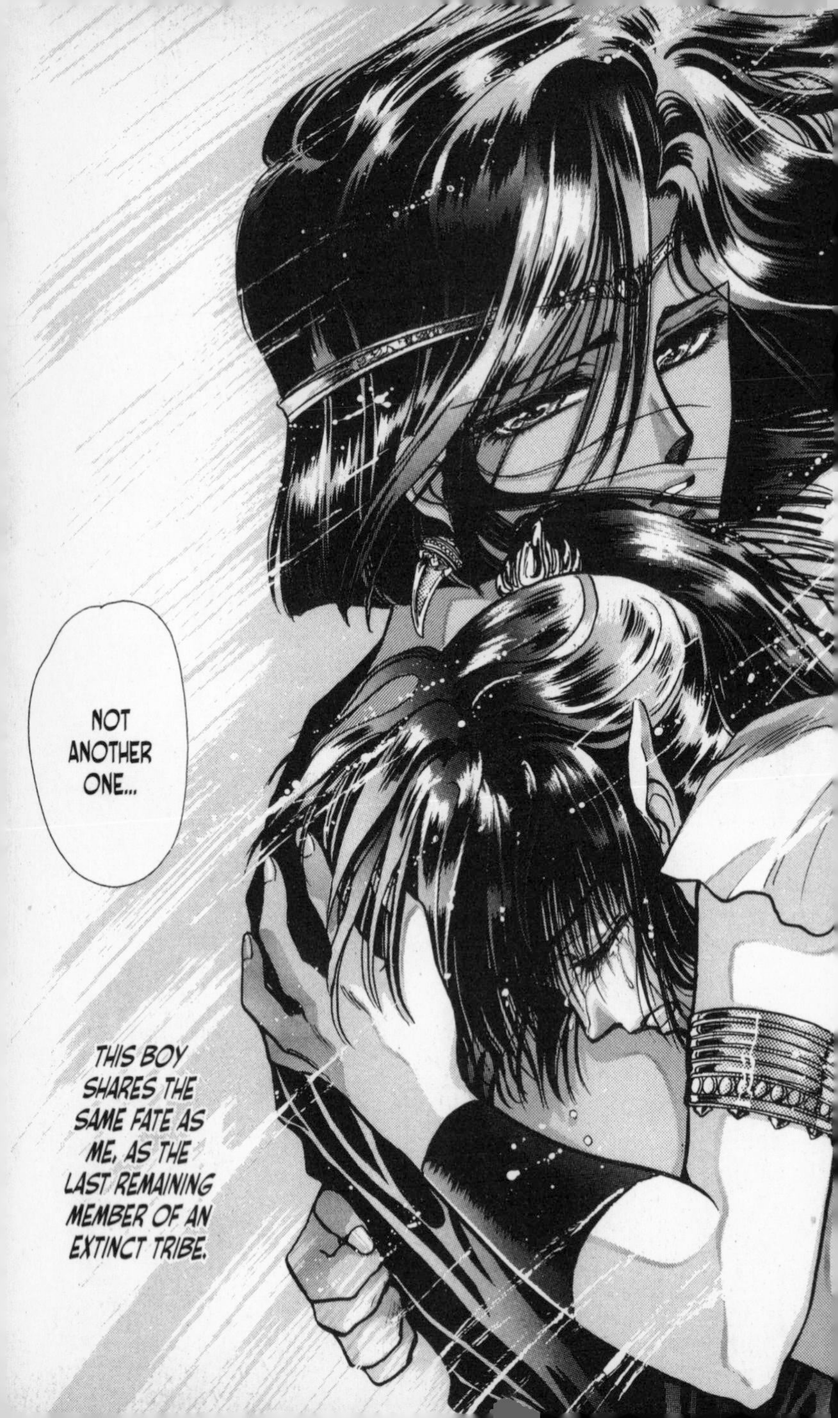
NOT ANOTHER ONE...
THIS BOY SHARES THE SAME FATE AS ME, AS THE LAST REMAINING MEMBER OF AN EXTINCT TRIBE.

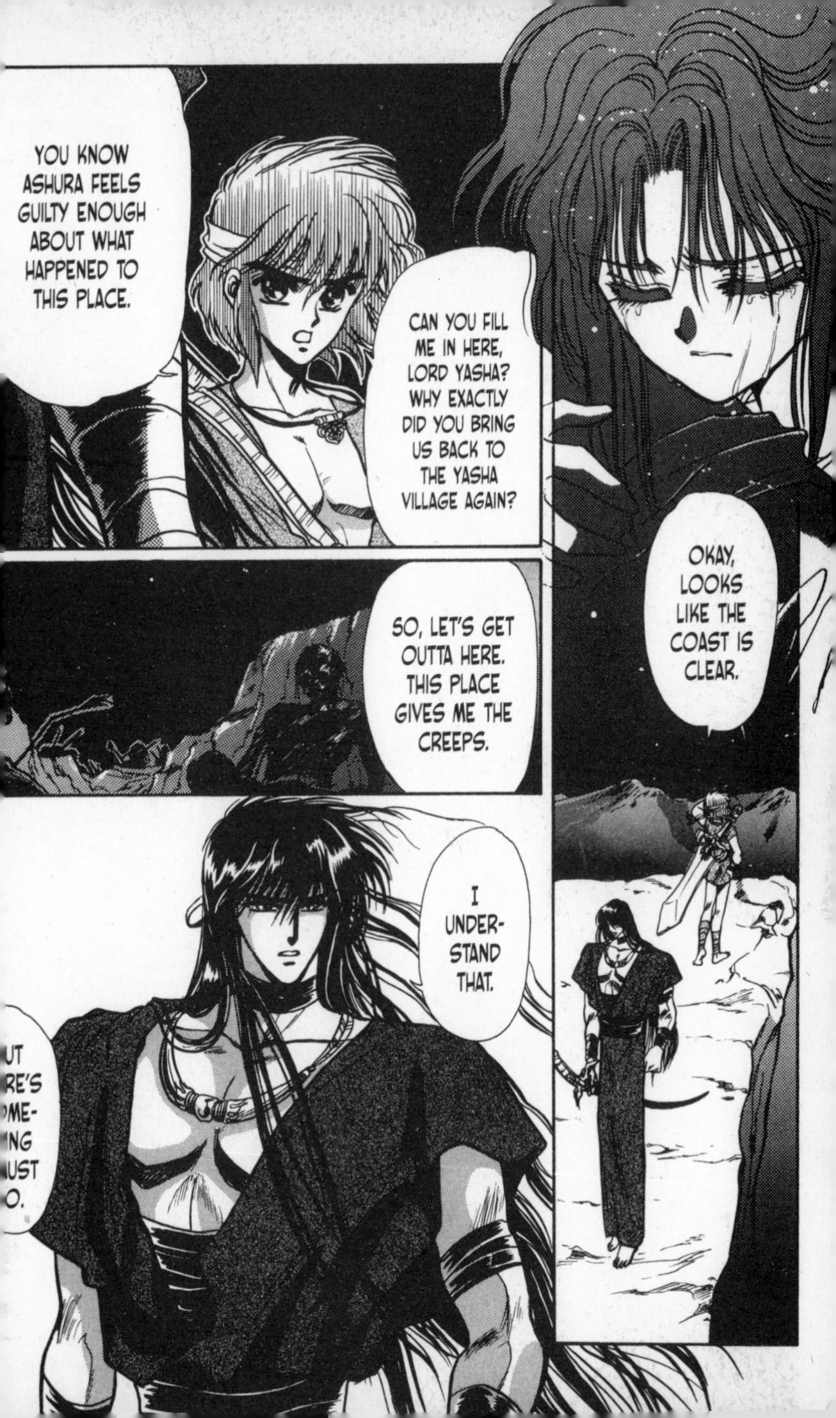
CAN YOU FILL ME IN HERE, LORD YASHA? WHY EXACTLY DID YOU BRING US BACK TO THE YASHA VILLAGE AGAIN?
YOU KNOW ASHURA FEELS GUILTY ENOUGH ABOUT WHAT HAPPENED TO THIS PLACE.
OKAY, LOOKS LIKE THE COAST IS CLEAR.
SO, LET'S GET OUTTA HERE. THIS PLACE GIVES ME THE CREEPS.
I UNDER- STAND THAT.
UT RE'S ME- NG UST O.

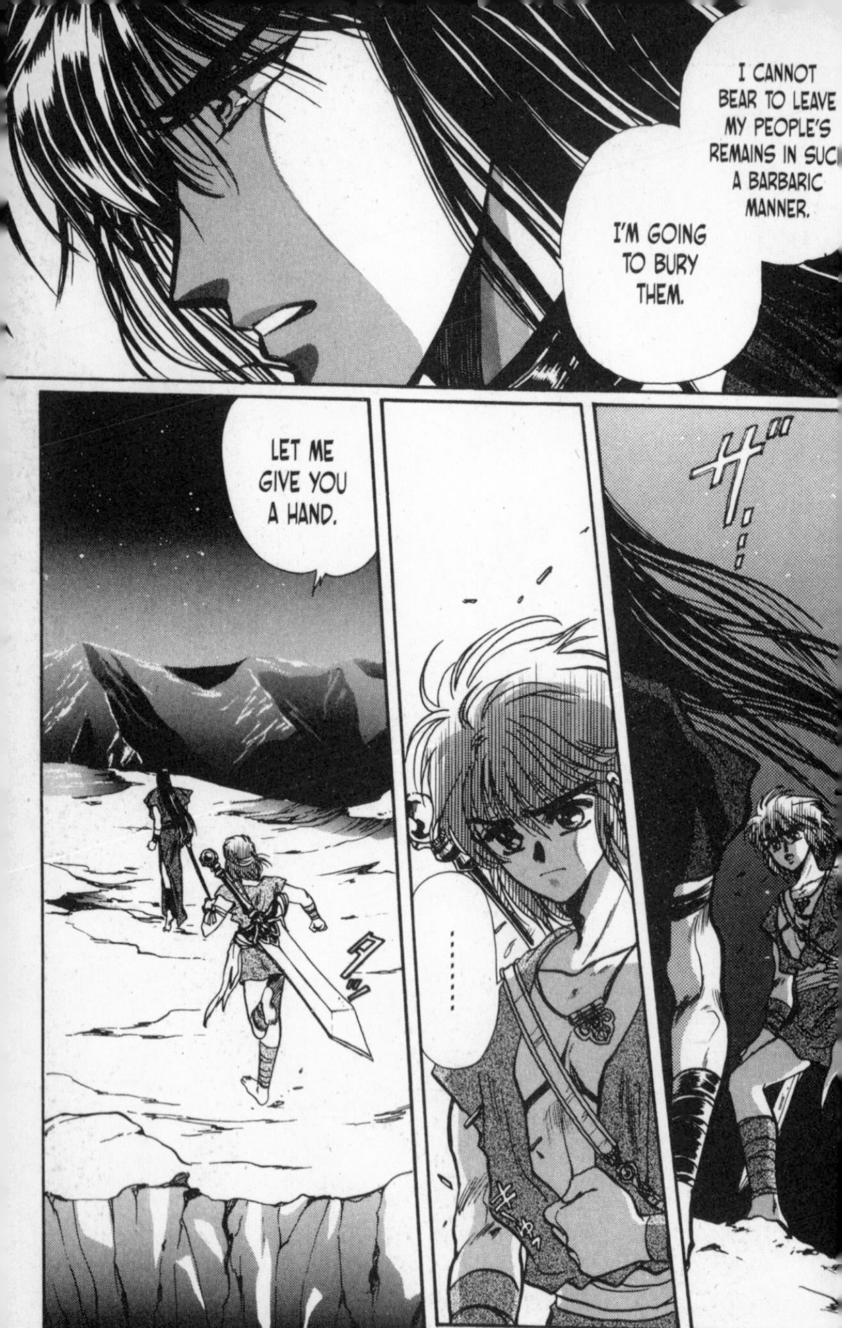
I CANNOT BEAR TO LEAVE MY PEOPLE'S REMAINS IN SUC A BARBARIC MANNER.
I'M GOING TO BURY THEM.
......
LET ME GIVE YOU A HAND.

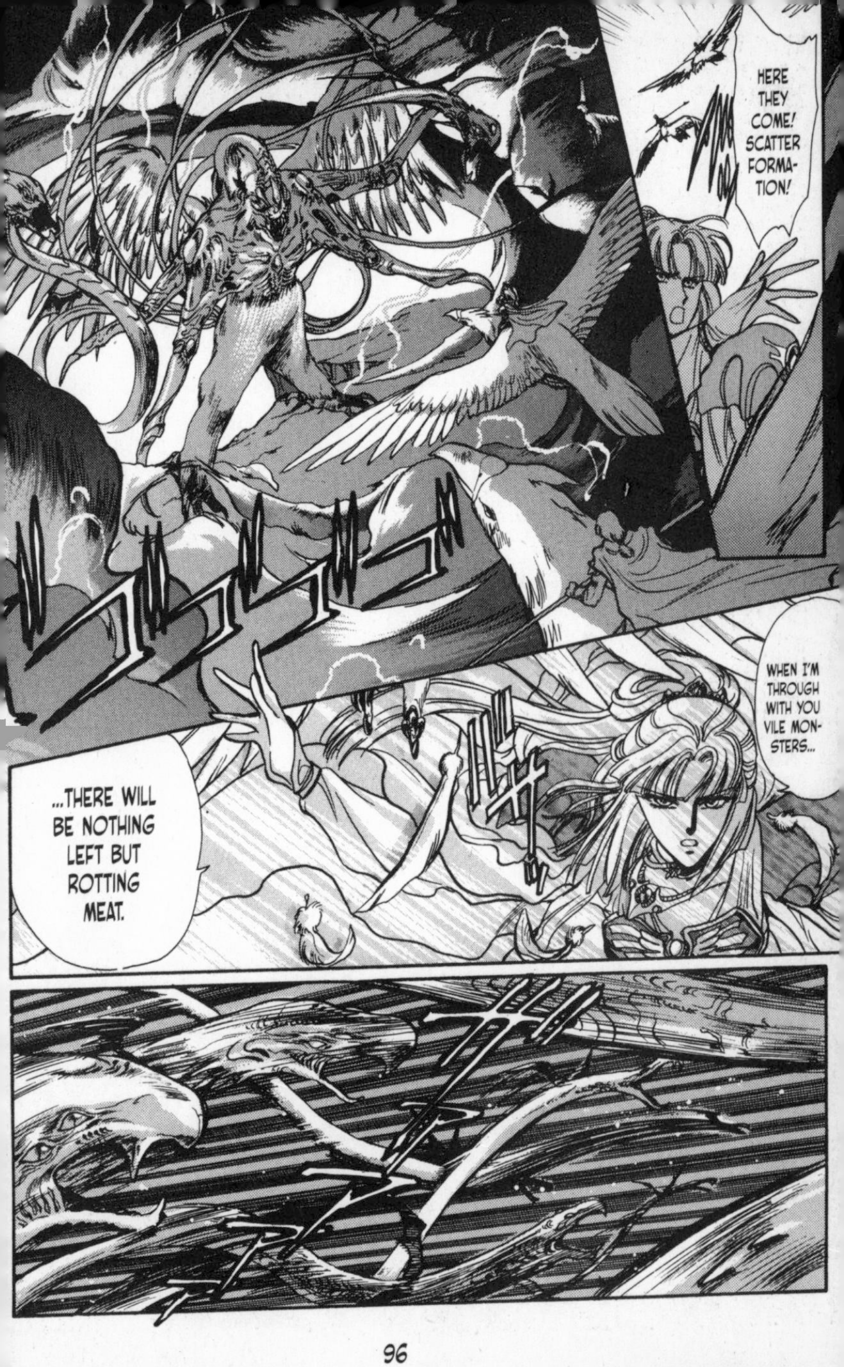
HERE THEY COME! SCATTER FORMATION!
WHEN I'M THROUGH WITH YOU VILE MONSTERS...
...THERE WILL BE NOTHING LEFT BUT ROTTING MEAT.

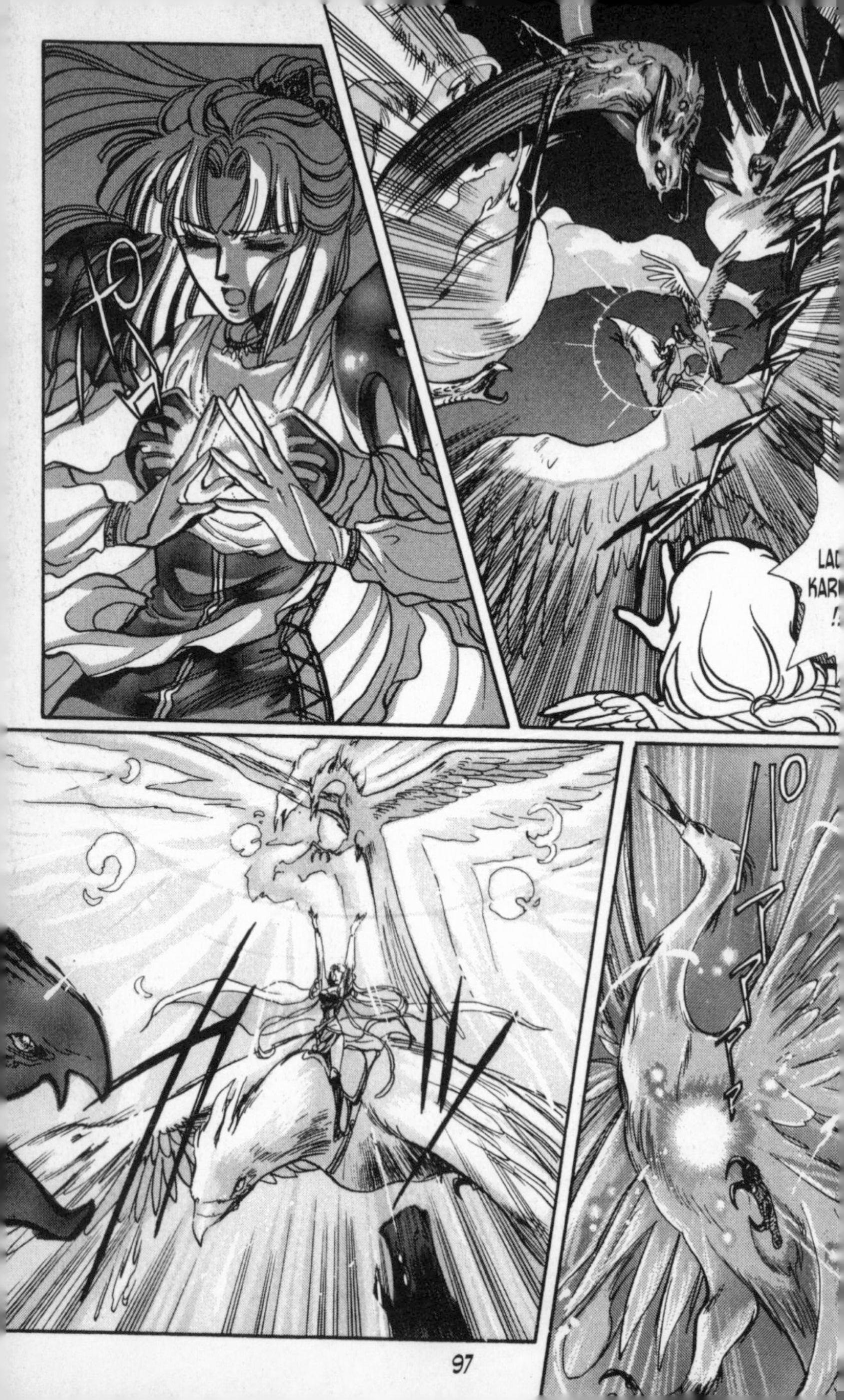

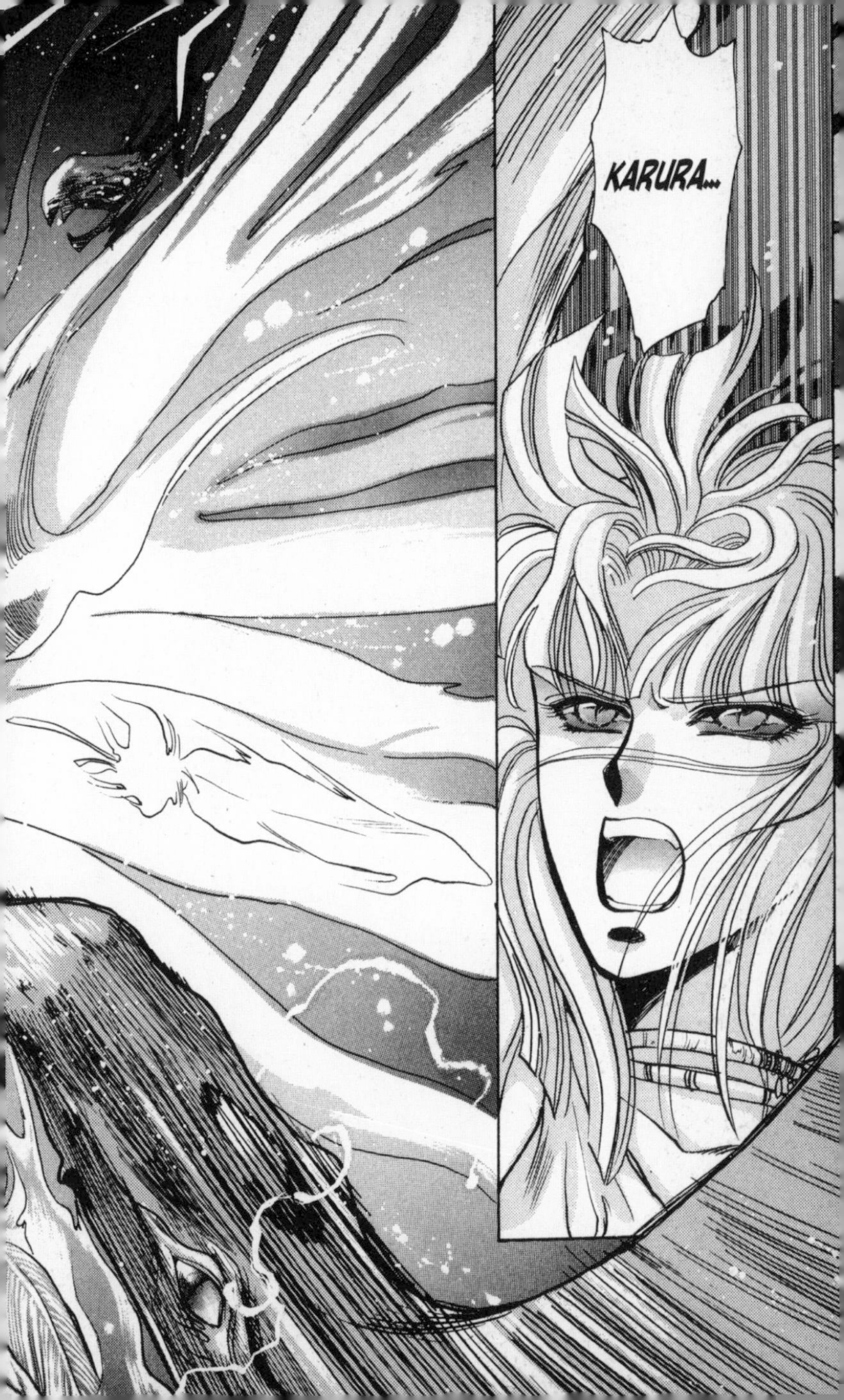
KARURA...

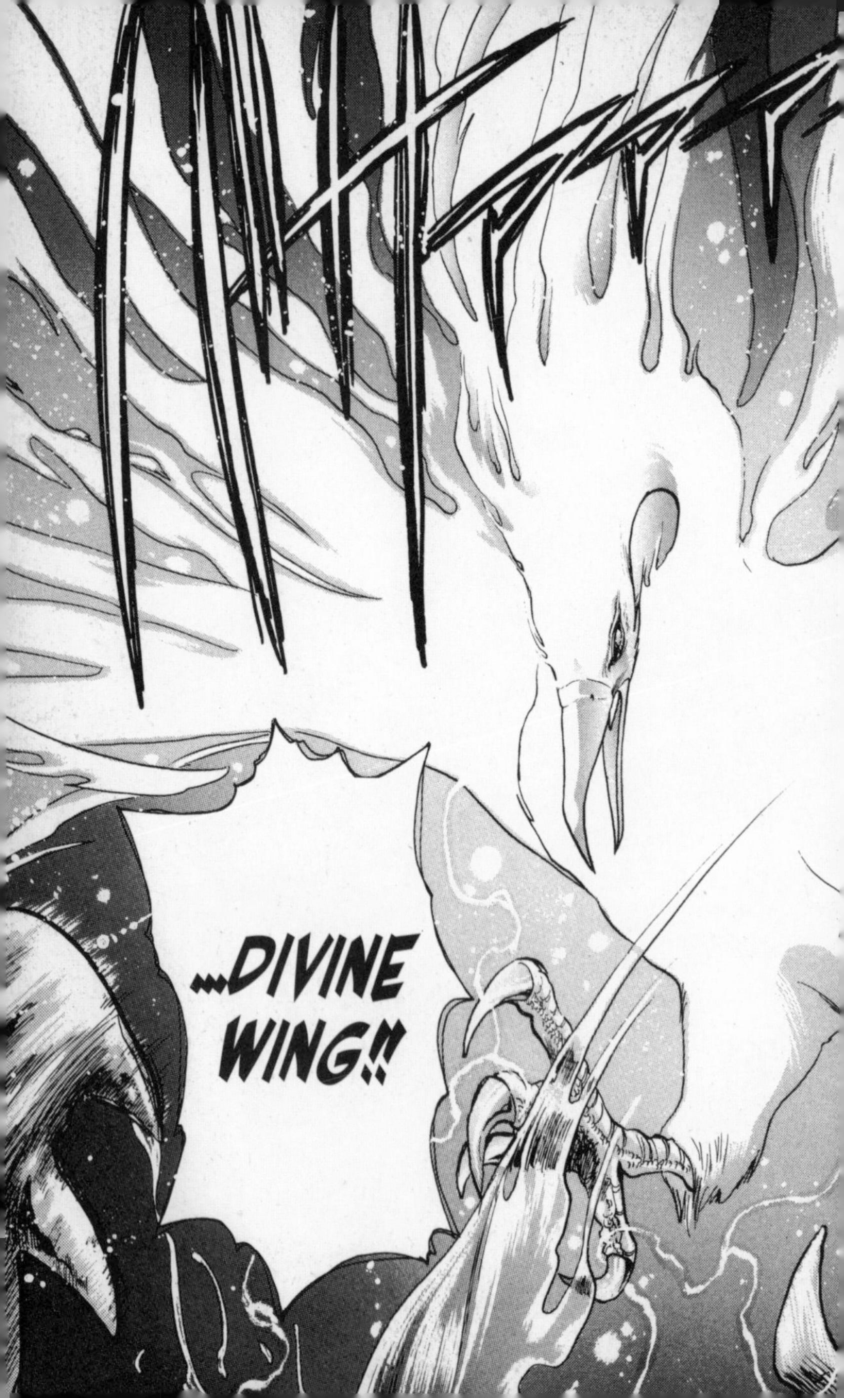
...DIVINE WING!!

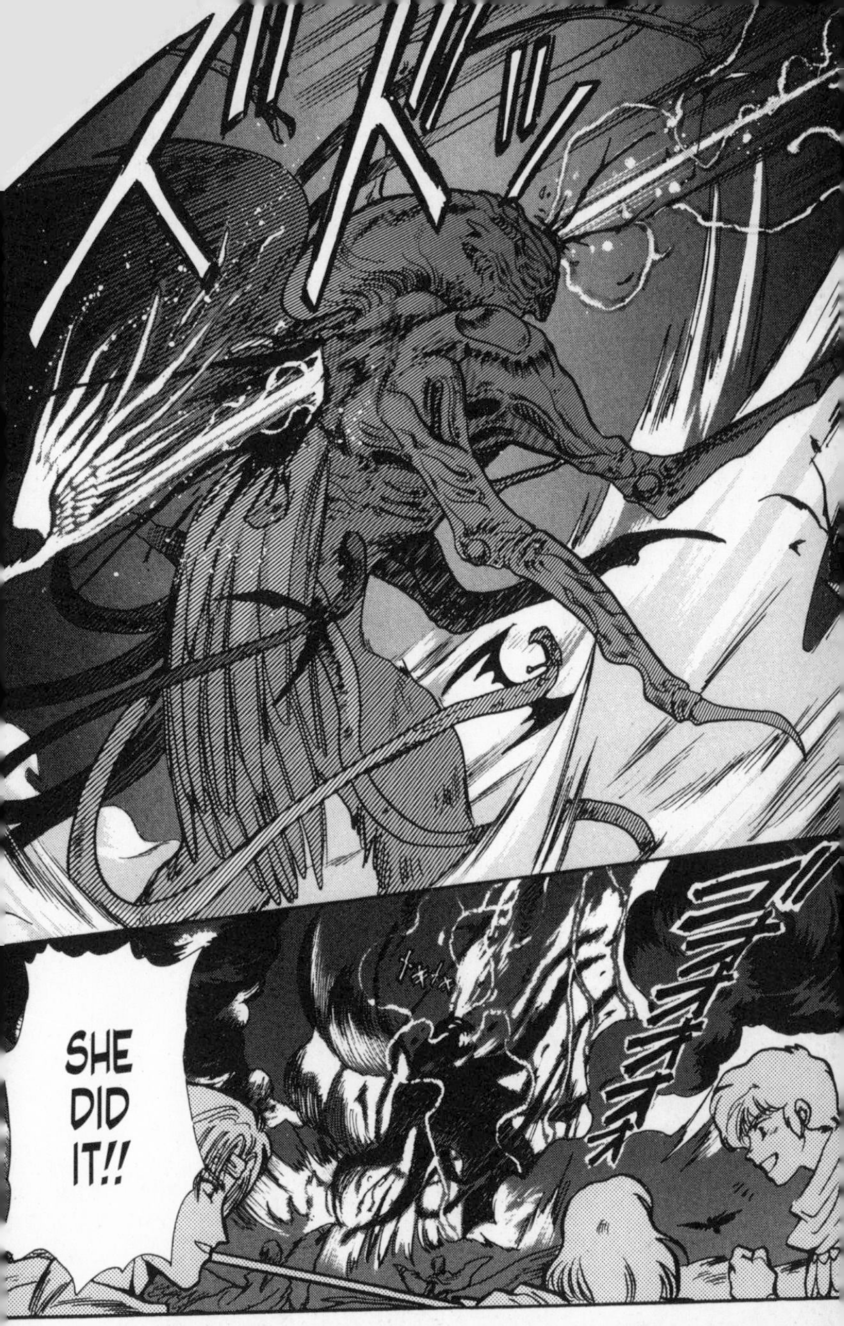
SHE DID IT!!

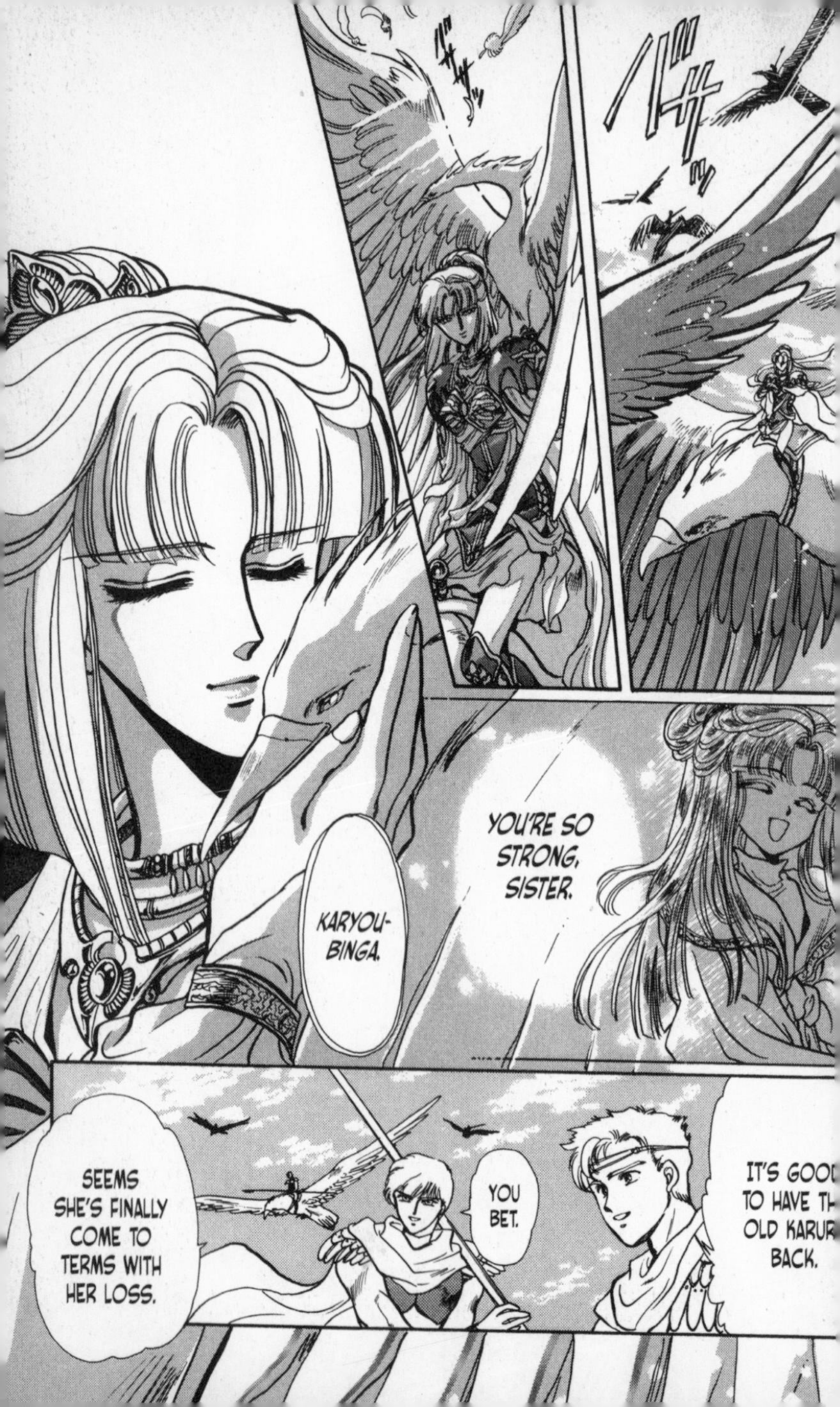
バサッ
YOU'RE SO STRONG, SISTER.
KARYOU-BINGA.
IT'S GOOD TO HAVE TH OLD KARUR BACK.
YOU BET.
SEEMS SHE'S FINALLY COME TO TERMS WITH HER LOSS.

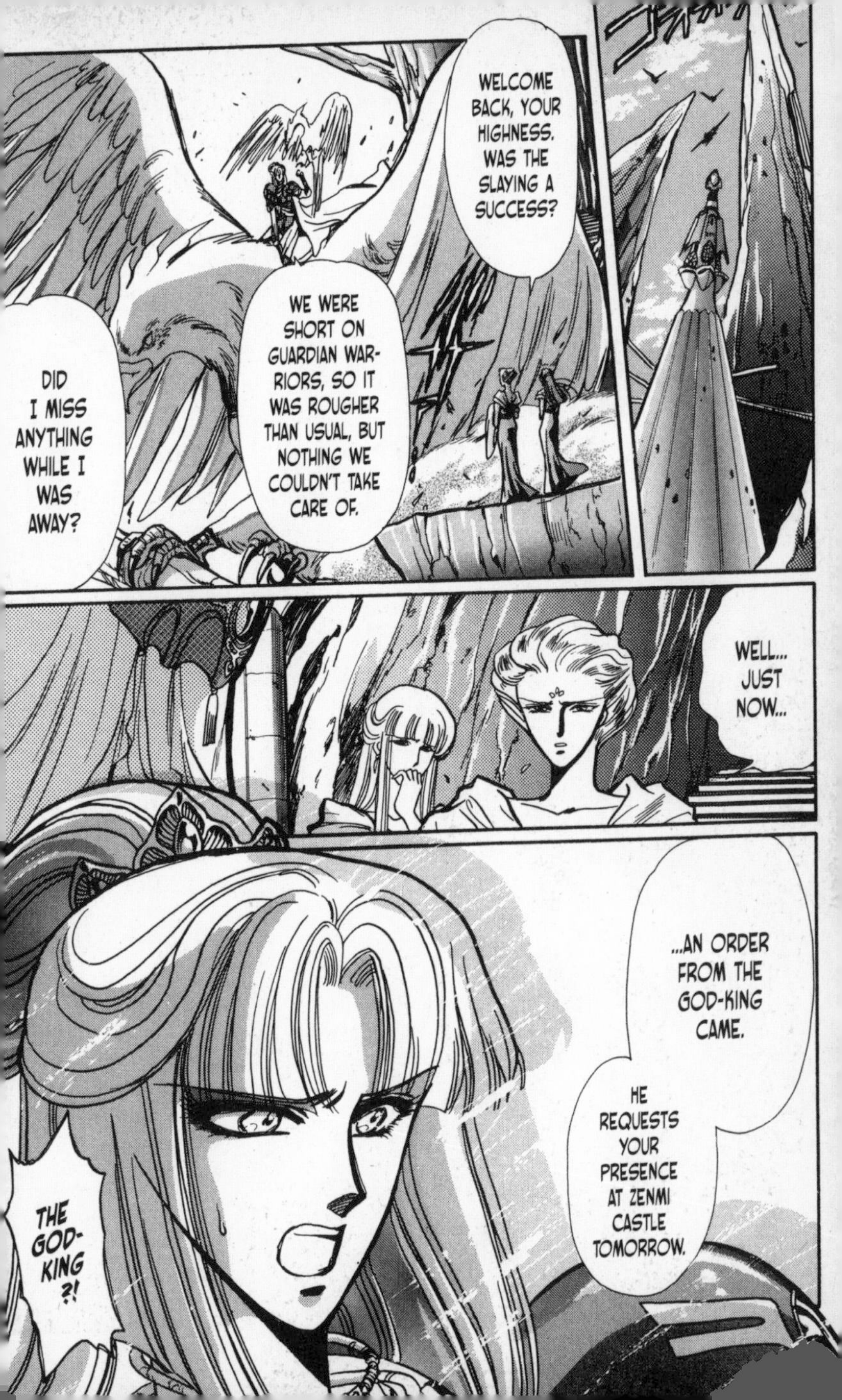
WELCOME BACK, YOUR HIGHNESS. WAS THE SLAYING A SUCCESS?
WE WERE SHORT ON GUARDIAN WAR-RIORS, SO IT WAS ROUGHER THAN USUAL, BUT NOTHING WE COULDN'T TAKE CARE OF.
DID I MISS ANYTHING WHILE I WAS AWAY?
WELL... JUST NOW...
...AN ORDER FROM THE GOD-KING CAME.
HE REQUESTS YOUR PRESENCE AT ZENMI CASTLE TOMORROW.
THE GOD-KING?!

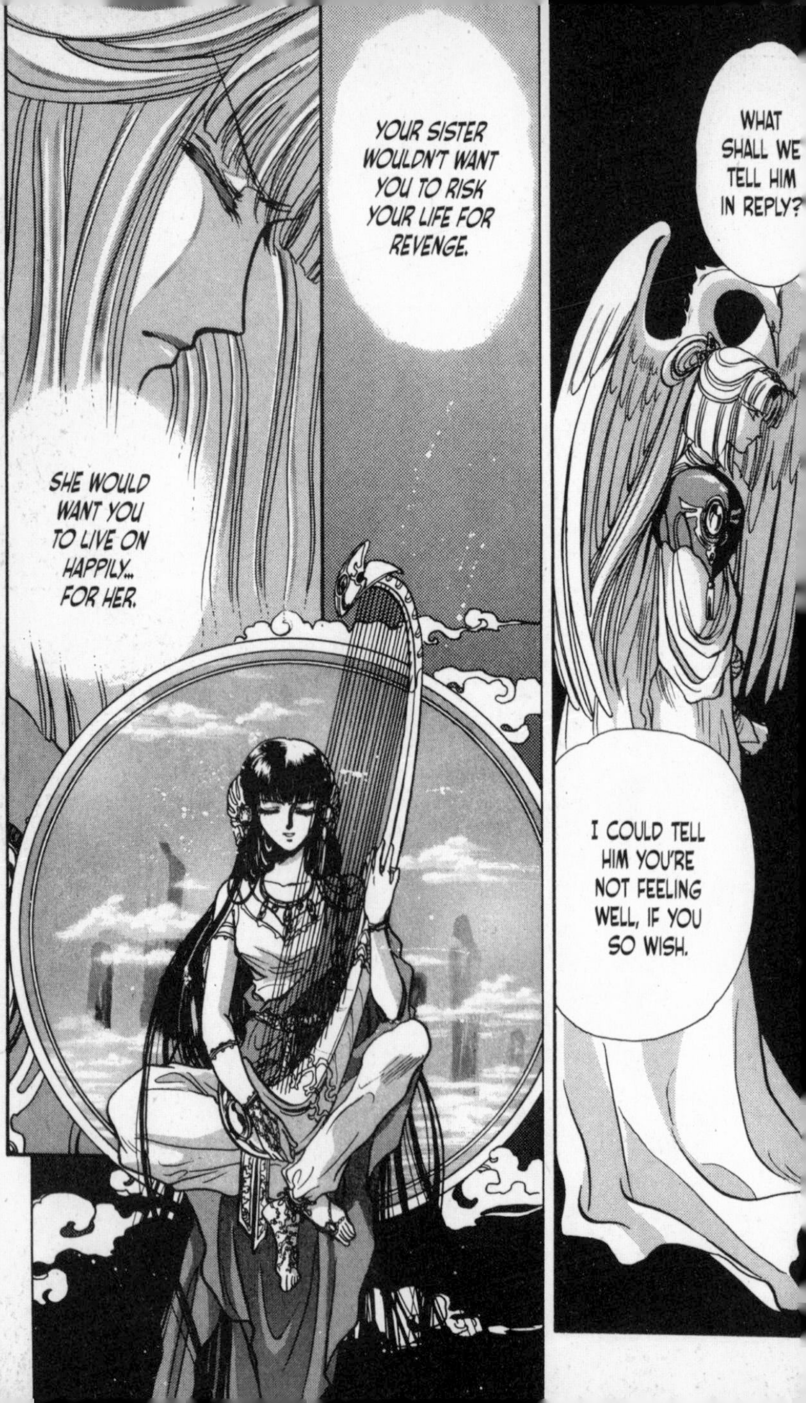
WHAT SHALL WE TELL HIM IN REPLY?
I COULD TELL HIM YOU'RE NOT FEELING WELL, IF YOU SO WISH.
YOUR SISTER WOULDN'T WANT YOU TO RISK YOUR LIFE FOR REVENGE.
SHE WOULD WANT YOU TO LIVE ON HAPPILY... FOR HER.

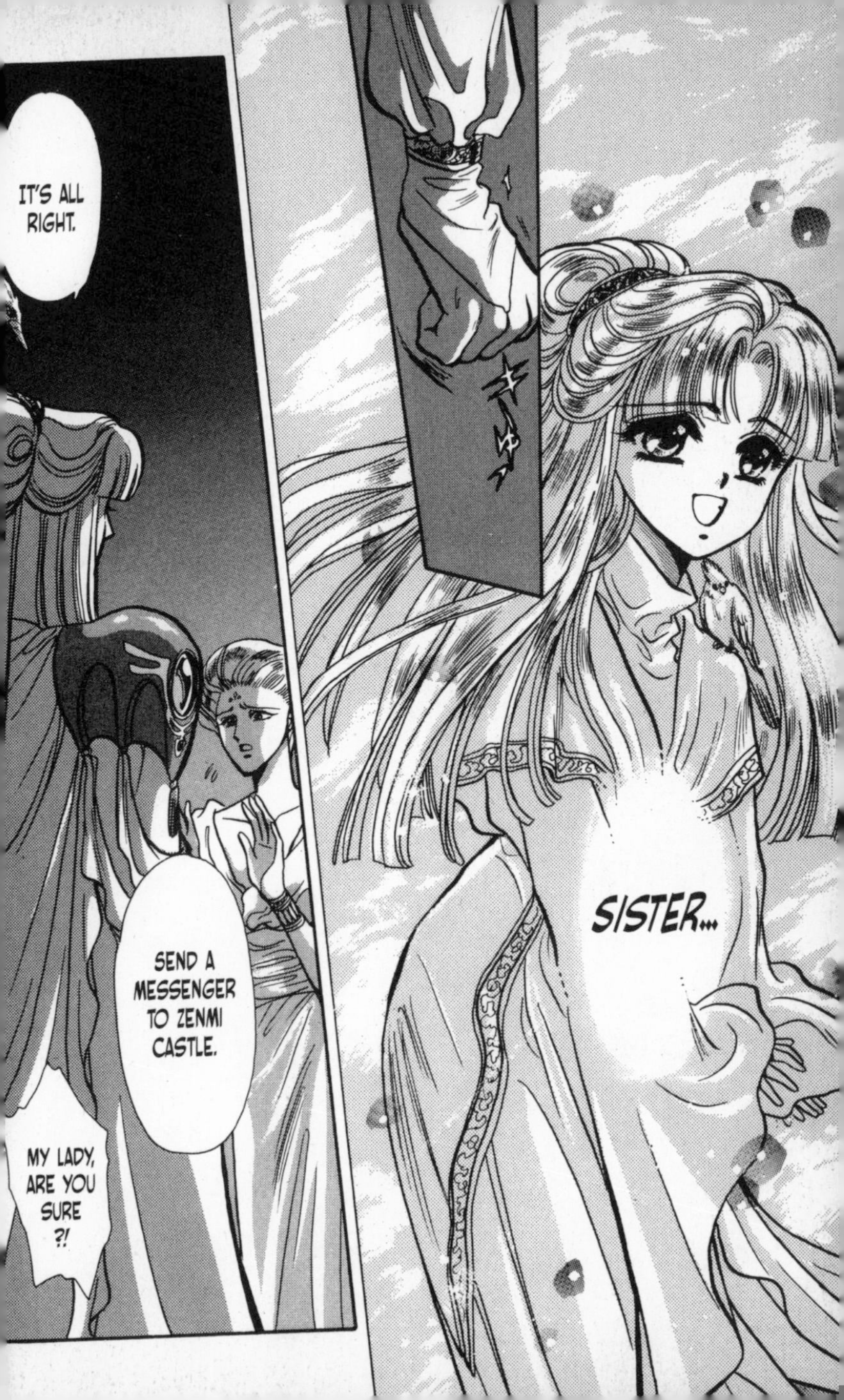
SISTER...
SEND A MESSENGER TO ZENMI CASTLE.
MY LADY, ARE YOU SURE ?!
IT'S ALL RIGHT.

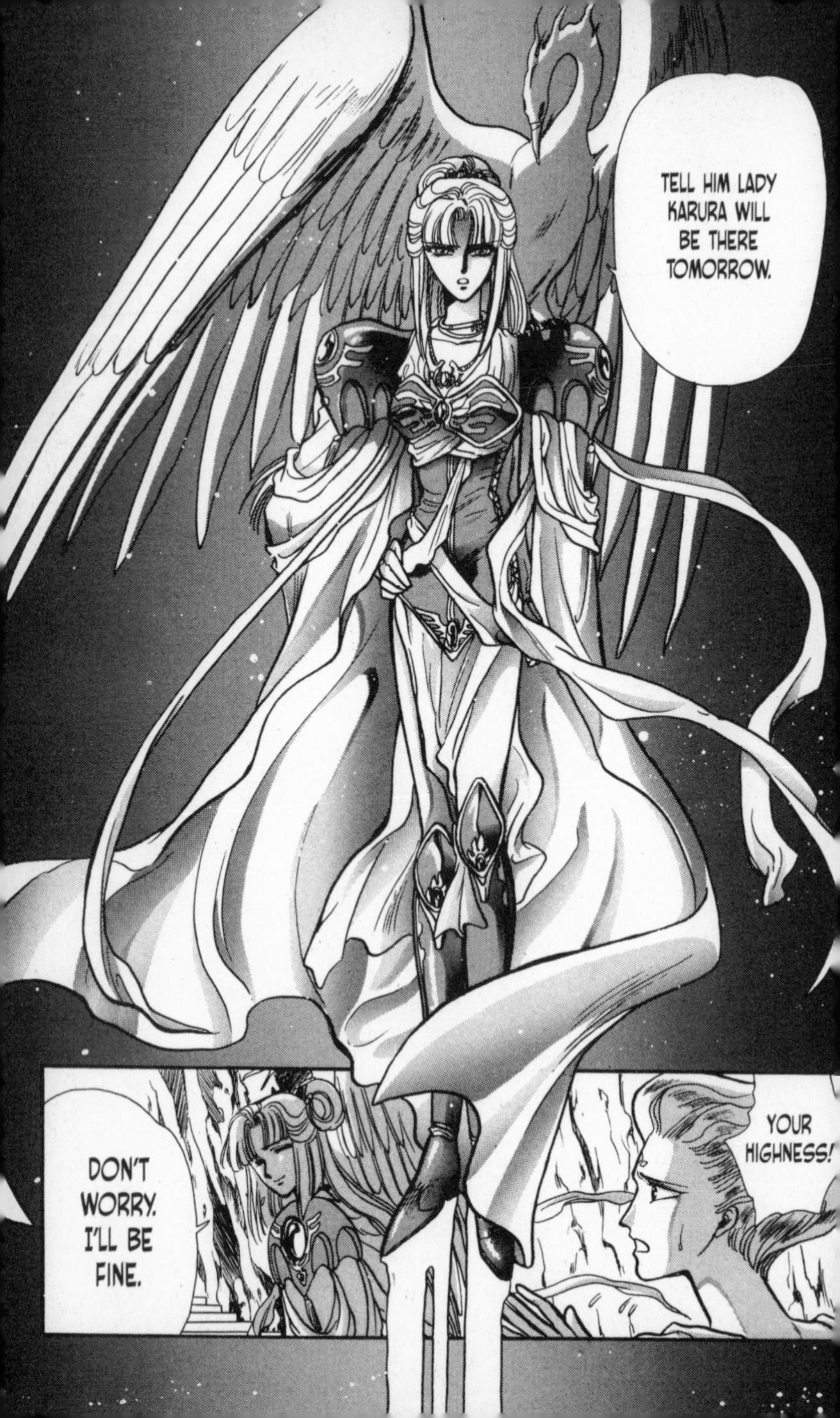
TELL HIM LADY KARURA WILL BE THERE TOMORROW.
YOUR HIGHNESS!
DON'T WORRY. I'LL BE FINE.

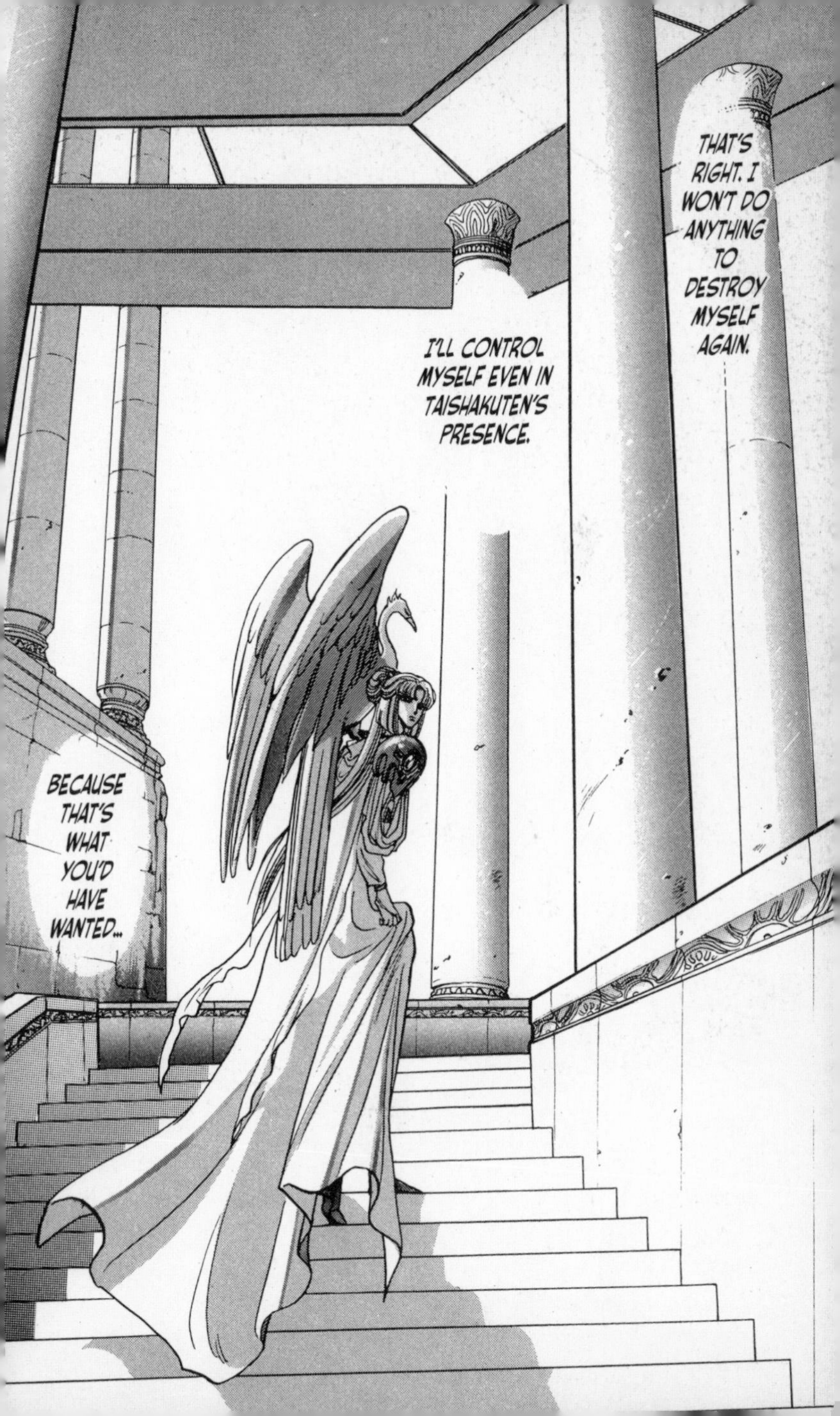
THAT'S RIGHT. I WON'T DO ANYTHING TO DESTROY MYSELF AGAIN.
I'LL CONTROL MYSELF EVEN IN TAISHAKUTEN'S PRESENCE.
BECAUSE THAT'S WHAT YOU'D HAVE WANTED...

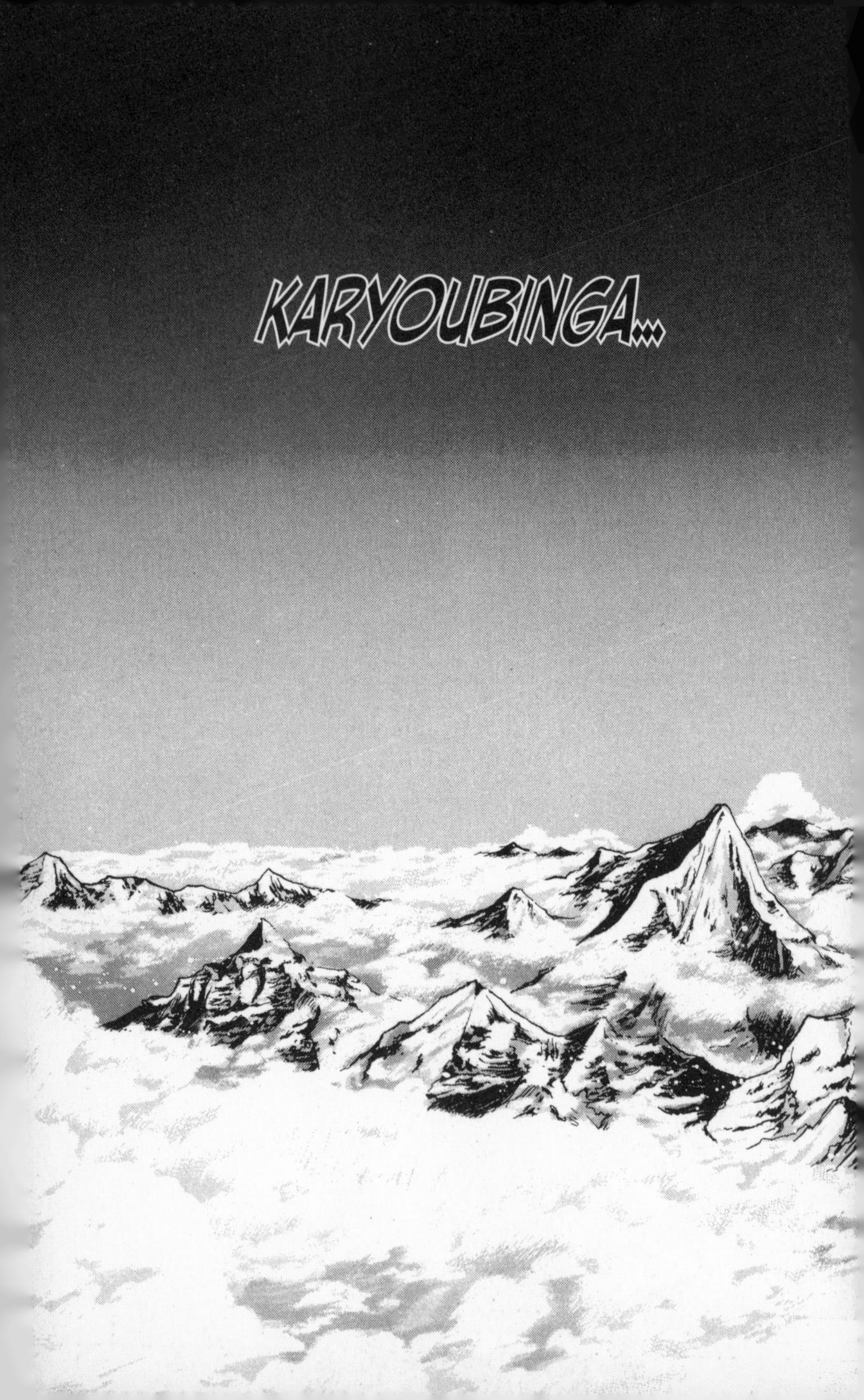
KARYOUBINGA...

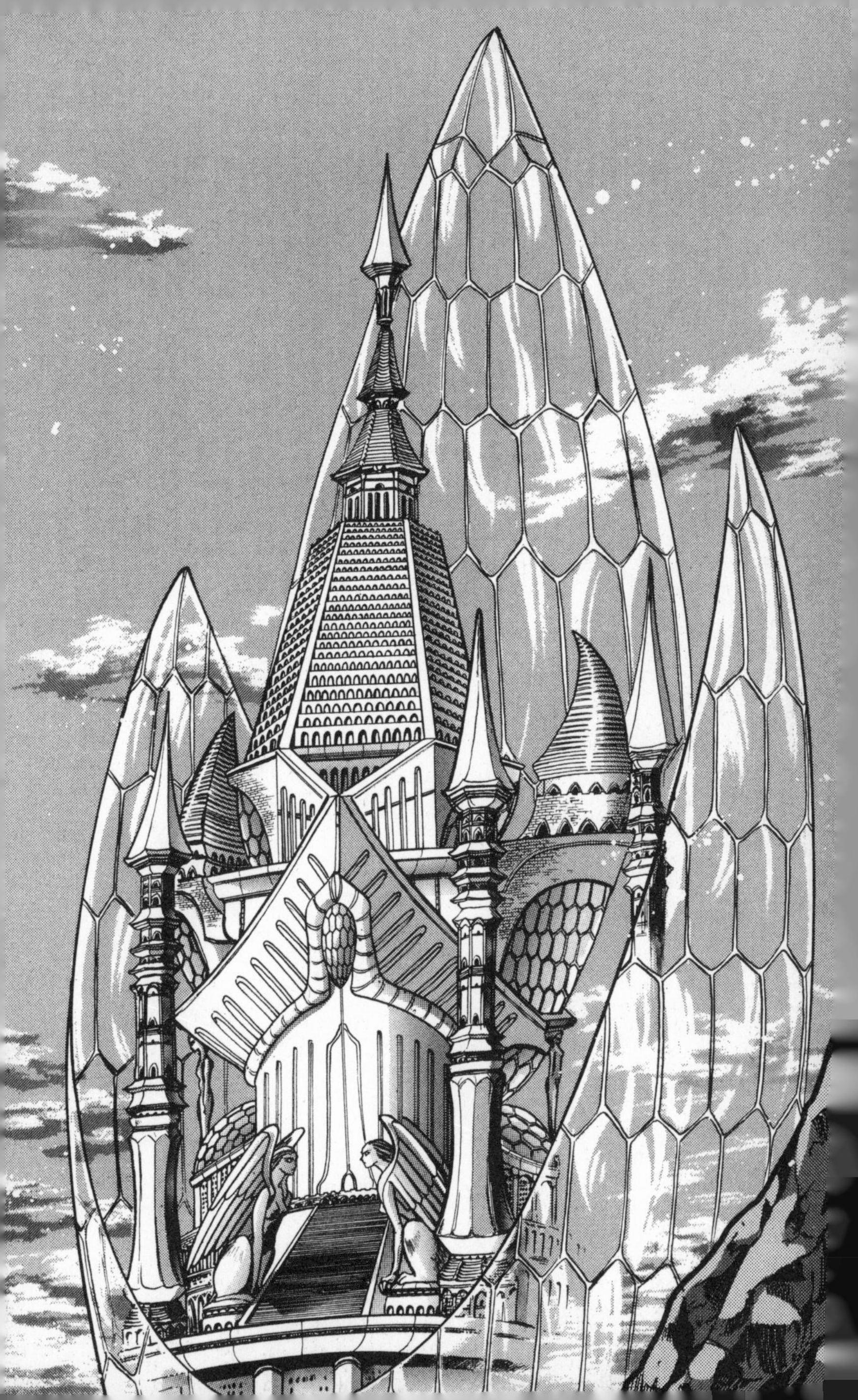

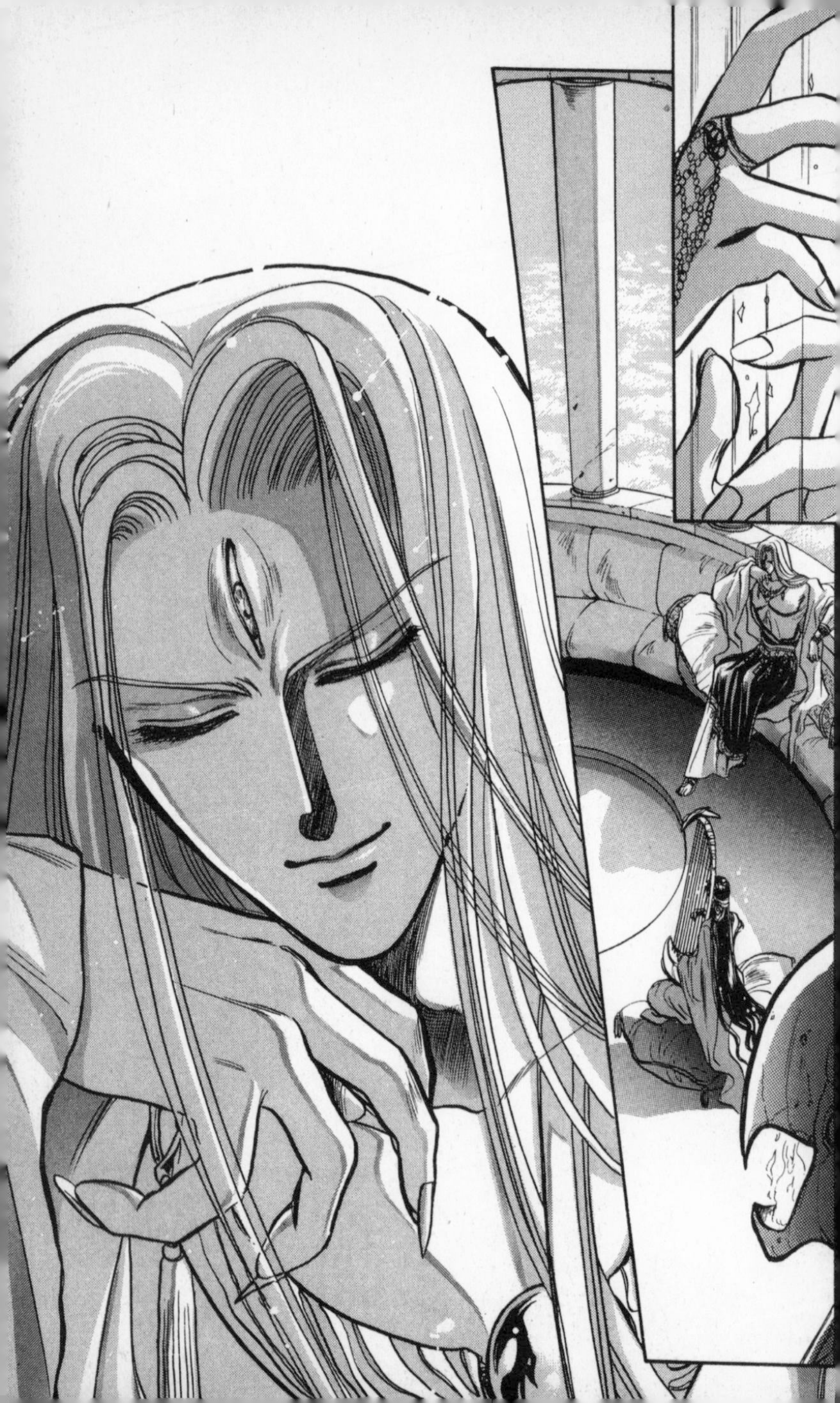

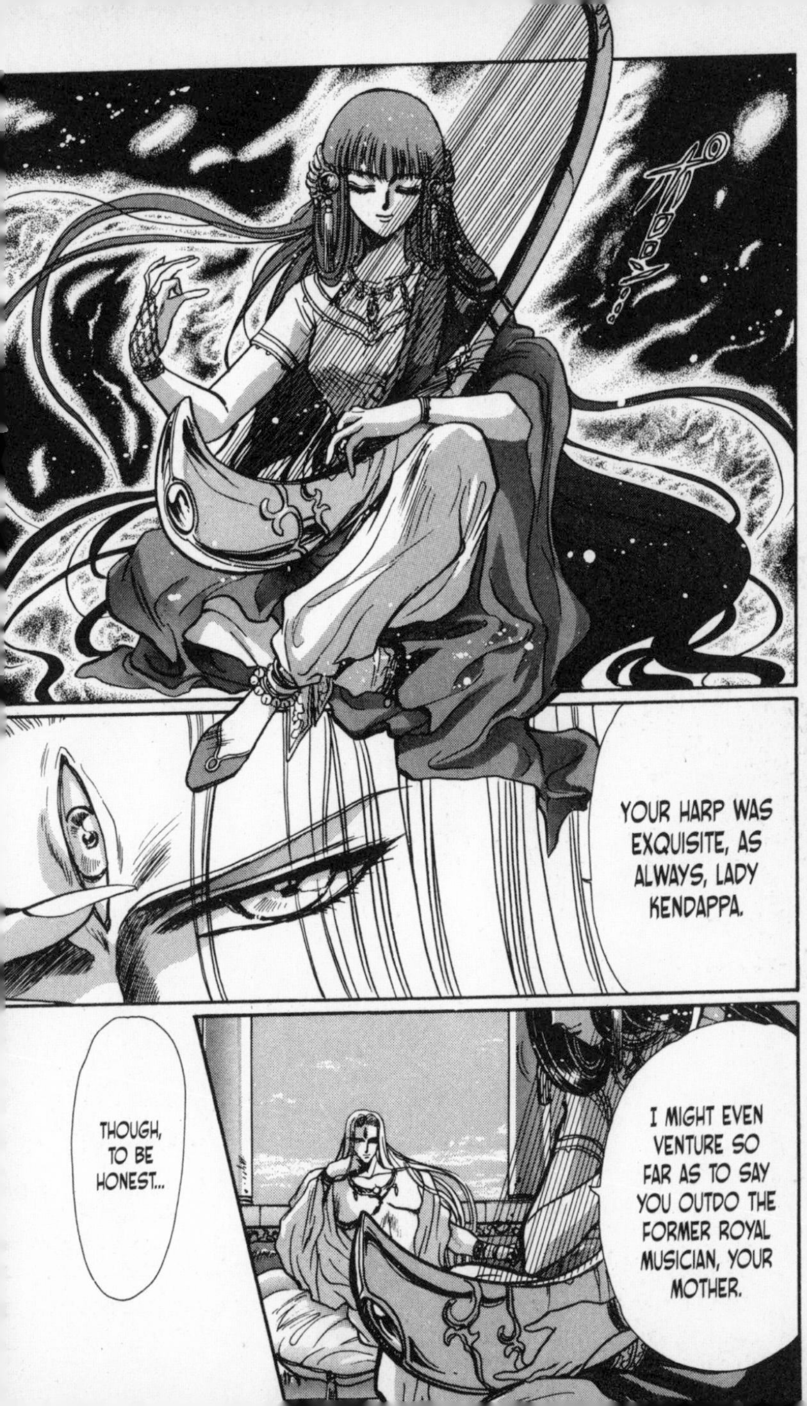
YOUR HARP WAS EXQUISITE, AS ALWAYS, LADY KENDAPPA.
I MIGHT EVEN VENTURE SO FAR AS TO SAY YOU OUTDO THE FORMER ROYAL MUSICIAN, YOUR MOTHER.
THOUGH, TO BE HONEST...

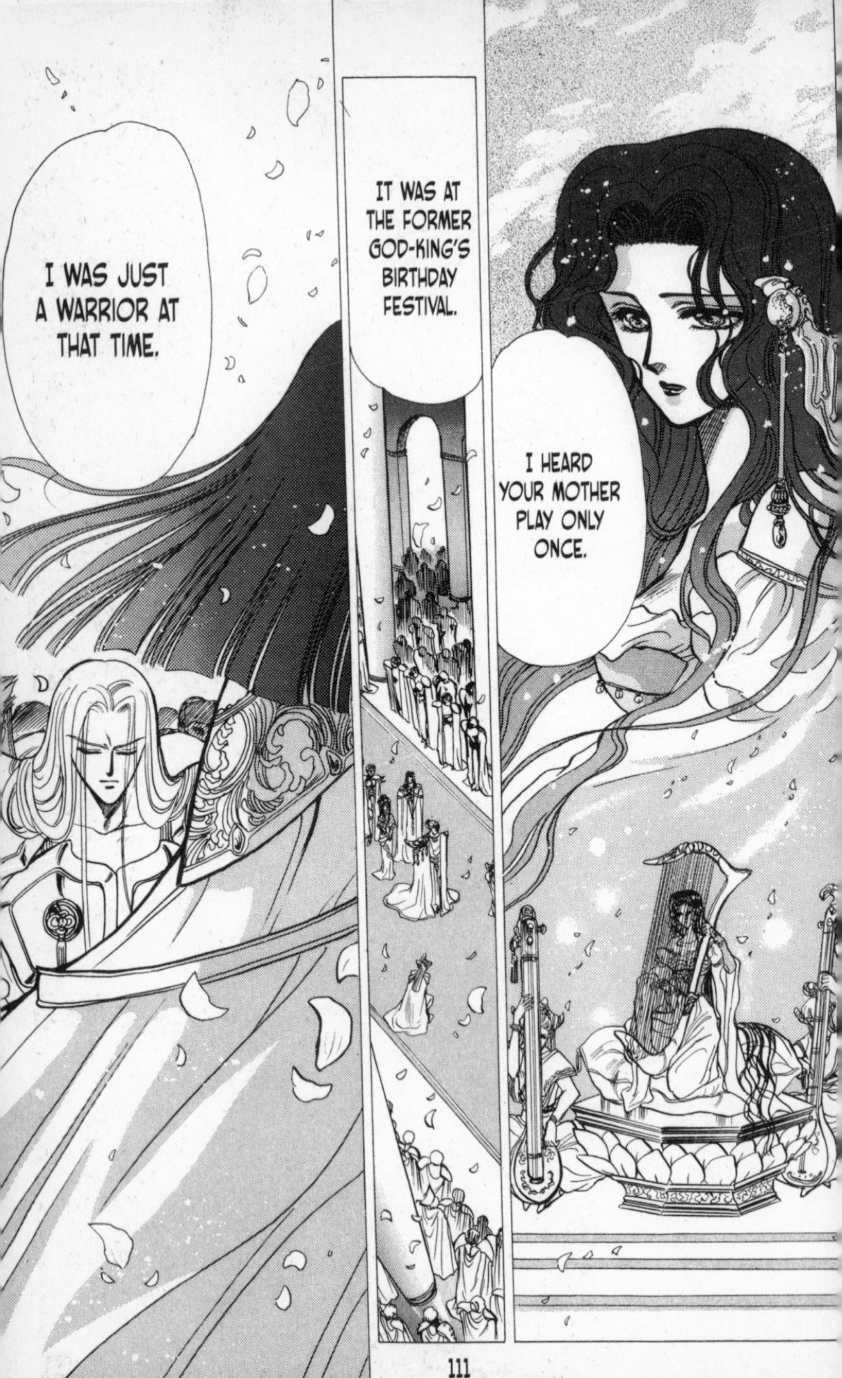
I HEARD YOUR MOTHER PLAY ONLY ONCE.
IT WAS AT THE FORMER GOD-KING'S BIRTHDAY FESTIVAL.
I WAS JUST A WARRIOR AT THAT TIME.

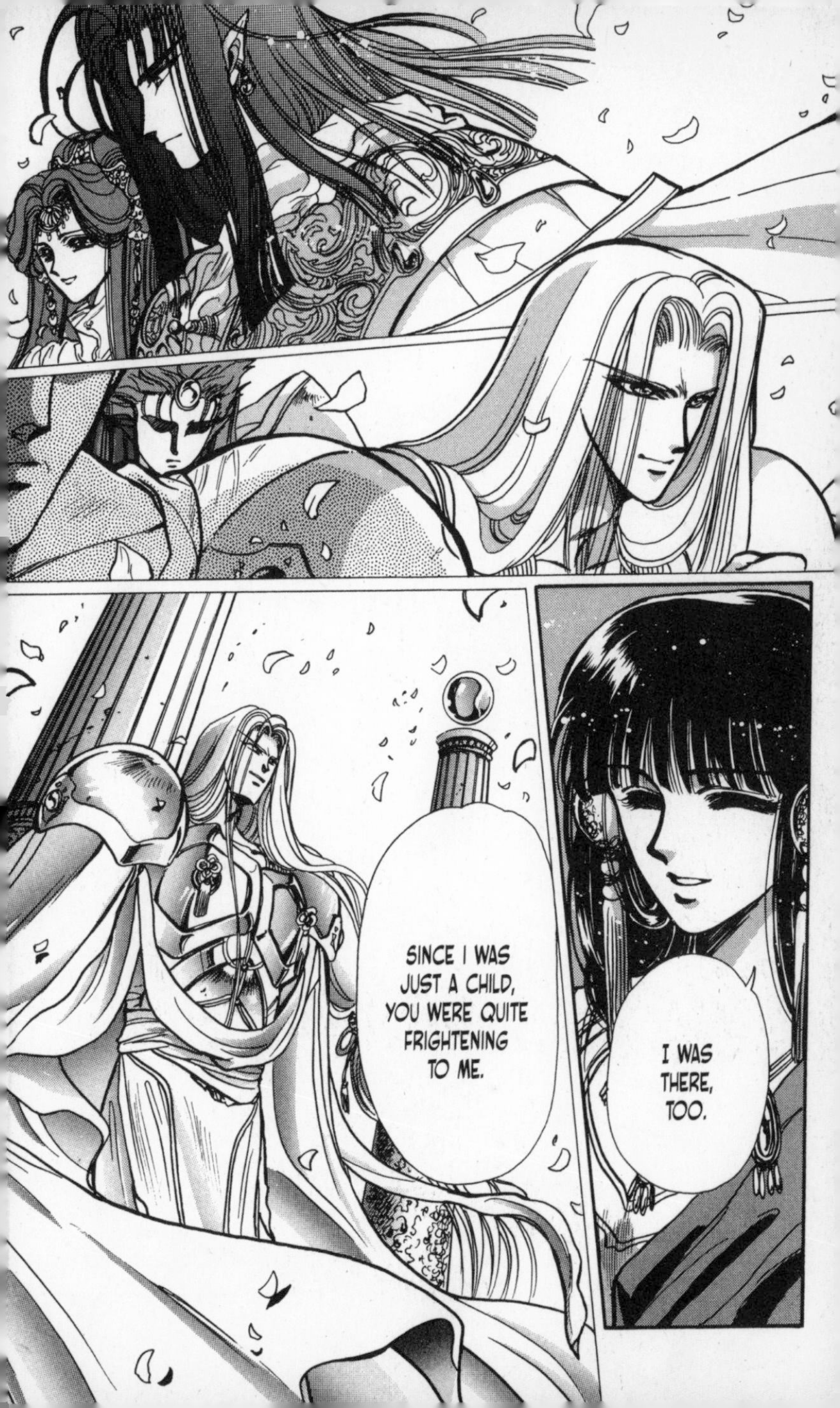
I WAS THERE, TOO.
SINCE I WAS JUST A CHILD, YOU WERE QUITE FRIGHTENING TO ME.

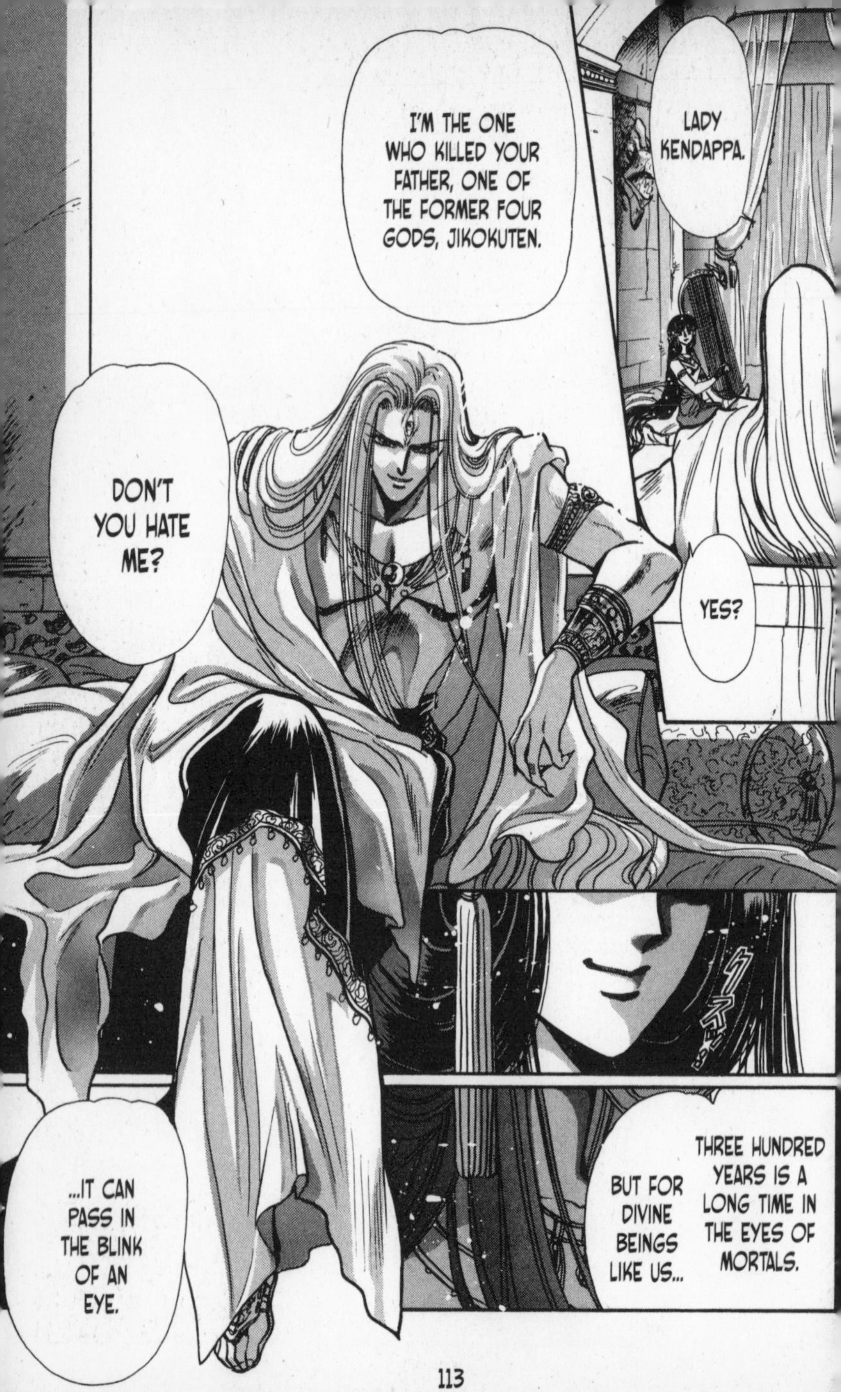
LADY KENDAPPA.
YES?
I'M THE ONE WHO KILLED YOUR FATHER, ONE OF THE FORMER FOUR GODS, JIKOKUTEN.
DON'T YOU HATE ME?
THREE HUNDRED YEARS IS A LONG TIME IN THE EYES OF MORTALS.
BUT FOR DIVINE BEINGS LIKE US...
...IT CAN PASS IN THE BLINK OF AN EYE.

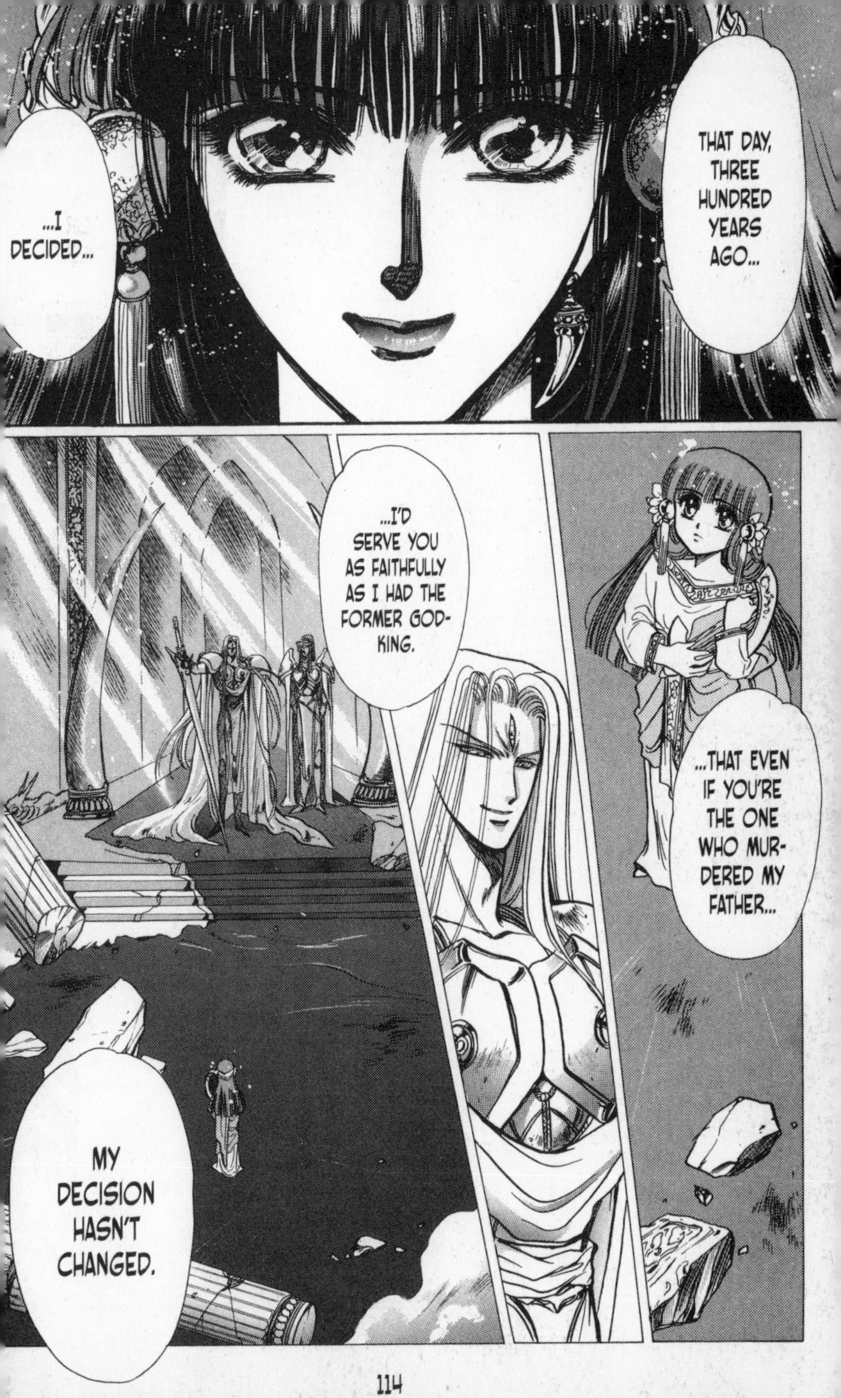
THAT DAY, THREE HUNDRED YEARS AGO...
...I DECIDED...
...THAT EVEN IF YOU'RE THE ONE WHO MURDERED MY FATHER...
...I'D SERVE YOU AS FAITHFULLY AS I HAD THE FORMER GOD-KING.
MY DECISION HASN'T CHANGED.

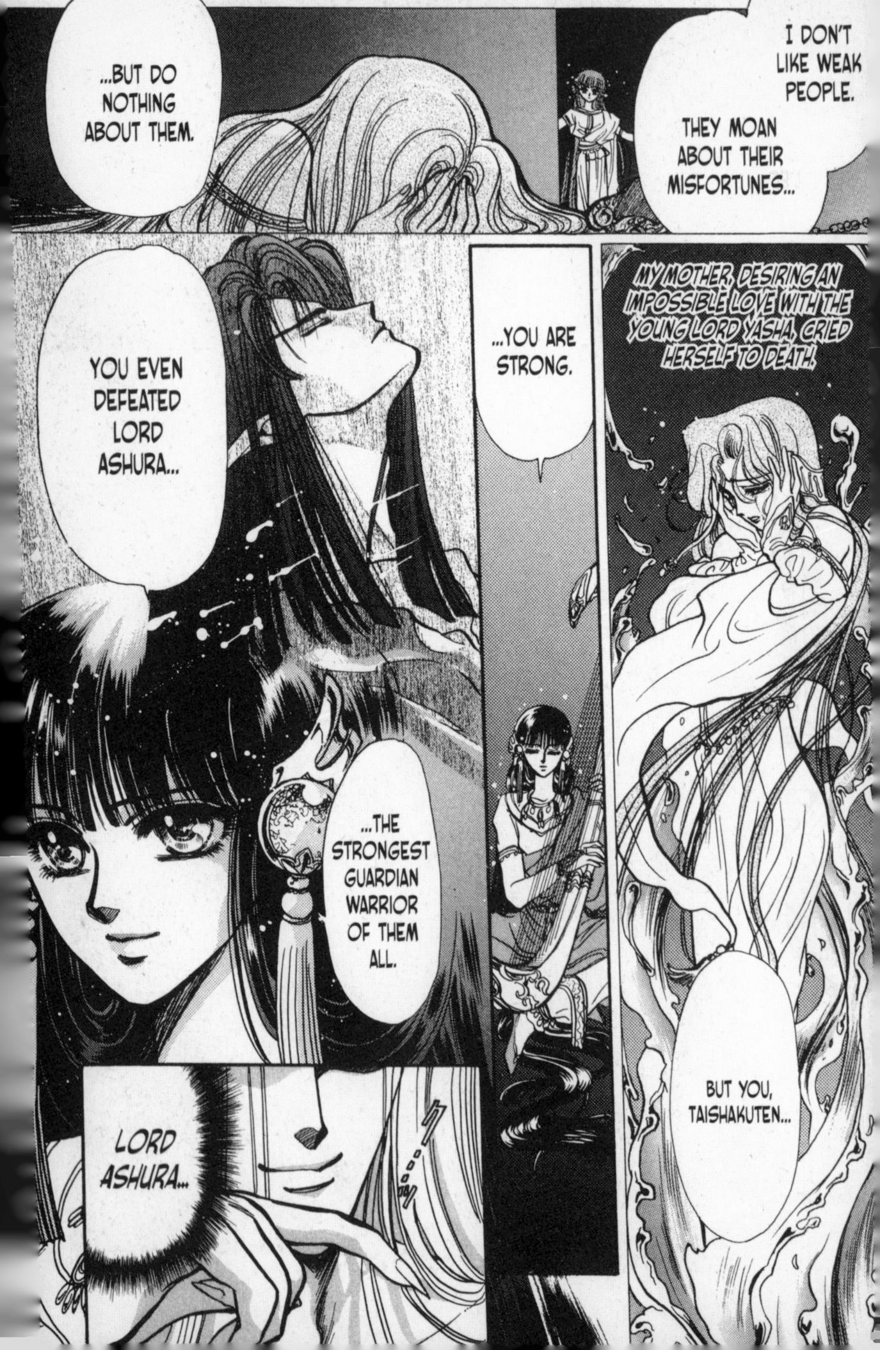
I DON'T LIKE WEAK PEOPLE.
THEY MOAN ABOUT THEIR MISFORTUNES...
...BUT DO NOTHING ABOUT THEM.
MY MOTHER, DESIRING AN IMPOSSIBLE LOVE WITH THE YOUNG LORD YASHA, CRIED HERSELF TO DEATH.
BUT YOU, TAISHAKUTEN...
...YOU ARE STRONG.
YOU EVEN DEFEATED LORD ASHURA...
...THE STRONGEST GUARDIAN WARRIOR OF THEM ALL.
LORD ASHURA...

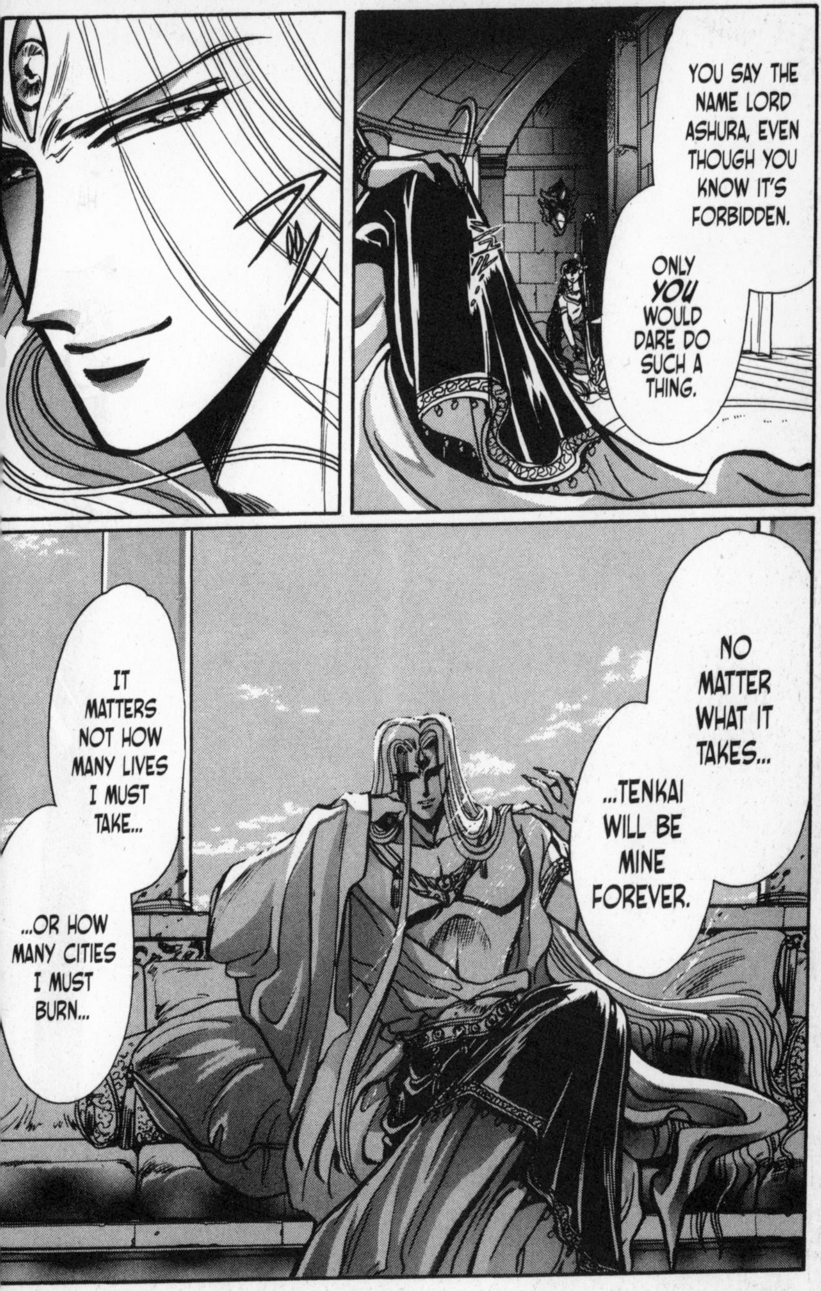
YOU SAY THE NAME LORD ASHURA, EVEN THOUGH YOU KNOW IT'S FORBIDDEN.
ONLY *YOU* WOULD DARE DO SUCH A THING.
NO MATTER WHAT IT TAKES...
...TENKAI WILL BE MINE FOREVER.
IT MATTERS NOT HOW MANY LIVES I MUST TAKE...
...OR HOW MANY CITIES I MUST BURN...

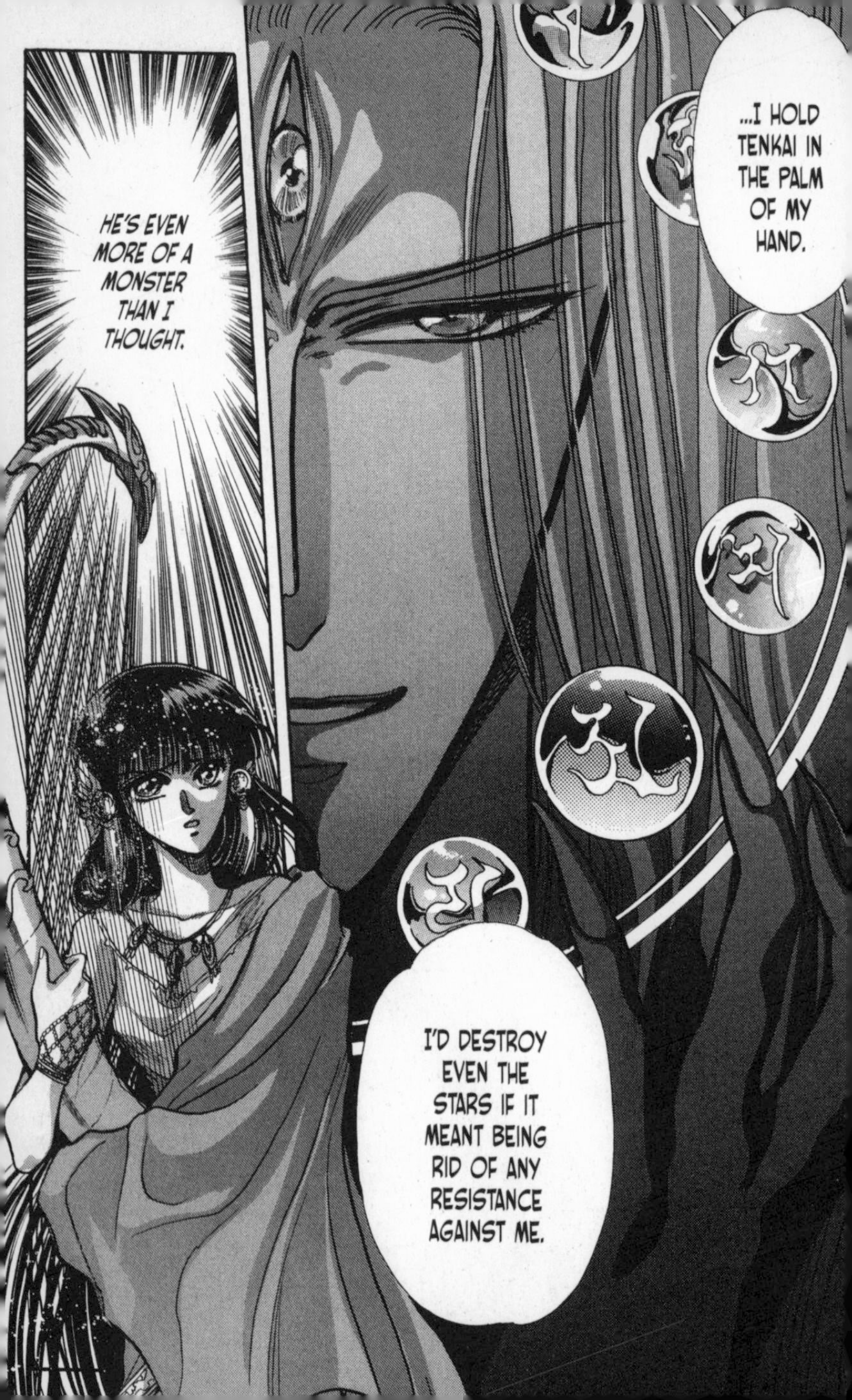
...I HOLD TENKAI IN THE PALM OF MY HAND.
I'D DESTROY EVEN THE STARS IF IT MEANT BEING RID OF ANY RESISTANCE AGAINST ME.
HE'S EVEN MORE OF A MONSTER THAN I THOUGHT.

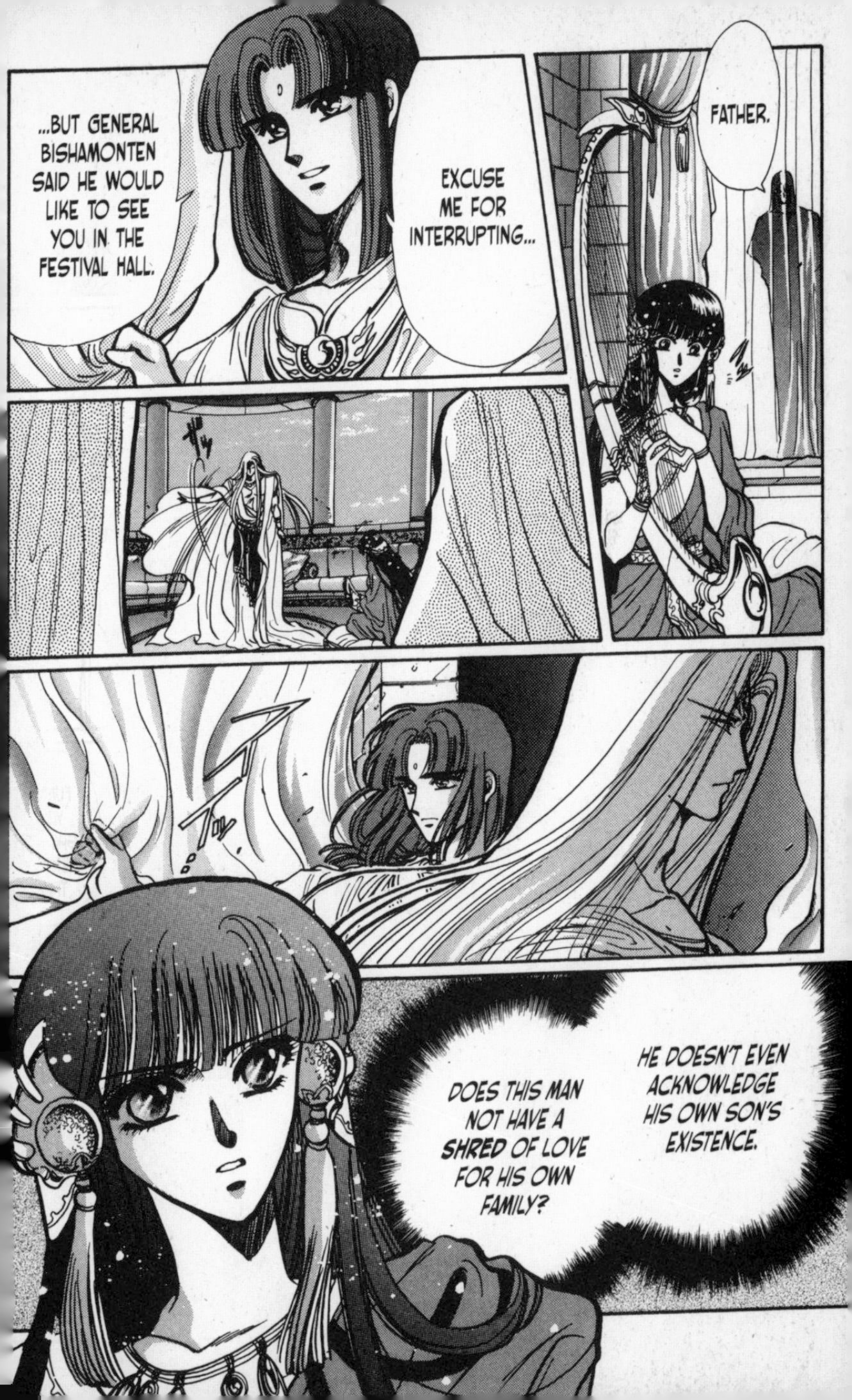
FATHER.
EXCUSE ME FOR INTERRUPTING...
...BUT GENERAL BISHAMONTEN SAID HE WOULD LIKE TO SEE YOU IN THE FESTIVAL HALL.
HE DOESN'T EVEN ACKNOWLEDGE HIS OWN SON'S EXISTENCE.
DOES THIS MAN NOT HAVE A SHRED OF LOVE FOR HIS OWN FAMILY?

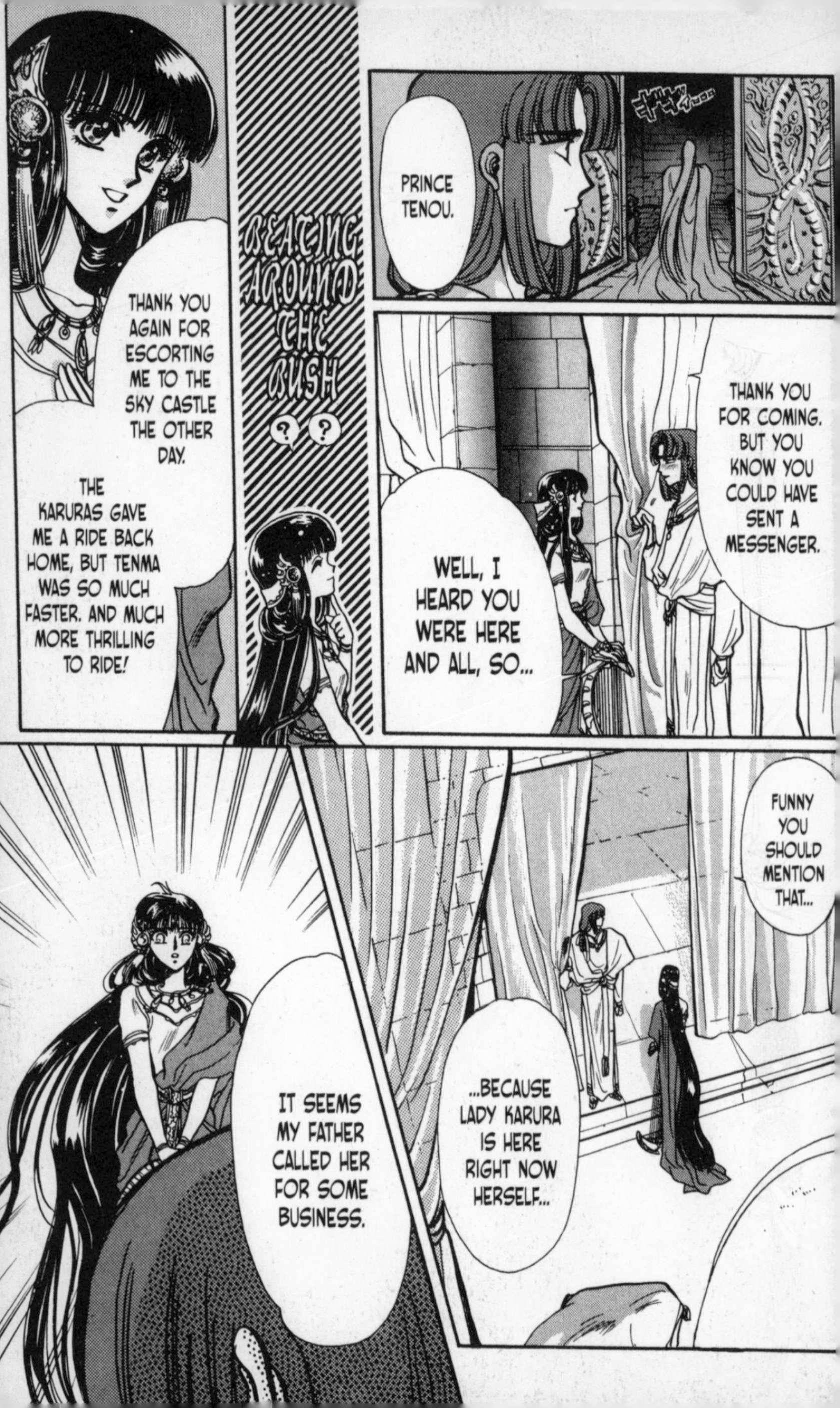
PRINCE TENOU.
THANK YOU FOR COMING. BUT YOU KNOW YOU COULD HAVE SENT A MESSENGER.
WELL, I HEARD YOU WERE HERE AND ALL, SO...
BEATING AROUND THE BUSH
? ?
THANK YOU AGAIN FOR ESCORTING ME TO THE SKY CASTLE THE OTHER DAY.
THE KARURAS GAVE ME A RIDE BACK HOME, BUT TENMA WAS SO MUCH FASTER. AND MUCH MORE THRILLING TO RIDE!
FUNNY YOU SHOULD MENTION THAT...
...BECAUSE LADY KARURA IS HERE RIGHT NOW HERSELF...
IT SEEMS MY FATHER CALLED HER FOR SOME BUSINESS.

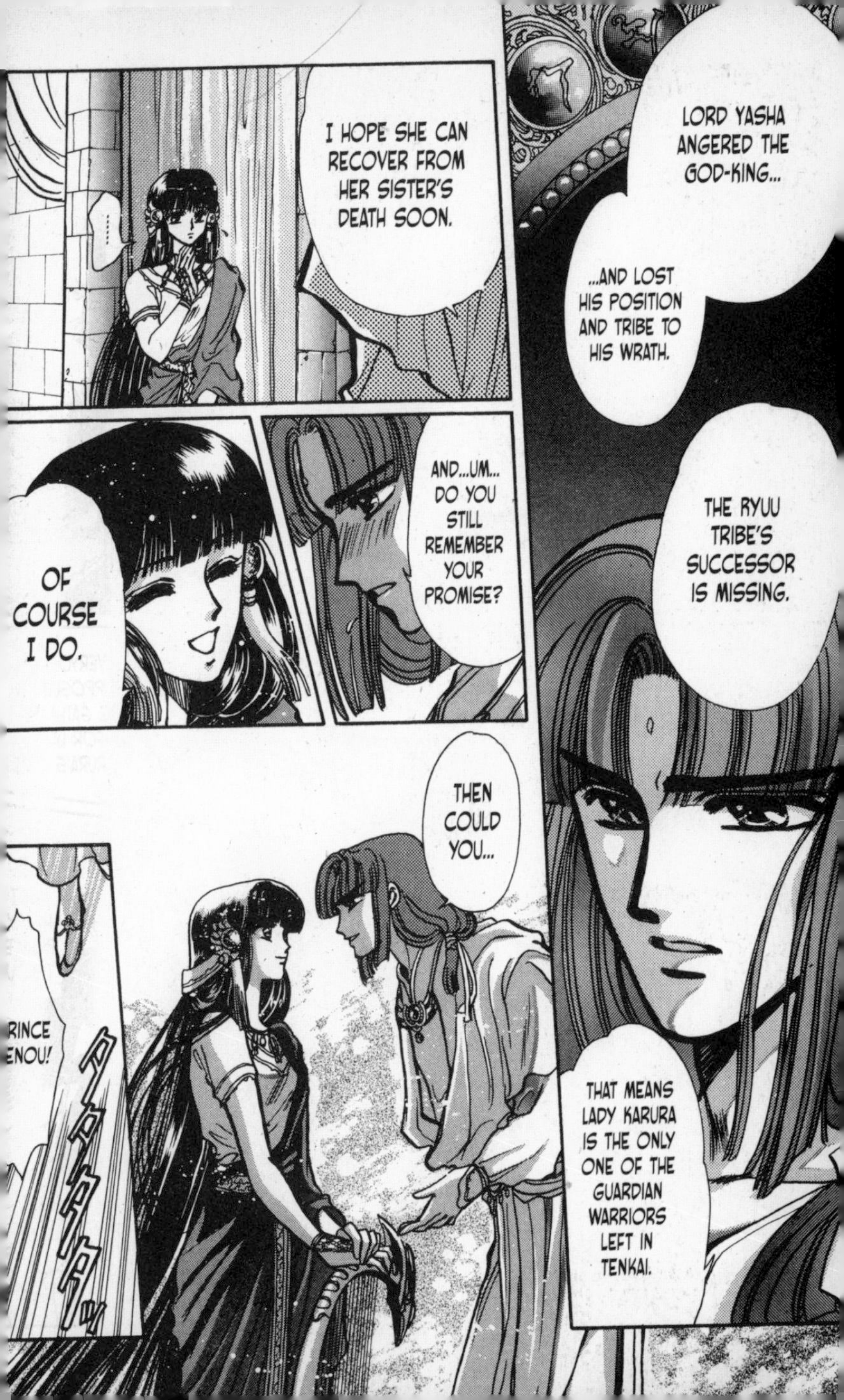
LORD YASHA ANGERED THE GOD-KING...
...AND LOST HIS POSITION AND TRIBE TO HIS WRATH.
THE RYUU TRIBE'S SUCCESSOR IS MISSING.
THAT MEANS LADY KARURA IS THE ONLY ONE OF THE GUARDIAN WARRIORS LEFT IN TENKAI.
I HOPE SHE CAN RECOVER FROM HER SISTER'S DEATH SOON.
......
AND...UM... DO YOU STILL REMEMBER YOUR PROMISE?
OF COURSE I DO.
THEN COULD YOU...
RINCE ENOU!

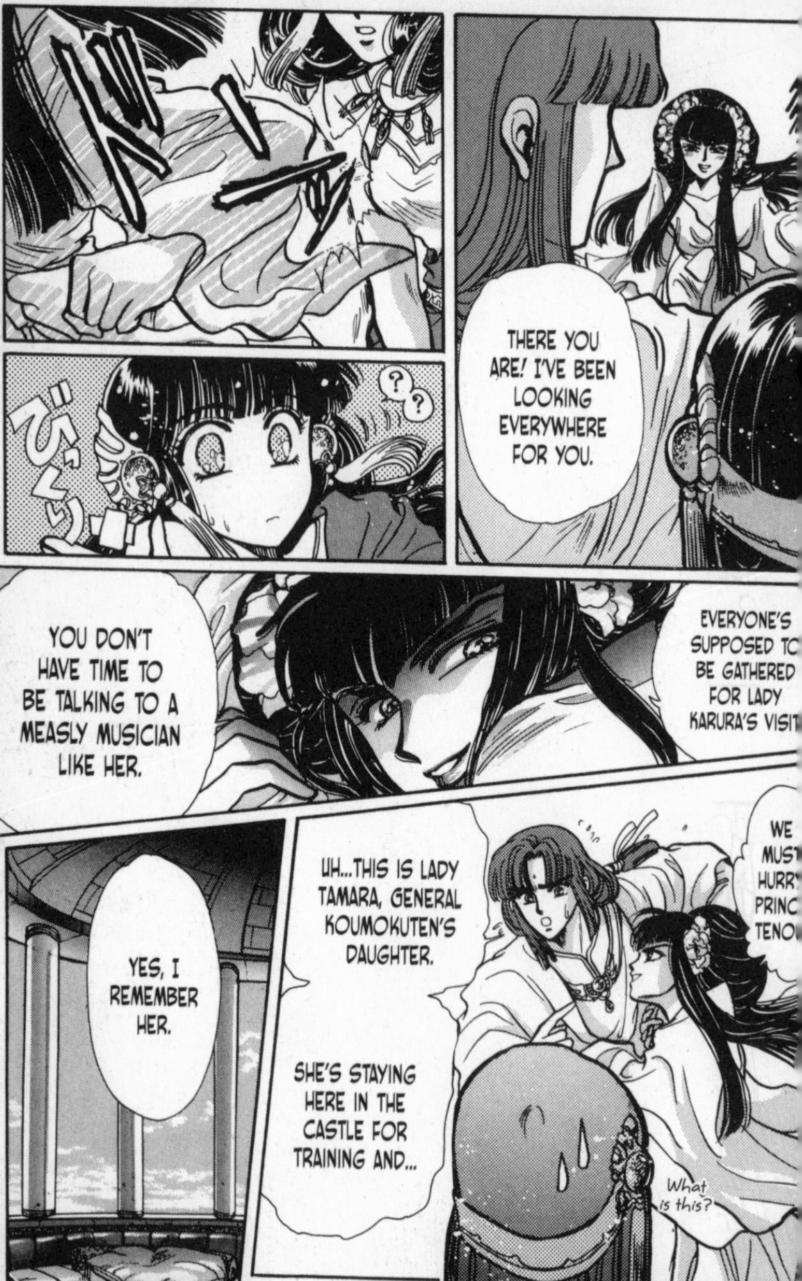
THERE YOU ARE! I'VE BEEN LOOKING EVERYWHERE FOR YOU.
? ?
EVERYONE'S SUPPOSED TO BE GATHERED FOR LADY KARURA'S VISIT
YOU DON'T HAVE TIME TO BE TALKING TO A MEASLY MUSICIAN LIKE HER.
WE MUST HURRY PRINC TENO
UH...THIS IS LADY TAMARA, GENERAL KOUMOKUTEN'S DAUGHTER.
SHE'S STAYING HERE IN THE CASTLE FOR TRAINING AND...
What is this?
YES, I REMEMBER HER.

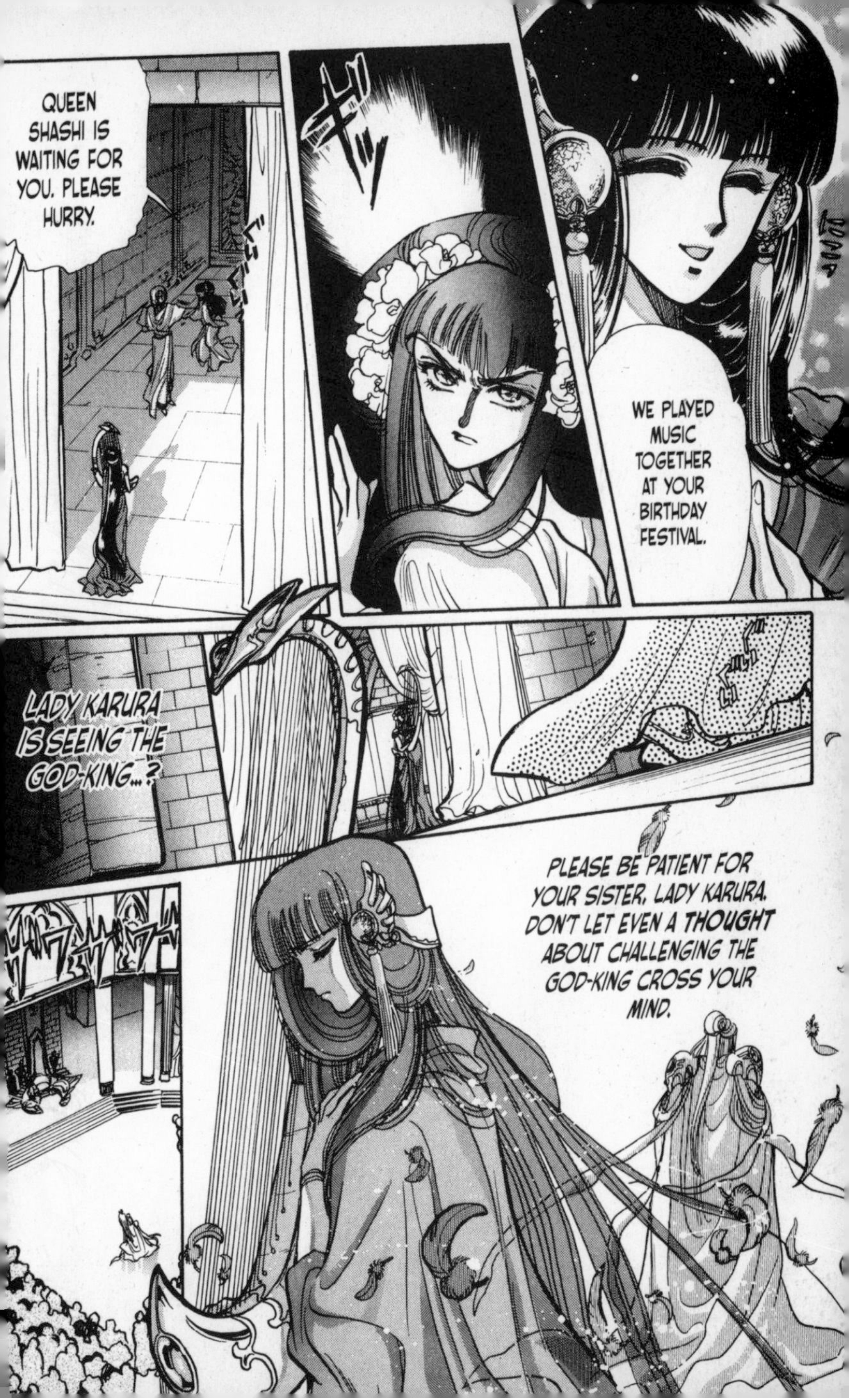
WE PLAYED MUSIC TOGETHER AT YOUR BIRTHDAY FESTIVAL.
QUEEN SHASHI IS WAITING FOR YOU. PLEASE HURRY.
LADY KARURA IS SEEING THE GOD-KING...?
PLEASE BE PATIENT FOR YOUR SISTER, LADY KARURA. DON'T LET EVEN A THOUGHT ABOUT CHALLENGING THE GOD-KING CROSS YOUR MIND.

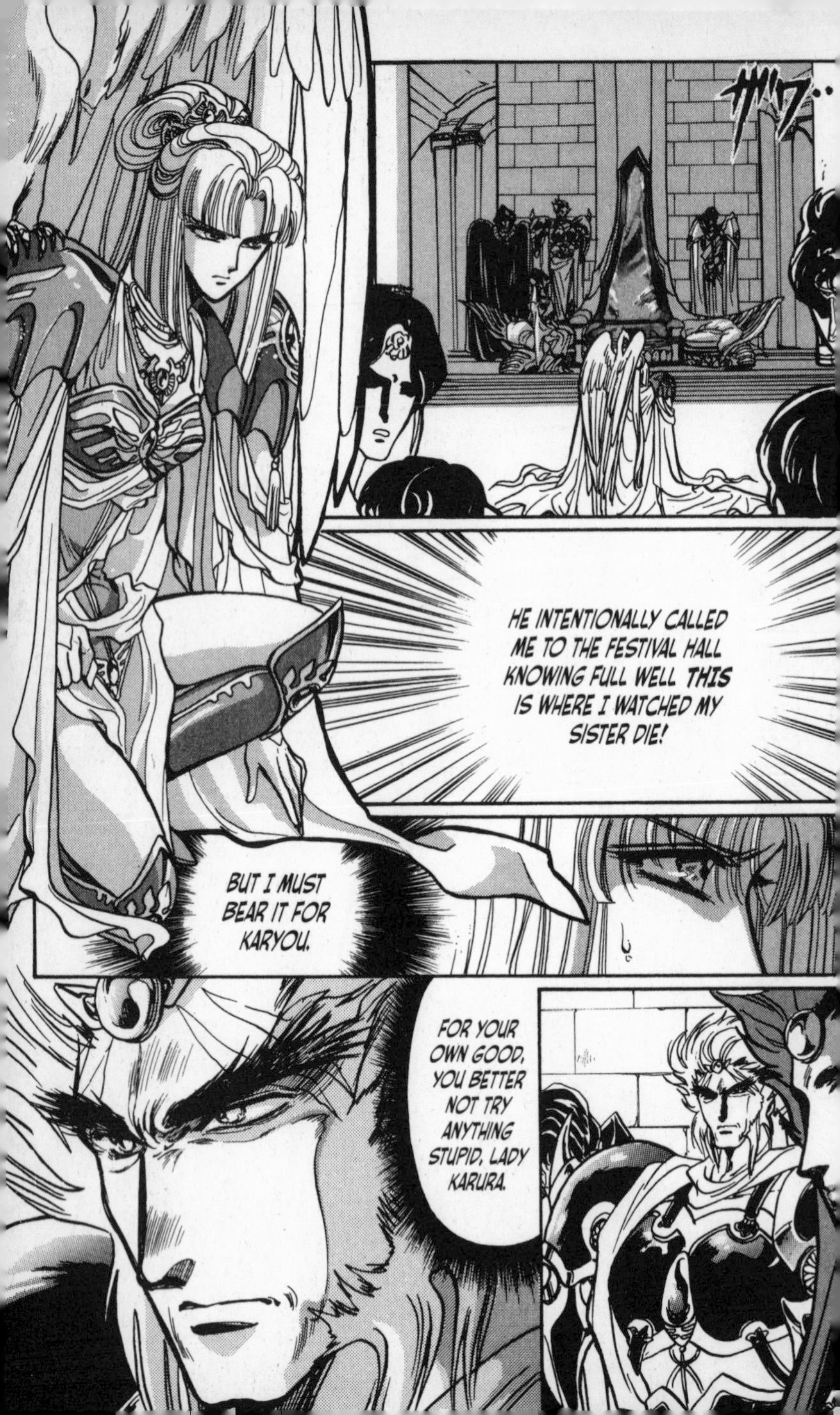

ザワ…
HE INTENTIONALLY CALLED ME TO THE FESTIVAL HALL KNOWING FULL WELL THIS IS WHERE I WATCHED MY SISTER DIE!
BUT I MUST BEAR IT FOR KARYOU.
FOR YOUR OWN GOOD, YOU BETTER NOT TRY ANYTHING STUPID, LADY KARURA.

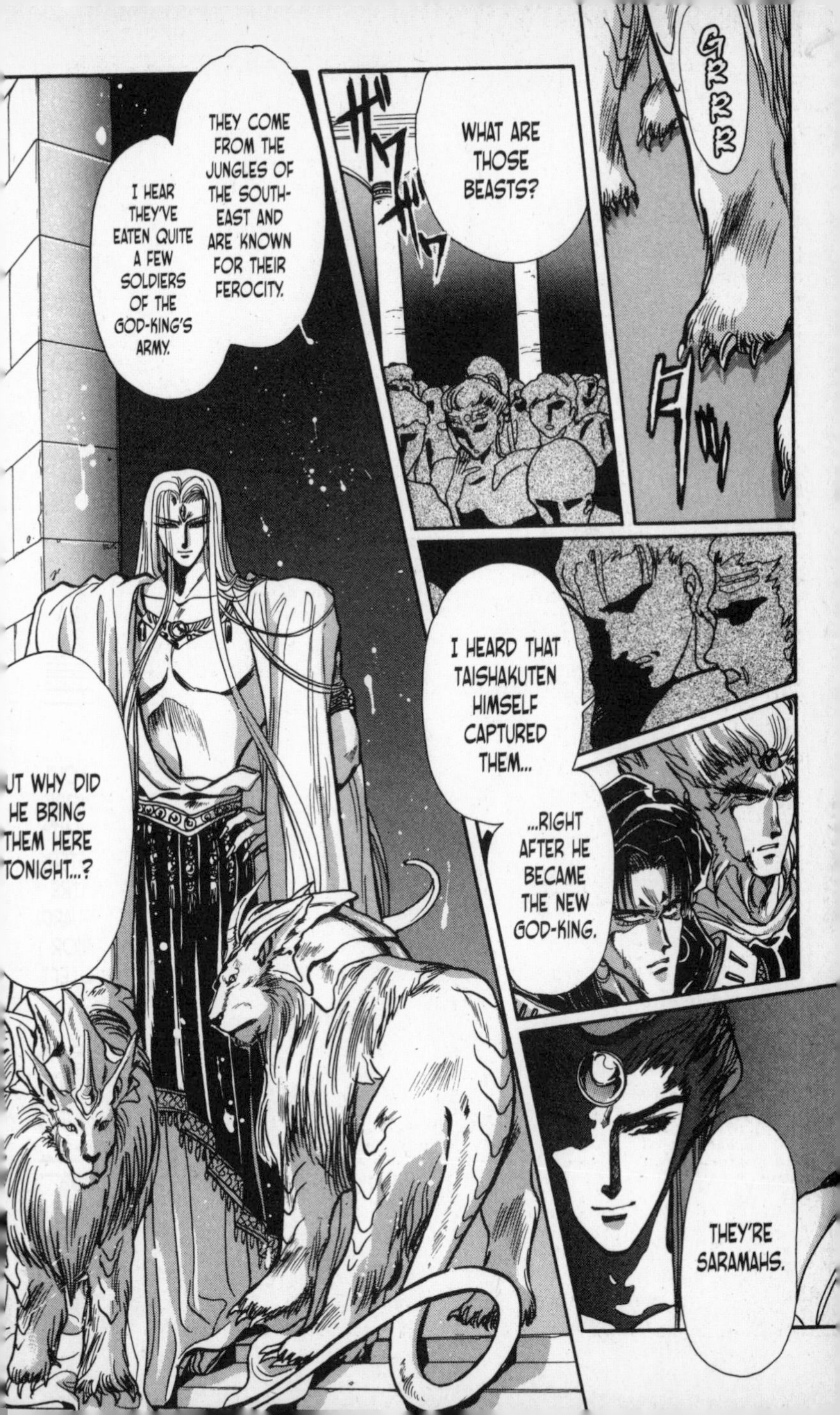
GRRR
WHAT ARE THOSE BEASTS?
I HEARD THAT TAISHAKUTEN HIMSELF CAPTURED THEM...
...RIGHT AFTER HE BECAME THE NEW GOD-KING.
THEY'RE SARAMAHS.
THEY COME FROM THE JUNGLES OF THE SOUTH-EAST AND ARE KNOWN FOR THEIR FEROCITY.
I HEAR THEY'VE EATEN QUITE A FEW SOLDIERS OF THE GOD-KING'S ARMY.
UT WHY DID HE BRING THEM HERE TONIGHT...?

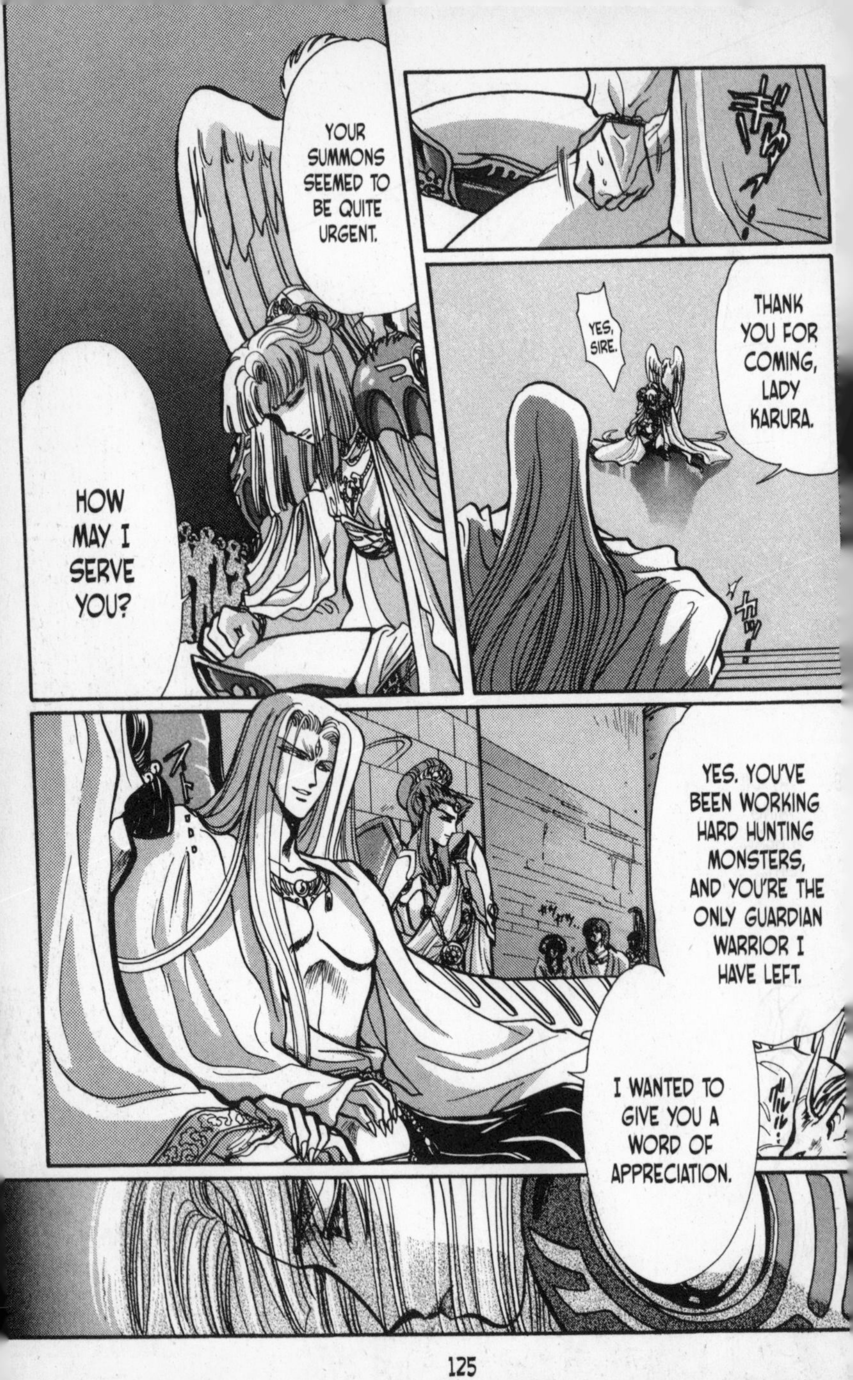
THANK YOU FOR COMING, LADY KARURA.
YES, SIRE.
YOUR SUMMONS SEEMED TO BE QUITE URGENT.
HOW MAY I SERVE YOU?
YES. YOU'VE BEEN WORKING HARD HUNTING MONSTERS, AND YOU'RE THE ONLY GUARDIAN WARRIOR I HAVE LEFT.
I WANTED TO GIVE YOU A WORD OF APPRECIATION.

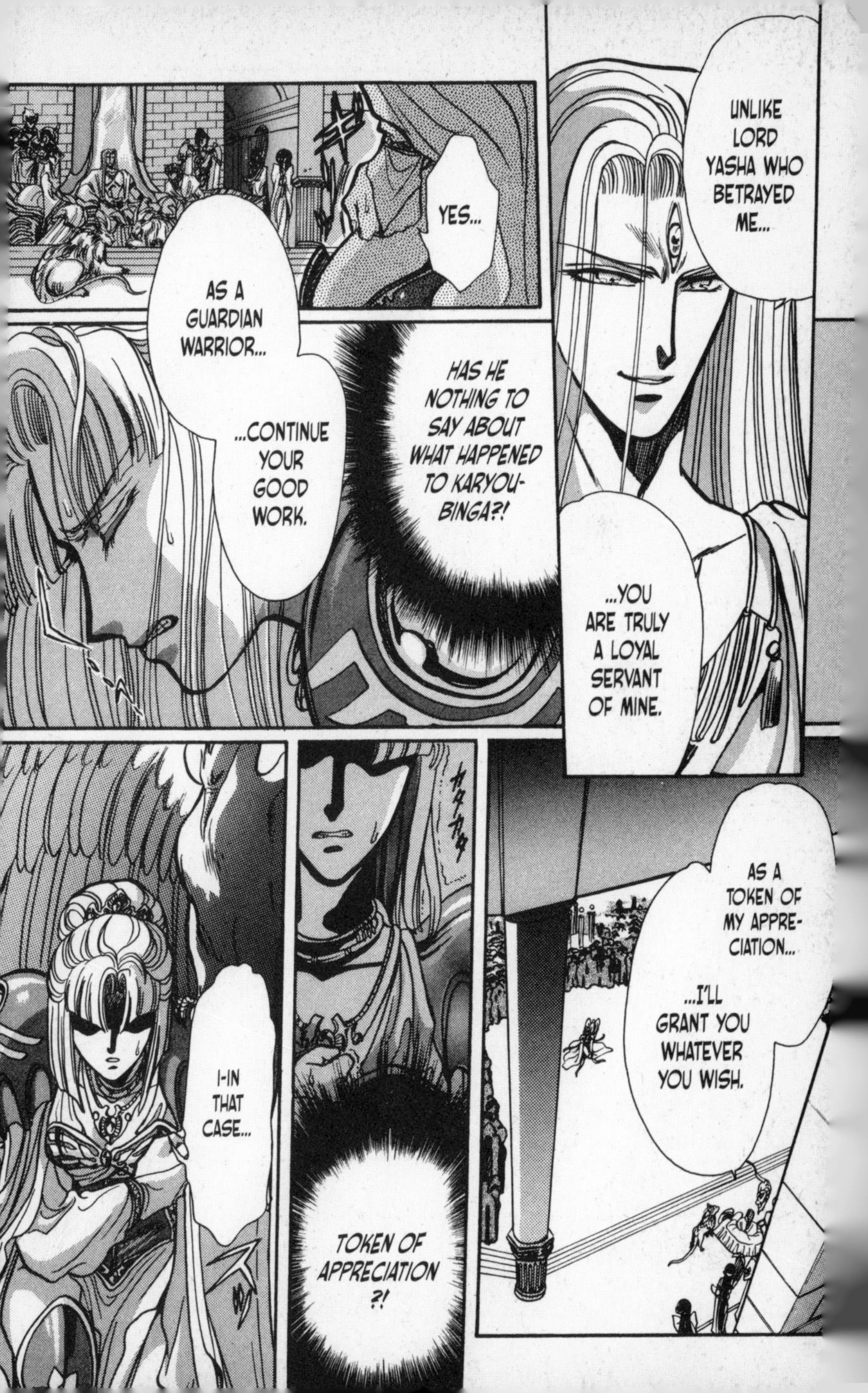
UNLIKE LORD YASHA WHO BETRAYED ME...
...YOU ARE TRULY A LOYAL SERVANT OF MINE.
YES...
AS A GUARDIAN WARRIOR...
HAS HE NOTHING TO SAY ABOUT WHAT HAPPENED TO KARYOU-BINGA?!
...CONTINUE YOUR GOOD WORK.
AS A TOKEN OF MY APPRE-CIATION...
...I'LL GRANT YOU WHATEVER YOU WISH.
カタカタ
TOKEN OF APPRECIATION?!
I-IN THAT CASE...

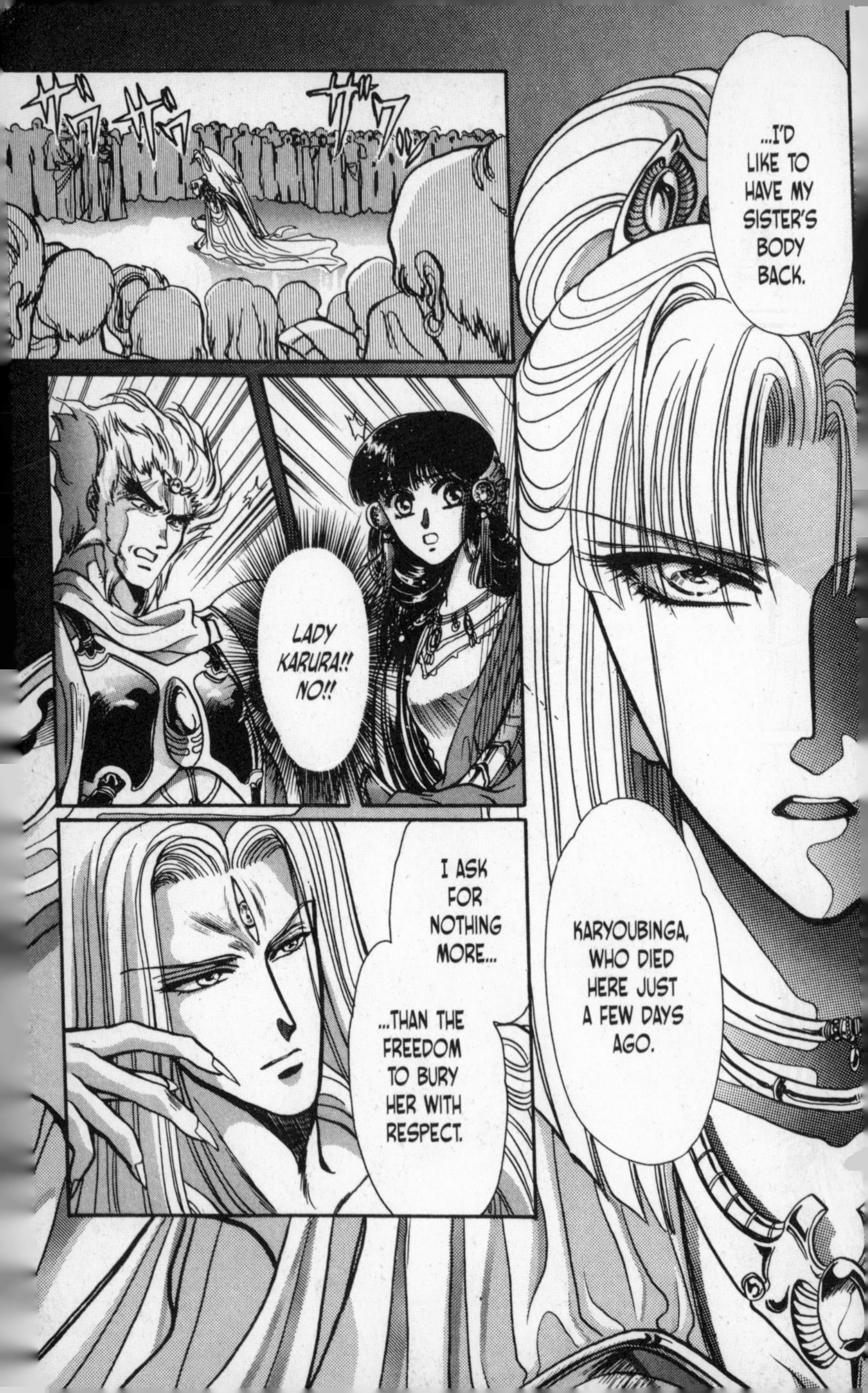
...I'D LIKE TO HAVE MY SISTER'S BODY BACK.
KARYOUBINGA, WHO DIED HERE JUST A FEW DAYS AGO.
ザワ ザワ
ザワッ
LADY KARURA!! NO!!
I ASK FOR NOTHING MORE...
...THAN THE FREEDOM TO BURY HER WITH RESPECT.

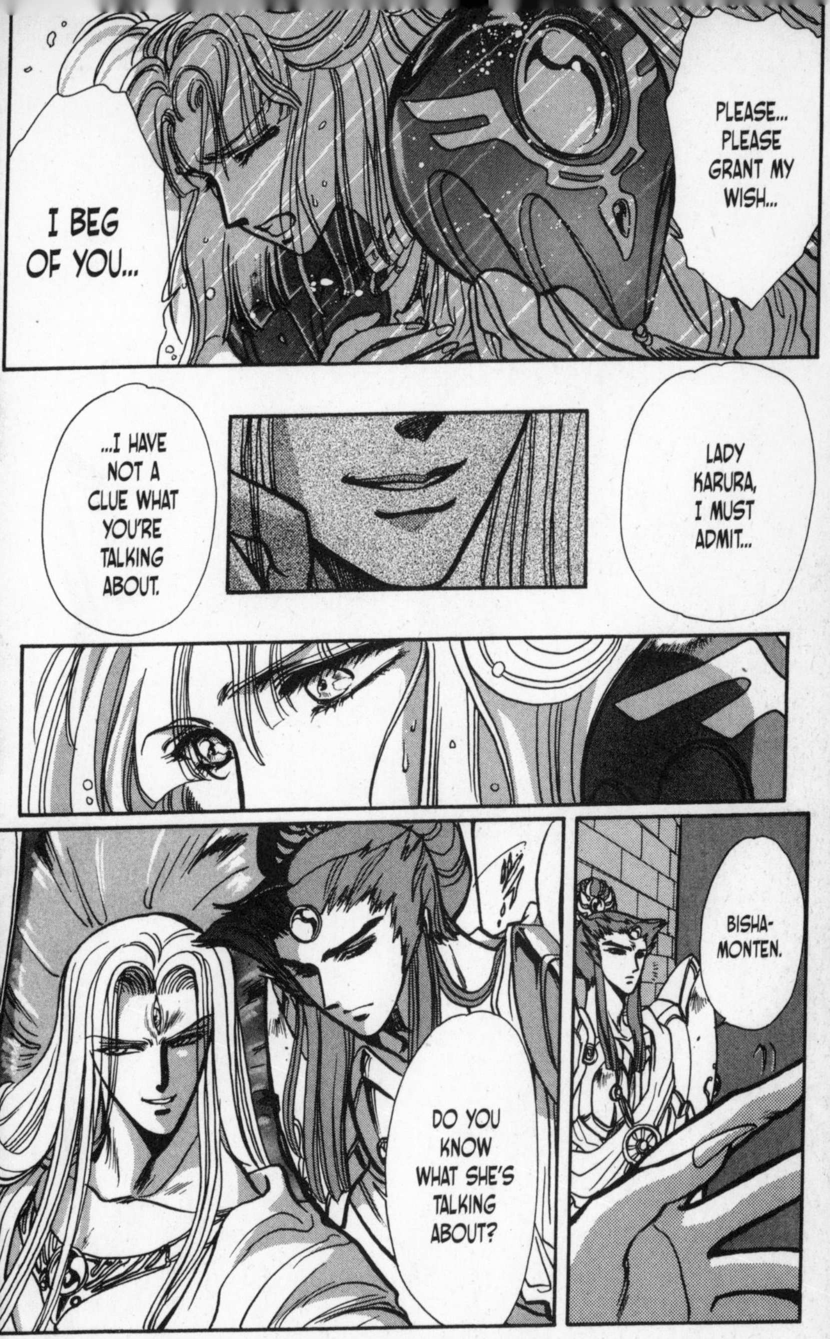
PLEASE... PLEASE GRANT MY WISH...
I BEG OF YOU...
LADY KARURA, I MUST ADMIT...
...I HAVE NOT A CLUE WHAT YOU'RE TALKING ABOUT.
BISHA-MONTEN.
DO YOU KNOW WHAT SHE'S TALKING ABOUT?

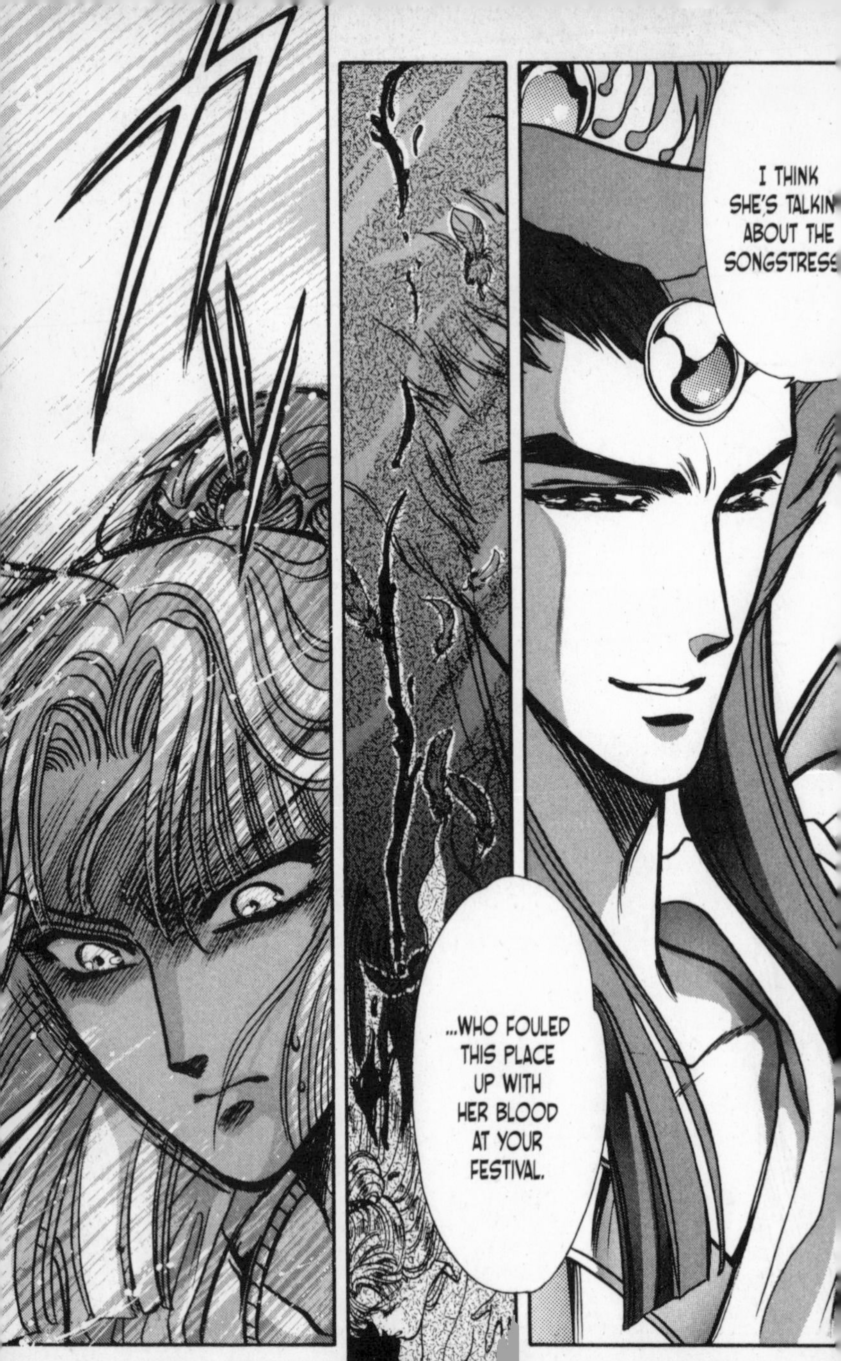
I THINK SHE'S TALKIN ABOUT THE SONGSTRES
...WHO FOULED THIS PLACE UP WITH HER BLOOD AT YOUR FESTIVAL.

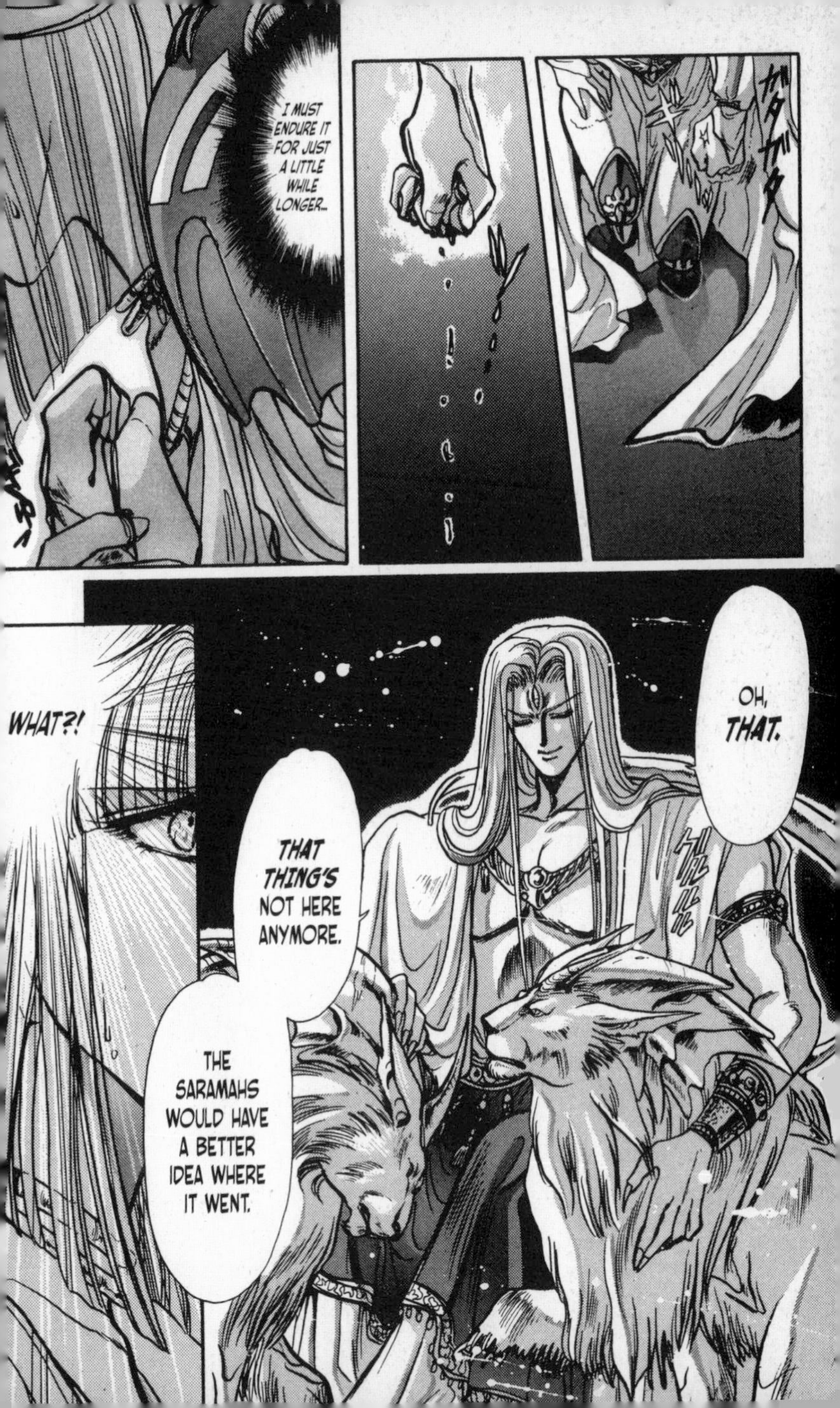
I MUST ENDURE IT FOR JUST A LITTLE WHILE LONGER...
OH, THAT.
THAT THING'S NOT HERE ANYMORE.
THE SARAMAHS WOULD HAVE A BETTER IDEA WHERE IT WENT.
WHAT?!

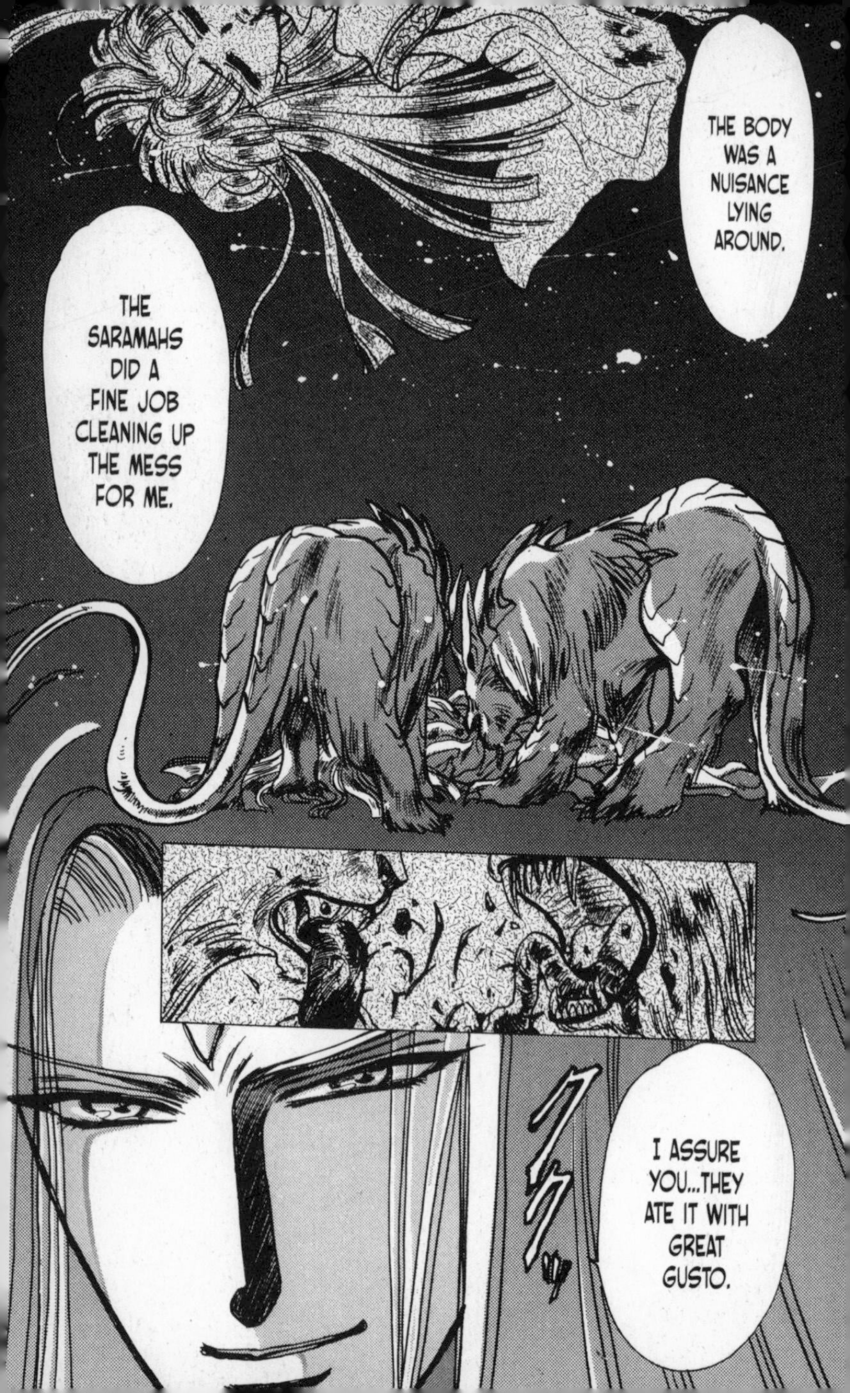

THE BODY WAS A NUISANCE LYING AROUND.
THE SARAMAHS DID A FINE JOB CLEANING UP THE MESS FOR ME.
I ASSURE YOU...THEY ATE IT WITH GREAT GUSTO.

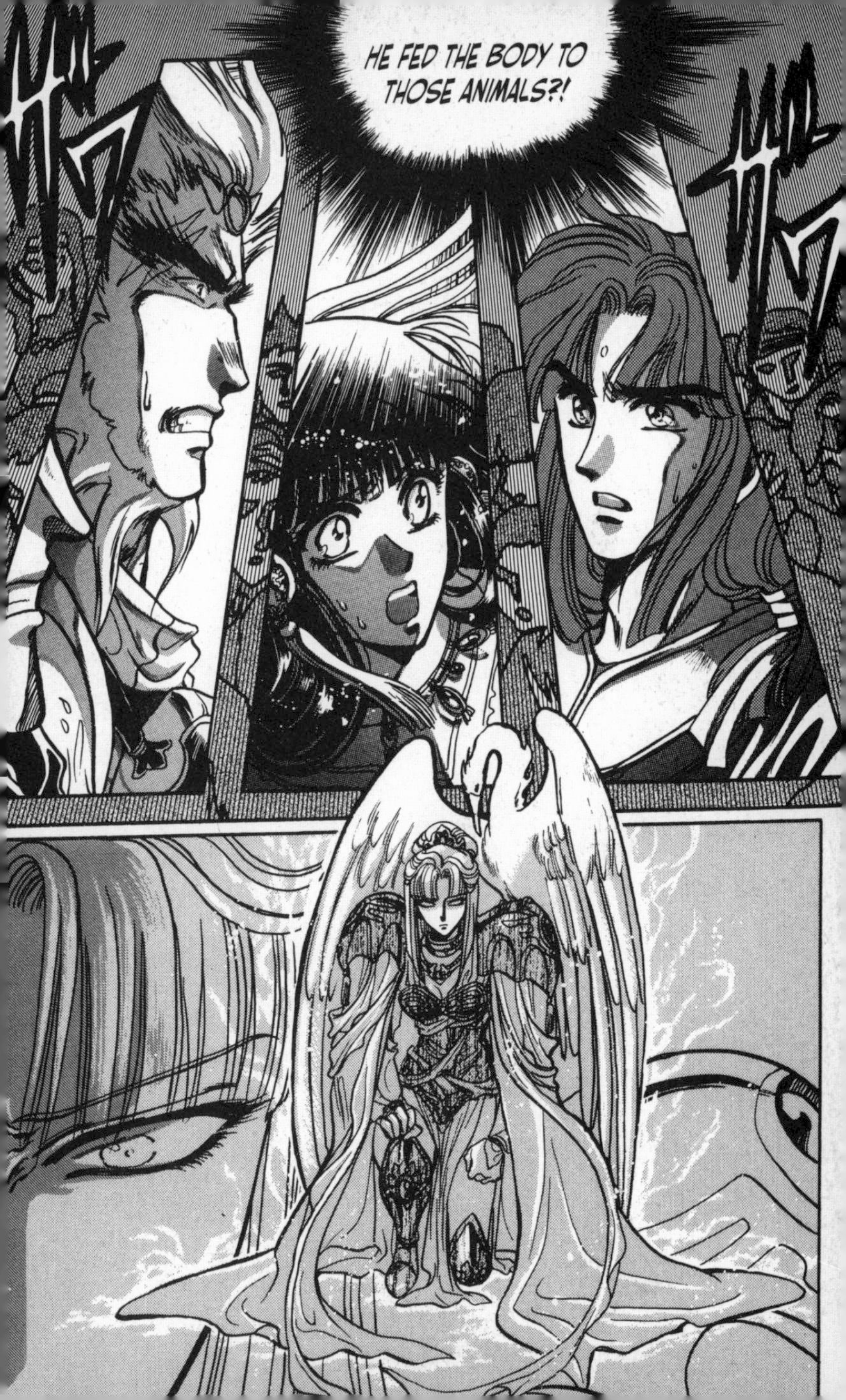
HE FED THE BODY TO
THOSE ANIMALS?!

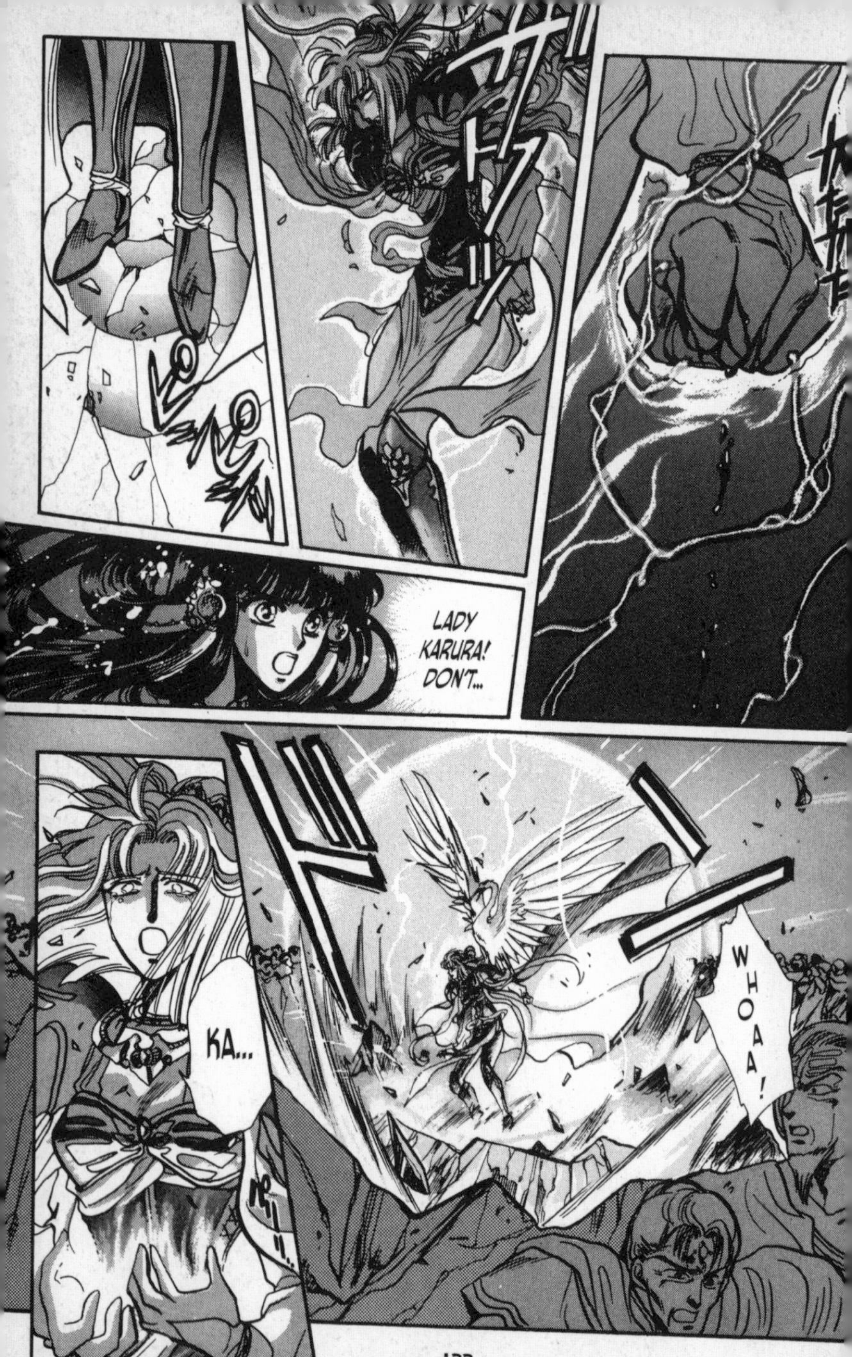
LADY KARURA! DON'T...
WHOA!
KA...

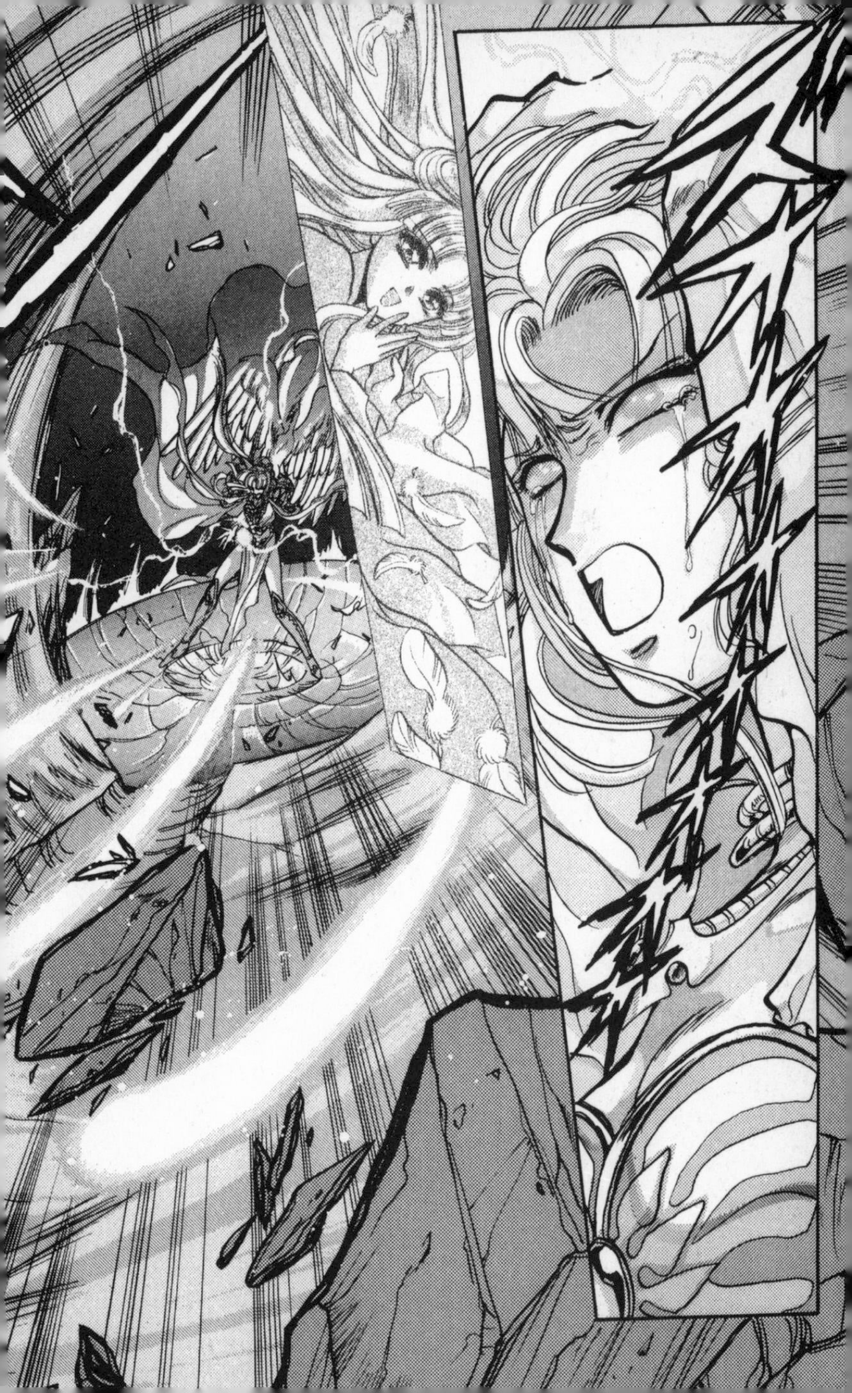

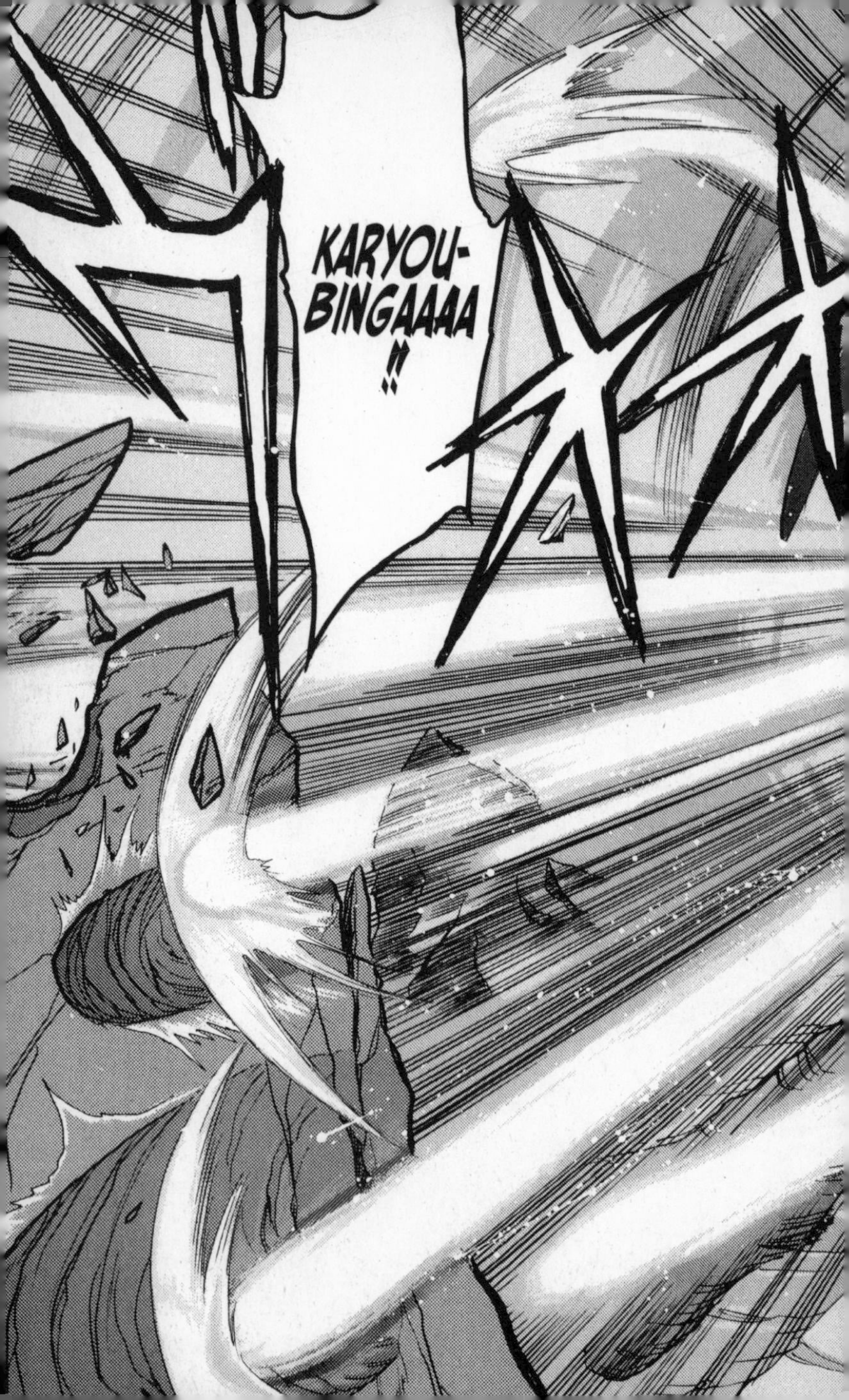
KARYOU-BINGAAAA!!

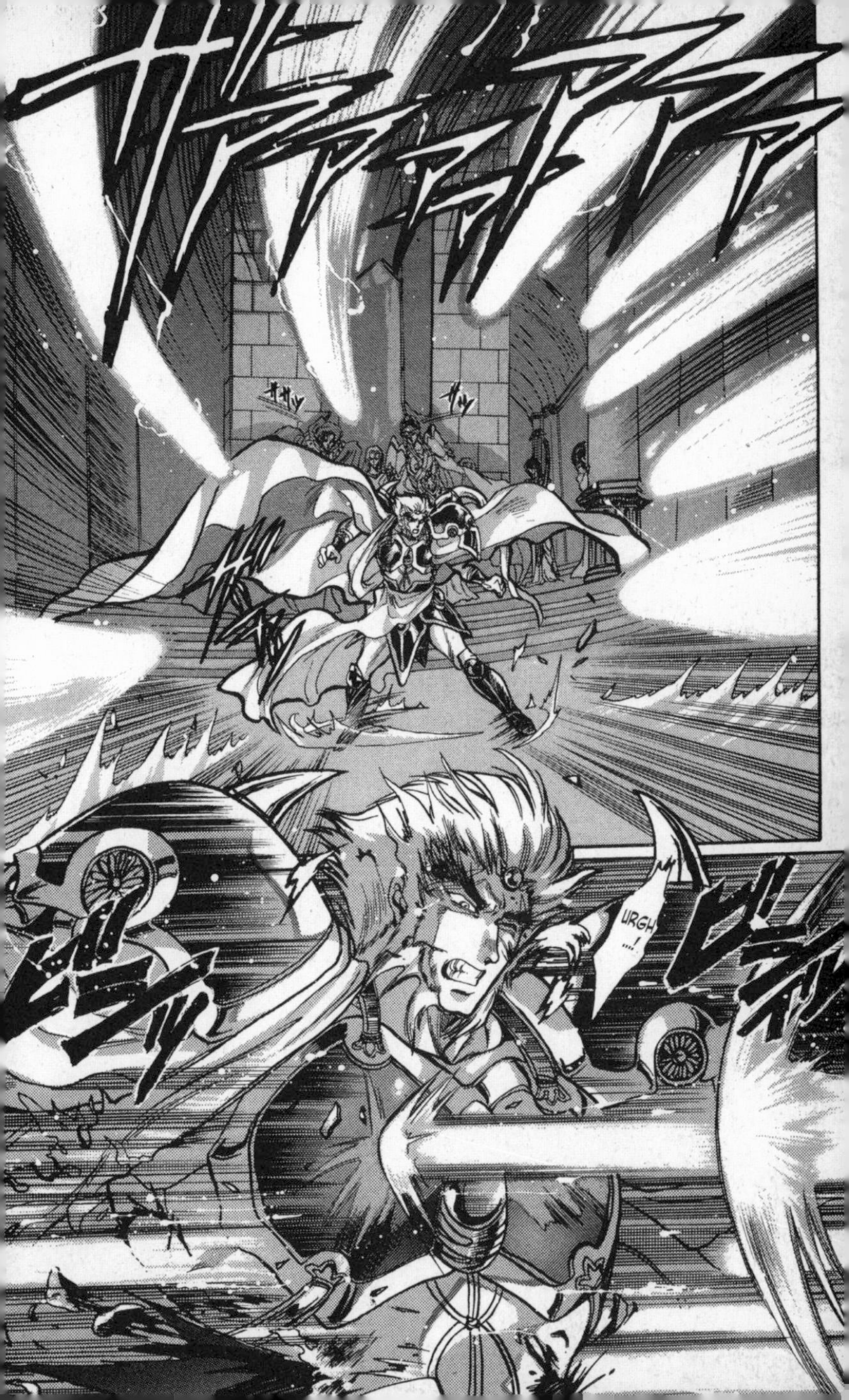
URGH ...!

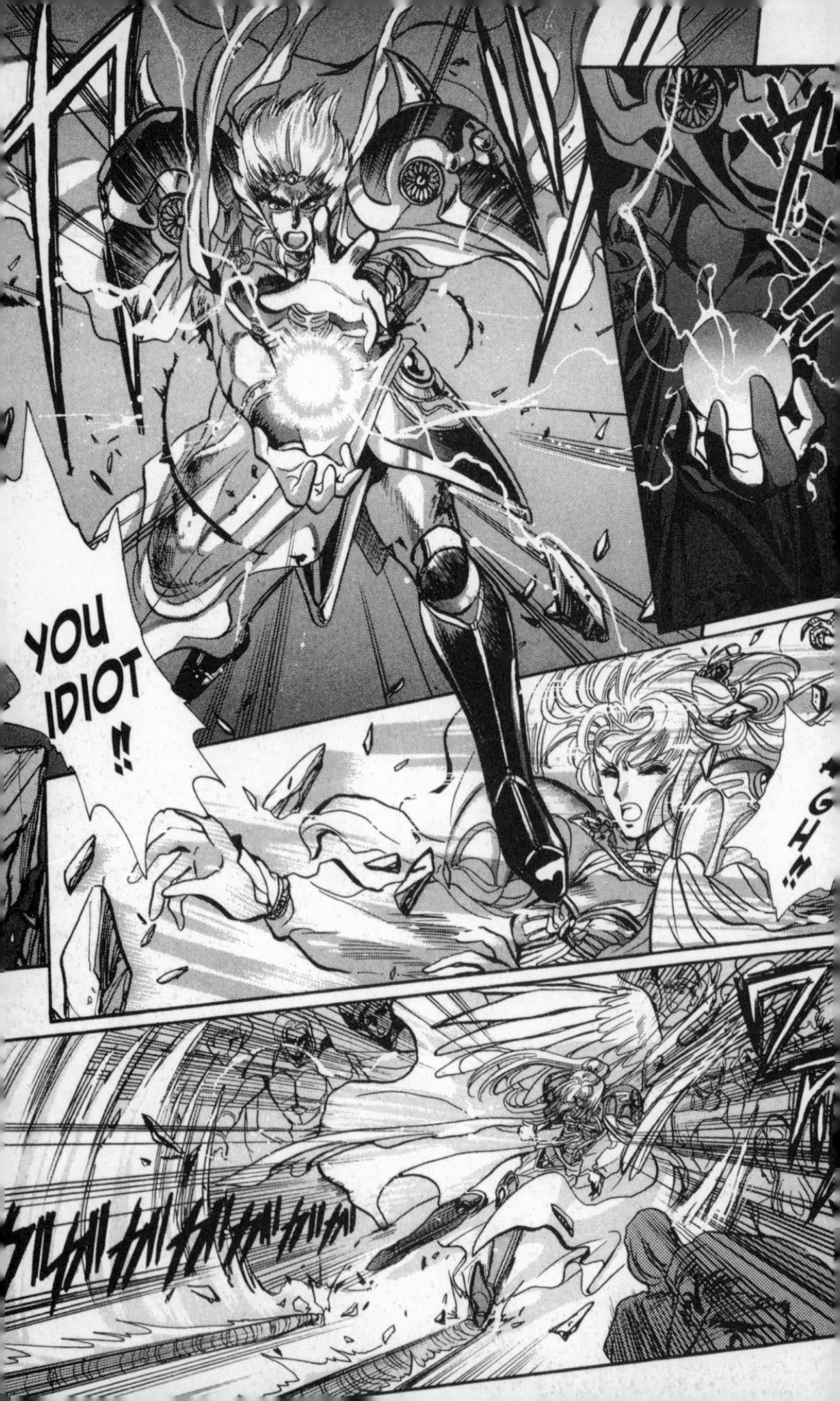
YOU IDIOT!!
AGH!!

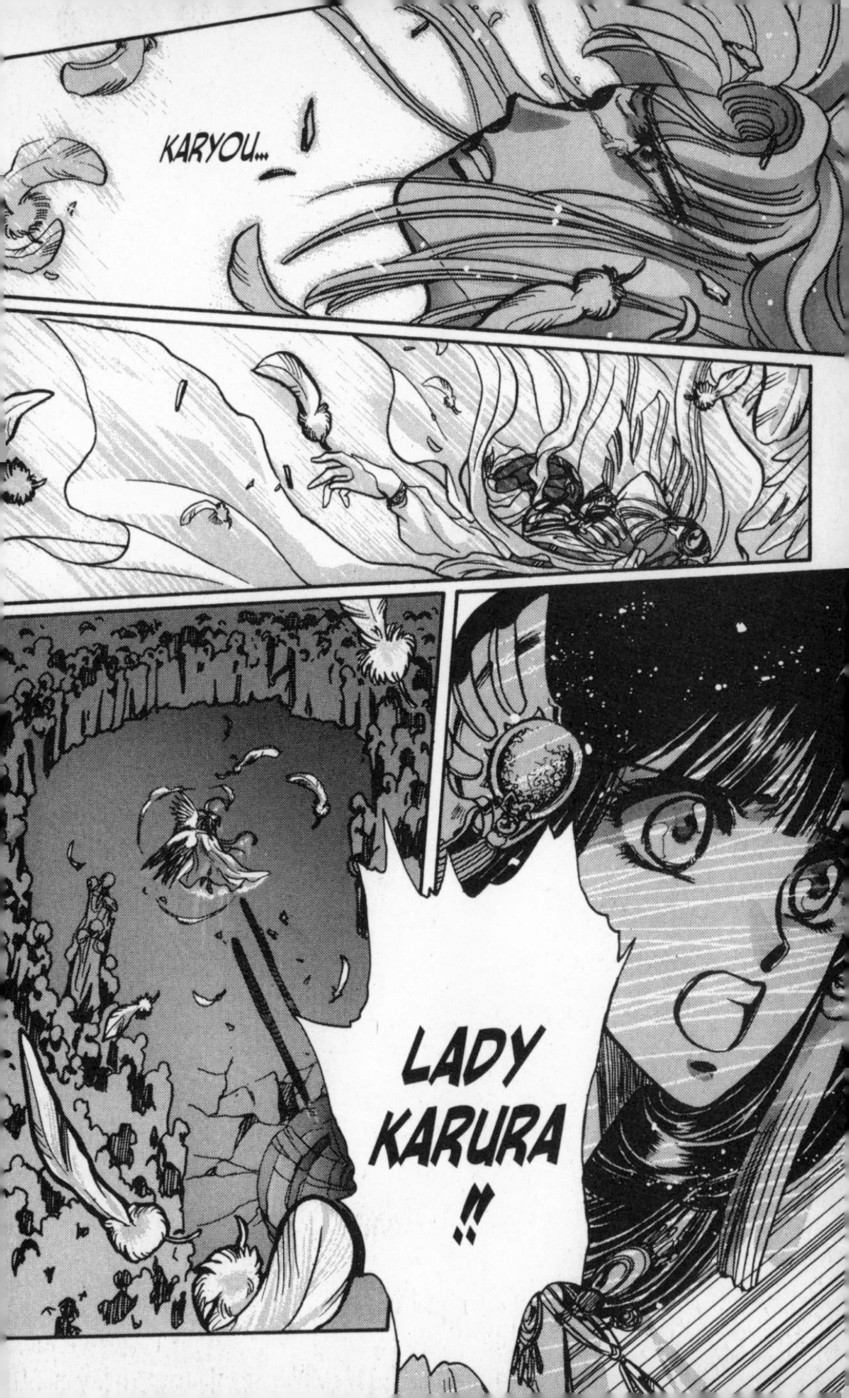
KARYOU...
LADY KARURA !!

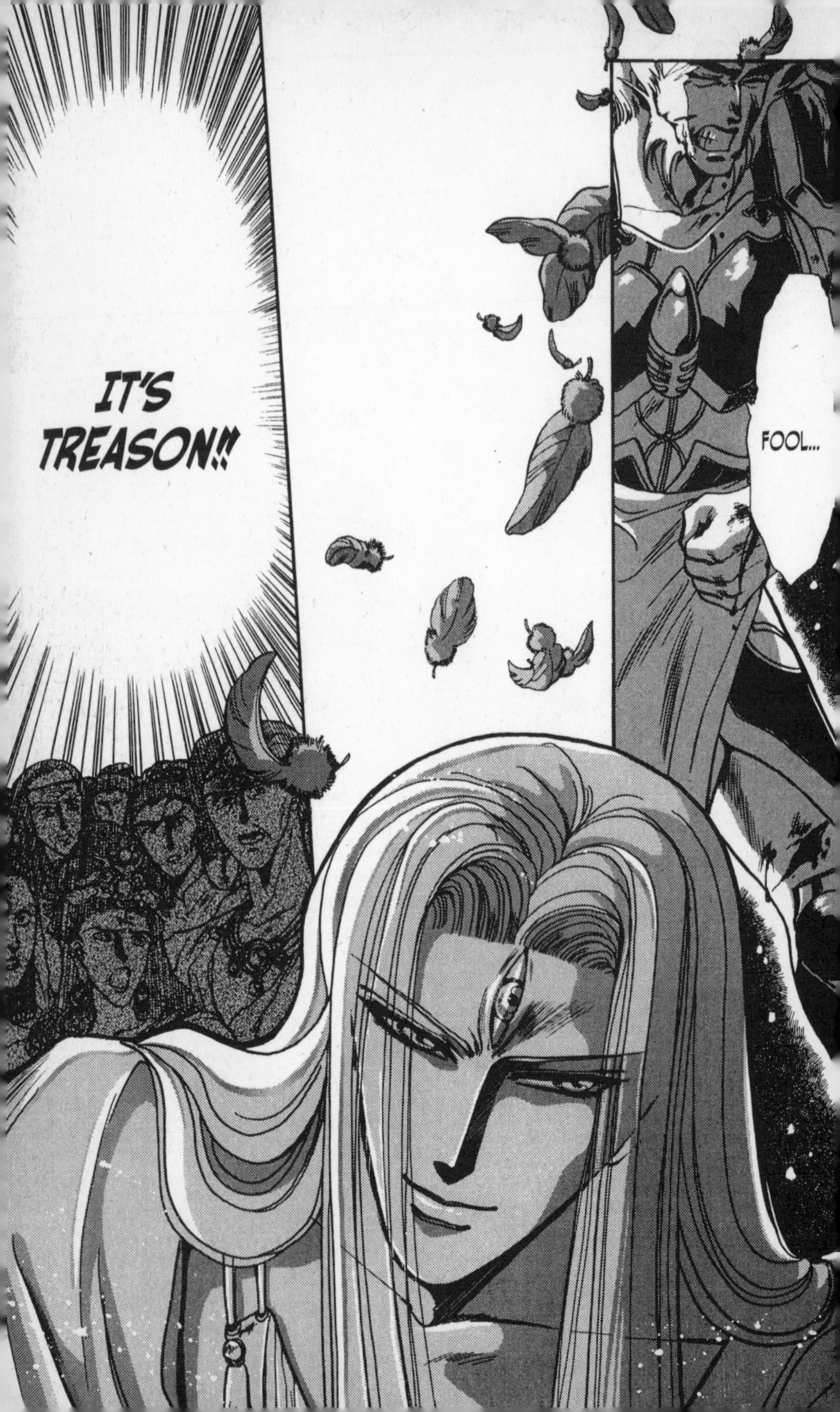
FOOL...
IT'S TREASON!!

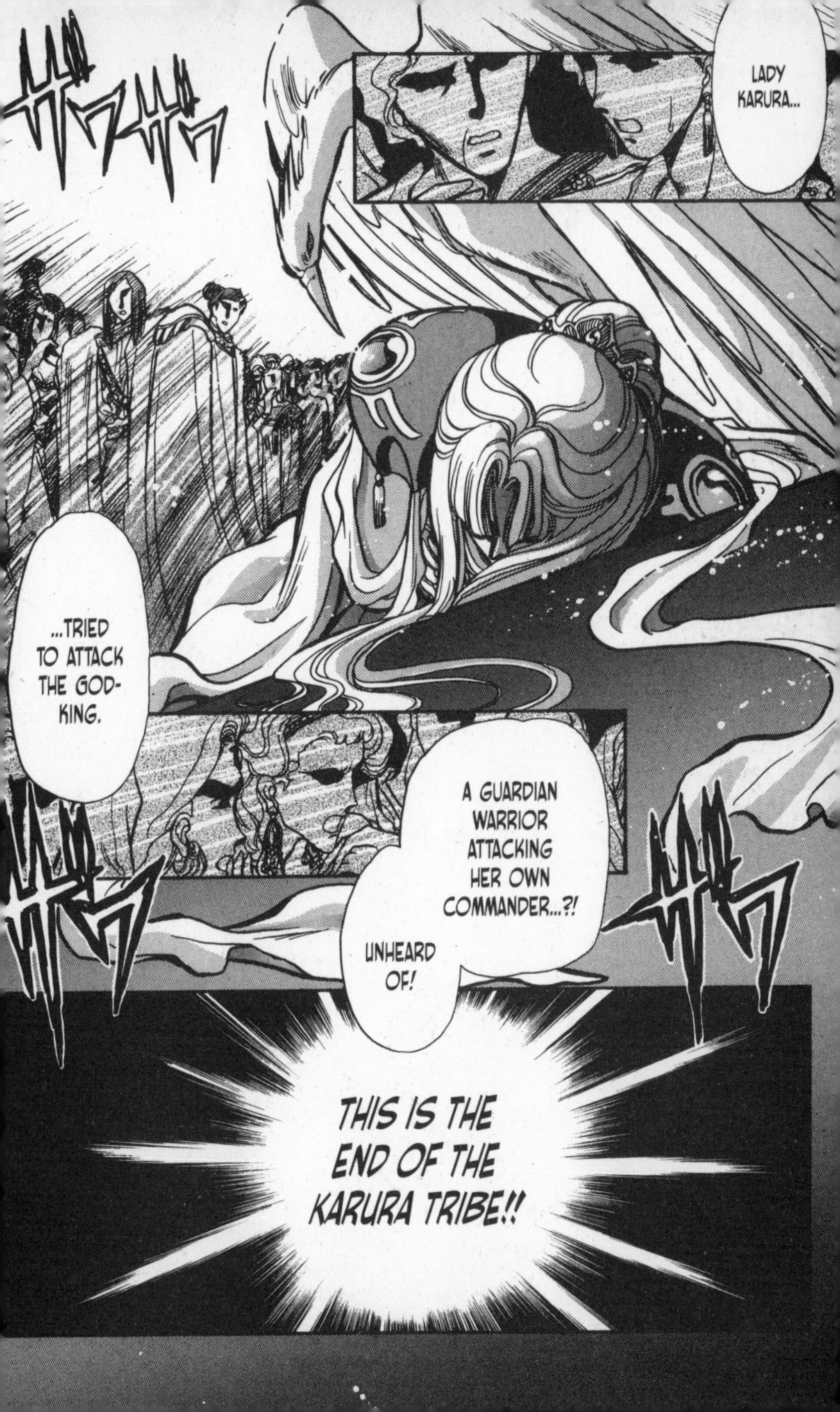
LADY KARURA...
...TRIED TO ATTACK THE GOD-KING.
A GUARDIAN WARRIOR ATTACKING HER OWN COMMANDER...?!
UNHEARD OF!
THIS IS THE END OF THE KARURA TRIBE!!

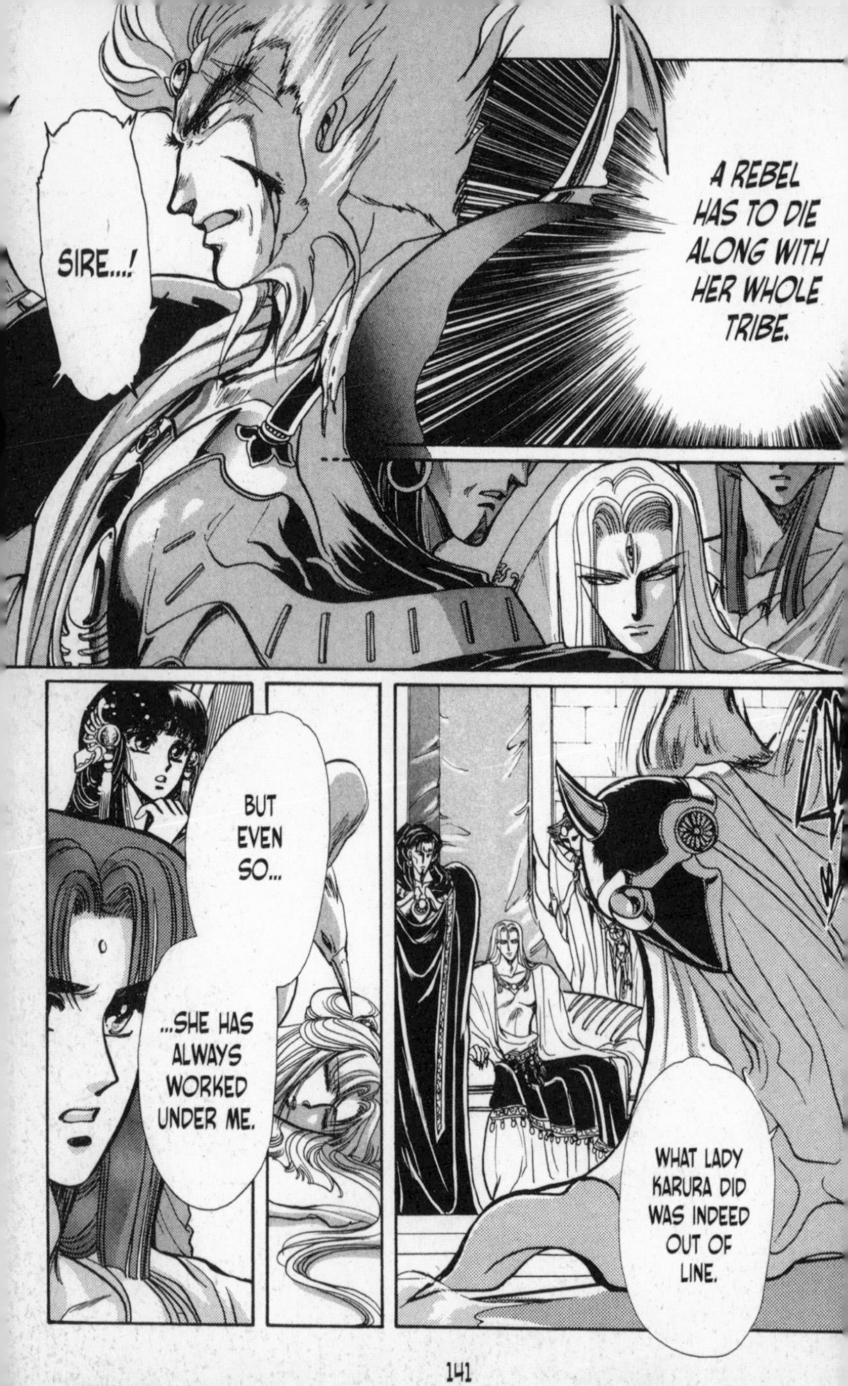
A REBEL HAS TO DIE ALONG WITH HER WHOLE TRIBE.
SIRE...!
WHAT LADY KARURA DID WAS INDEED OUT OF LINE.
BUT EVEN SO...
...SHE HAS ALWAYS WORKED UNDER ME.

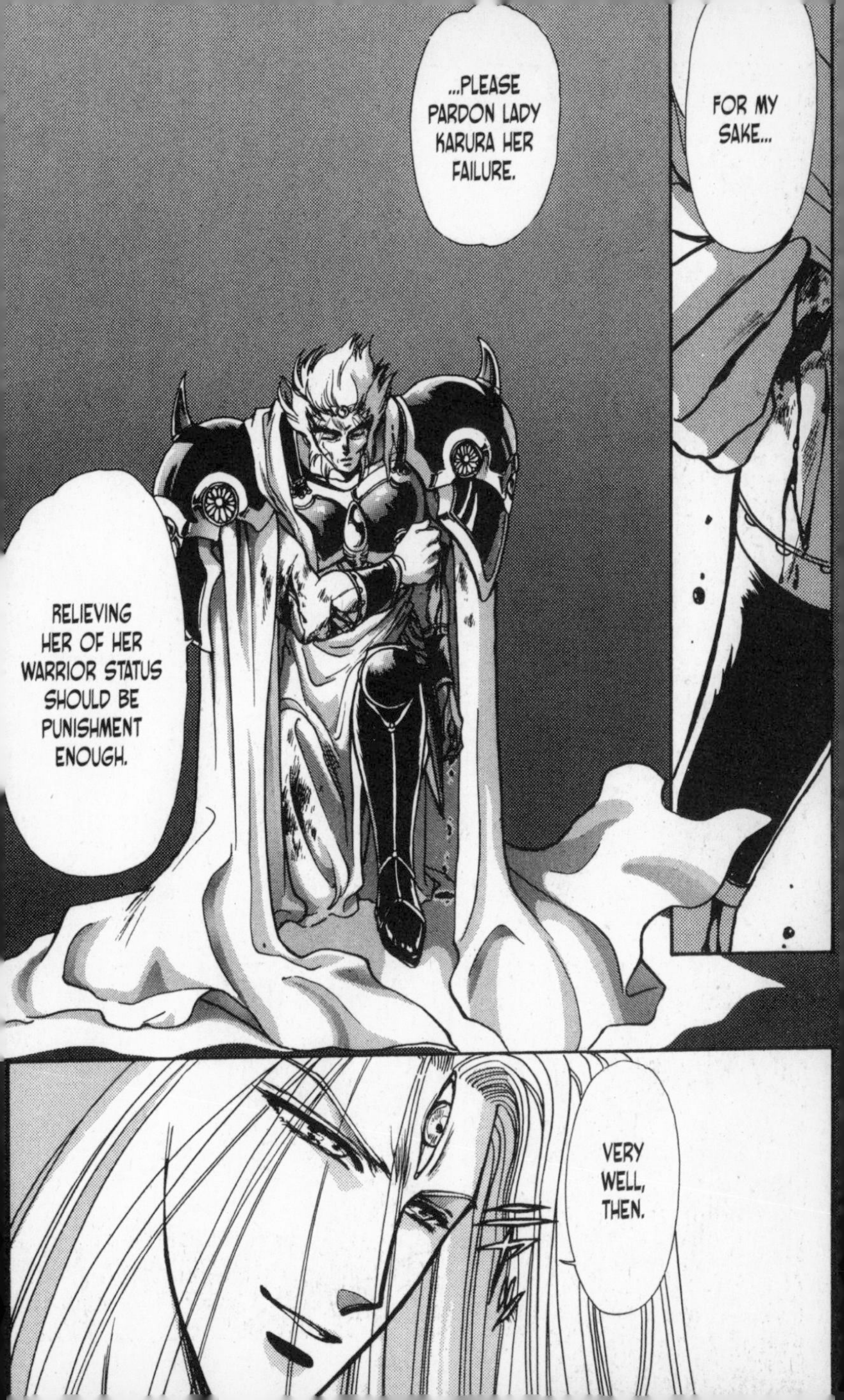
FOR MY SAKE...
...PLEASE PARDON LADY KARURA HER FAILURE.
RELIEVING HER OF HER WARRIOR STATUS SHOULD BE PUNISHMENT ENOUGH.
VERY WELL, THEN.

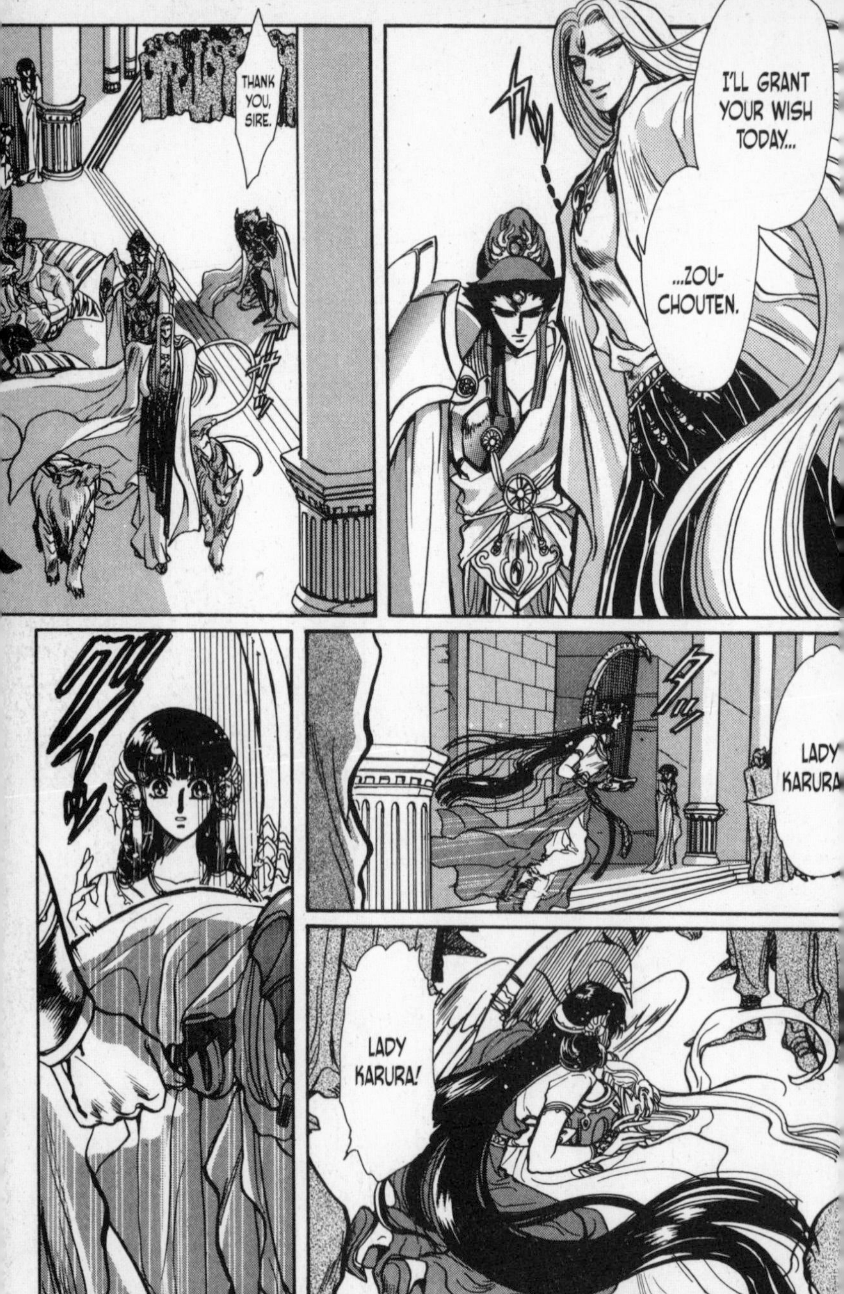
I'LL GRANT YOUR WISH TODAY...
...ZOU-CHOUTEN.
THANK YOU, SIRE.
LADY KARURA
LADY KARURA!

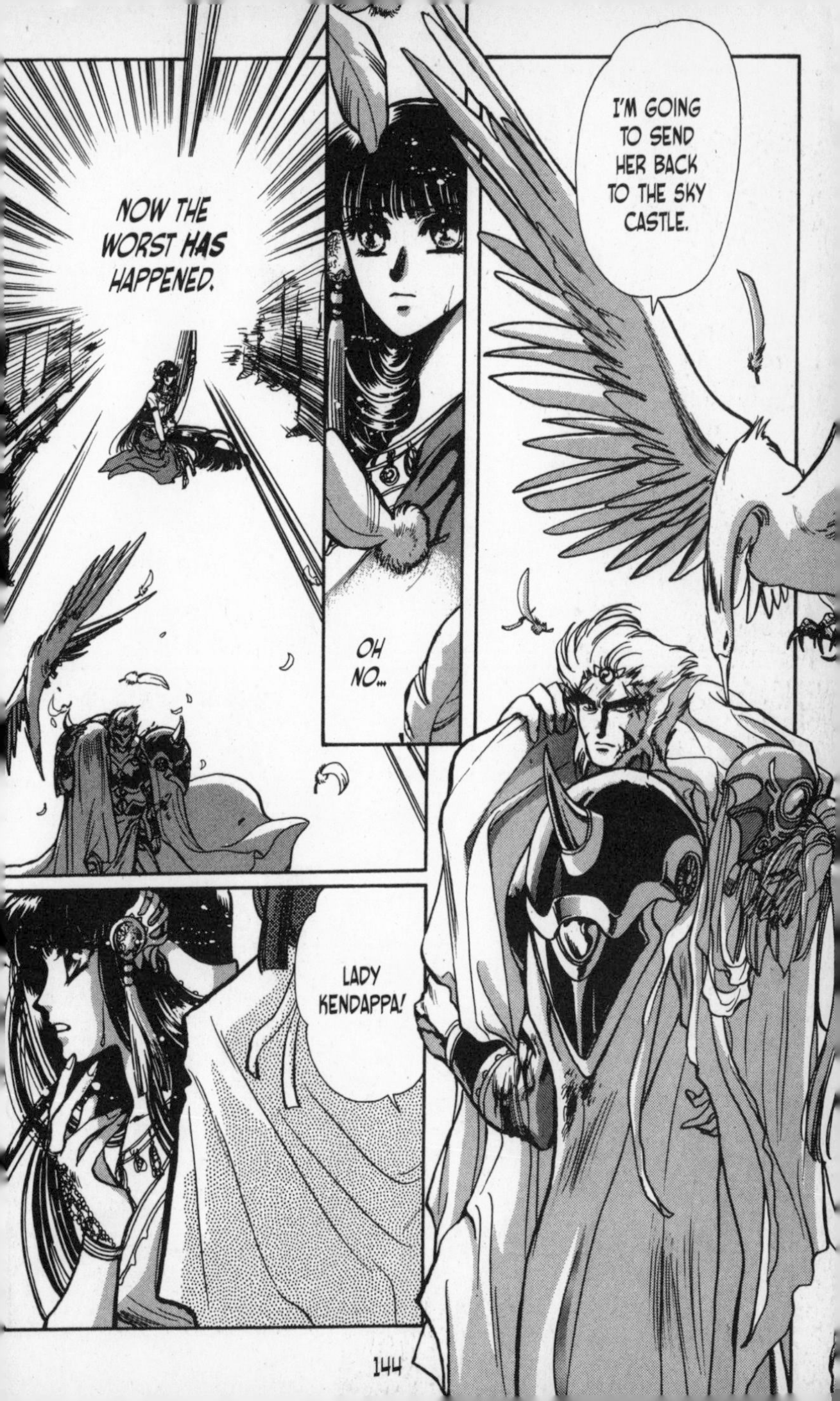
I'M GOING TO SEND HER BACK TO THE SKY CASTLE.
OH NO...
NOW THE WORST HAS HAPPENED.
LADY KENDAPPA!

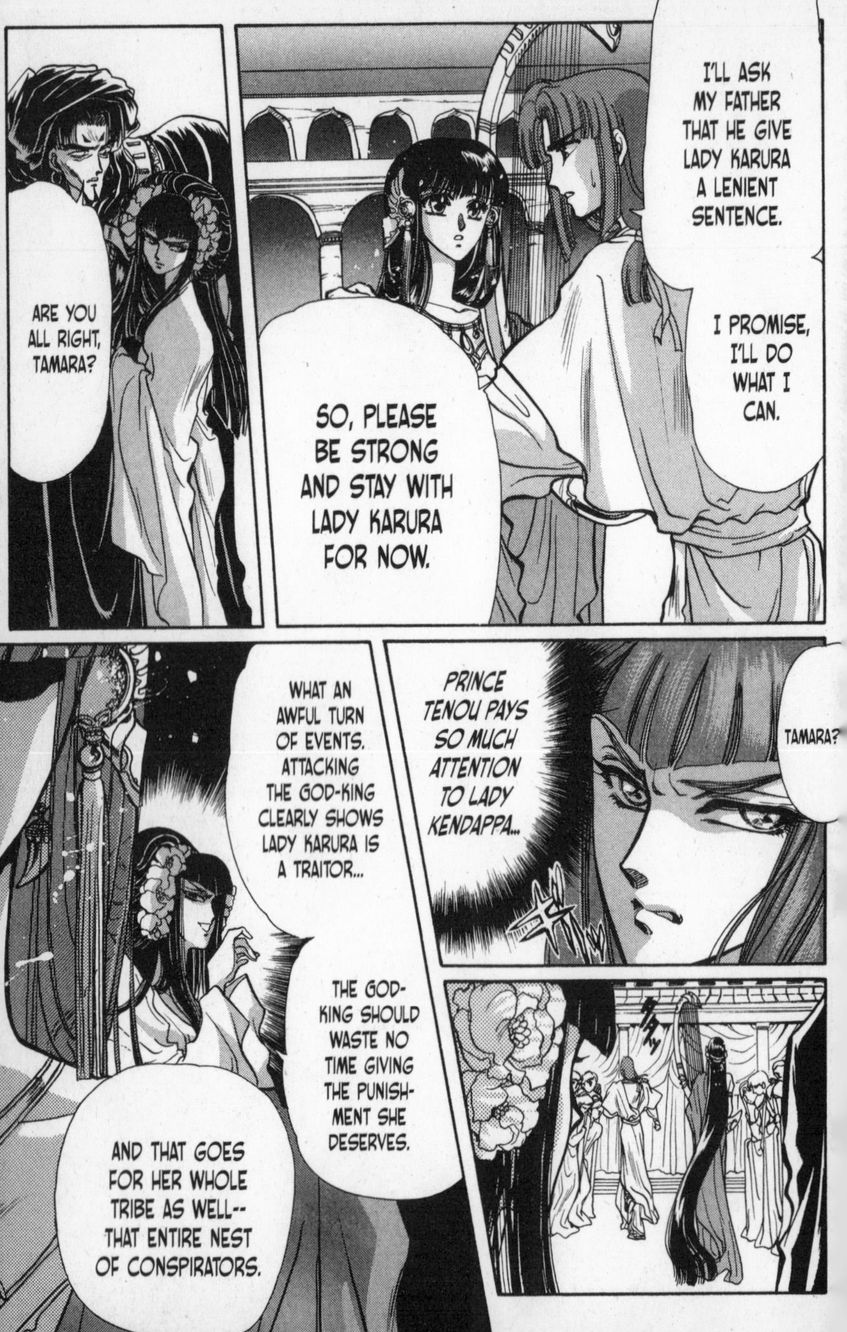
I'LL ASK MY FATHER THAT HE GIVE LADY KARURA A LENIENT SENTENCE.
I PROMISE, I'LL DO WHAT I CAN.
SO, PLEASE BE STRONG AND STAY WITH LADY KARURA FOR NOW.
ARE YOU ALL RIGHT, TAMARA?
TAMARA?
PRINCE TENOU PAYS SO MUCH ATTENTION TO LADY KENDAPPA...
WHAT AN AWFUL TURN OF EVENTS. ATTACKING THE GOD-KING CLEARLY SHOWS LADY KARURA IS A TRAITOR...
THE GOD-KING SHOULD WASTE NO TIME GIVING THE PUNISHMENT SHE DESERVES.
AND THAT GOES FOR HER WHOLE TRIBE AS WELL--THAT ENTIRE NEST OF CONSPIRATORS.

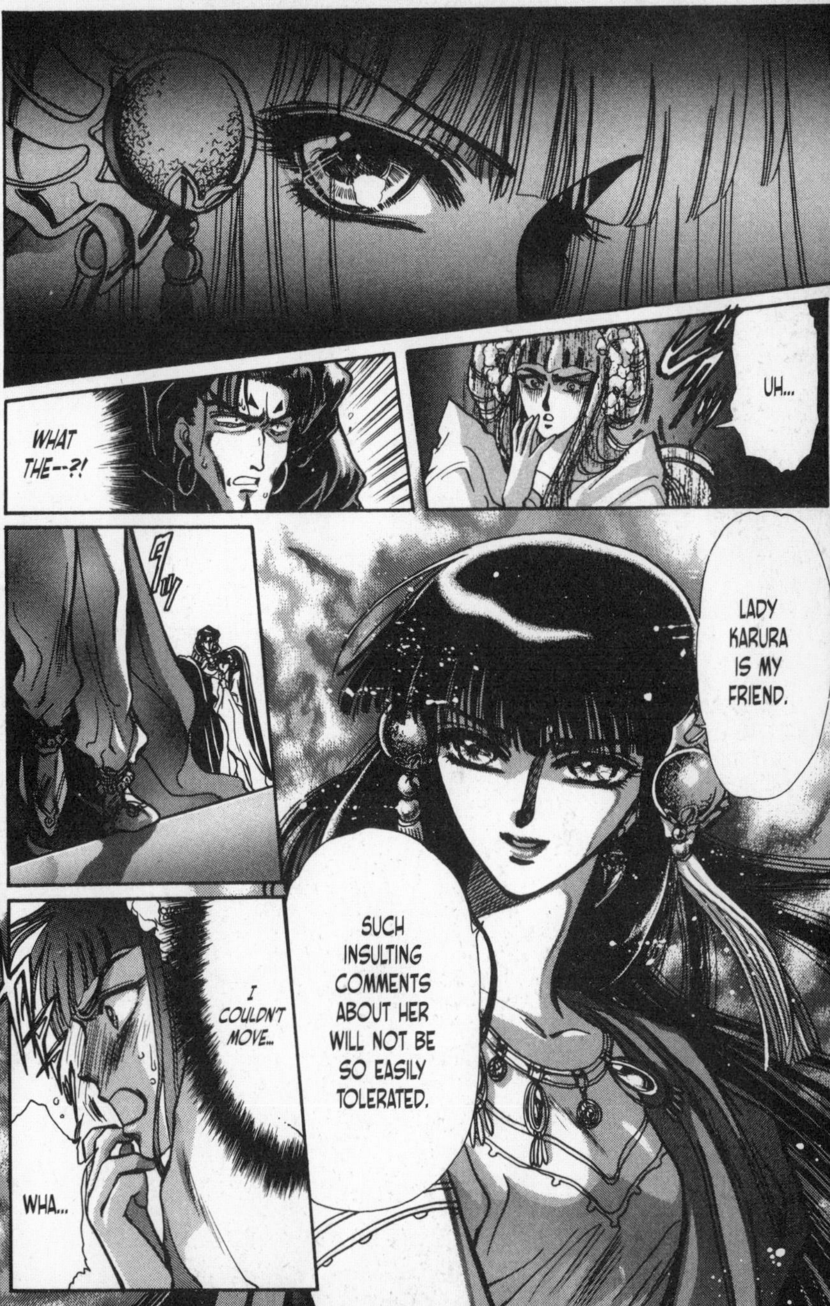
UH...
WHAT THE--?!
LADY KARURA IS MY FRIEND.
SUCH INSULTING COMMENTS ABOUT HER WILL NOT BE SO EASILY TOLERATED.
I COULDN'T MOVE...
WHA...

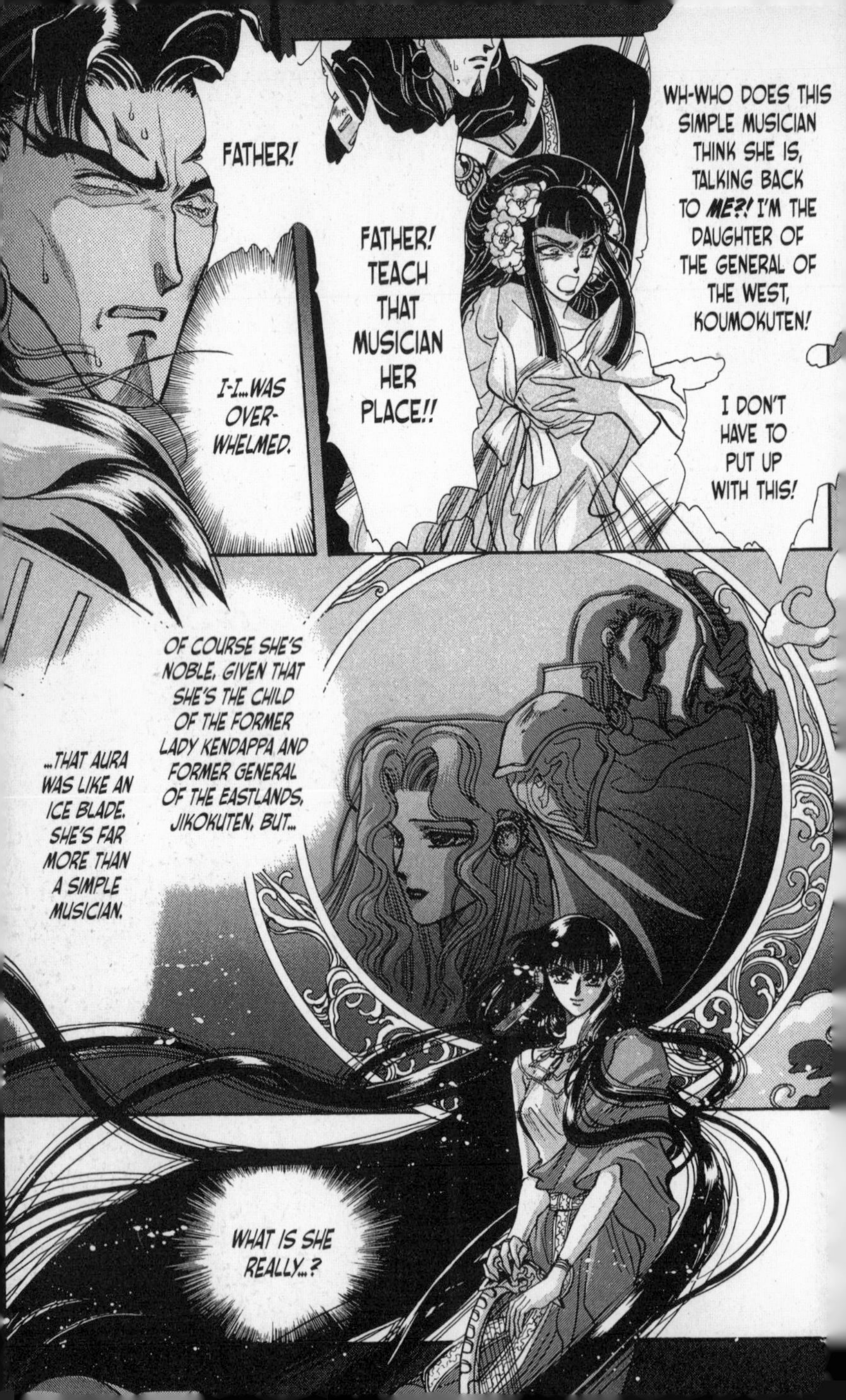
WH-WHO DOES THIS SIMPLE MUSICIAN THINK SHE IS, TALKING BACK TO ME?! I'M THE DAUGHTER OF THE GENERAL OF THE WEST, KOUMOKUTEN!
I DON'T HAVE TO PUT UP WITH THIS!
FATHER! TEACH THAT MUSICIAN HER PLACE!!
FATHER!
I-I...WAS OVERWHELMED.
OF COURSE SHE'S NOBLE, GIVEN THAT SHE'S THE CHILD OF THE FORMER LADY KENDAPPA AND FORMER GENERAL OF THE EASTLANDS, JIKOKUTEN, BUT...
...THAT AURA WAS LIKE AN ICE BLADE. SHE'S FAR MORE THAN A SIMPLE MUSICIAN.
WHAT IS SHE REALLY...?

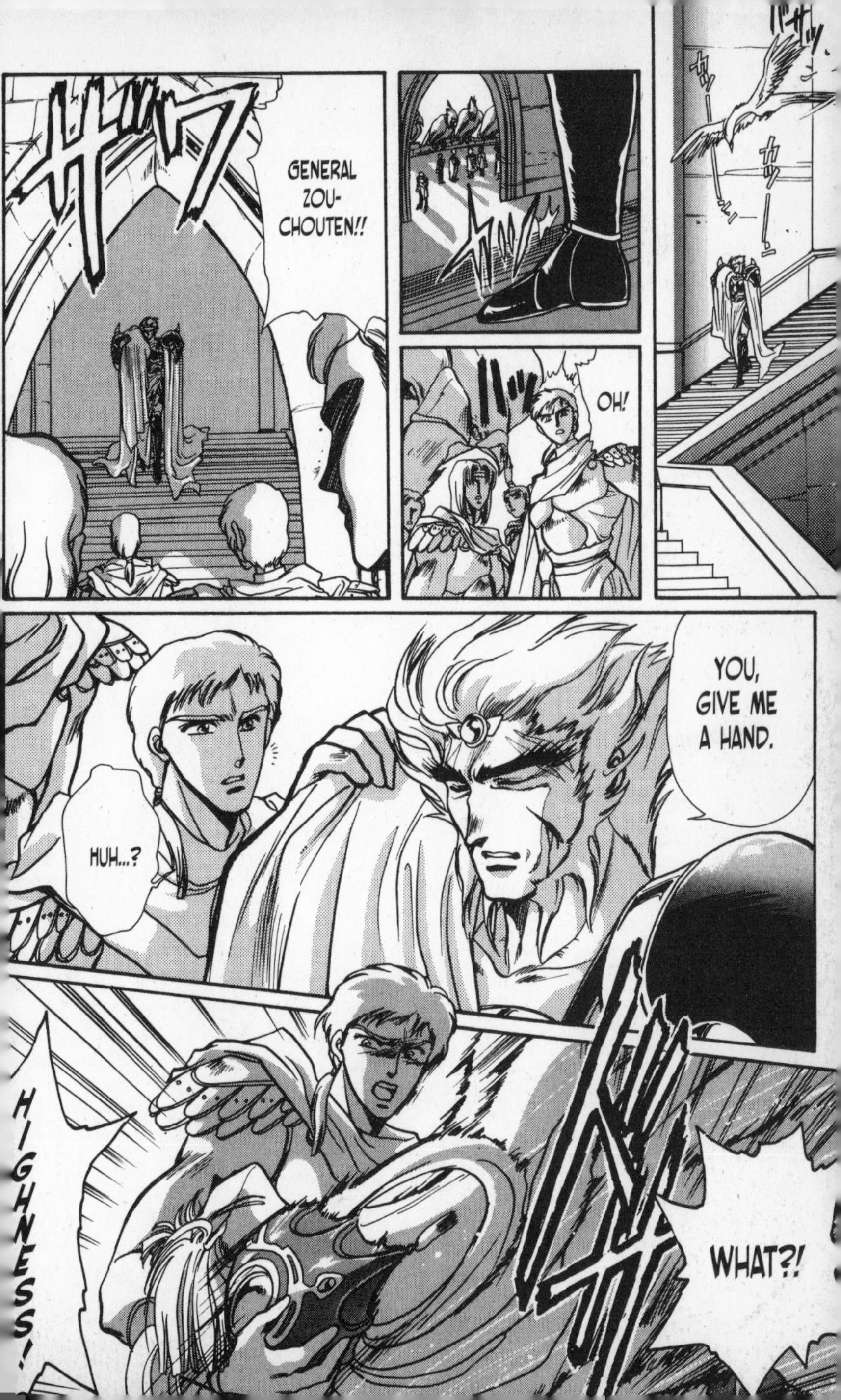
OH!
GENERAL ZOU-CHOUTEN!!
YOU, GIVE ME A HAND.
HUH...?
WHAT?!
HIGHNESS!

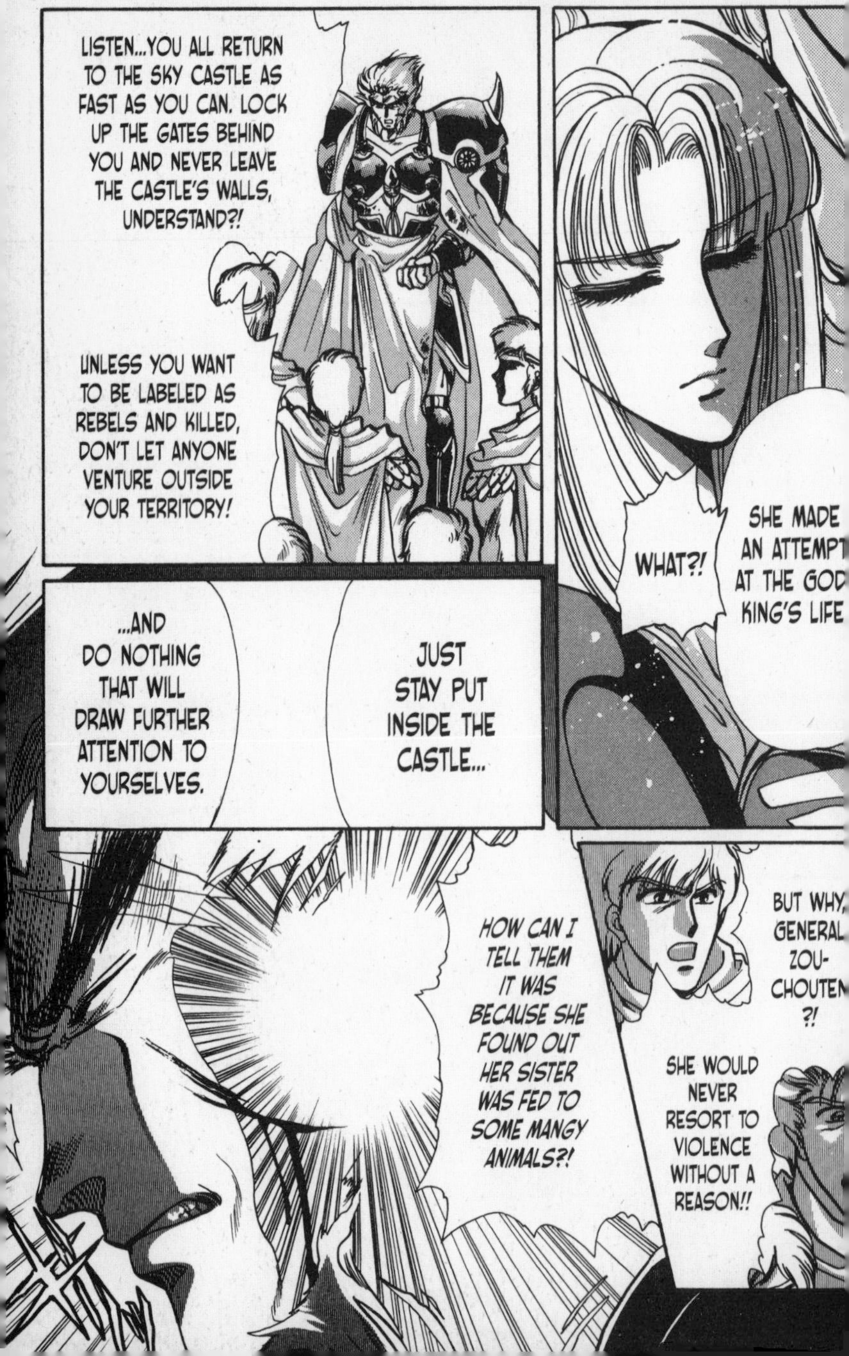

SHE MADE AN ATTEMPT AT THE GOD KING'S LIFE
WHAT?!
LISTEN...YOU ALL RETURN TO THE SKY CASTLE AS FAST AS YOU CAN. LOCK UP THE GATES BEHIND YOU AND NEVER LEAVE THE CASTLE'S WALLS, UNDERSTAND?!
UNLESS YOU WANT TO BE LABELED AS REBELS AND KILLED, DON'T LET ANYONE VENTURE OUTSIDE YOUR TERRITORY!
JUST STAY PUT INSIDE THE CASTLE...
...AND DO NOTHING THAT WILL DRAW FURTHER ATTENTION TO YOURSELVES.
BUT WHY, GENERAL ZOU-CHOUTEN ?!
SHE WOULD NEVER RESORT TO VIOLENCE WITHOUT A REASON!!
HOW CAN I TELL THEM IT WAS BECAUSE SHE FOUND OUT HER SISTER WAS FED TO SOME MANGY ANIMALS?!

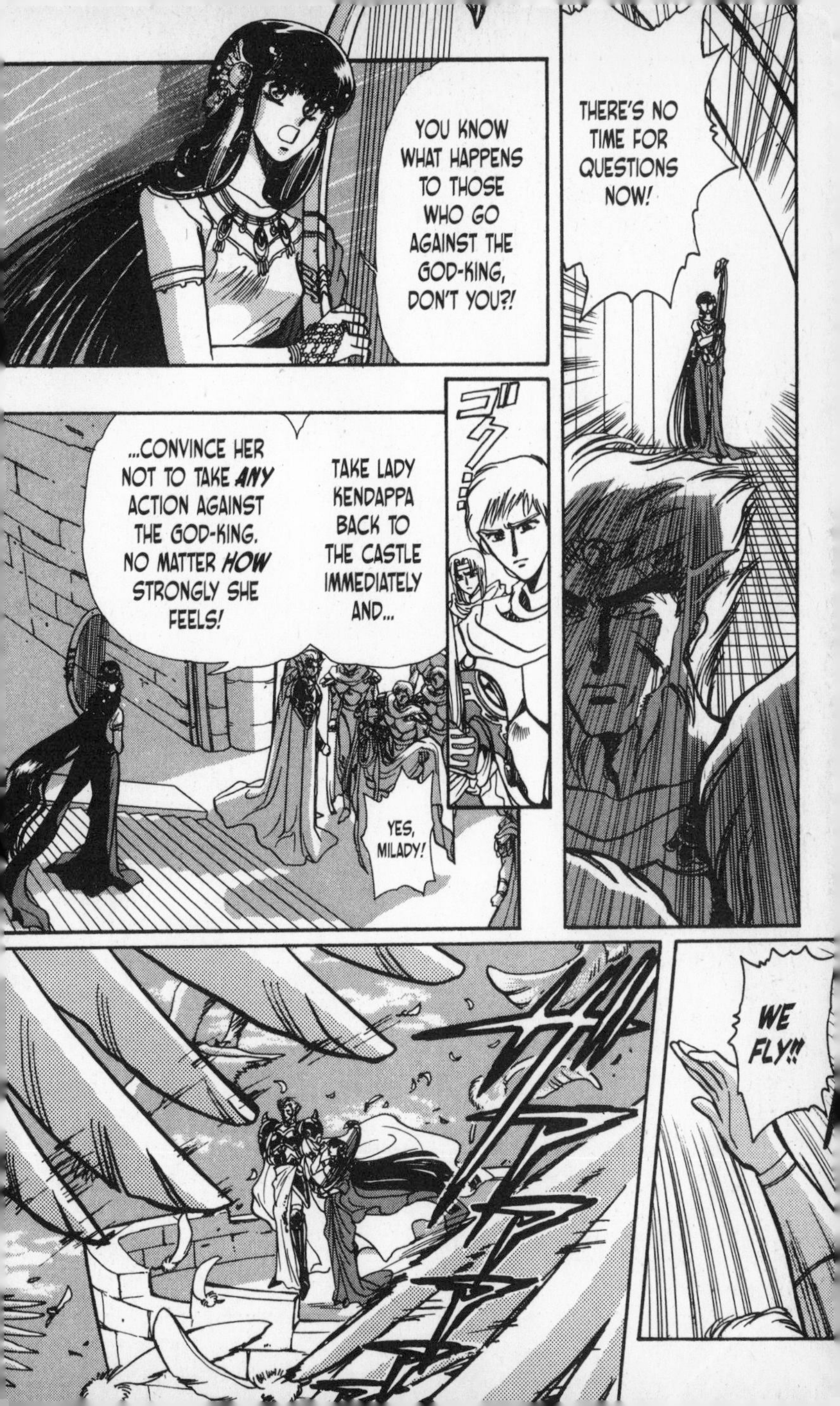
THERE'S NO TIME FOR QUESTIONS NOW!
YOU KNOW WHAT HAPPENS TO THOSE WHO GO AGAINST THE GOD-KING, DON'T YOU?!
TAKE LADY KENDAPPA BACK TO THE CASTLE IMMEDIATELY AND...
...CONVINCE HER NOT TO TAKE *ANY* ACTION AGAINST THE GOD-KING. NO MATTER *HOW* STRONGLY SHE FEELS!
YES, MILADY!
WE FLY!!

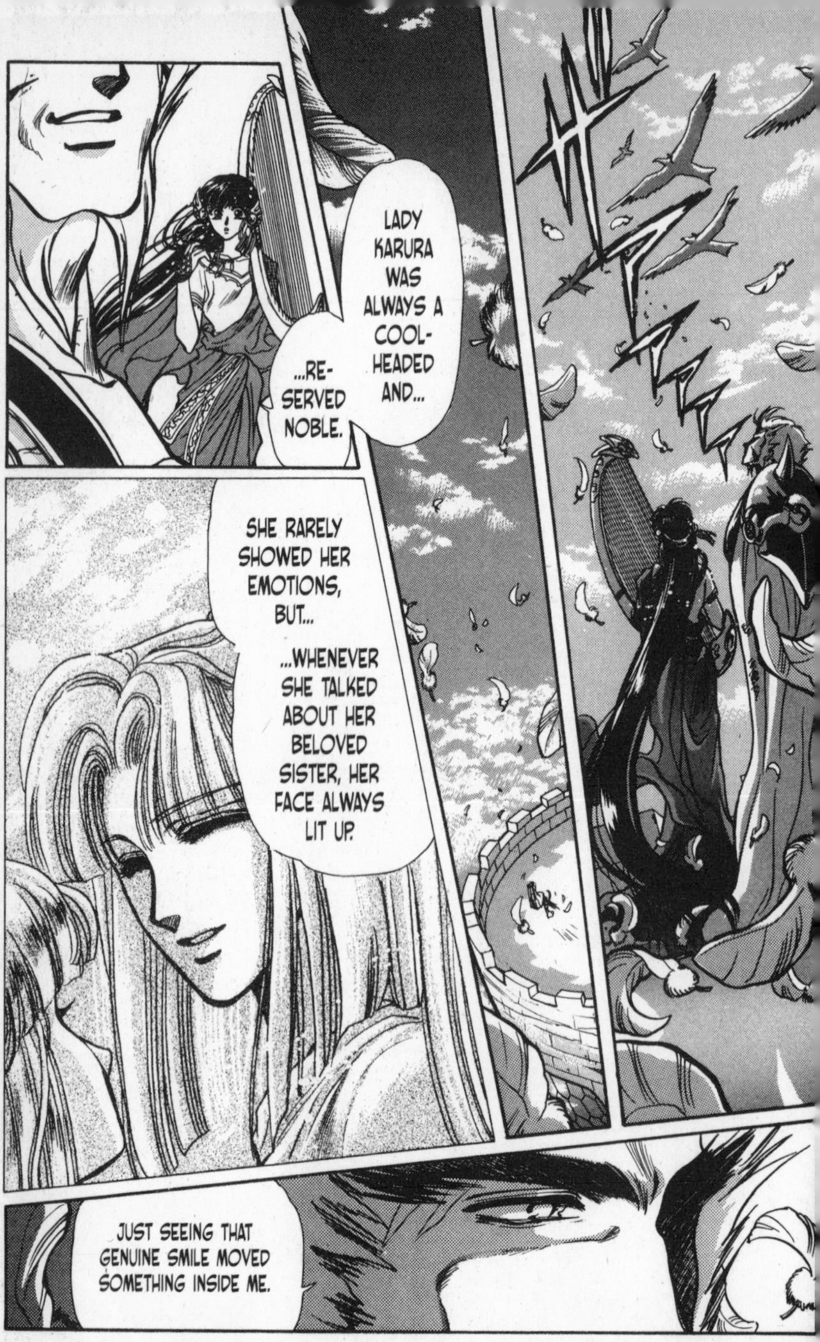
LADY KARURA WAS ALWAYS A COOL-HEADED AND...
...RE-SERVED NOBLE.
SHE RARELY SHOWED HER EMOTIONS, BUT...
...WHENEVER SHE TALKED ABOUT HER BELOVED SISTER, HER FACE ALWAYS LIT UP.
JUST SEEING THAT GENUINE SMILE MOVED SOMETHING INSIDE ME.

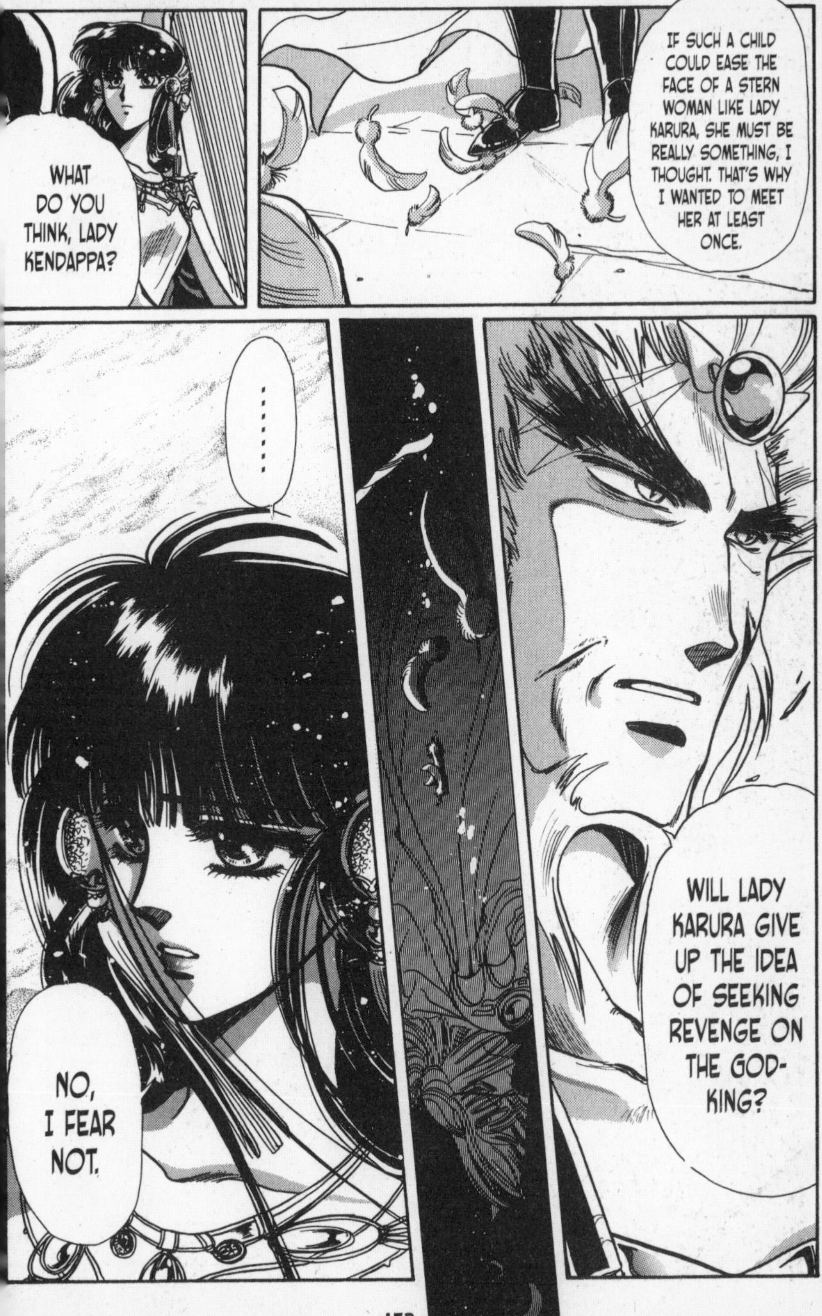
IF SUCH A CHILD COULD EASE THE FACE OF A STERN WOMAN LIKE LADY KARURA, SHE MUST BE REALLY SOMETHING, I THOUGHT. THAT'S WHY I WANTED TO MEET HER AT LEAST ONCE.
WHAT DO YOU THINK, LADY KENDAPPA?
WILL LADY KARURA GIVE UP THE IDEA OF SEEKING REVENGE ON THE GOD-KING?
......
NO, I FEAR NOT.

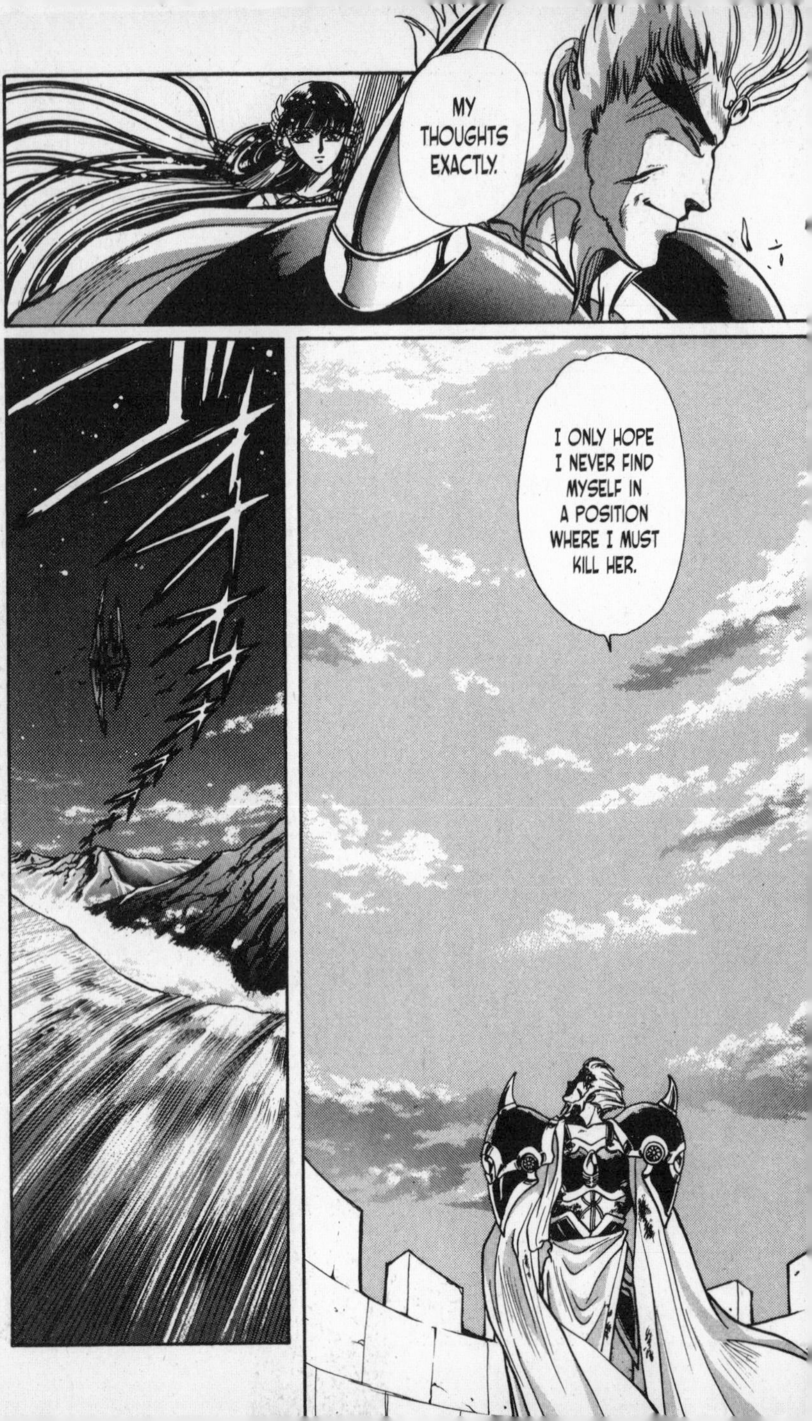
MY THOUGHTS EXACTLY.
I ONLY HOPE I NEVER FIND MYSELF IN A POSITION WHERE I MUST KILL HER.

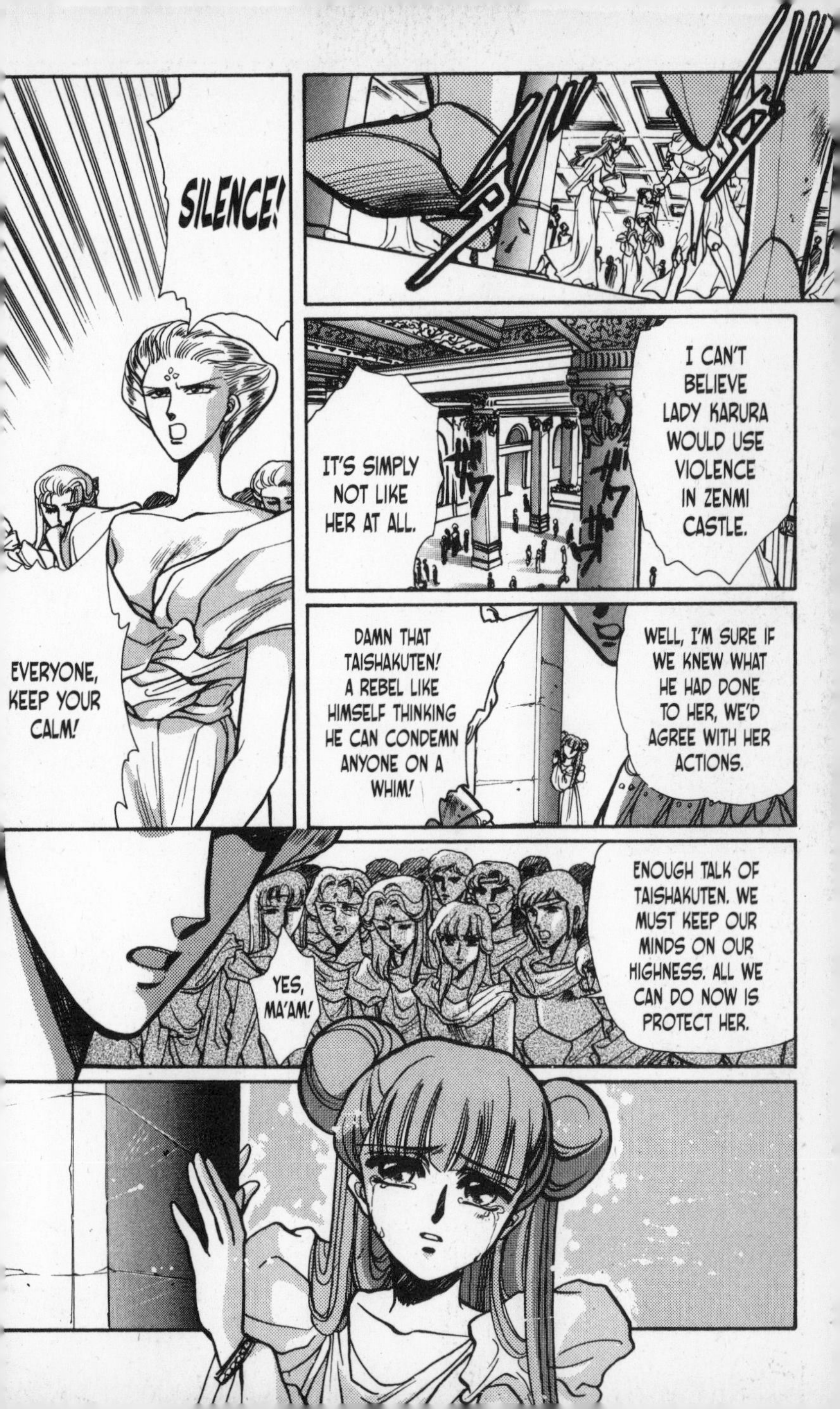
I CAN'T BELIEVE LADY KARURA WOULD USE VIOLENCE IN ZENMI CASTLE.
IT'S SIMPLY NOT LIKE HER AT ALL.
WELL, I'M SURE IF WE KNEW WHAT HE HAD DONE TO HER, WE'D AGREE WITH HER ACTIONS.
DAMN THAT TAISHAKUTEN! A REBEL LIKE HIMSELF THINKING HE CAN CONDEMN ANYONE ON A WHIM!
SILENCE!
EVERYONE, KEEP YOUR CALM!
ENOUGH TALK OF TAISHAKUTEN. WE MUST KEEP OUR MINDS ON OUR HIGHNESS. ALL WE CAN DO NOW IS PROTECT HER.
YES, MA'AM!

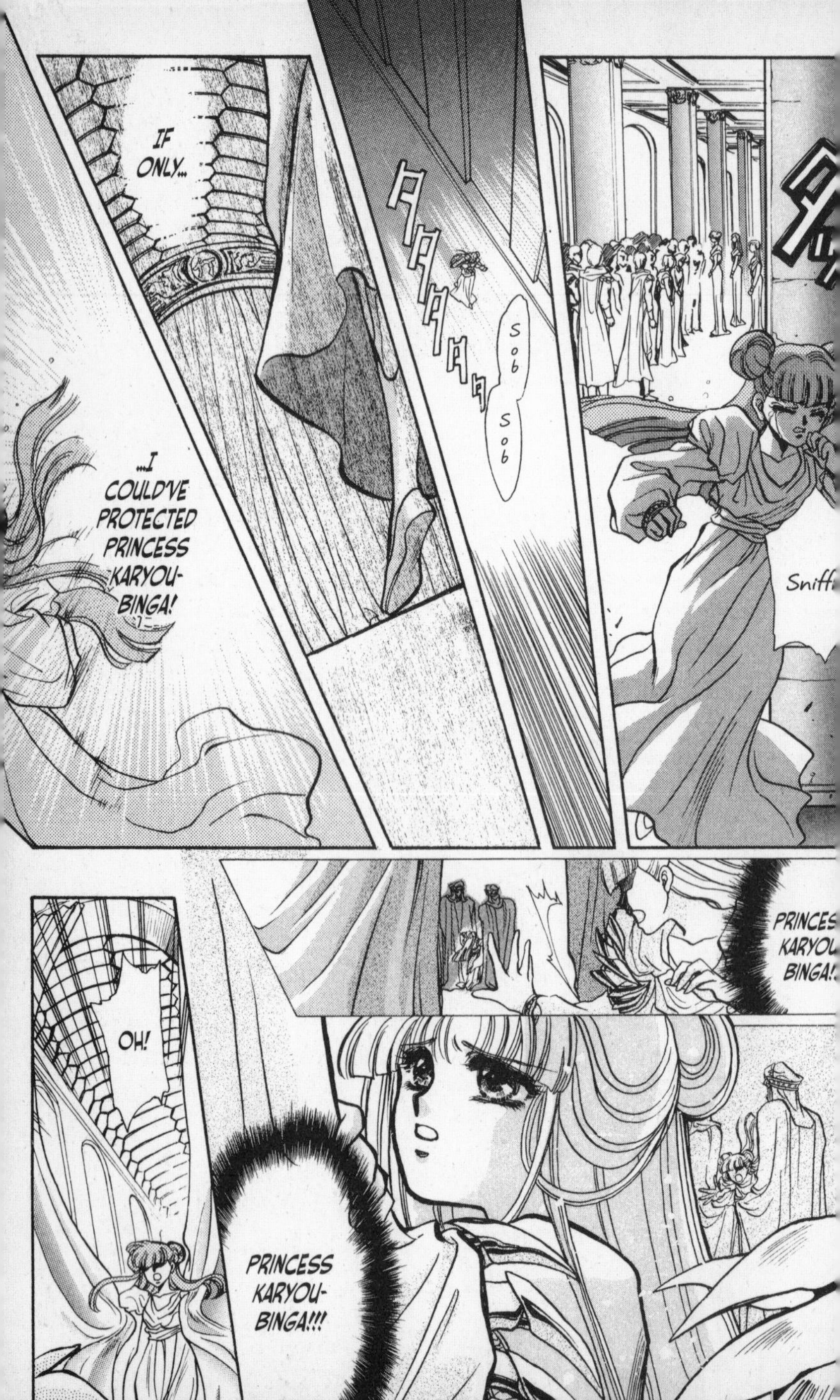

Sniff
Sob sob
IF ONLY...
...I COULD'VE PROTECTED PRINCESS KARYOU-BINGA!
PRINCES KARYOU-BINGA!
PRINCESS KARYOU-BINGA!!!
OH!

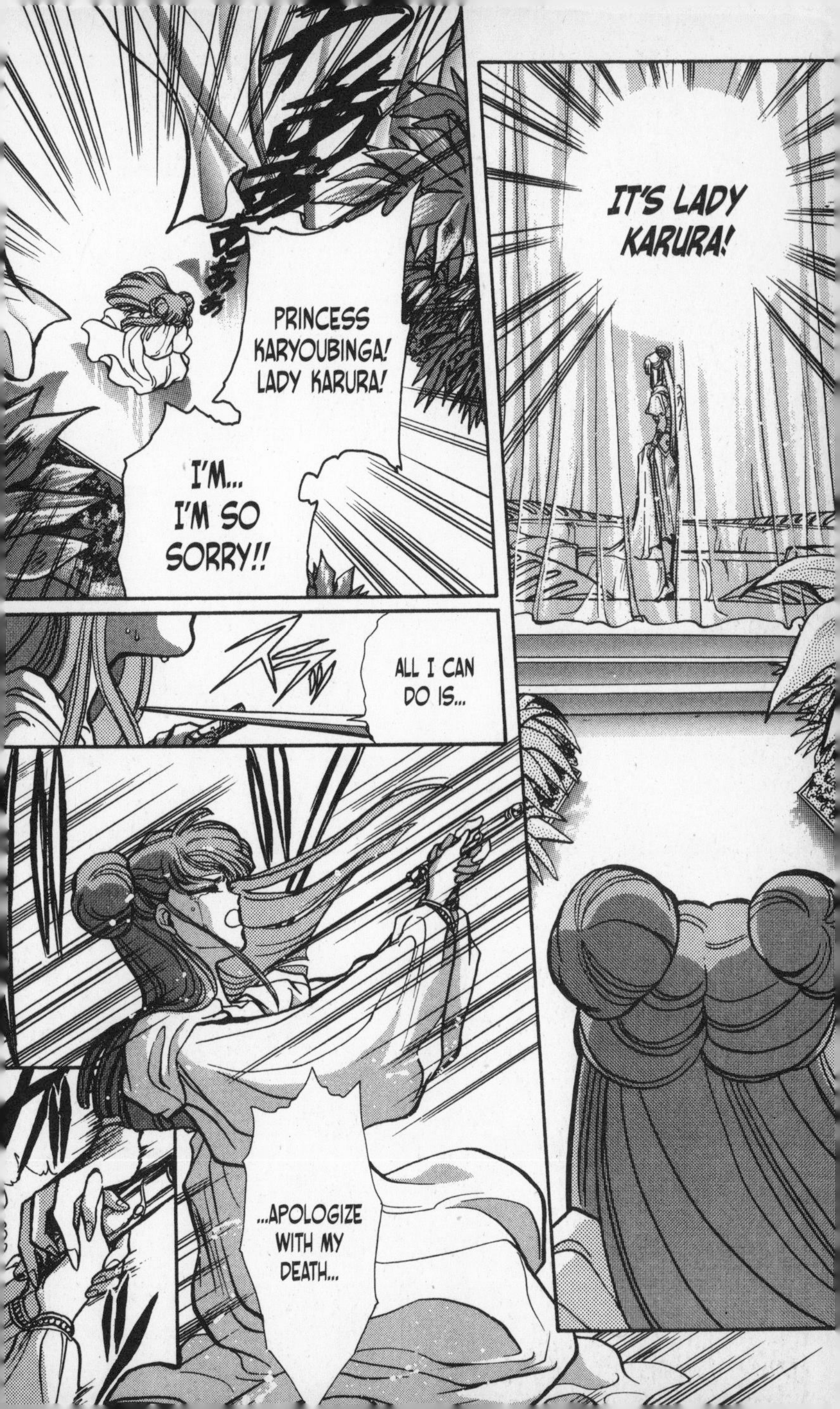
IT'S LADY KARURA!
PRINCESS KARYOUBINGA! LADY KARURA!
I'M... I'M SO SORRY!!
ALL I CAN DO IS...
...APOLOGIZE WITH MY DEATH...

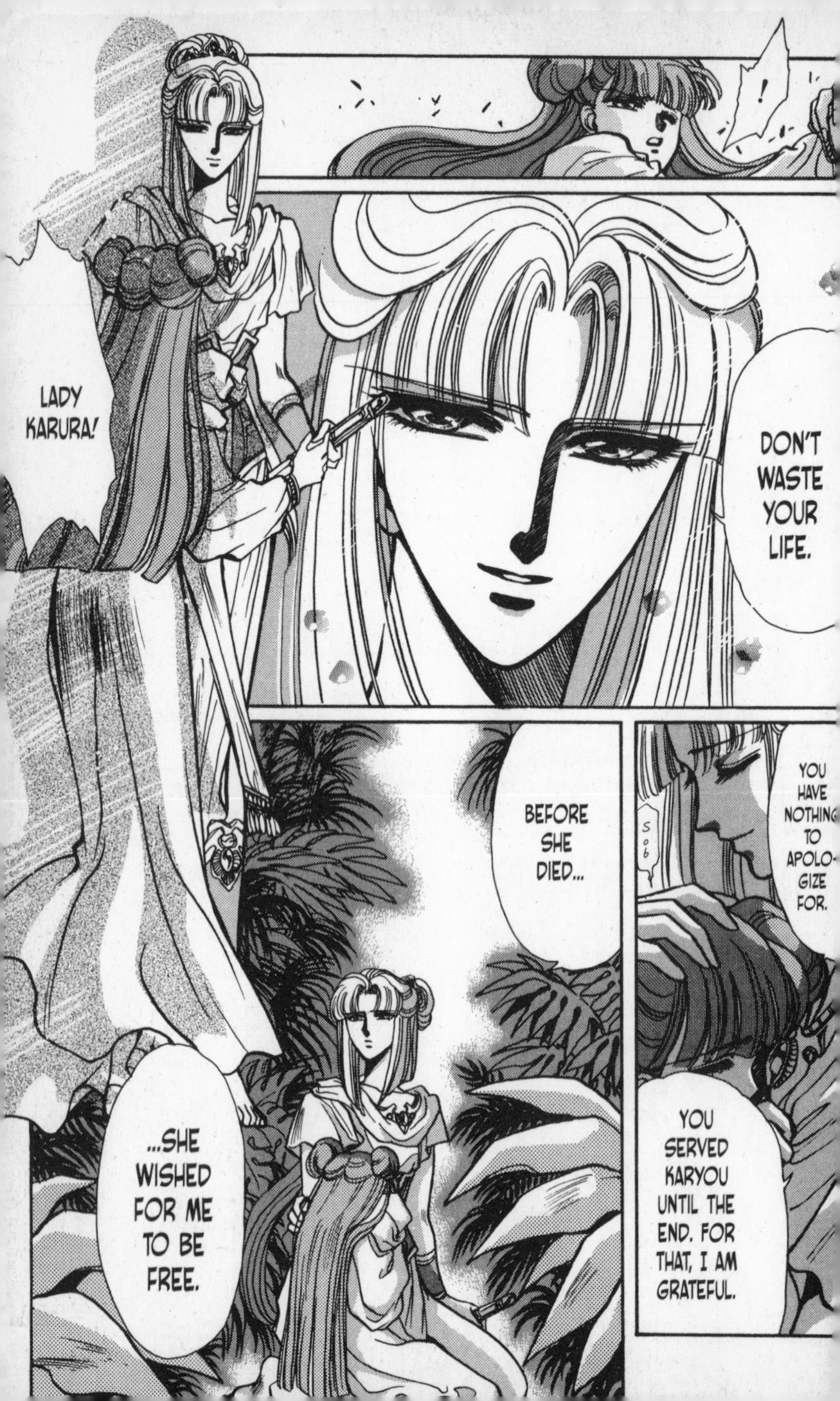
!
DON'T WASTE YOUR LIFE.
LADY KARURA!
Sob
YOU HAVE NOTHING TO APOLOGIZE FOR.
YOU SERVED KARYOU UNTIL THE END. FOR THAT, I AM GRATEFUL.
BEFORE SHE DIED...
...SHE WISHED FOR ME TO BE FREE.

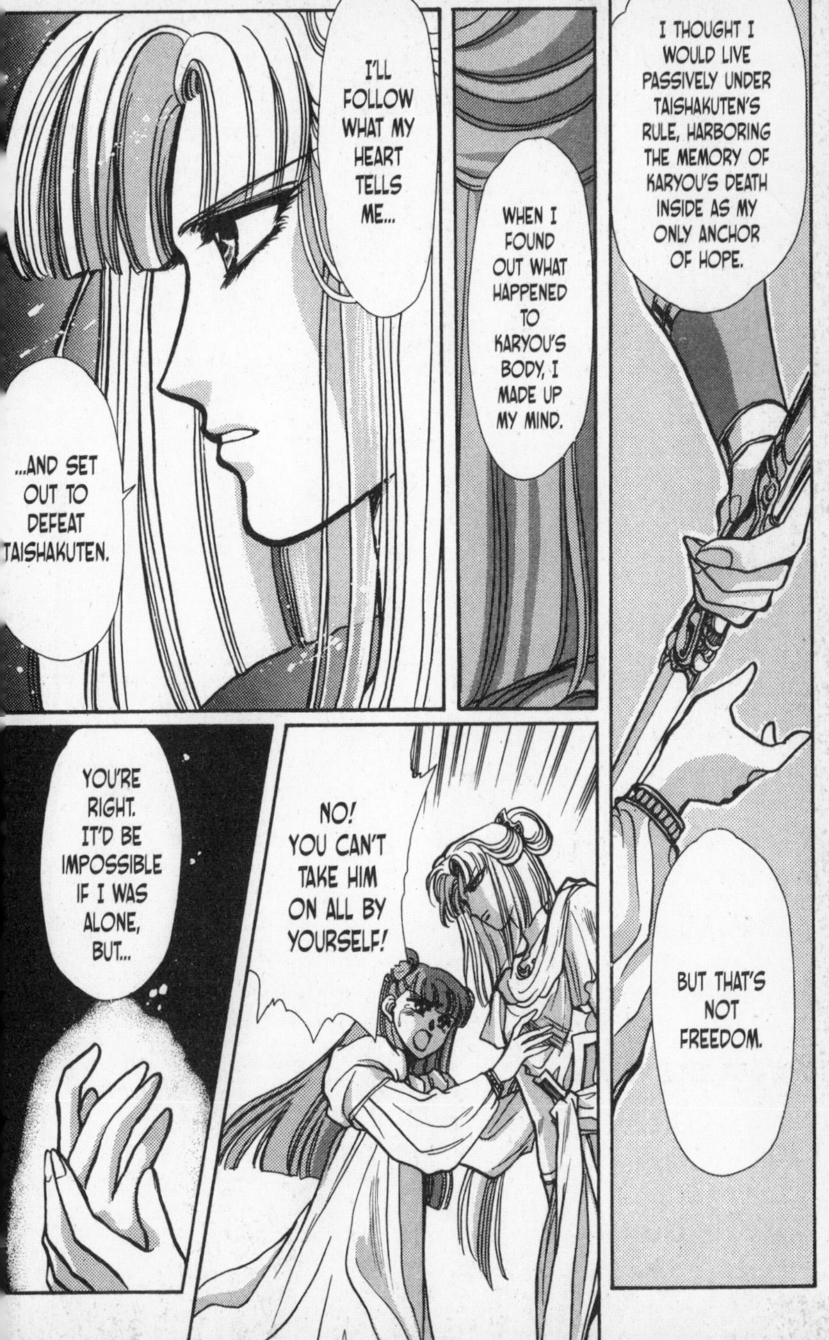
I THOUGHT I WOULD LIVE PASSIVELY UNDER TAISHAKUTEN'S RULE, HARBORING THE MEMORY OF KARYOU'S DEATH INSIDE AS MY ONLY ANCHOR OF HOPE.
BUT THAT'S NOT FREEDOM.
WHEN I FOUND OUT WHAT HAPPENED TO KARYOU'S BODY, I MADE UP MY MIND.
I'LL FOLLOW WHAT MY HEART TELLS ME...
...AND SET OUT TO DEFEAT TAISHAKUTEN.
NO! YOU CAN'T TAKE HIM ON ALL BY YOURSELF!
YOU'RE RIGHT. IT'D BE IMPOSSIBLE IF I WAS ALONE, BUT...

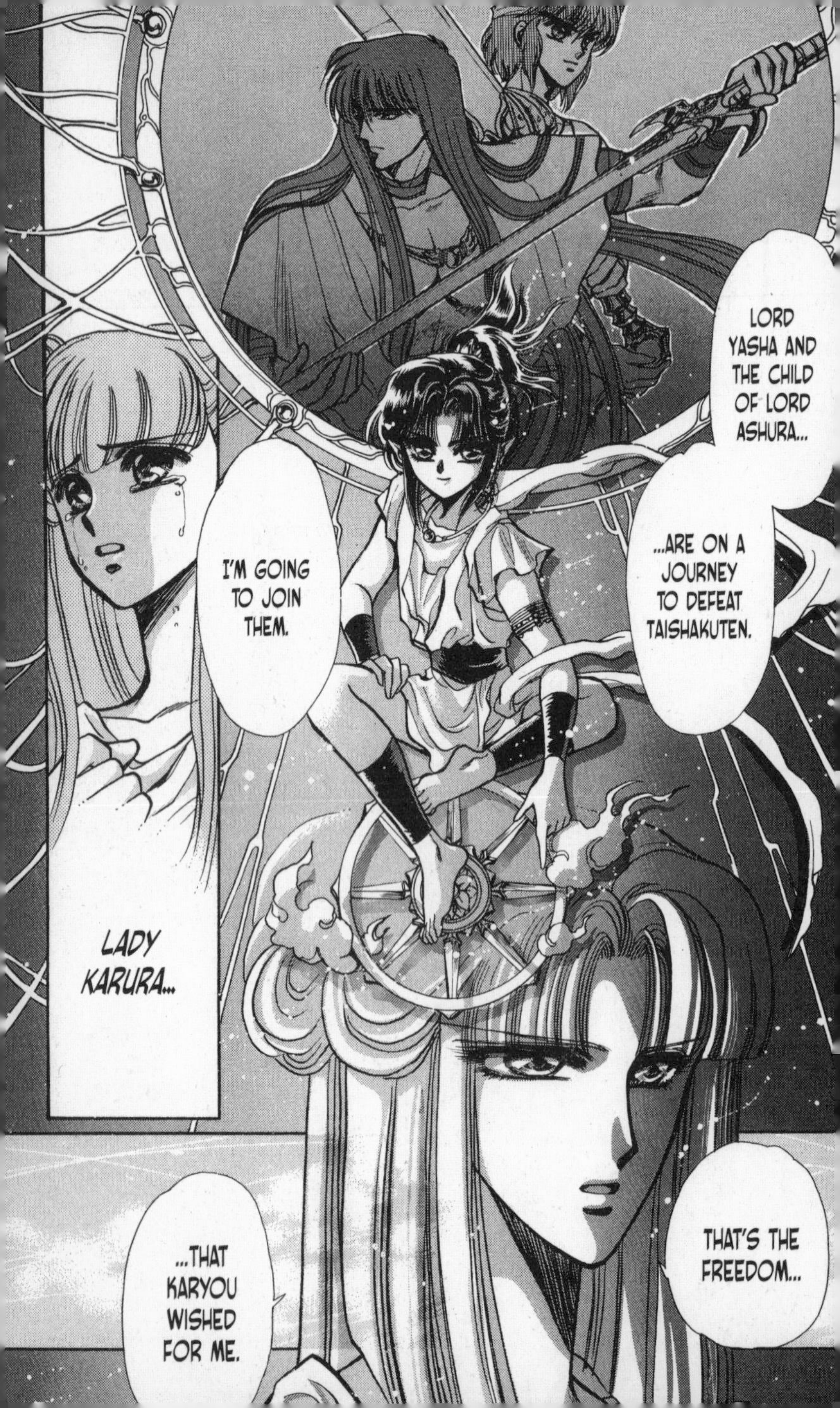
LORD YASHA AND THE CHILD OF LORD ASHURA...
...ARE ON A JOURNEY TO DEFEAT TAISHAKUTEN.
I'M GOING TO JOIN THEM.
LADY KARURA...
THAT'S THE FREEDOM...
...THAT KARYOU WISHED FOR ME.

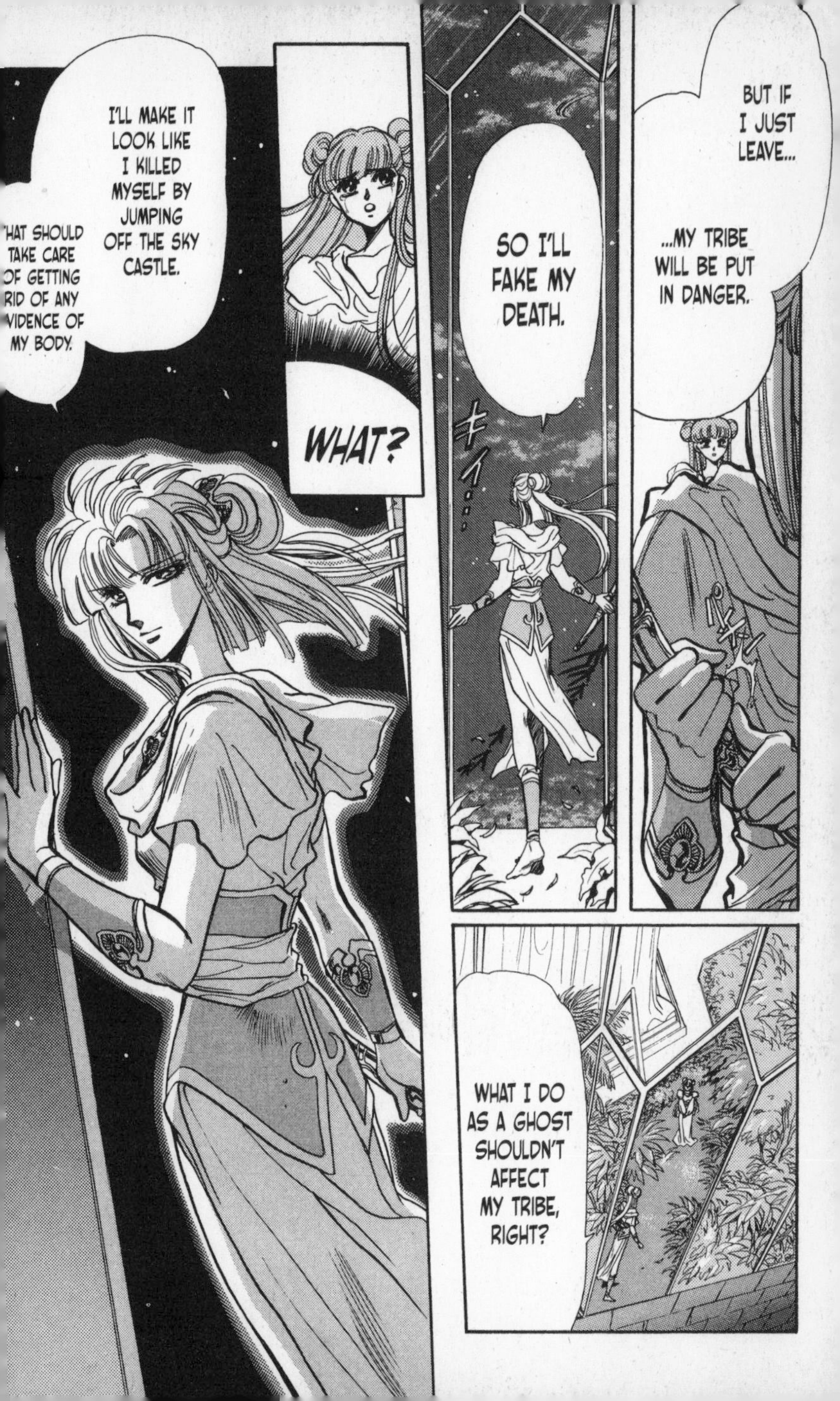
BUT IF I JUST LEAVE...
...MY TRIBE WILL BE PUT IN DANGER.
SO I'LL FAKE MY DEATH.
WHAT I DO AS A GHOST SHOULDN'T AFFECT MY TRIBE, RIGHT?
I'LL MAKE IT LOOK LIKE I KILLED MYSELF BY JUMPING OFF THE SKY CASTLE.
HAT SHOULD TAKE CARE OF GETTING RID OF ANY VIDENCE OF MY BODY.
WHAT?

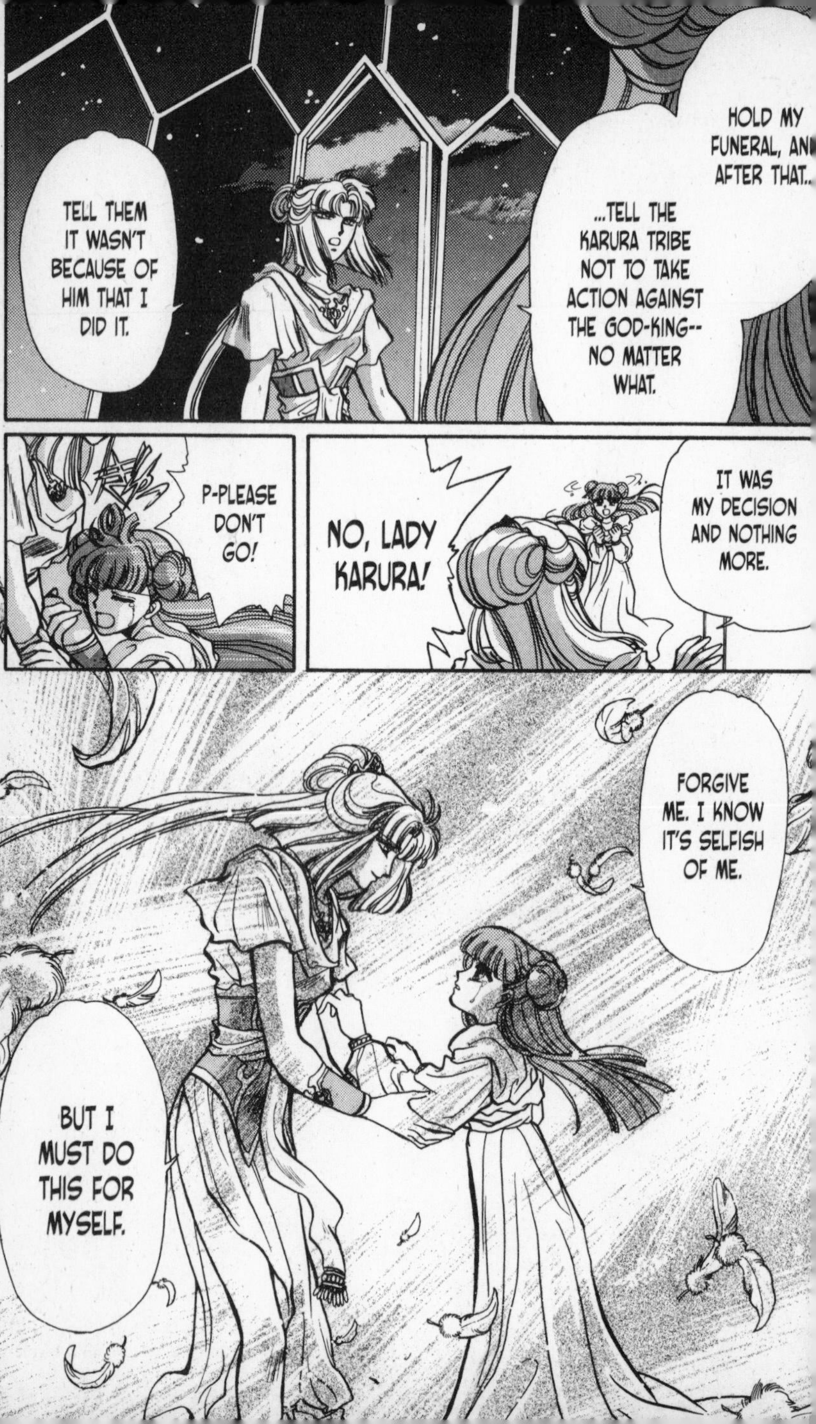
HOLD MY FUNERAL, AN AFTER THAT..
...TELL THE KARURA TRIBE NOT TO TAKE ACTION AGAINST THE GOD-KING-- NO MATTER WHAT.
TELL THEM IT WASN'T BECAUSE OF HIM THAT I DID IT.
IT WAS MY DECISION AND NOTHING MORE.
NO, LADY KARURA!
P-PLEASE DON'T GO!
FORGIVE ME. I KNOW IT'S SELFISH OF ME.
BUT I MUST DO THIS FOR MYSELF.

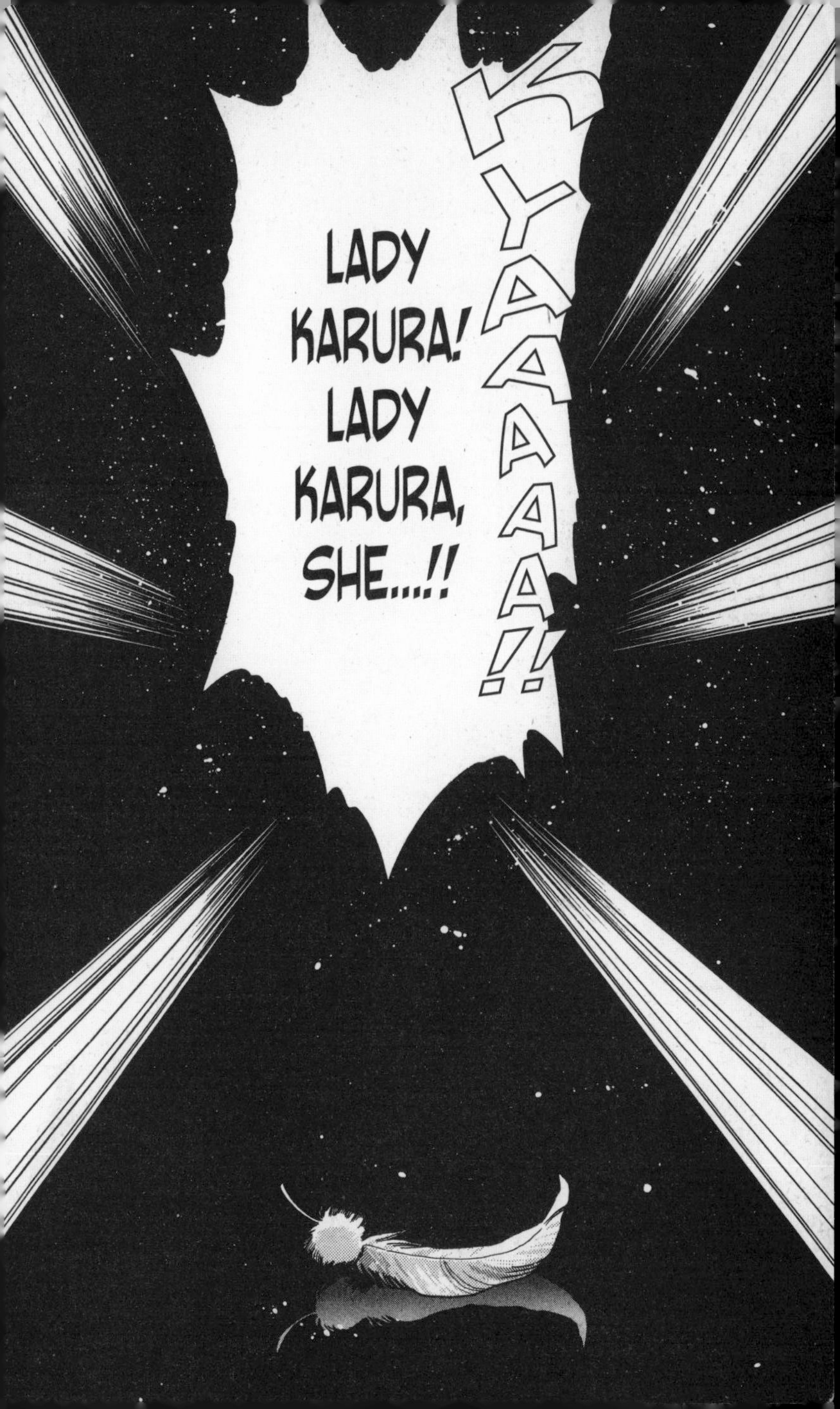
KYAAAAA!!
LADY KARURA! LADY KARURA, SHE...!!

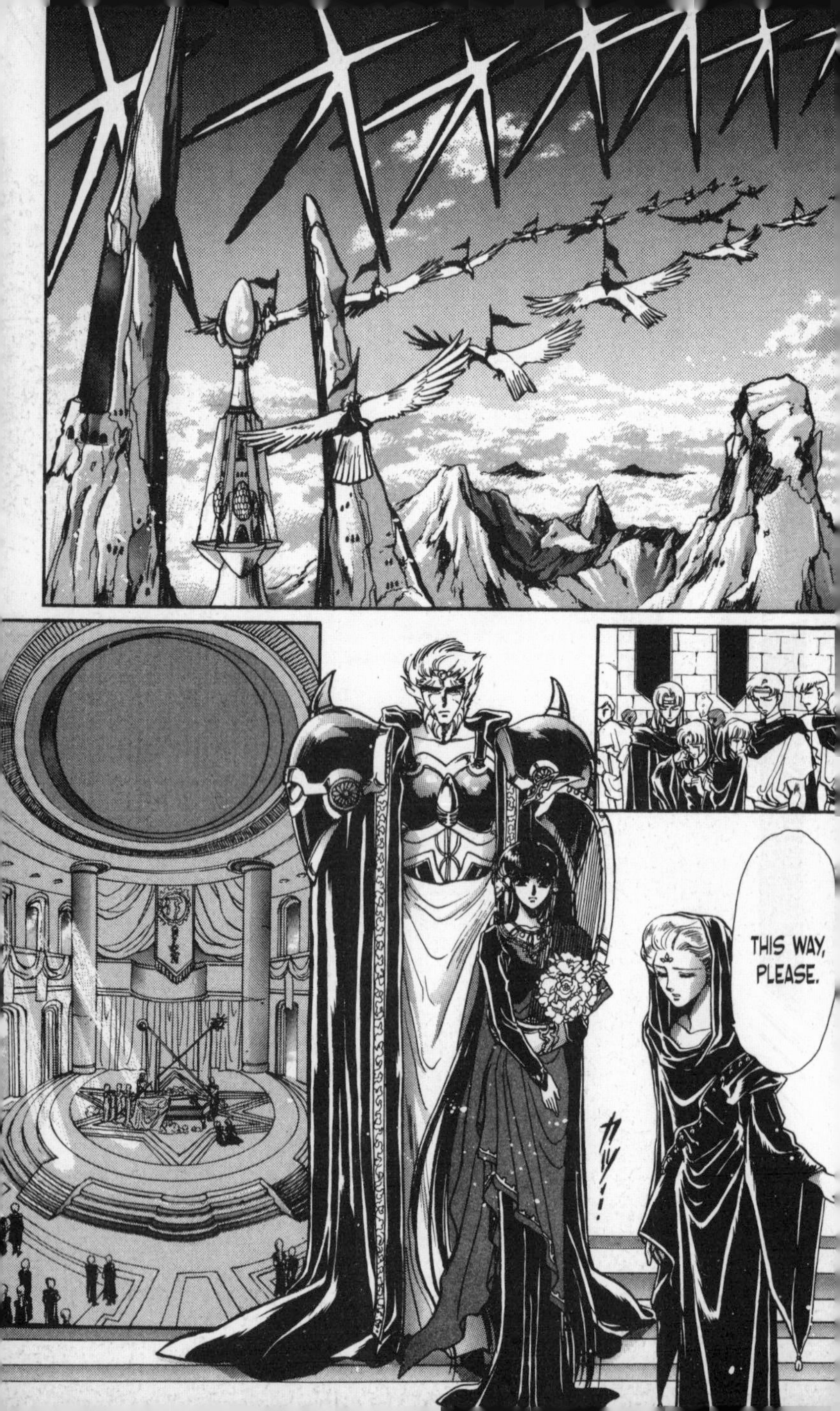
THIS WAY, PLEASE.
カッ!!

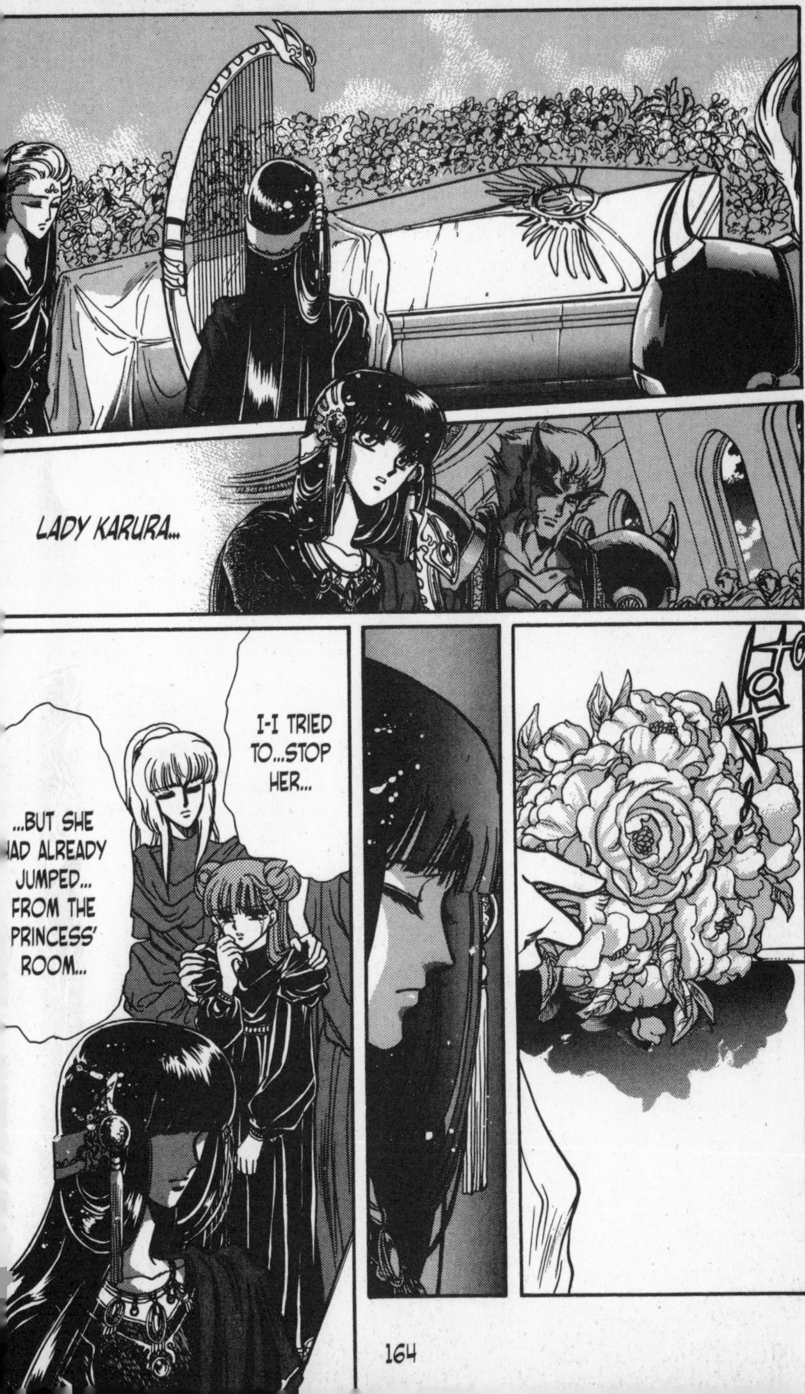
LADY KARURA...
I-I TRIED TO...STOP HER...
...BUT SHE HAD ALREADY JUMPED... FROM THE PRINCESS' ROOM...

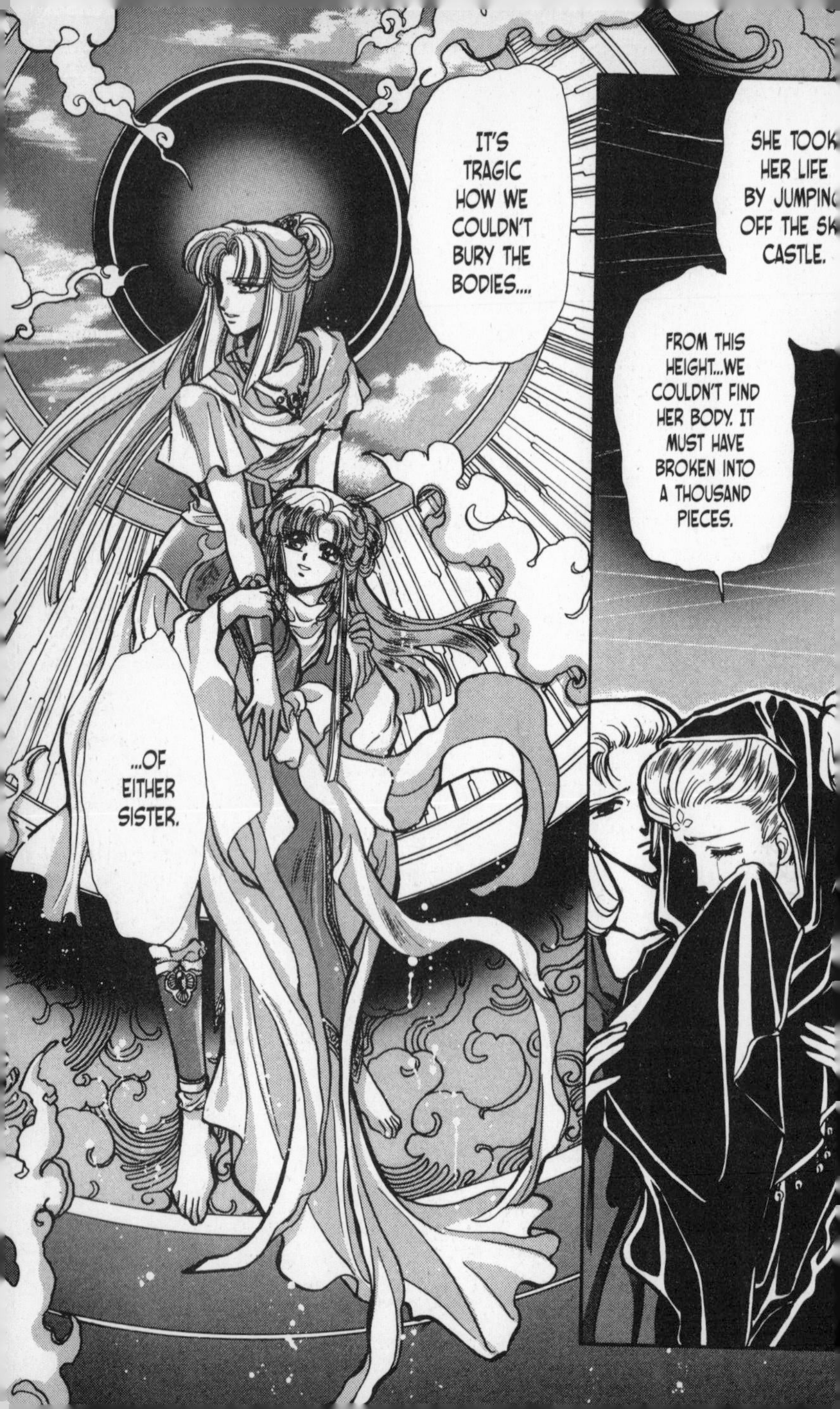
SHE TOOK HER LIFE BY JUMPIN OFF THE SK CASTLE.
FROM THIS HEIGHT...WE COULDN'T FIND HER BODY. IT MUST HAVE BROKEN INTO A THOUSAND PIECES.
IT'S TRAGIC HOW WE COULDN'T BURY THE BODIES....
...OF EITHER SISTER.

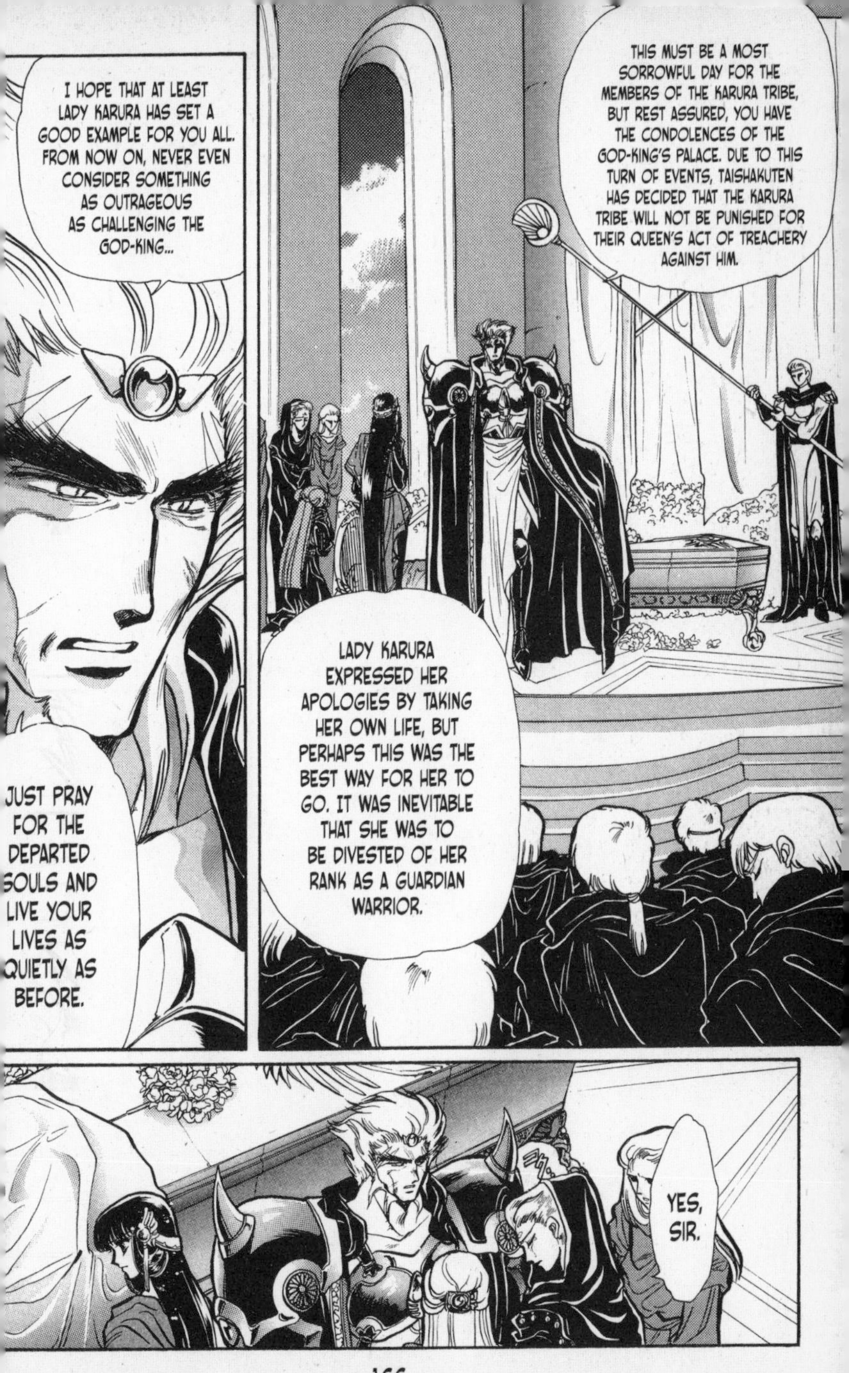
THIS MUST BE A MOST SORROWFUL DAY FOR THE MEMBERS OF THE KARURA TRIBE, BUT REST ASSURED, YOU HAVE THE CONDOLENCES OF THE GOD-KING'S PALACE. DUE TO THIS TURN OF EVENTS, TAISHAKUTEN HAS DECIDED THAT THE KARURA TRIBE WILL NOT BE PUNISHED FOR THEIR QUEEN'S ACT OF TREACHERY AGAINST HIM.
LADY KARURA EXPRESSED HER APOLOGIES BY TAKING HER OWN LIFE, BUT PERHAPS THIS WAS THE BEST WAY FOR HER TO GO. IT WAS INEVITABLE THAT SHE WAS TO BE DIVESTED OF HER RANK AS A GUARDIAN WARRIOR.
I HOPE THAT AT LEAST LADY KARURA HAS SET A GOOD EXAMPLE FOR YOU ALL. FROM NOW ON, NEVER EVEN CONSIDER SOMETHING AS OUTRAGEOUS AS CHALLENGING THE GOD-KING...
JUST PRAY FOR THE DEPARTED SOULS AND LIVE YOUR LIVES AS QUIETLY AS BEFORE.
YES, SIR.

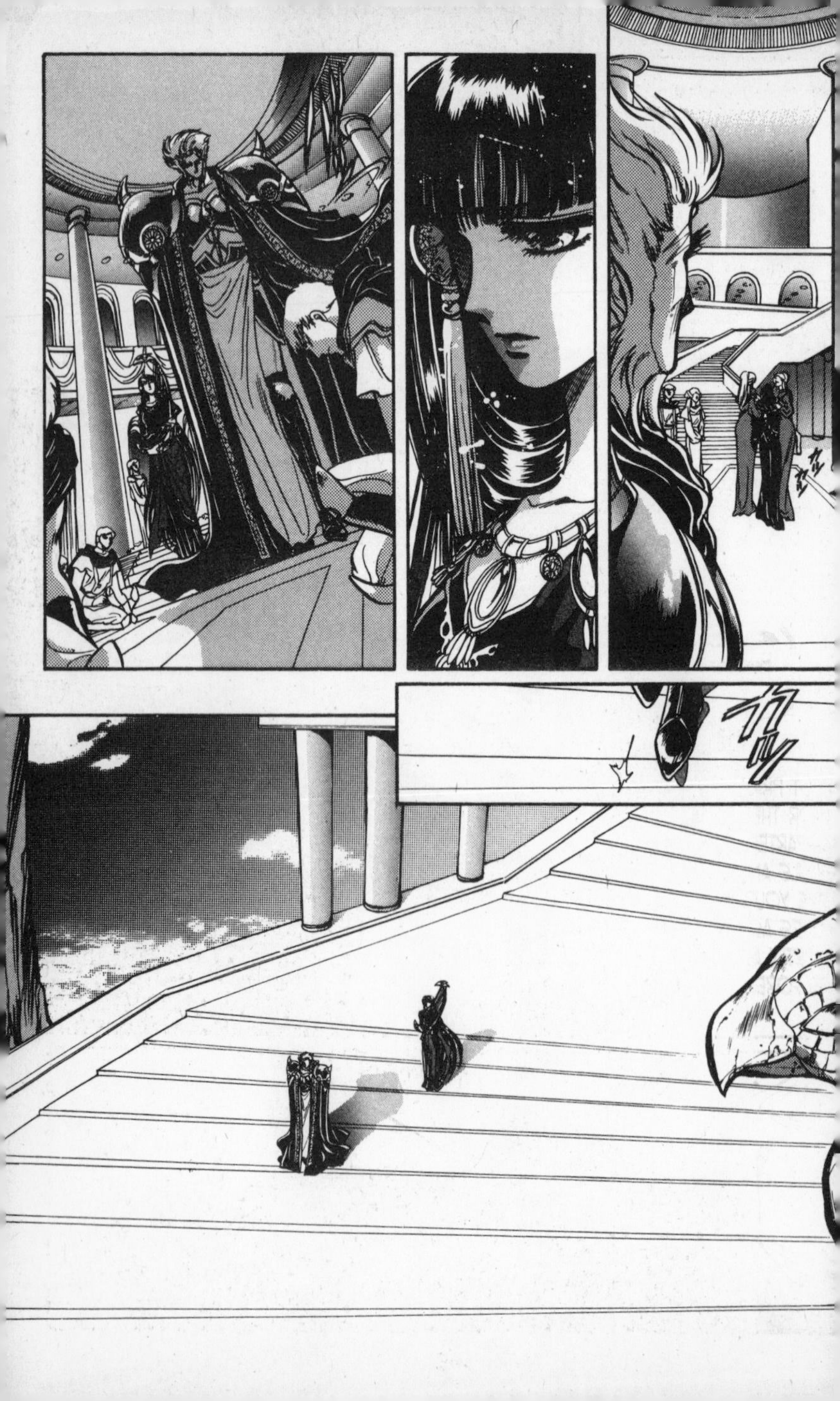
カツ
コツ
カッ

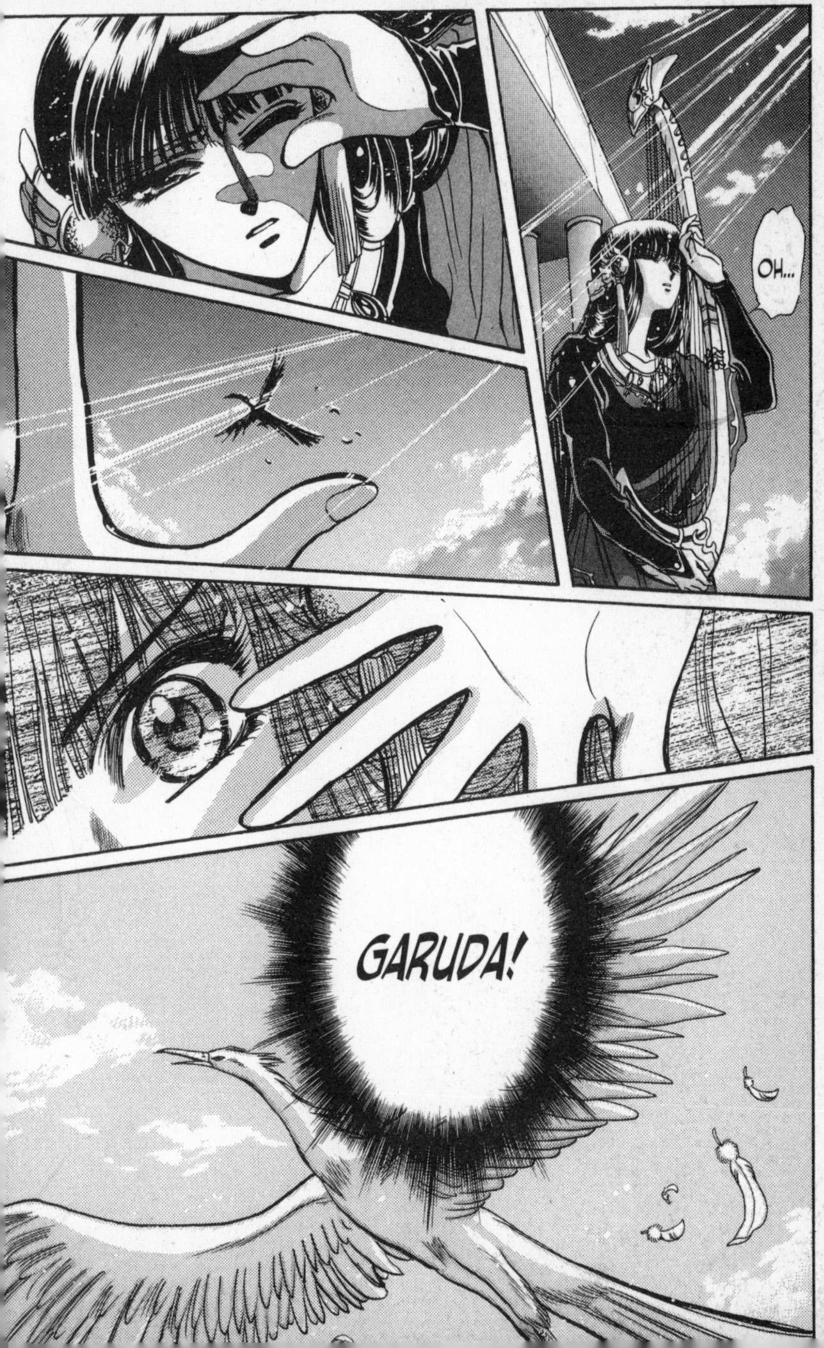

OH...
GARUDA!

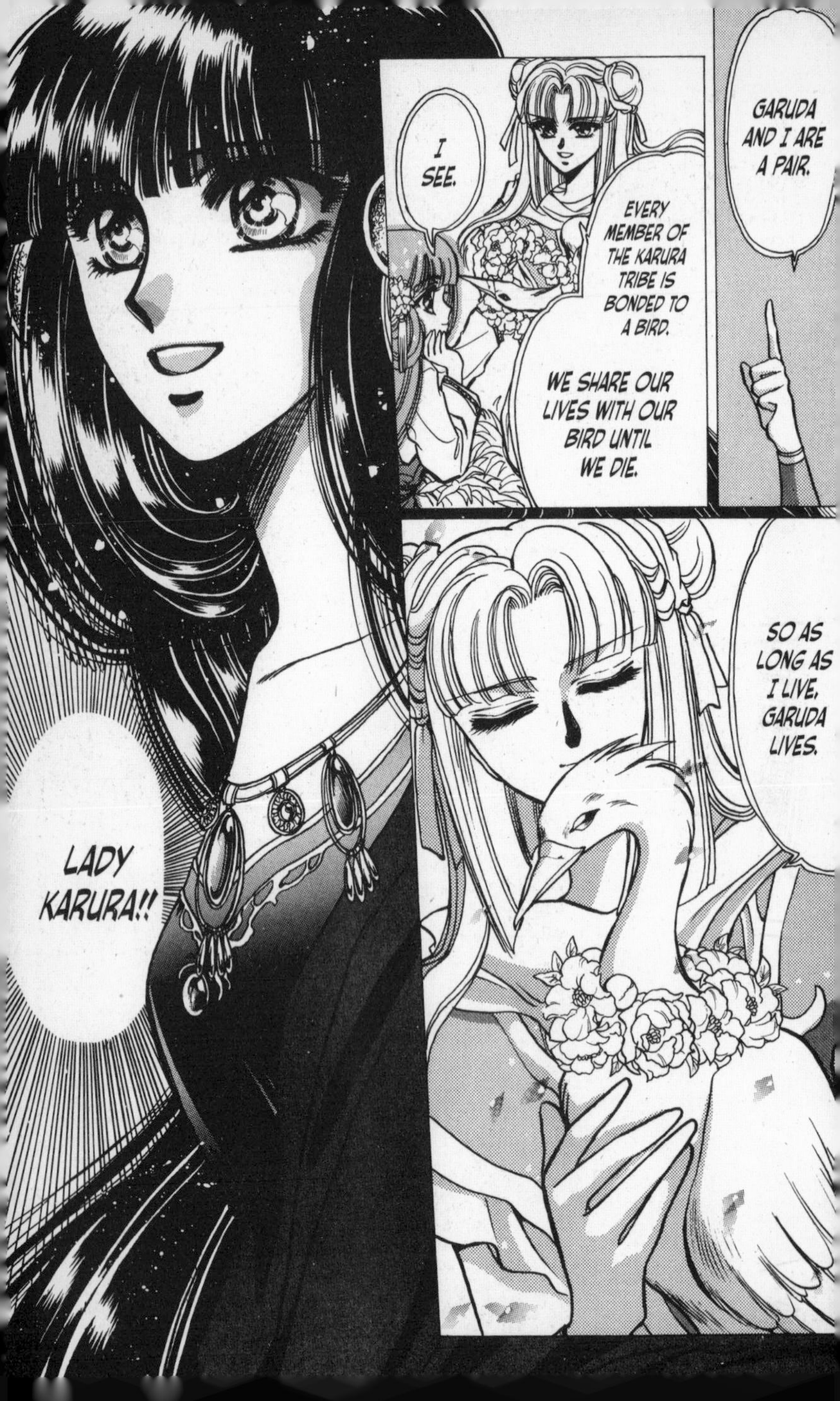
GARUDA AND I ARE A PAIR.
I SEE.
EVERY MEMBER OF THE KARURA TRIBE IS BONDED TO A BIRD.
WE SHARE OUR LIVES WITH OUR BIRD UNTIL WE DIE.
SO AS LONG AS I LIVE, GARUDA LIVES.
LADY KARURA!!

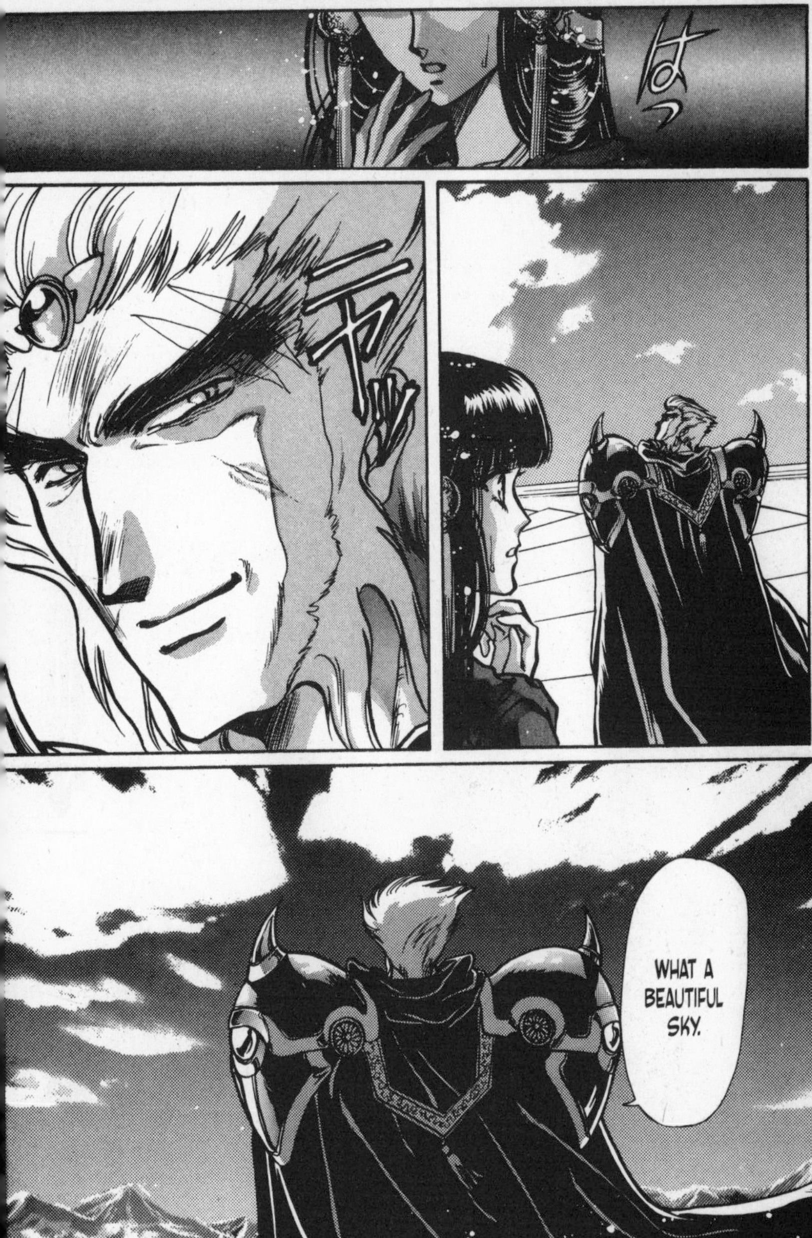
はっ
ニヤッ
WHAT A BEAUTIFUL SKY.

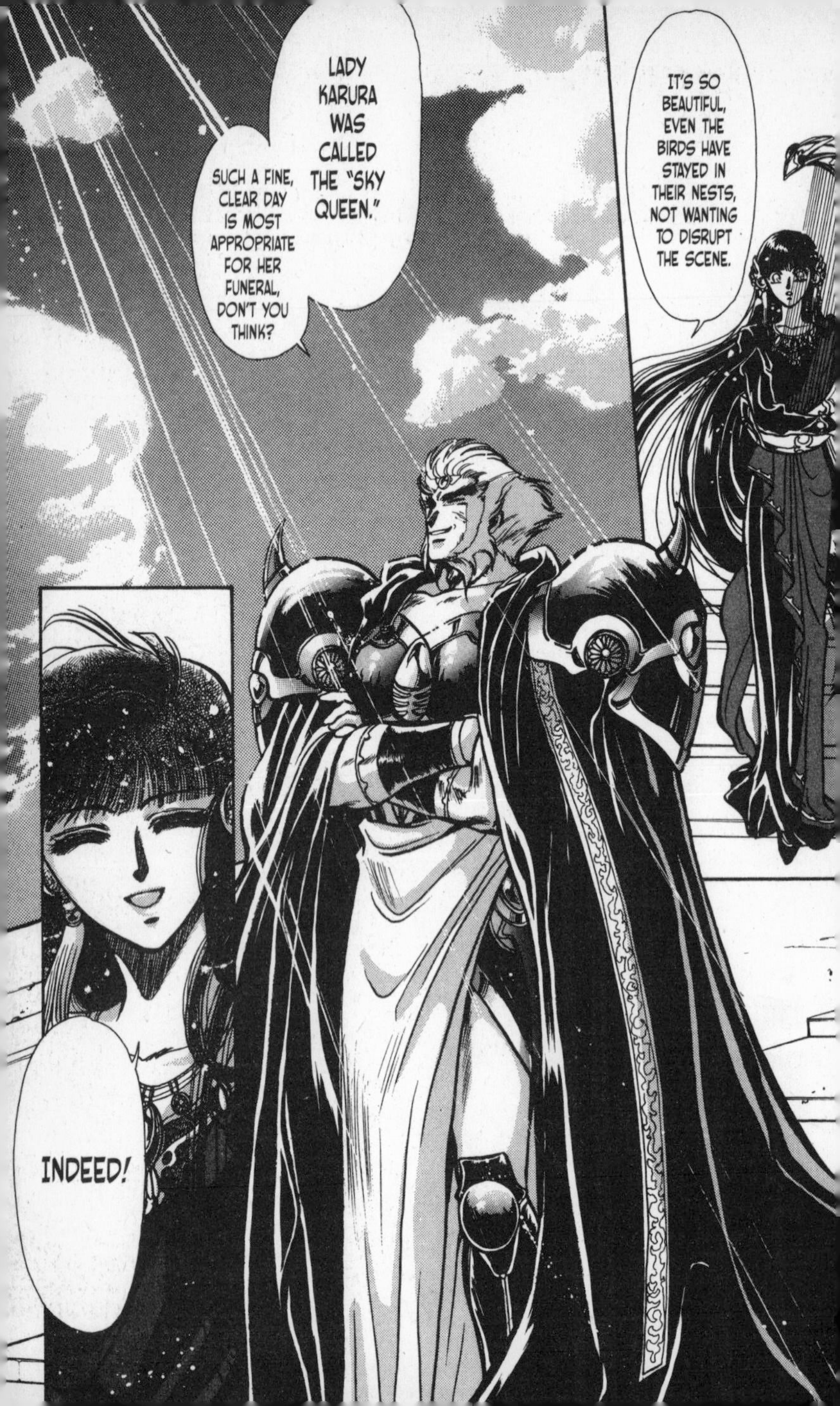
IT'S SO BEAUTIFUL, EVEN THE BIRDS HAVE STAYED IN THEIR NESTS, NOT WANTING TO DISRUPT THE SCENE.
LADY KARURA WAS CALLED THE "SKY QUEEN."
SUCH A FINE, CLEAR DAY IS MOST APPROPRIATE FOR HER FUNERAL, DON'T YOU THINK?
INDEED!

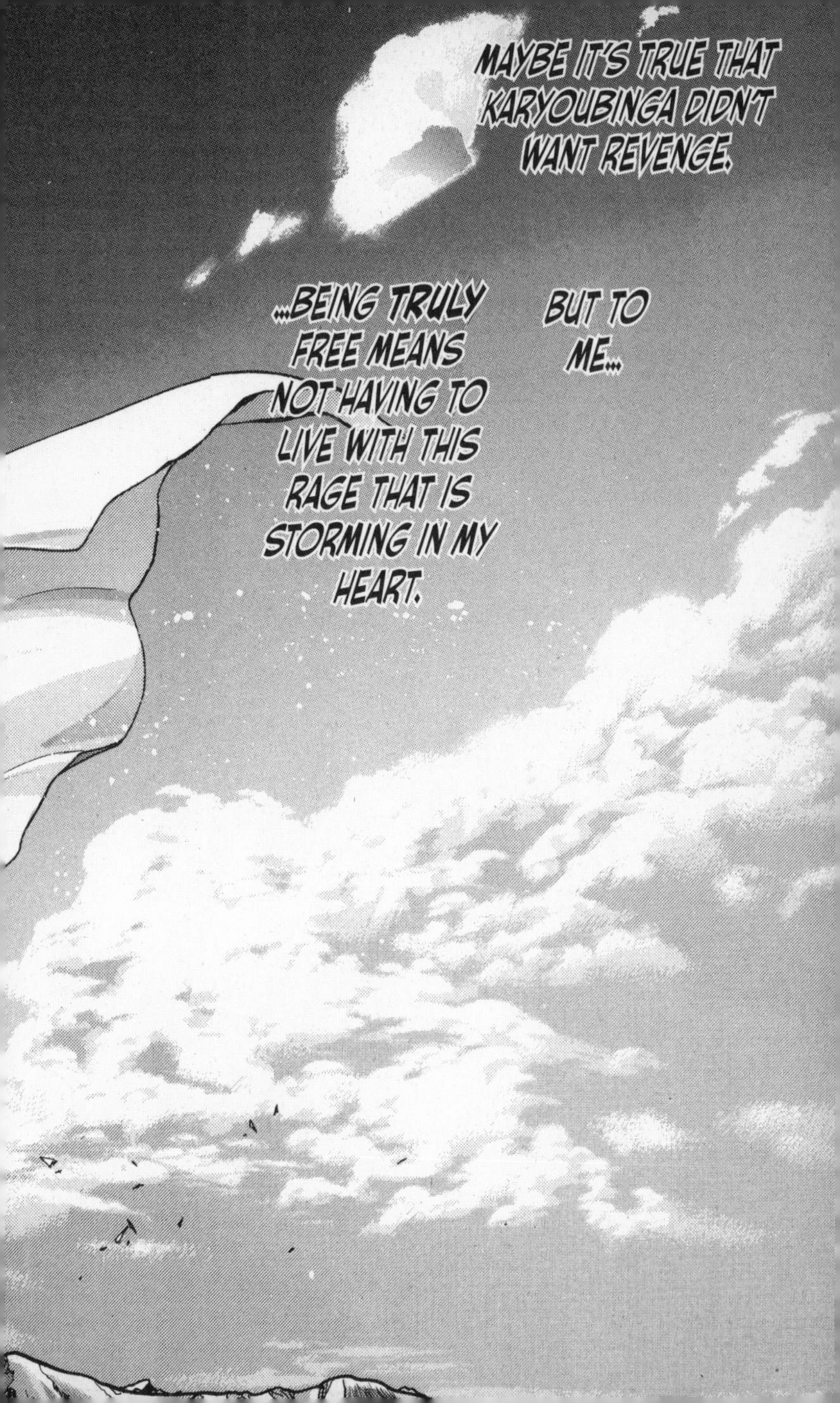
MAYBE IT'S TRUE THAT KARYOUBINGA DIDN'T WANT REVENGE.
BUT TO ME...
...BEING TRULY FREE MEANS NOT HAVING TO LIVE WITH THIS RAGE THAT IS STORMING IN MY HEART.

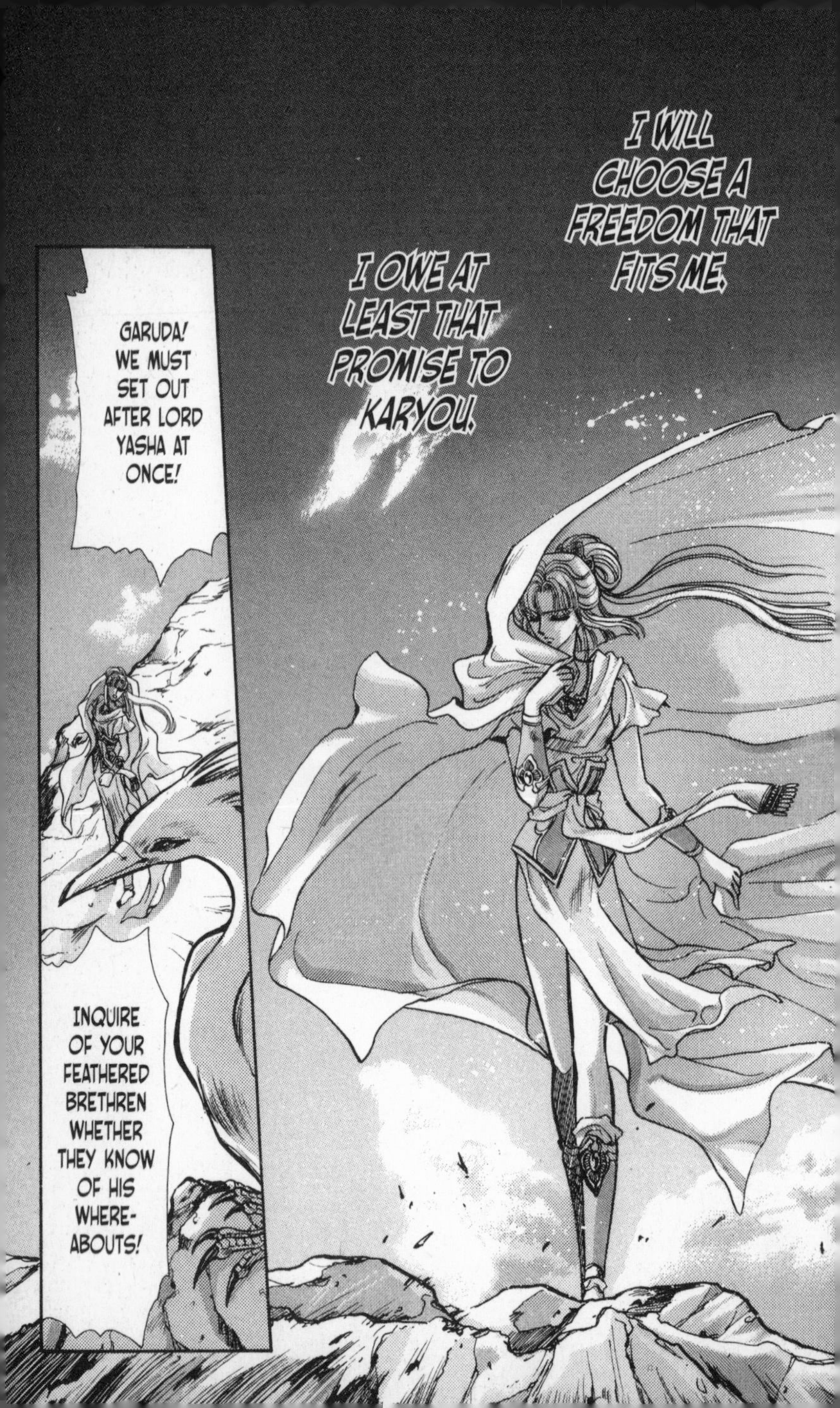

I WILL CHOOSE A FREEDOM THAT FITS ME.
I OWE AT LEAST THAT PROMISE TO KARYOU.
GARUDA! WE MUST SET OUT AFTER LORD YASHA AT ONCE!
INQUIRE OF YOUR FEATHERED BRETHREN WHETHER THEY KNOW OF HIS WHERE-ABOUTS!

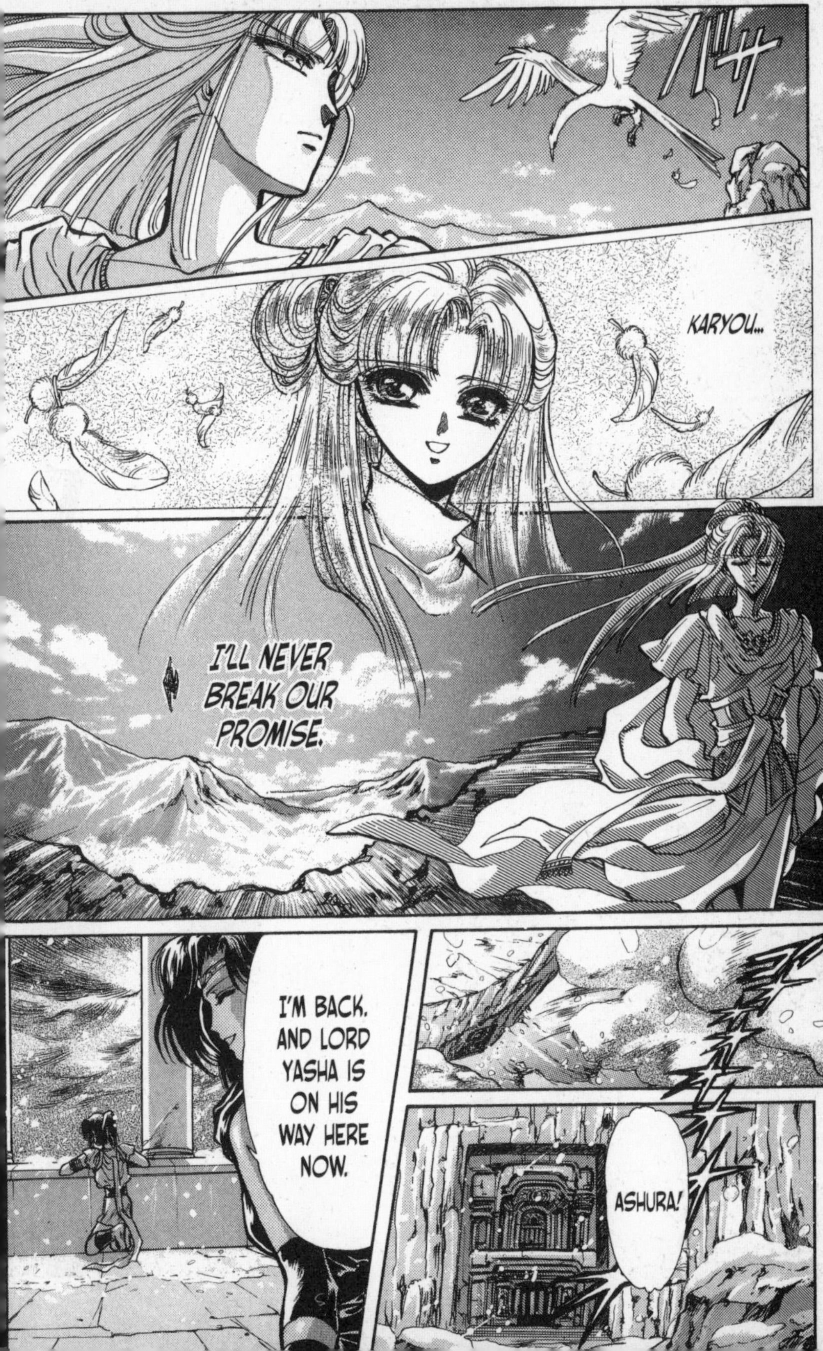
KARYOU...
I'LL NEVER BREAK OUR PROMISE.
ASHURA!
I'M BACK. AND LORD YASHA IS ON HIS WAY HERE NOW.

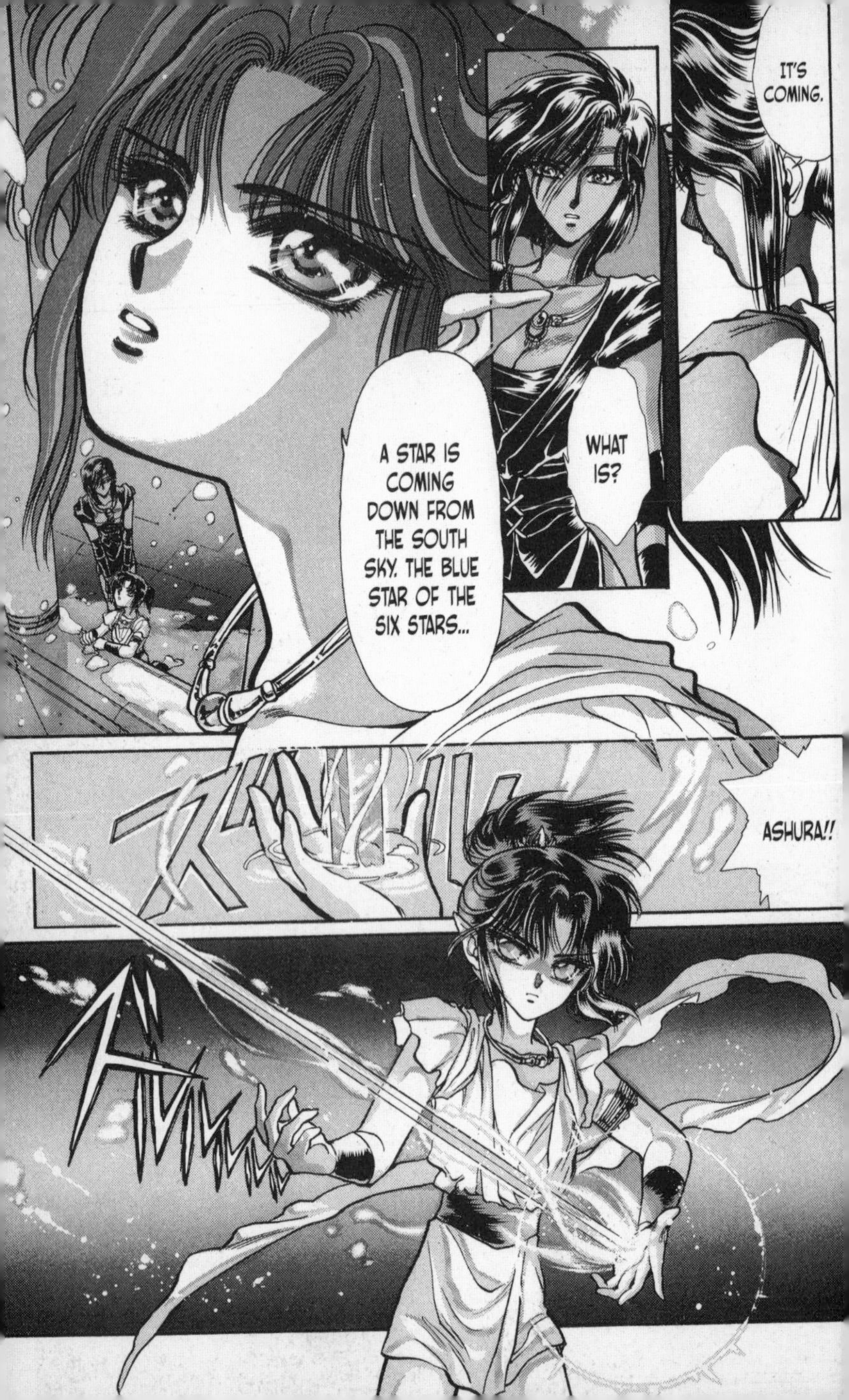
IT'S COMING.
WHAT IS?
A STAR IS COMING DOWN FROM THE SOUTH SKY. THE BLUE STAR OF THE SIX STARS...
ASHURA!!

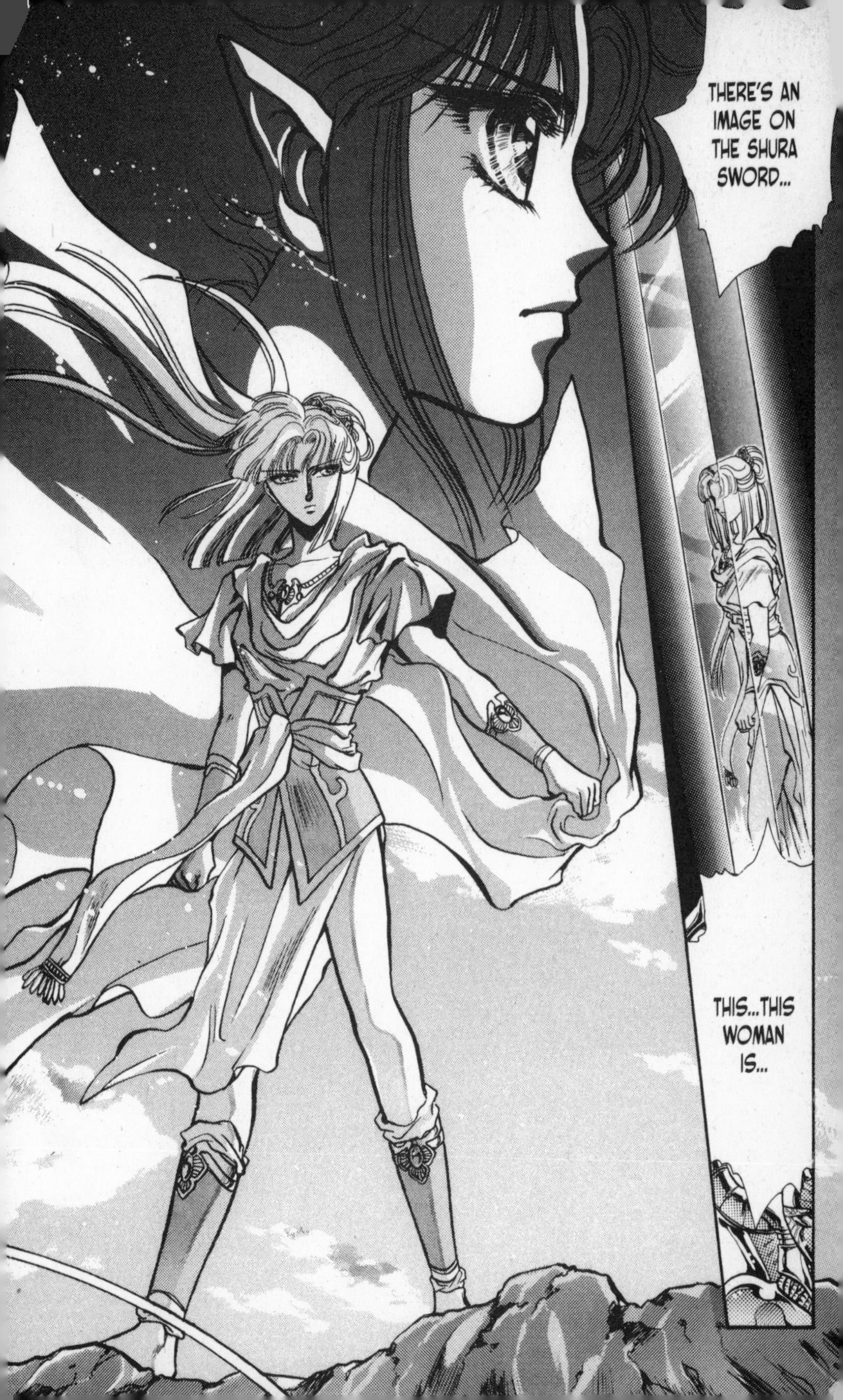
THERE'S AN IMAGE ON THE SHURA SWORD...
THIS...THIS WOMAN IS...

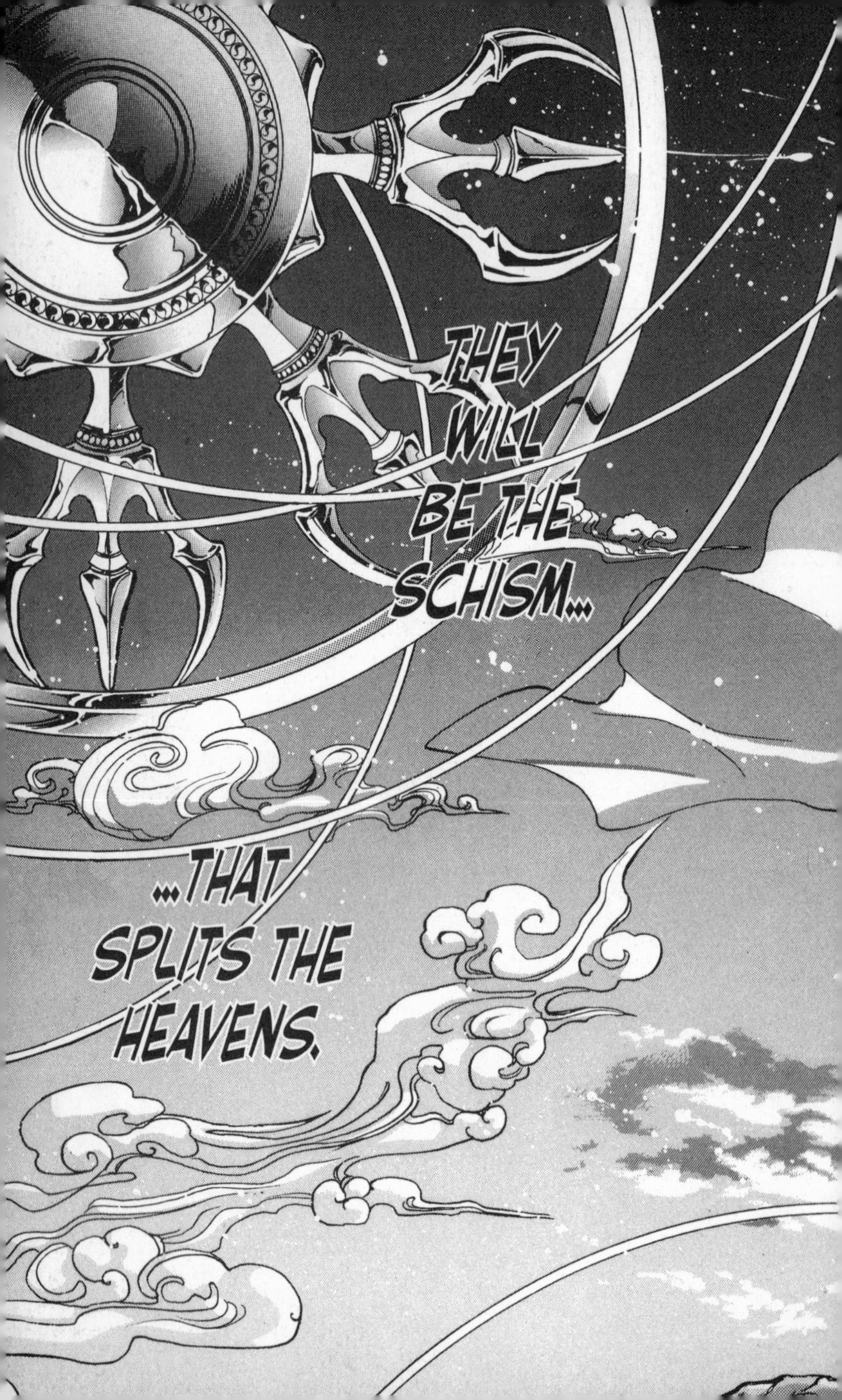
THEY WILL BE THE SCHISM...
...THAT SPLITS THE HEAVENS.

R G   VEDA

聖 伝

SKY QUEEN, FLY AWAY

END

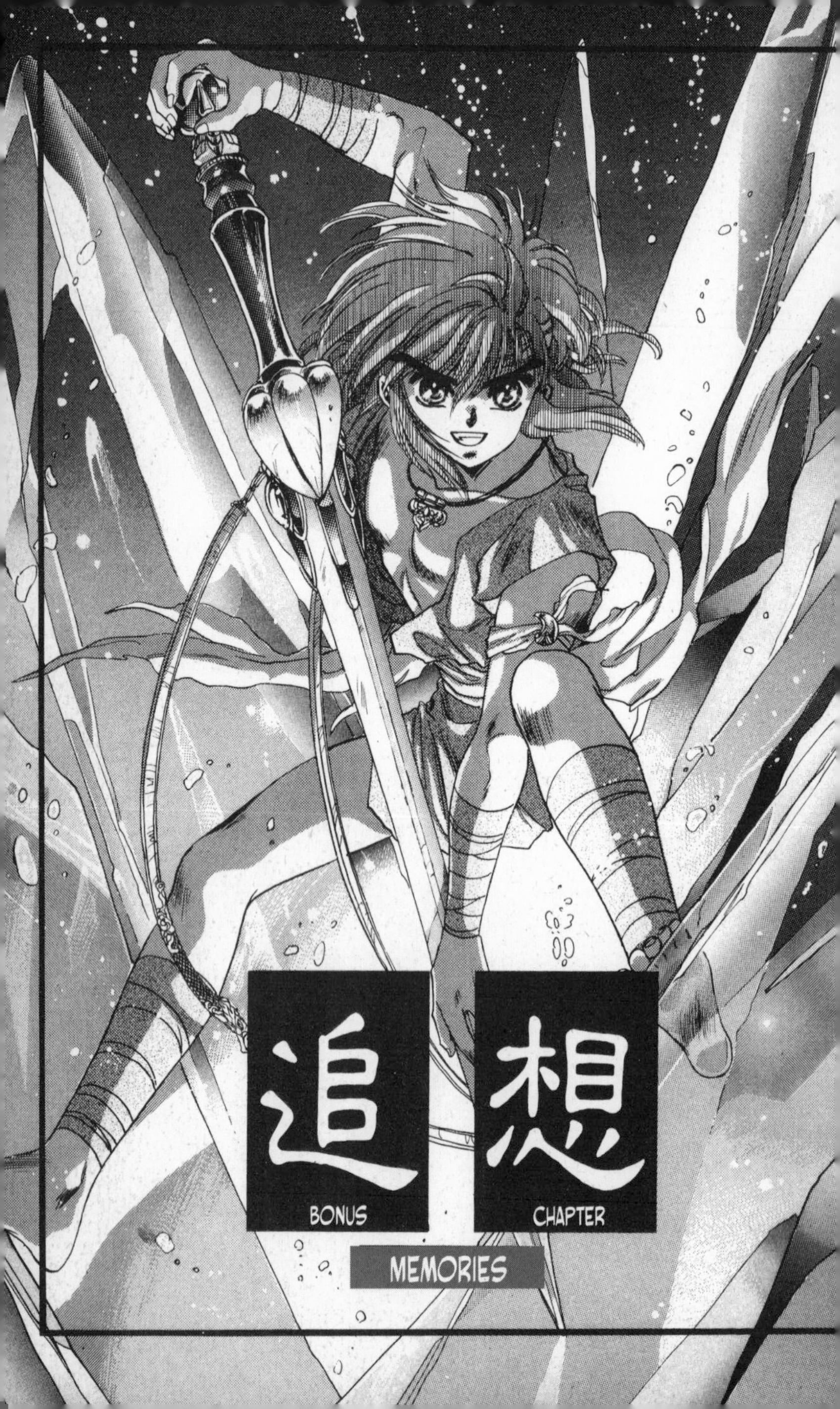
追想
BONUS
CHAPTER
MEMORIES

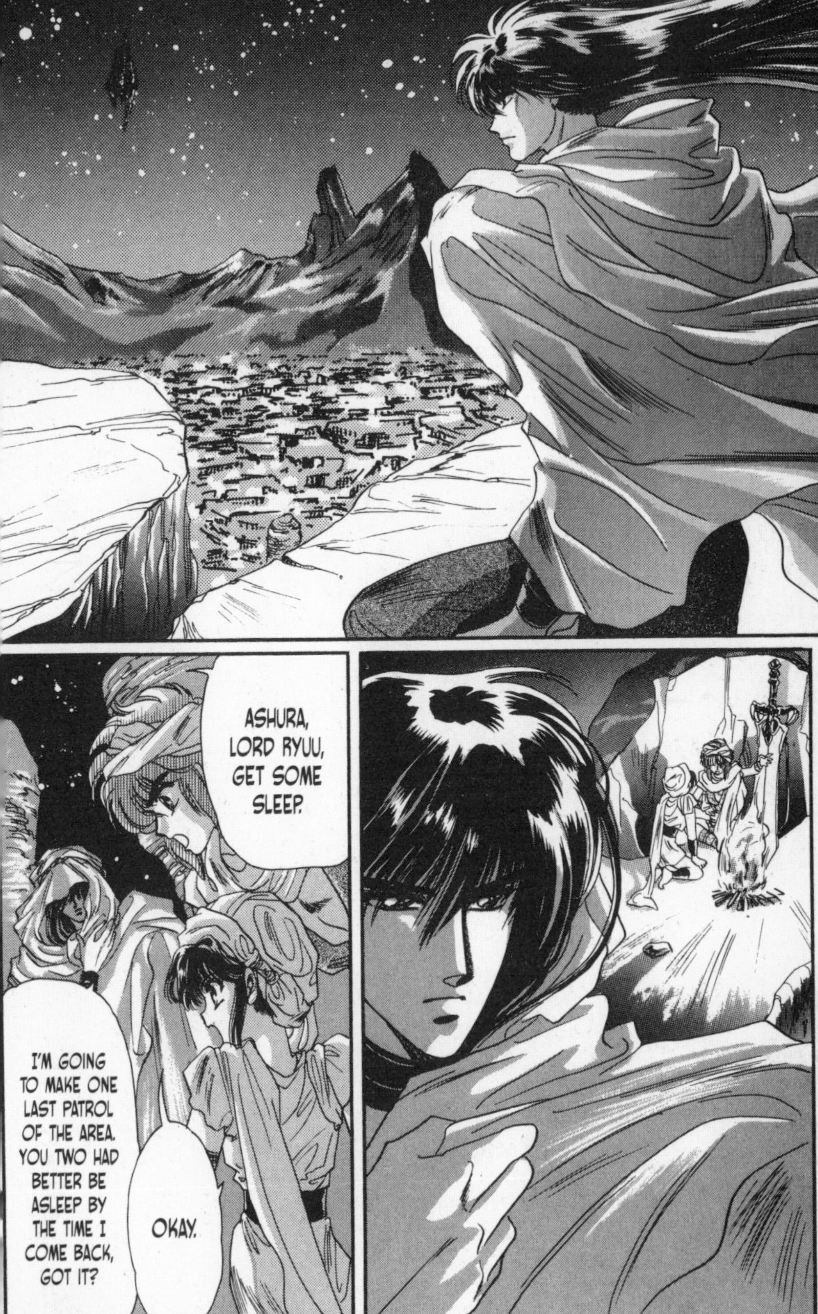
ASHURA, LORD RYUU, GET SOME SLEEP.
I'M GOING TO MAKE ONE LAST PATROL OF THE AREA. YOU TWO HAD BETTER BE ASLEEP BY THE TIME I COME BACK, GOT IT?
OKAY.

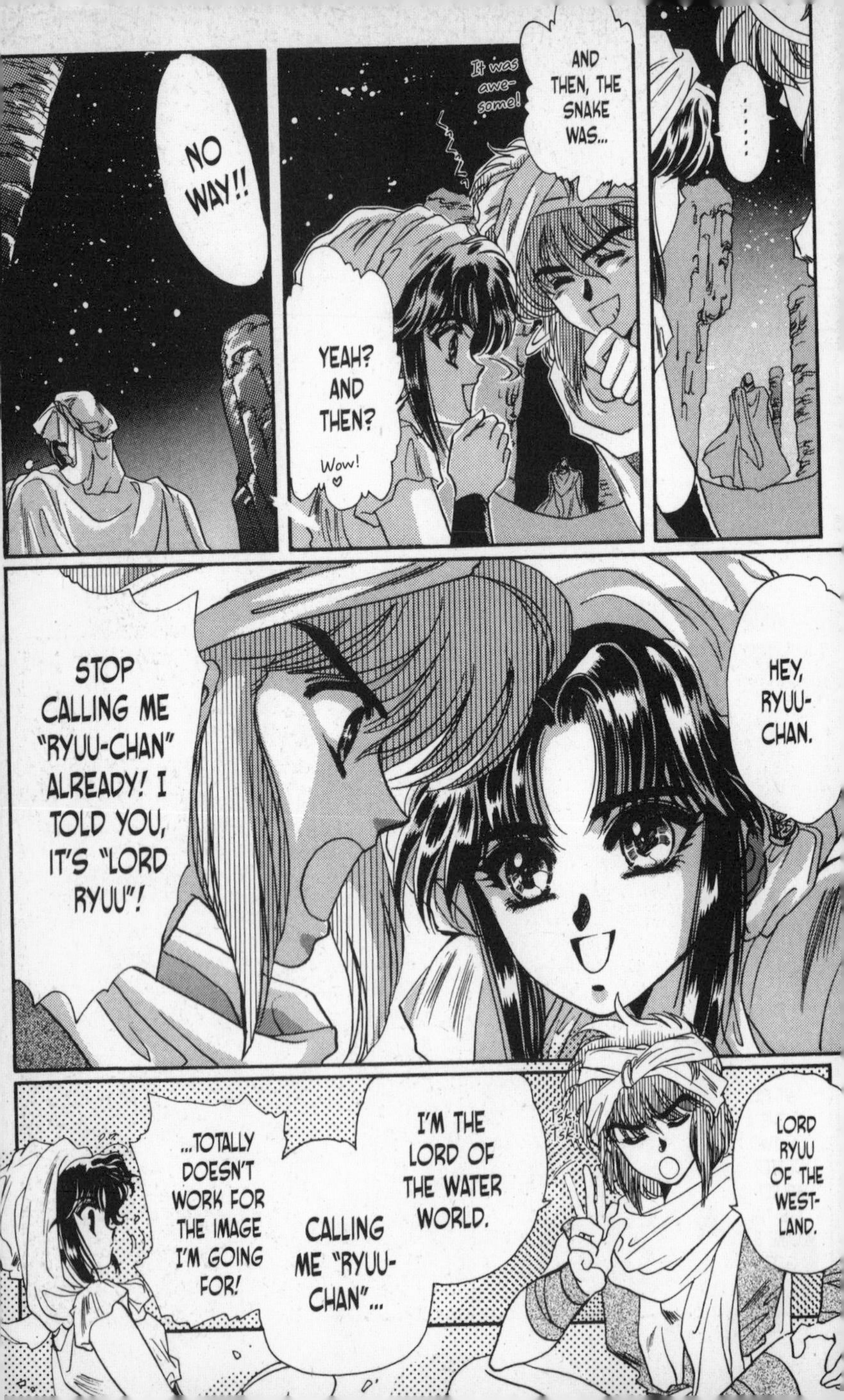
……
AND THEN, THE SNAKE WAS...
It was awe-some!
YEAH? AND THEN?
Wow! ♥
NO WAY!!
HEY, RYUU-CHAN.
STOP CALLING ME "RYUU-CHAN" ALREADY! I TOLD YOU, IT'S "LORD RYUU"!
LORD RYUU OF THE WEST-LAND.
Tsk, Tsk
I'M THE LORD OF THE WATER WORLD.
CALLING ME "RYUU-CHAN"...
...TOTALLY DOESN'T WORK FOR THE IMAGE I'M GOING FOR!

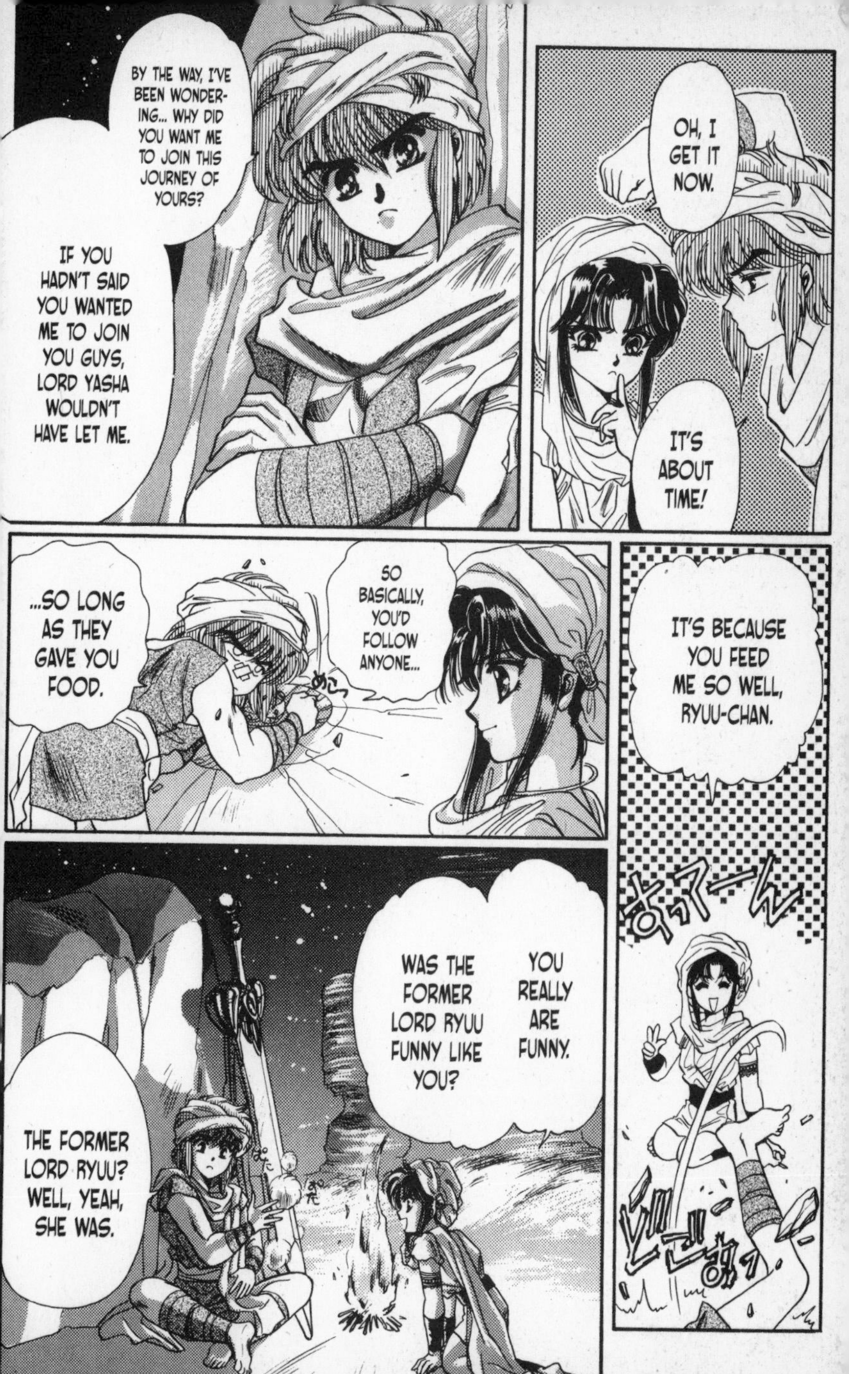
OH, I GET IT NOW.
IT'S ABOUT TIME!
BY THE WAY, I'VE BEEN WONDERING... WHY DID YOU WANT ME TO JOIN THIS JOURNEY OF YOURS?
IF YOU HADN'T SAID YOU WANTED ME TO JOIN YOU GUYS, LORD YASHA WOULDN'T HAVE LET ME.
IT'S BECAUSE YOU FEED ME SO WELL, RYUU-CHAN.
SO BASICALLY, YOU'D FOLLOW ANYONE...
...SO LONG AS THEY GAVE YOU FOOD.
YOU REALLY ARE FUNNY.
WAS THE FORMER LORD RYUU FUNNY LIKE YOU?
THE FORMER LORD RYUU? WELL, YEAH, SHE WAS.

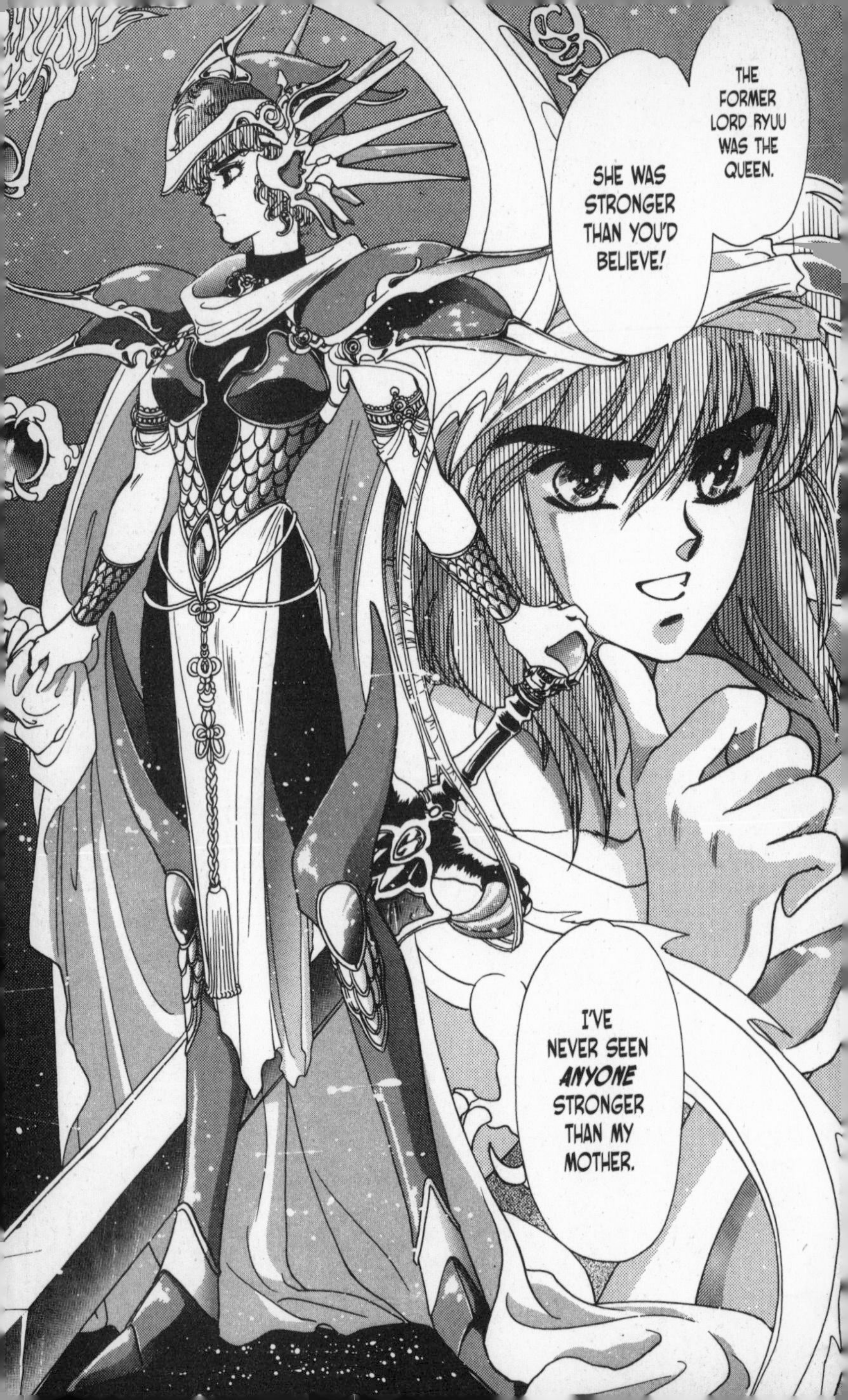
THE FORMER LORD RYUU WAS THE QUEEN.
SHE WAS STRONGER THAN YOU'D BELIEVE!
I'VE NEVER SEEN ***ANYONE*** STRONGER THAN MY MOTHER.

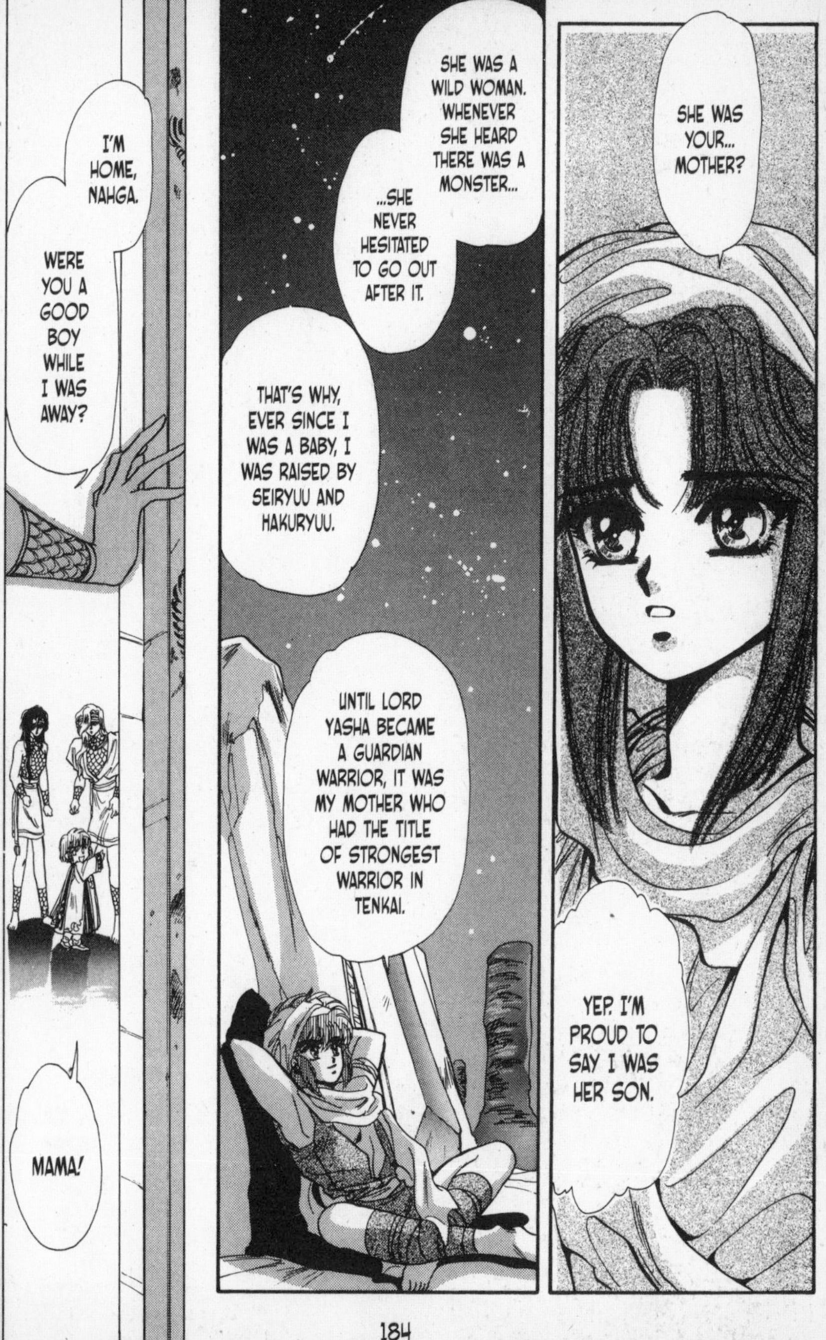
SHE WAS YOUR... MOTHER?
YEP. I'M PROUD TO SAY I WAS HER SON.
SHE WAS A WILD WOMAN. WHENEVER SHE HEARD THERE WAS A MONSTER...
...SHE NEVER HESITATED TO GO OUT AFTER IT.
THAT'S WHY, EVER SINCE I WAS A BABY, I WAS RAISED BY SEIRYUU AND HAKURYUU.
UNTIL LORD YASHA BECAME A GUARDIAN WARRIOR, IT WAS MY MOTHER WHO HAD THE TITLE OF STRONGEST WARRIOR IN TENKAI.
I'M HOME, NAHGA.
WERE YOU A GOOD BOY WHILE I WAS AWAY?
MAMA!

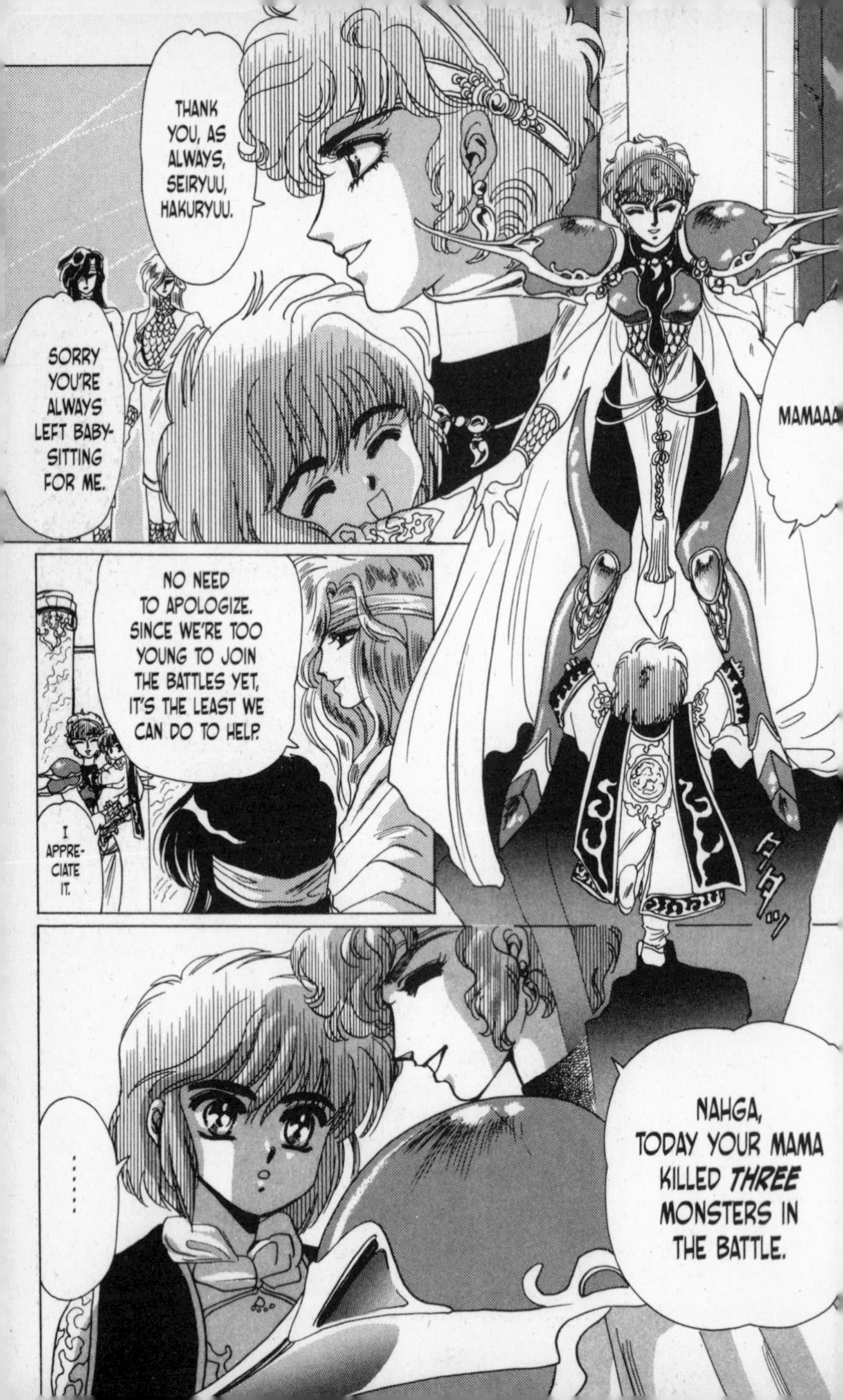
MAMAAA
THANK YOU, AS ALWAYS, SEIRYUU, HAKURYUU.
SORRY YOU'RE ALWAYS LEFT BABY-SITTING FOR ME.
NO NEED TO APOLOGIZE. SINCE WE'RE TOO YOUNG TO JOIN THE BATTLES YET, IT'S THE LEAST WE CAN DO TO HELP.
I APPRE-CIATE IT.
NAHGA, TODAY YOUR MAMA KILLED THREE MONSTERS IN THE BATTLE.
......

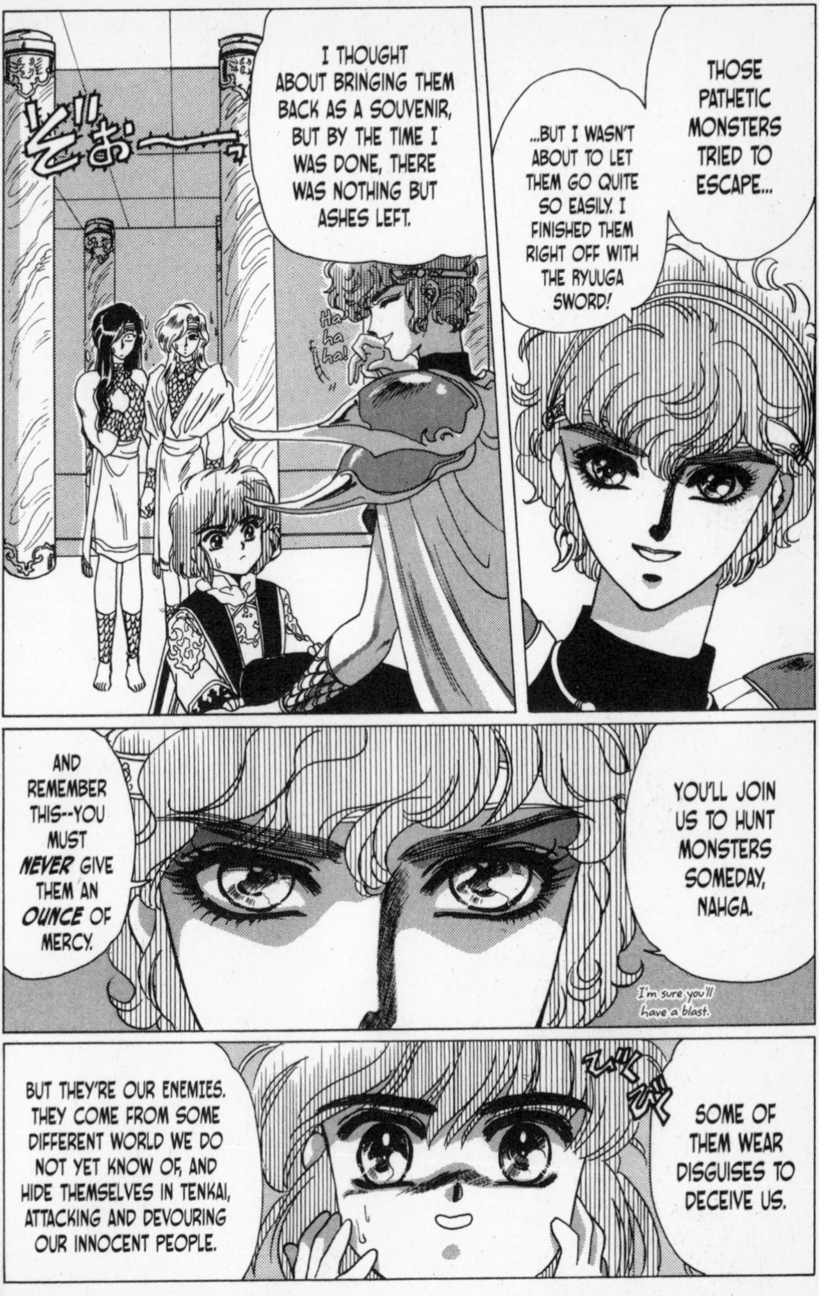
THOSE PATHETIC MONSTERS TRIED TO ESCAPE...
...BUT I WASN'T ABOUT TO LET THEM GO QUITE SO EASILY. I FINISHED THEM RIGHT OFF WITH THE RYUUGA SWORD!
I THOUGHT ABOUT BRINGING THEM BACK AS A SOUVENIR, BUT BY THE TIME I WAS DONE, THERE WAS NOTHING BUT ASHES LEFT.
Ha ha ha!
YOU'LL JOIN US TO HUNT MONSTERS SOMEDAY, NAHGA.
I'm sure you'll have a blast.
AND REMEMBER THIS--YOU MUST NEVER GIVE THEM AN OUNCE OF MERCY.
SOME OF THEM WEAR DISGUISES TO DECEIVE US.
BUT THEY'RE OUR ENEMIES. THEY COME FROM SOME DIFFERENT WORLD WE DO NOT YET KNOW OF, AND HIDE THEMSELVES IN TENKAI, ATTACKING AND DEVOURING OUR INNOCENT PEOPLE.

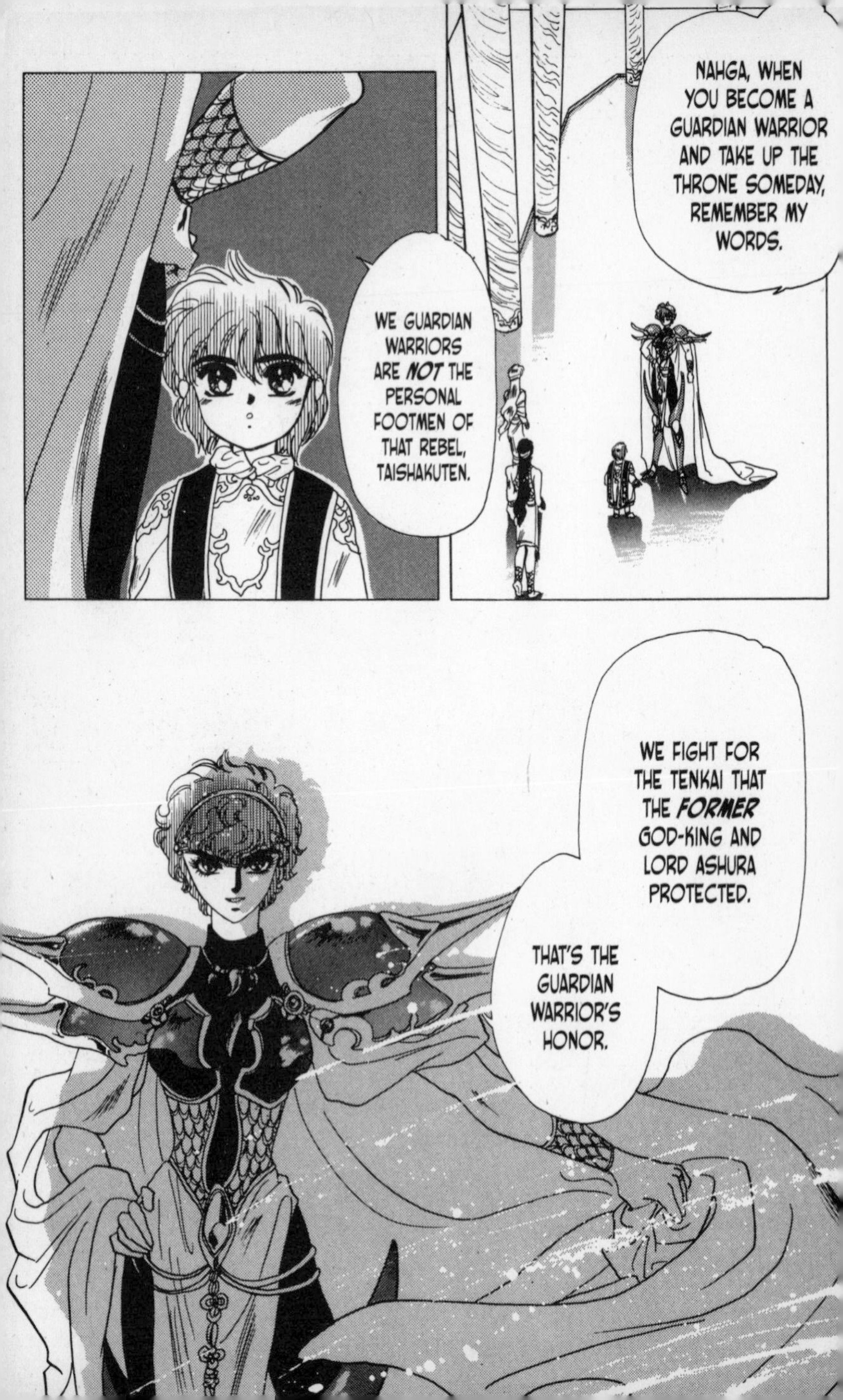
NAHGA, WHEN YOU BECOME A GUARDIAN WARRIOR AND TAKE UP THE THRONE SOMEDAY, REMEMBER MY WORDS.
WE GUARDIAN WARRIORS ARE *NOT* THE PERSONAL FOOTMEN OF THAT REBEL, TAISHAKUTEN.
WE FIGHT FOR THE TENKAI THAT THE *FORMER* GOD-KING AND LORD ASHURA PROTECTED.
THAT'S THE GUARDIAN WARRIOR'S HONOR.

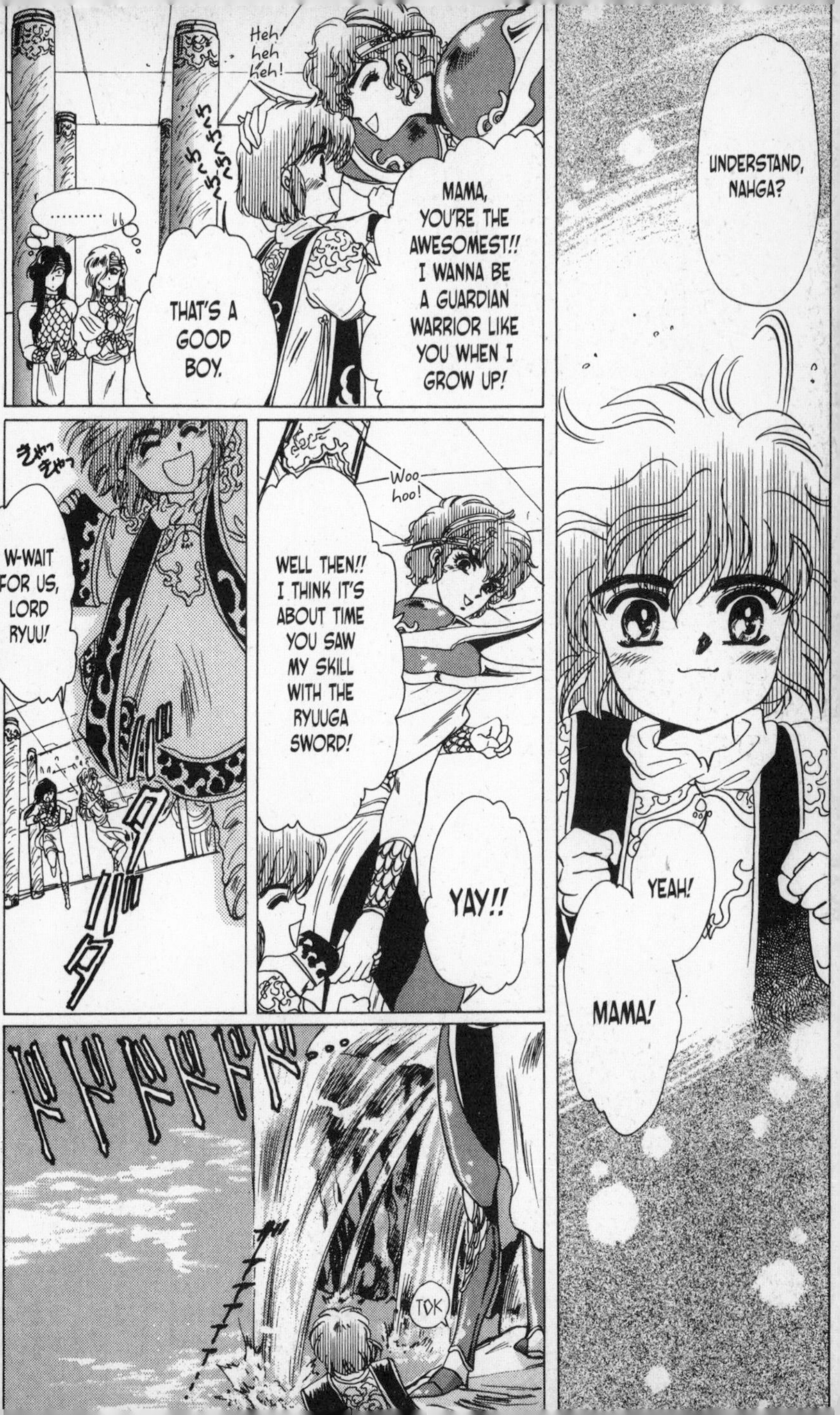
UNDERSTAND, NAHGA?
YEAH!
MAMA!
Heh heh heh!
MAMA, YOU'RE THE AWESOMEST!! I WANNA BE A GUARDIAN WARRIOR LIKE YOU WHEN I GROW UP!
THAT'S A GOOD BOY.
....
Woo hoo!
WELL THEN!! I THINK IT'S ABOUT TIME YOU SAW MY SKILL WITH THE RYUUGA SWORD!
YAY!!
W-WAIT FOR US, LORD RYUU!
TOK

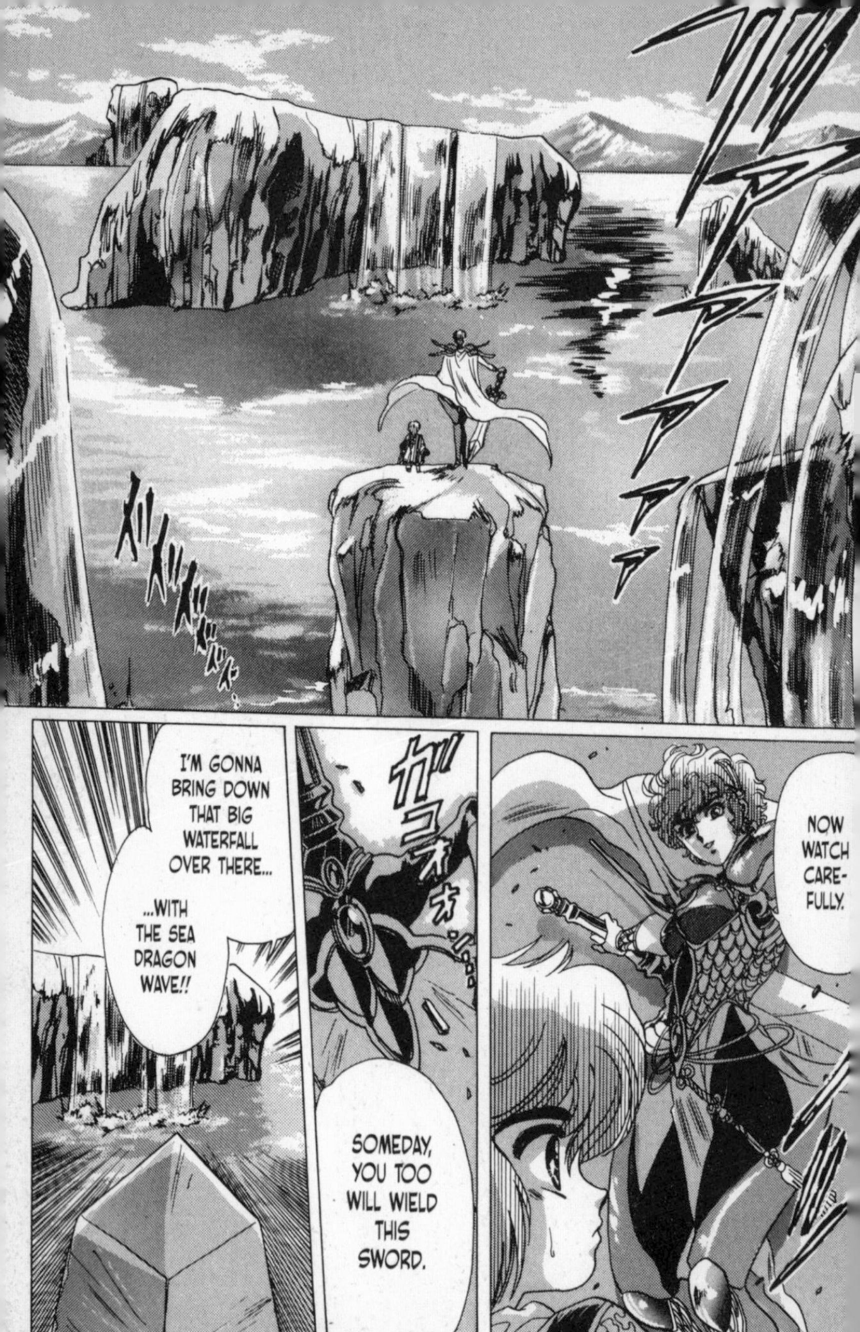
NOW WATCH CARE-FULLY.
SOMEDAY, YOU TOO WILL WIELD THIS SWORD.
I'M GONNA BRING DOWN THAT BIG WATERFALL OVER THERE...
...WITH THE SEA DRAGON WAVE!!

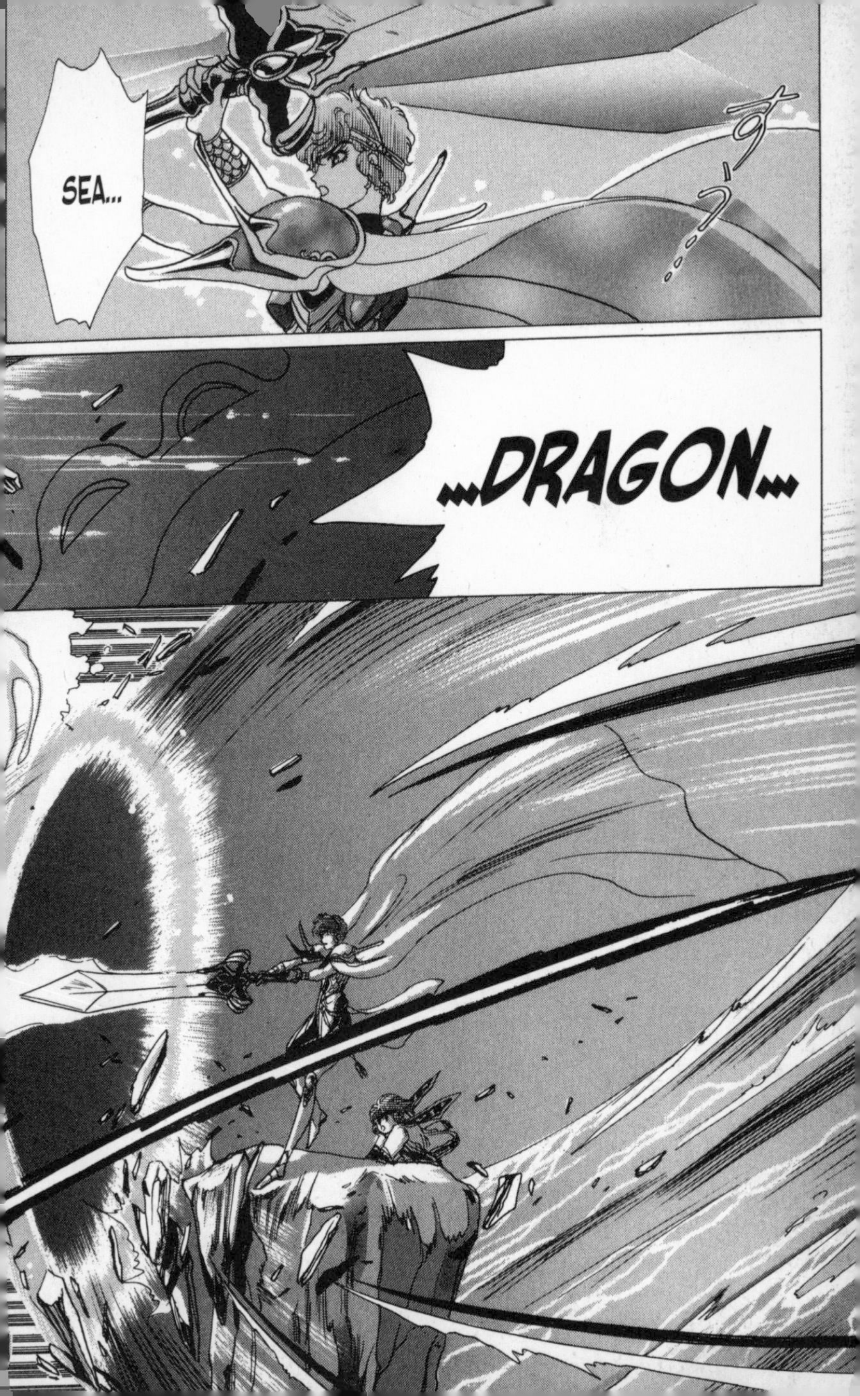
すぅっ…
SEA...
...DRAGON...

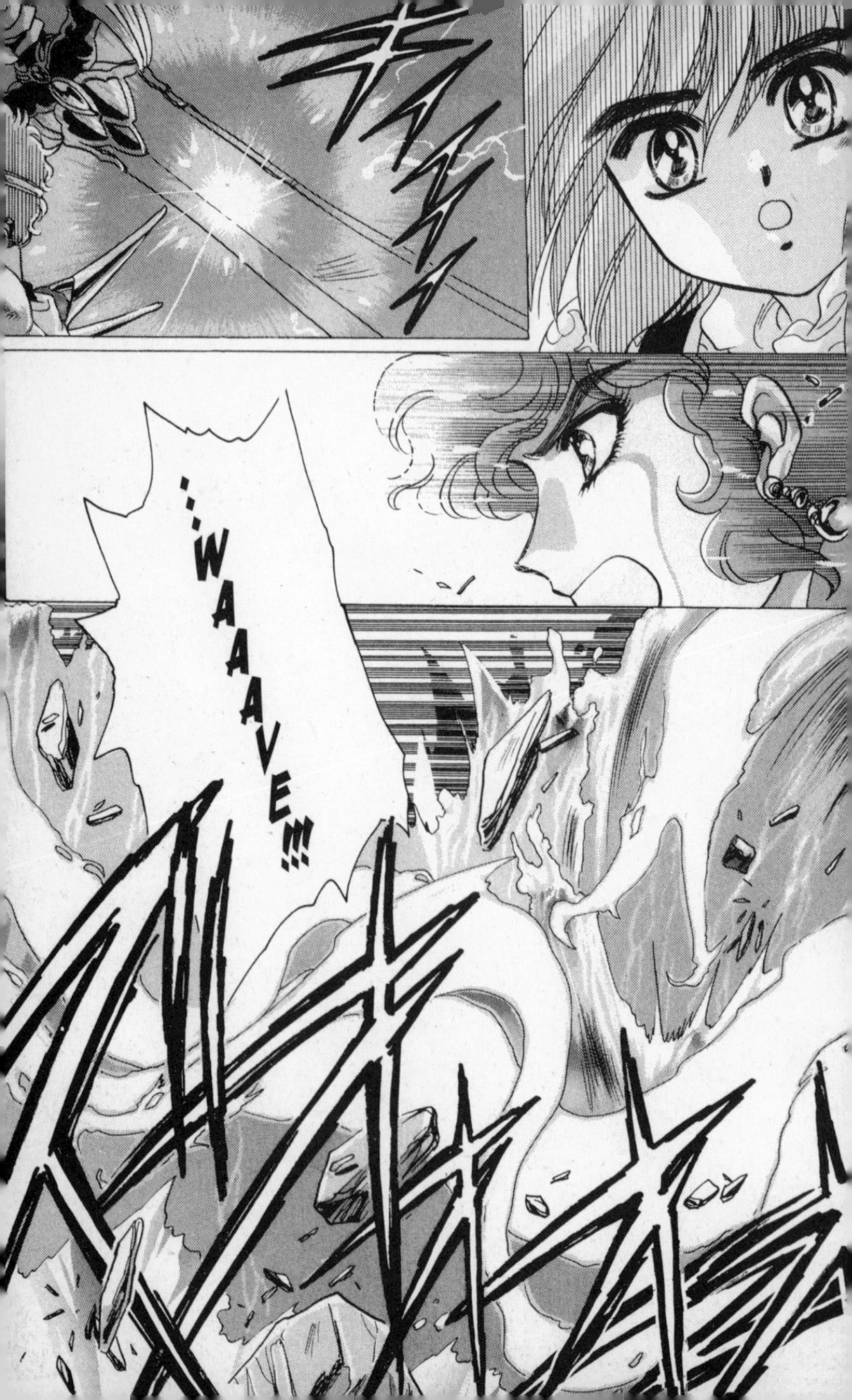
...WAAAAVE!!!

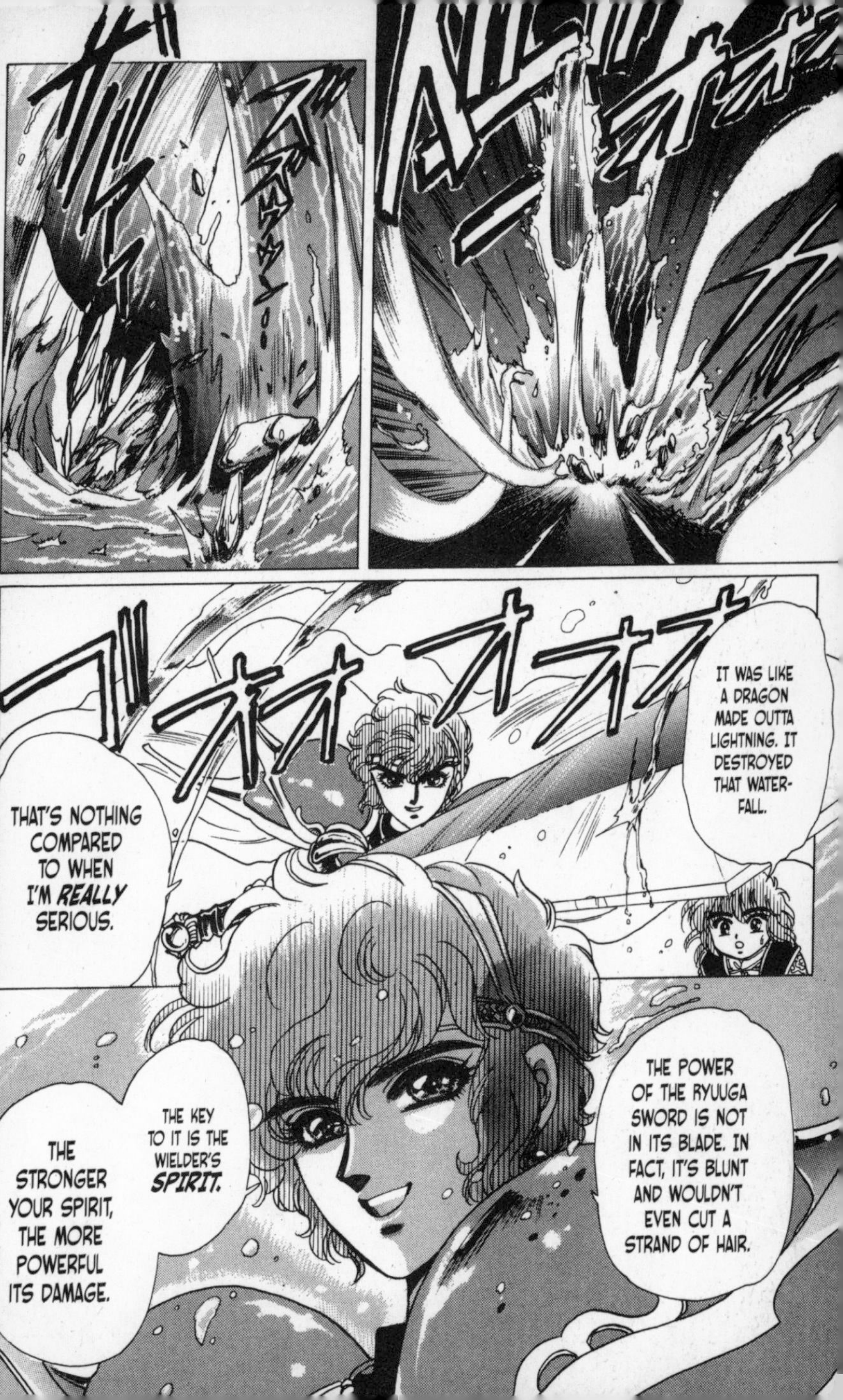
IT WAS LIKE A DRAGON MADE OUTTA LIGHTNING. IT DESTROYED THAT WATER-FALL.
THAT'S NOTHING COMPARED TO WHEN I'M ***REALLY*** SERIOUS.
THE POWER OF THE RYUUGA SWORD IS NOT IN ITS BLADE. IN FACT, IT'S BLUNT AND WOULDN'T EVEN CUT A STRAND OF HAIR.
THE KEY TO IT IS THE WIELDER'S ***SPIRIT.***
THE STRONGER YOUR SPIRIT, THE MORE POWERFUL ITS DAMAGE.

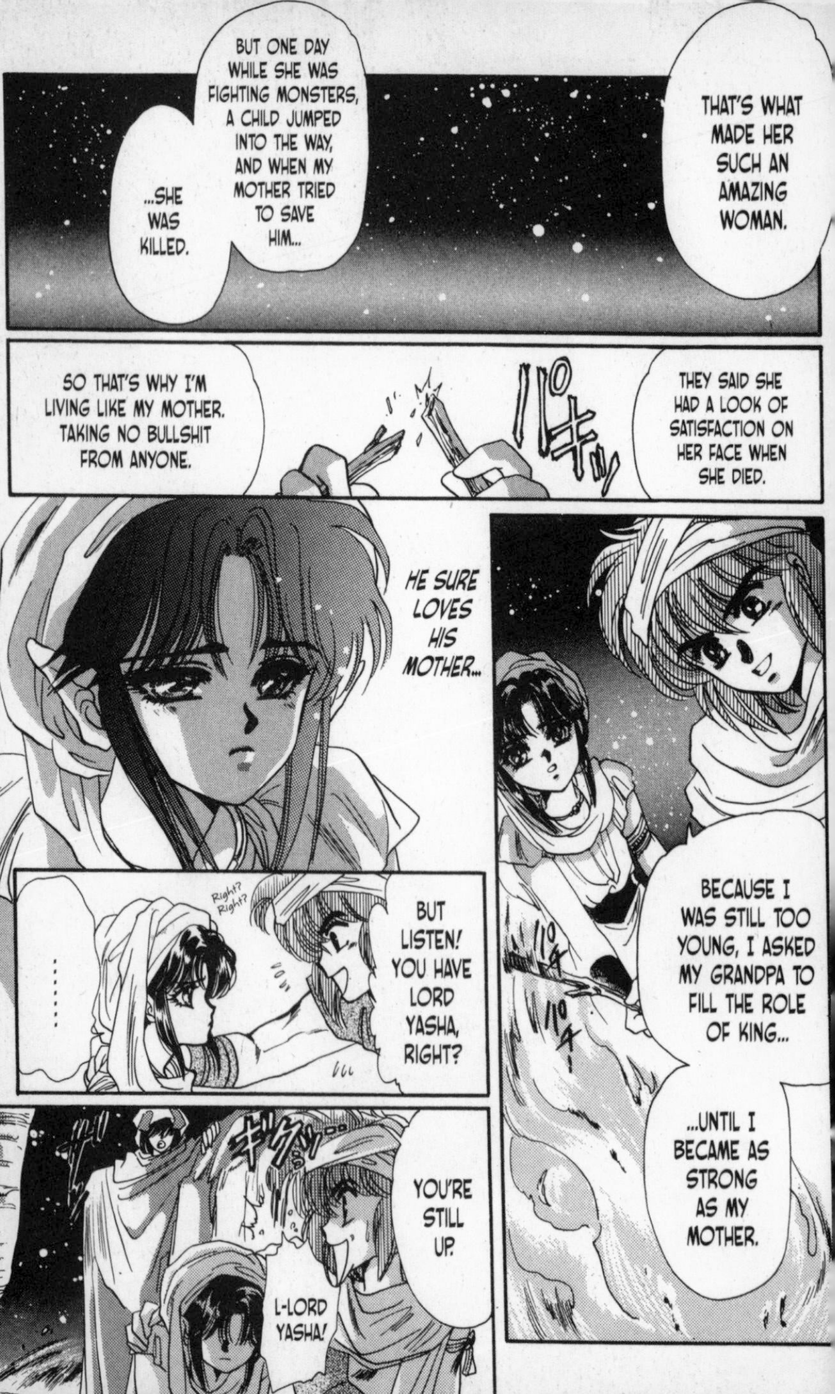
THAT'S WHAT MADE HER SUCH AN AMAZING WOMAN.
BUT ONE DAY WHILE SHE WAS FIGHTING MONSTERS, A CHILD JUMPED INTO THE WAY, AND WHEN MY MOTHER TRIED TO SAVE HIM...
...SHE WAS KILLED.
THEY SAID SHE HAD A LOOK OF SATISFACTION ON HER FACE WHEN SHE DIED.
パキッ
SO THAT'S WHY I'M LIVING LIKE MY MOTHER. TAKING NO BULLSHIT FROM ANYONE.
パチ
パチ
BECAUSE I WAS STILL TOO YOUNG, I ASKED MY GRANDPA TO FILL THE ROLE OF KING...
...UNTIL I BECAME AS STRONG AS MY MOTHER.
HE SURE LOVES HIS MOTHER...
BUT LISTEN! YOU HAVE LORD YASHA, RIGHT?
Right? Right?
......
ギクッ
YOU'RE STILL UP.
L-LORD YASHA!

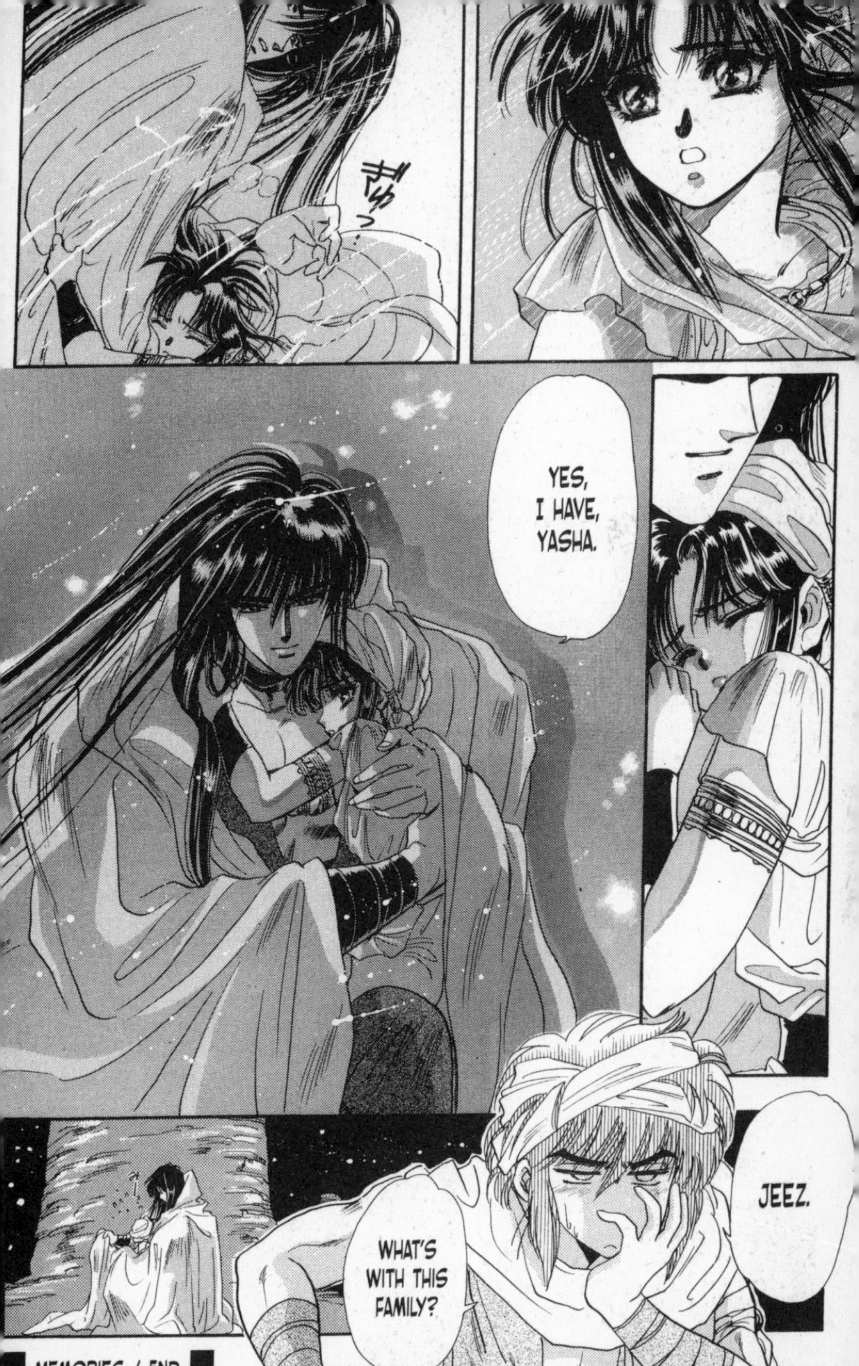
ぎゅっ
YES, I HAVE, YASHA.
JEEZ.
WHAT'S WITH THIS FAMILY?

MEMORIES / END

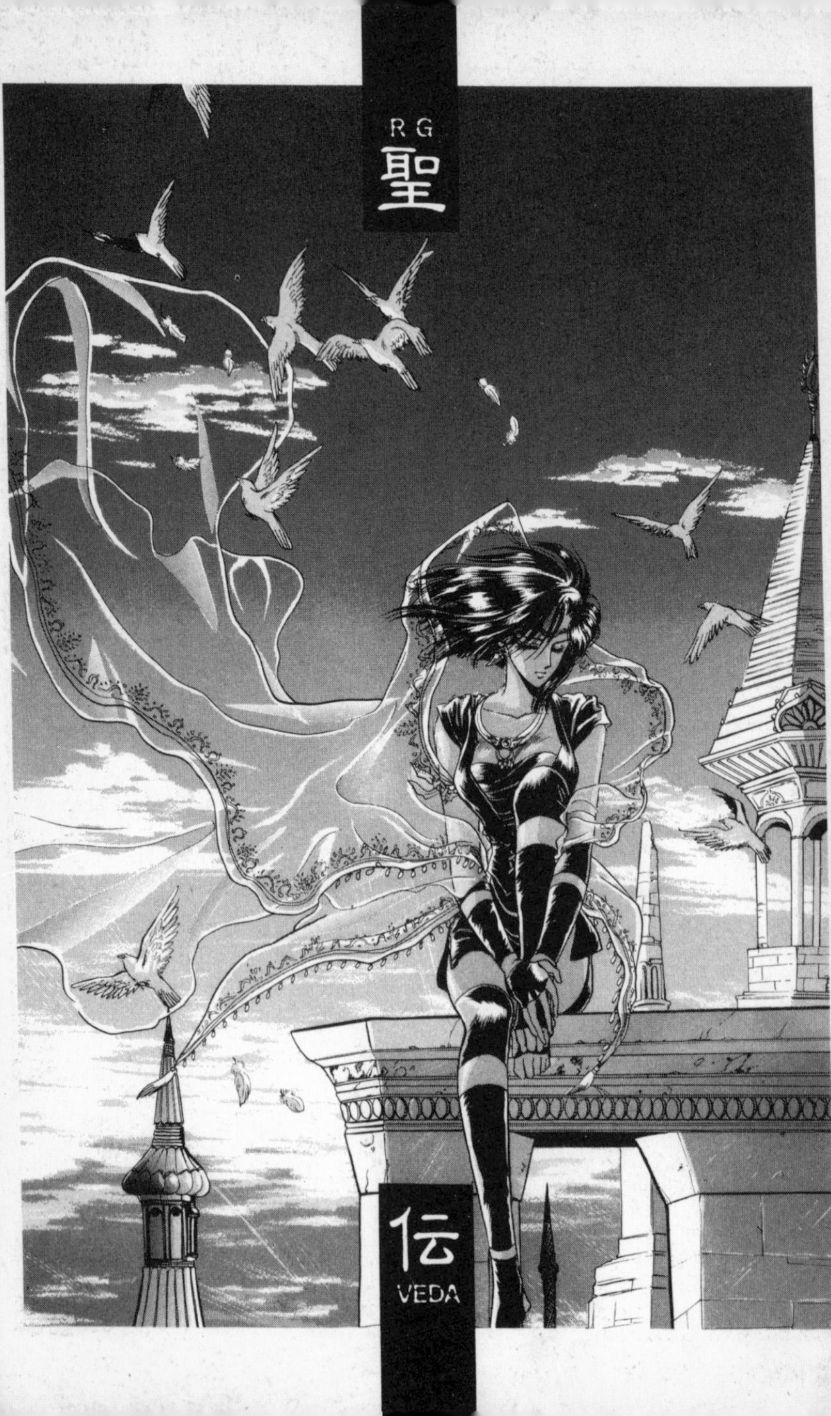
RG
聖
伝
VEDA

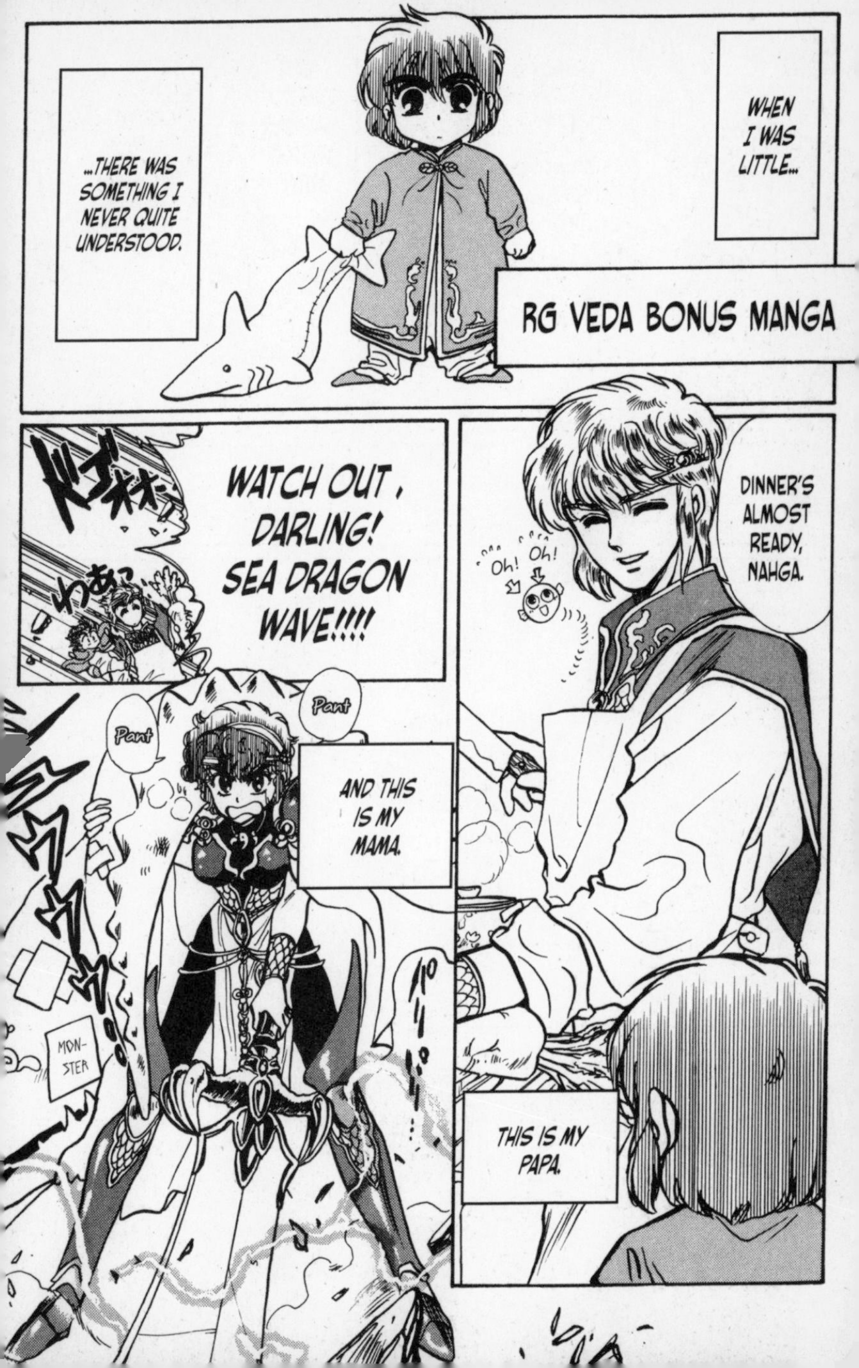

WHEN I WAS LITTLE...
RG VEDA BONUS MANGA
...THERE WAS SOMETHING I NEVER QUITE UNDERSTOOD.
DINNER'S ALMOST READY, NAHGA.
Oh! Oh!
THIS IS MY PAPA.
WATCH OUT, DARLING! SEA DRAGON WAVE!!!!
Pant
Pant
AND THIS IS MY MAMA.
MON-STER

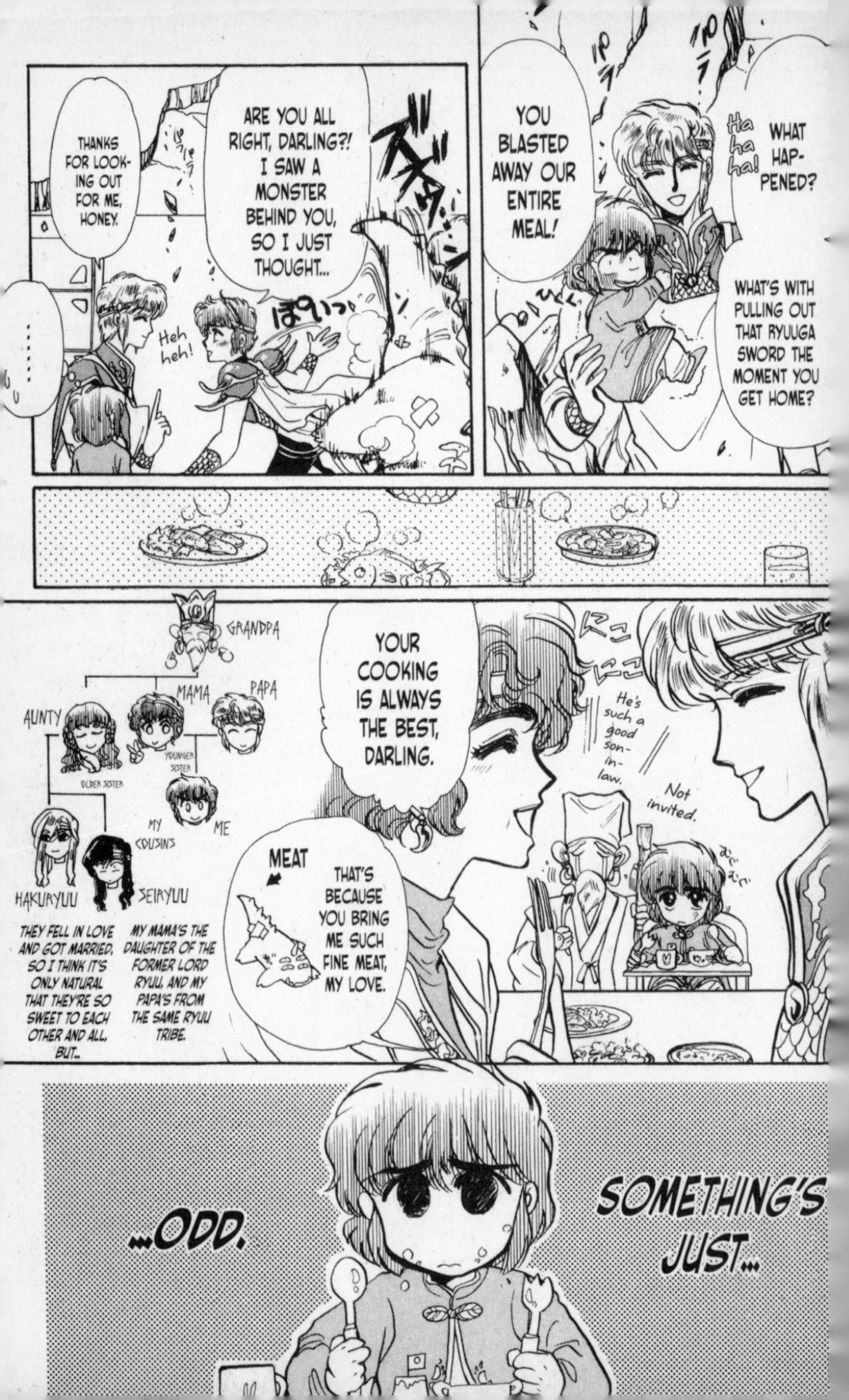
Ha ha ha!
WHAT HAP-PENED?
WHAT'S WITH PULLING OUT THAT RYUUGA SWORD THE MOMENT YOU GET HOME?
YOU BLASTED AWAY OUR ENTIRE MEAL!
ARE YOU ALL RIGHT, DARLING?! I SAW A MONSTER BEHIND YOU, SO I JUST THOUGHT...
Heh heh!
THANKS FOR LOOK-ING OUT FOR ME, HONEY.
......
He's such a good son-in-law.
Not invited.
YOUR COOKING IS ALWAYS THE BEST, DARLING.
THAT'S BECAUSE YOU BRING ME SUCH FINE MEAT, MY LOVE.
MEAT
GRANDPA
PAPA
MAMA
AUNTY
YOUNGER SISTER
OLDER SISTER
ME
MY COUSINS
HAKURYUU
SEIRYUU
MY MAMA'S THE DAUGHTER OF THE FORMER LORD RYUU, AND MY PAPA'S FROM THE SAME RYUU TRIBE.
THEY FELL IN LOVE AND GOT MARRIED, SO I THINK IT'S ONLY NATURAL THAT THEY'RE SO SWEET TO EACH OTHER AND ALL, BUT...
SOMETHING'S JUST...
...ODD.

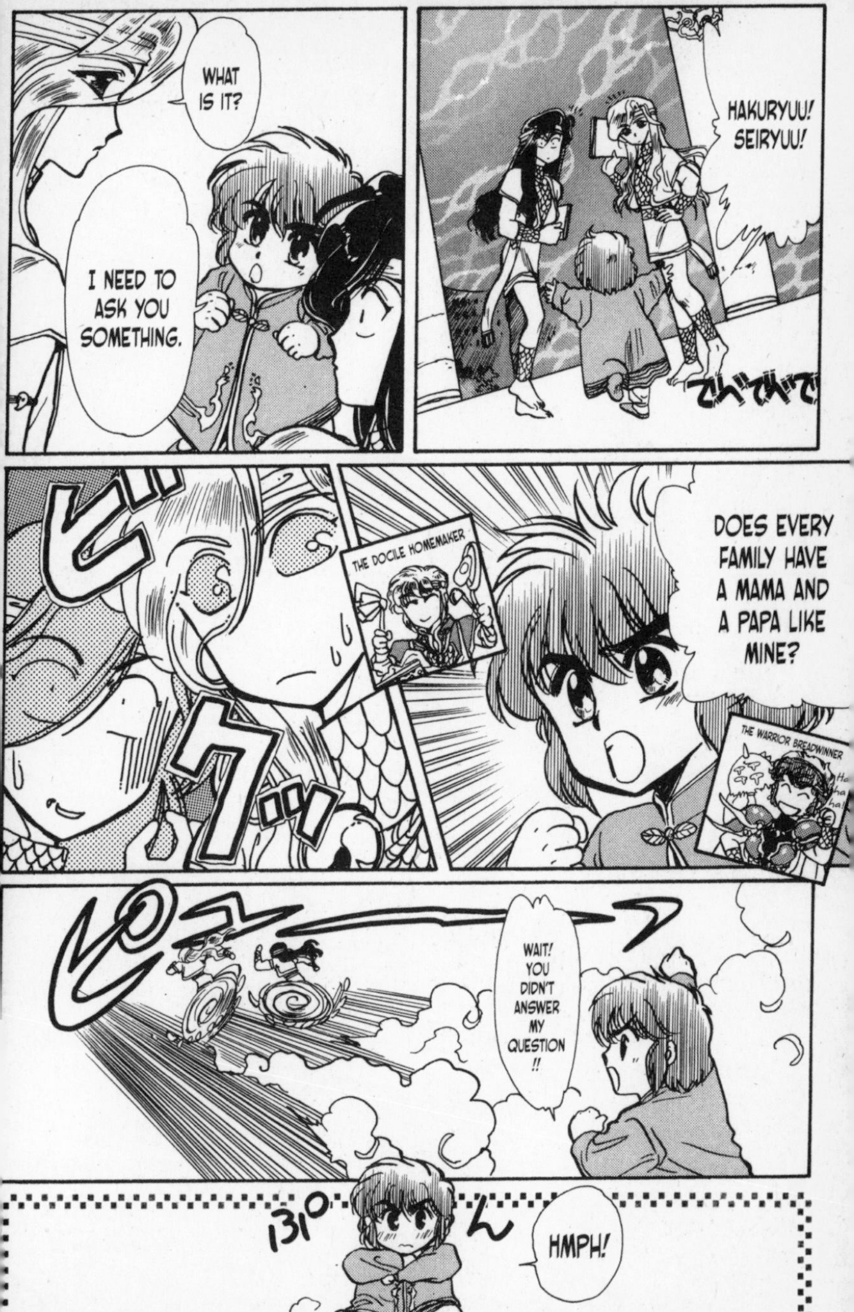
HAKURYUU! SEIRYUU!
WHAT IS IT?
I NEED TO ASK YOU SOMETHING.
DOES EVERY FAMILY HAVE A MAMA AND A PAPA LIKE MINE?
THE DOCILE HOMEMAKER
THE WARRIOR BREADWINNER
Ha ha ha!
WAIT! YOU DIDN'T ANSWER MY QUESTION!!
HMPH!

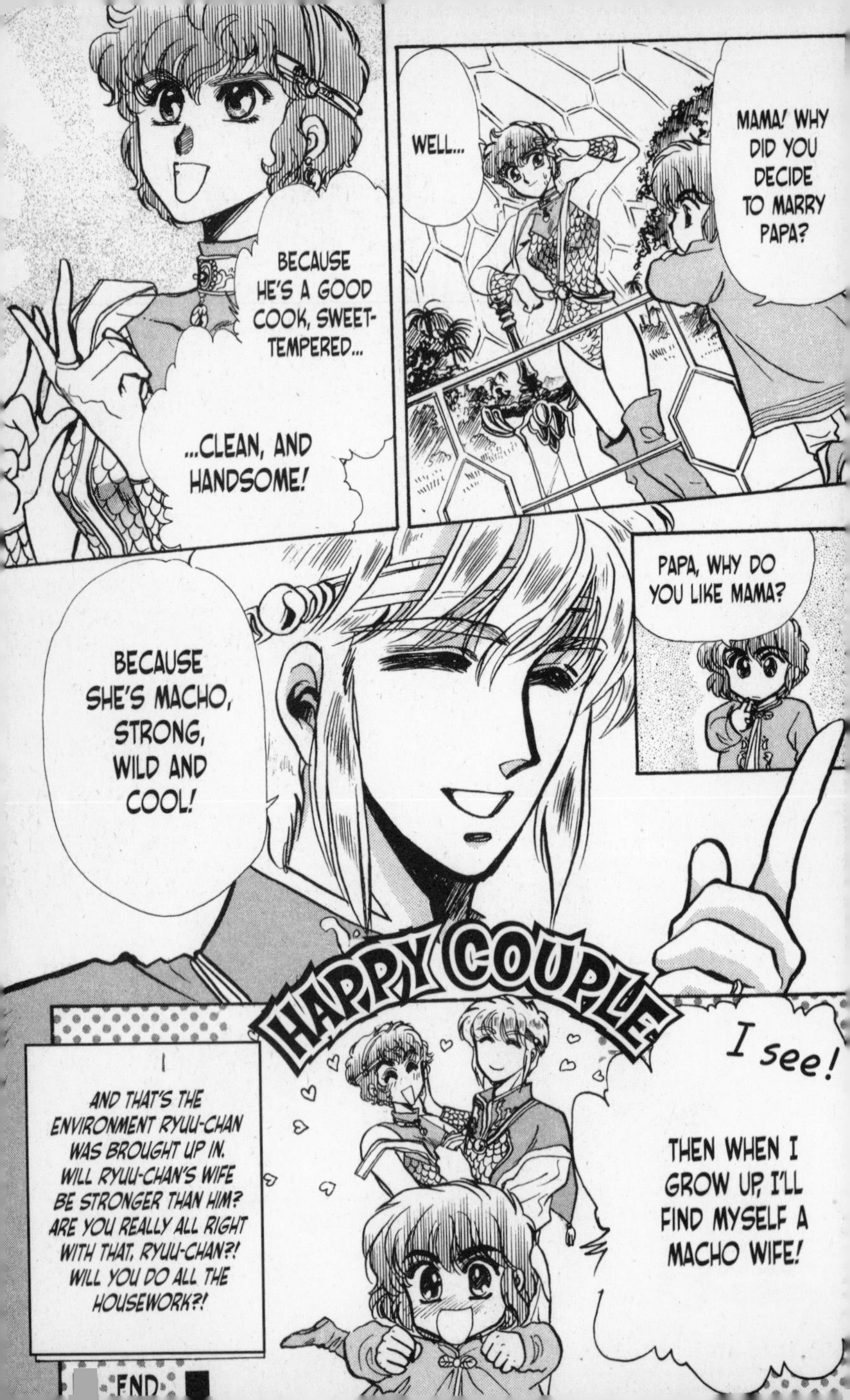
MAMA! WHY DID YOU DECIDE TO MARRY PAPA?
WELL...
BECAUSE HE'S A GOOD COOK, SWEET-TEMPERED...
...CLEAN, AND HANDSOME!
PAPA, WHY DO YOU LIKE MAMA?
BECAUSE SHE'S MACHO, STRONG, WILD AND COOL!
HAPPY COUPLE
I see!
THEN WHEN I GROW UP, I'LL FIND MYSELF A MACHO WIFE!
AND THAT'S THE ENVIRONMENT RYUU-CHAN WAS BROUGHT UP IN. WILL RYUU-CHAN'S WIFE BE STRONGER THAN HIM? ARE YOU REALLY ALL RIGHT WITH THAT, RYUU-CHAN?! WILL YOU DO ALL THE HOUSEWORK?!
END

NEXT TIME IN RG VEDA

AT THE RUINS OF HIS FORMER VILLAGE, YASHA MEETS HIS LONG-LOST BROTHER, RASETSU...WHO ATTACKS YASHA TO AVENGE THE PEOPLE HE ABANDONED! BUT KOUMOKUTEN'S ARMY IS CLOSE BEHIND. WILL RASETSU RISE TO DEFEND THE BROTHER HE ONCE LOVED?

COMING SOON!

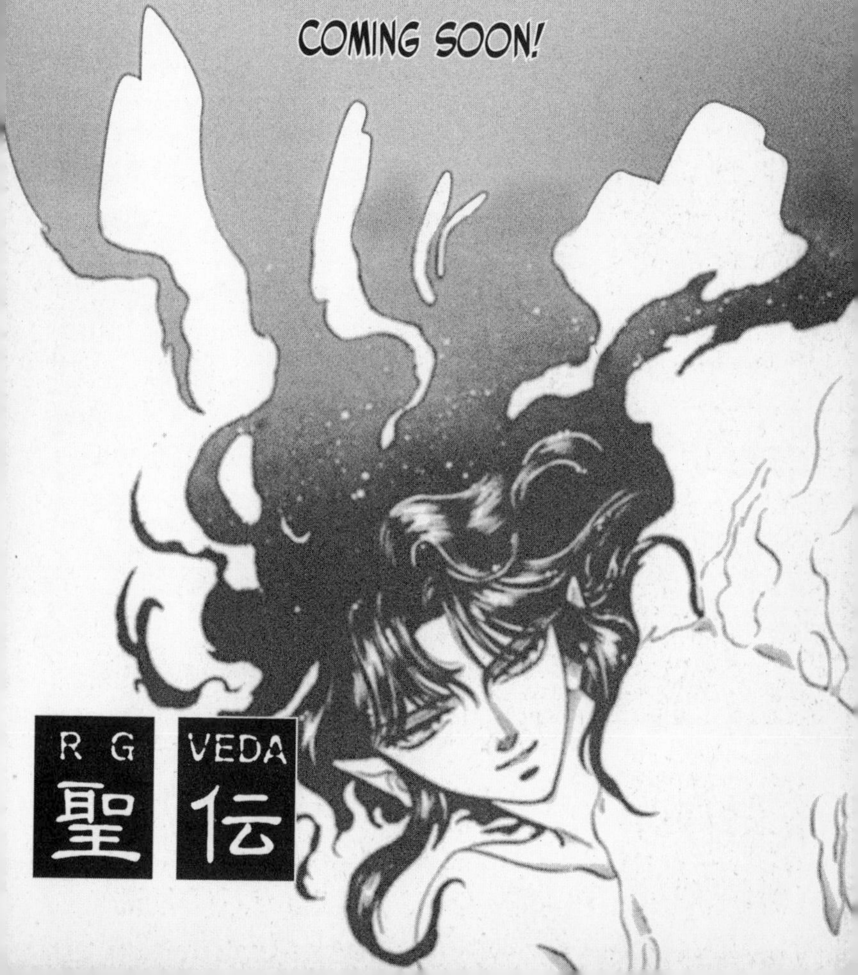
RG VEDA
聖伝

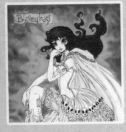
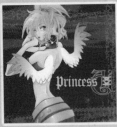

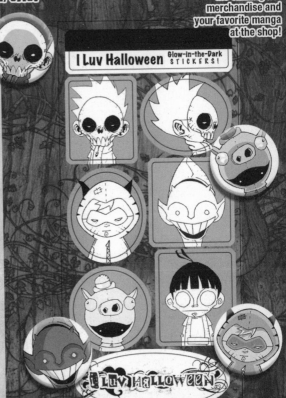

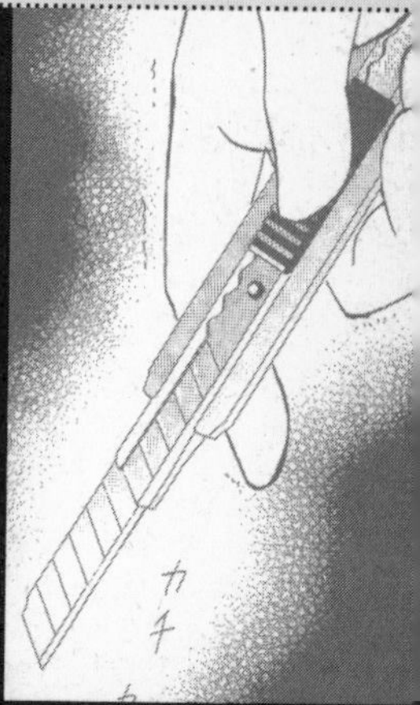
カチ

Ayumu struggles with her studies, and the all-important high school entrance exams are approaching. Fortunately, she has help from her best bud Shii-chan, who is at the top of the class. But when the test results come back, the friends are surprised: Ayumu surpasses Shii-chan's scores and gets into the school of her choice—without Shii-chan! Losing her friend is so painful for Ayumu that she starts cutting herself to ease her sorrow. Finally, Ayumu seeks comfort in a new friend, Manami. But will Manami prove to be the friend that Ayumu truly needs? Or will Ayumu continue down a dark path?

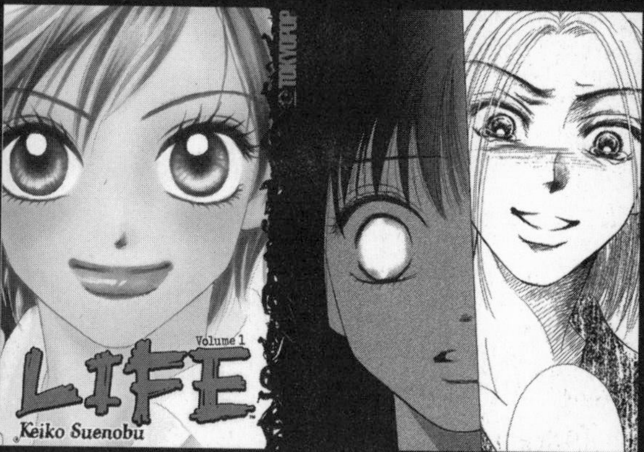
Volume 1
LIFE
Keiko Suenobu
©TOKYOPOP

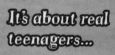

It's about real teenagers...

It's about real high school...

It's about real life.

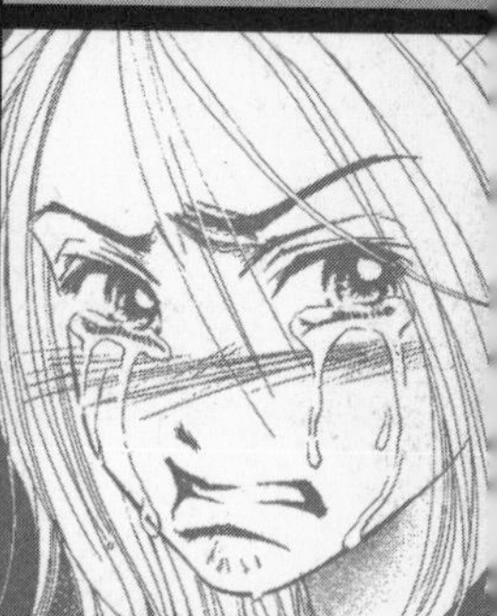

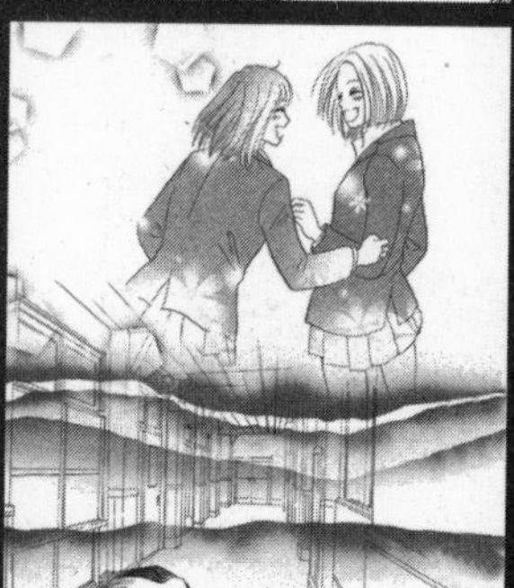

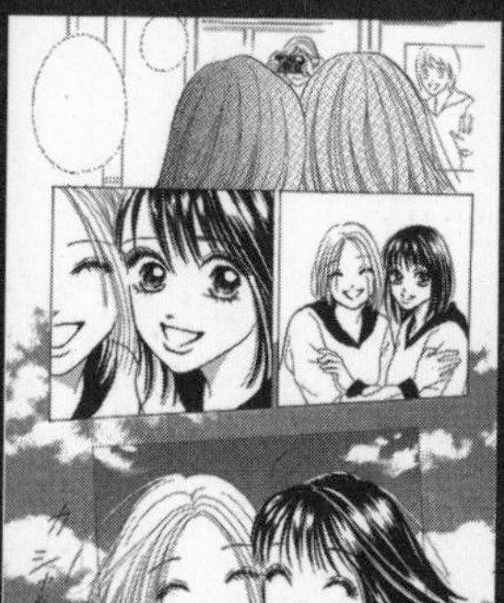

WWW.TOKYOPOP.COM/LIFE

LIFE
BY KEIKO SUENOBU

Ordinary high school teenagers...
Except that they're not.

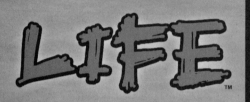

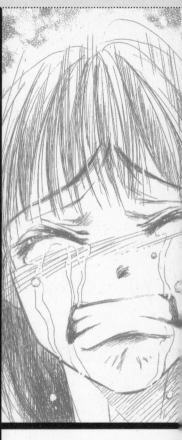

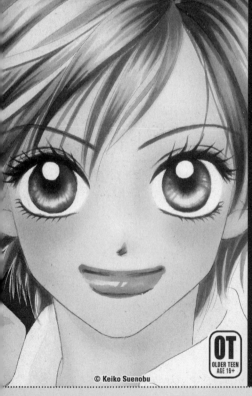

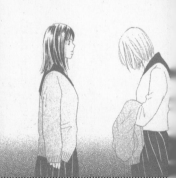

READ THE ENTIRE FIRST CHAPTER ONLINE FOR FREE:

that I'm not like other people...

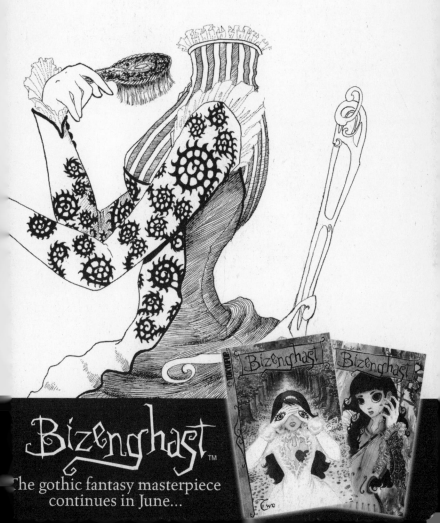

BIZENGHAST

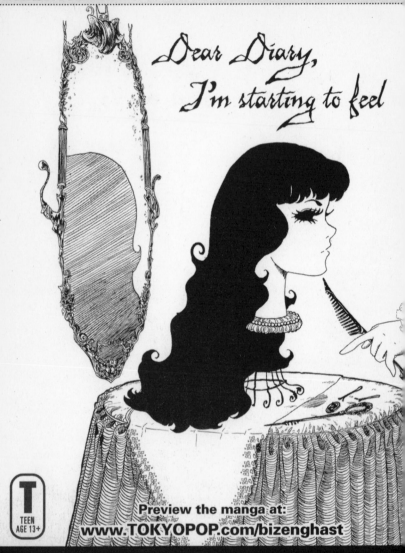

Dear Diary,
I'm starting to feel

THIS FALL, TOKYOPOP CREATES A FRESH, NEW CHAPTER IN TEEN NOVELS...

For Adventurers...

Witches' Forest:
The Adventures of Duan Surk

By Mishio Fukazawa
Duan Surk is a 16-year-old Level 2 fighter who embarks on the quest of a lifetime—battling mythical creatures and outwitting evil sorceresses, all in an impossible rescue mission in the spooky Witches' Forest!

BASED ON THE FAMOUS
FORTUNE QUEST **WORLD**

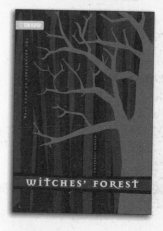

For Dreamers...

Magic Moon

By Wolfgang and Heike Hohlbein
Kim enters the enigmatic realm of Magic Moon, where he battles unthinkable monsters and fantastical creatures—in order to unravel the secret that keeps his sister locked in a coma.

THE WORLDWIDE BESTSELLING FANTASY
THRILLOGY **ARRIVES IN THE U.S.!**

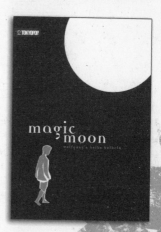

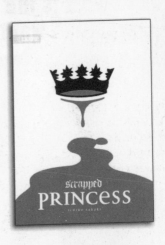
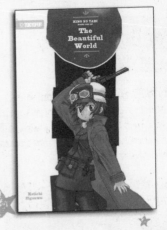

STOP!

This is the back of the book!

You wouldn't want to spoil a great ending!

This book is printed "manga-style," in the authentic Japanese right-to-left format. Since none of the artwork has been flipped or altered, readers get to experience the story just as the creator intended. You've been asking for it, so TOKYOPOP® delivered: authentic, hot-off-the-press, and far more fun!

DIRECTIONS

If this is your first time reading manga-style, here's a quick guide to help you understand how it works.

It's easy... just start in the top right panel and follow the numbers. Have fun, and look for more 100% authentic manga from TOKYOPOP®!

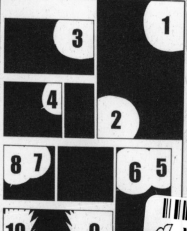

100% AUTHENTIC MANGA